EMPIRES AND WALLS

Studies in Critical Social Sciences Book Series

Haymarket Books is proud to be working with Brill Academic Publisher (www.brill.nl) to republish the *Studies in Critical Social Sciences* book series in pa perback editions. This peer-reviewed book series offers insights into our curren reality by exploring the content and consequences of power relationships unde capitalism, and by considering the spaces of opposition and resistance to thes changes that have been defining our new age. Our full catalog of *SCSS* volume can be viewed at www.haymarketbooks.org/category/scss-series.

Empires and Walls

Globalization, Migration, and Colonial Domination

Mohammad A. Chaichian

Haymarket
Books
Chicago, IL

First published in 2014 by Brill Academic Publishers, The Netherlands.
© 2014 Koninklijke Brill NV, Leiden, The Netherlands

Published in paperback in 2014 by
Haymarket Books
P.O. Box 180165
Chicago, IL 60618
773-583-7884
www.haymarketbooks.org

ISBN: 978-1-60846-422-7

Trade distribution:
In the U.S. through Consortium Book Sales, www.cbsd.com
In the UK, Turnaround Publisher Services, www.turnaround-psl.com
In all other countries by Publishers Group Worldwide, www.pgw.com

Cover design by Ragina Johnson.

This book was published with the generous support of Lannan Foundation
and the Wallace Action Fund.

Printed in Canada by union labor.

10 9 8 7 6 5 4 3 2 1

Library of Congress Cataloging-in-Publication Data is available.

To Dina and Yashaar

CONTENTS

List of Illustrations xi

Foreword by David Fasenfest xix

Preface xxiii

1 Walls, Borders, and Imperial Formations: In Search of an
   Explanation 1
   Borders, Walls and Globalization 15

PART ONE

THE IMPERIAL WALLS THAT ARE NO LONGER AROUND

2 Hadrian's Wall: An Ill-Fated Strategy for Tribal Management in
   Roman Britain 23
   Geopolitics of Hadrian's Wall 31
   Why Did Hadrian Build the Wall? 40
   Hadrian's Wall: Beginning of the End? 49

3 Red Snake: The Great Wall of Gorgan, Iran 53
   Was the *Red Snake* a Defensive Wall? 59
   The Wall's Architecture 66
   The Wall's Associated Hydraulic Structures and Functions ... 78
   The Red Snake as a Yet Unsolved Enigma 85

4 Clash of Empires: Prelude to the Berlin Wall 90
   The Rise and Fall of the German Empire 92
   Preparing Germans for Occupation, 1945–1947 97
   Emergence of the Two Germanys under Occupation,
     1947–1949 103
   Post-War Dependent Development of a Divided and
     Occupied Germany 110

5 Build the Wall: The Two German Economies are Now United! 119
   The Wall's Architecture 129
   Was the Wall a Sign of East Germany's Weakness? 139
   Concluding Remarks 147

PART TWO

ANTI-IMPERIALIST WALLS

6 Dismantling the Defensive Wall of the Colonized:
   Banning the Islamic Veil (*Hijab*) in French Schools 151
   The French Colonial Presence in North Africa 154
   French Republicanism and the Problematic "Collective
      Identity" 156
   Muslim Immigrants in France 157
   Social Spheres and the *Maghrebi* Muslim Identity:
      A New Frontier for Anti-colonial Resistance 161
   Hijab as the Last Defensive Tool of the Colonized:
      Soft as a Cloth, Tough as a Wall 163
   Conclusion 168

PART THREE

NEO-COLONIAL WALLS

7 An Empire in the Making: American Colonial Interests South
   of the Border 175
   Migration of Mexicans to the United States 179
   Maquiladoras, NAFTA, and the Evolution of Twin Cities
      along the U.S.-Mexico Border 195
   The Border is No Longer: Long Live the Border! 199

8 The Great Offensive Wall of Mexico: Border Blues 207
   Erecting the Offensive Barrier, or "The Great Wall of
      Mexico" 213
   The Fence/Wall Architecture 220
   Is the Border Fence/Wall Effective? Notes from the Field 235

9 Israel and Palestine: a Settler Colony is Born 246
   Israel: The Birth of a Nation 247
   Advancement of Zionist Settler Colonies in Palestine under
      British Occupation 254
   Zionist Colonization and the Land Question in Palestine 258

10 Bantustans, Maquiladoras, and the Separation Barrier
 Israeli Style 271
 Israel's First Expansion Phase, 1947–1949 271
 Israel's Second Expansion Phase, 1949–1967 275
 Israel's Third Expansion Phase, 1967–1991 277
 Israel's Fourth Expansion Phase, 1993–2000 281
 The Second *Intifada*: Prelude to the Wall/Fence 286
 Israel's Final Expansionist Offensive: The Separation Barrier 292
 The Separation Barrier's Architecture 296
 The Two Economies Are Now Fully Integrated:
 Erect the Separation Barrier! 304
 A "Villa in the Jungle"? From Jabotinsky's "Iron Wall" to the
 Separation Barrier 315

11 Epilogue: Conceptualizing Walls and borders—"Globalization
 from within" 320
 Post-Wall Berlin 324

References 333
Index 353

LIST OF ILLUSTRATIONS

Photos

1.1 Girl riding donkey in front of the Pavilions of Morocco on "a street in Cairo," Paris Exposition, 1889 7

1.2 Three Arab men sitting in front of Kabyle house, Paris Exposition, 1889 7

1.3 Hercules and the Lernaean Hydra 11

2.1 Cawfields Milecastle and Hadrian's Wall on the Great Whin Sill looking east 35

2.2 The Vallum crossing over the ditch at Benwell (near Newcastle) looking north towards the fort 38

2.3 A reconstructed model of the Segedunum Roman Fort and a settlement south of Hadrian's Wall at the eastern end of Hadrian's Wall ca. 200 AD 41

2.4 Author standing on the Wall's remains in Housesteads next to the Fort facing east 44

2.5 Author standing on top of the Wall's remains facing east next to the Cawfields milecastle 46

2.6 Sheep grazing at Housesteads Roman Fort along Hadrian's Wall 47

3.1 A profile of the brick Wall excavated in 2005 with an approximate height of 1.47 meters 69

3.2 A view of a section of the 2 meter-wide brick Wall (lower left) and one of the kilns (center right) located south of the barrier in Qara Deeb 70

3.3 Conceptualization of the ditch, the Gorgan Wall, and one Fort # 5 facing south. All that is left is a mound-like impression of this 196 kilometer-long ancient structure 72

3.4 Bricks salvaged from the Gorgan Wall used in construction of this house (top portion) in the village of Tamar Qara Quzli, northeast of the town of Kalaleh, Golestan Province 73

3.5 Two more houses built by bricks salvaged from the Gorgan Wall in the village of Tamar Qara Quzli, northeast of the town of Kalaleh, Golestan Province 73

3.6 The Gorgan Wall mound and the adjacent ditch on the extreme east end near the ancient Garkaz Dam 74

3.7   A view of Chai-Ghushan Kuchek Canal, facing northwest
       towards the Wall   81
3.8   Author standing on the Sadd-I Garkaz Dam facing east   82
5.1   A Berlin family separated by the newly laid out barbed wire
       on the corner of Bernauer and Schweder Straße, August 1961   121
5.2   Armed East German Combat Groups of the Working Class
       (*Kampfgruppen der Arbeiterklasse*) with water cannons
       behind them are deployed west of the Brandenburg Gate to
       secure the border between West and East Berlin,
       August 13, 1961   122
5.3   Aerial view of East Berlin under Soviet control in the
       aftermath of Allied bombing, July 1945   124
5.4   Berlin Wall blocking the historic Brandenburg Gate, 1963   125
5.5   The Wall, second generation: President John F. Kennedy
       views the Berlin Wall from an elevated platform at
       Checkpoint Charlie   130
5.6   The Wall, third generation: Remains of the Wall on the right,
       in St. Hedwig Cemetery on Liesen Straße   132
5.7   Fourth generation Berlin Wall concrete slabs, detail   133
5.8   The removed concrete sewer pipes on display at the
       Bernauer Straße Wall Museum   134
5.9   The Wall's Fourth Generation (1975–1989)   135
5.10   Inner German border with a control strip (first generation,
       1952–early 1960s)   141
5.11   Inner German border, second generation (1962)   141
7.1   Border Wall separating Nogales, Arizona on the U.S. side
       (left) from Nogales, Sonora on the Mexican side, 2009 (right)   200
7.2 & 7.3 Two sides of the Wall: border Wall and security road,
       Calexico, California (top) and a busy street next to the wall
       in Mexicali, Baja California on the Mexican side across from
       Calexico (bottom), 2009   201
7.4   Abandoned shopping carts by Mexican day-shoppers who
       hold Border Crossing Cards (BCCs) in San Luis, Arizona on
       the U.S. side of the border   204
7.5   Highly fortified entrance to U.S. Border Customs facility on
       the Mexican side of the border in Mexicali, Baja California   205
8.1   Ineffective Fencing in the San Diego-Tijuana Sector in the
       Early 1990s   209
8.2   A mobile border surveillance tower near the U.S-Mexico
       border in Nogales, Arizona   223

8.3   An example of picket-style fence in San Diego-Tijuana
      border, CA near Freedom Park on the U.S. side, with patrol
      road and soft pavement to track would-be intruders on
      the left 226

8.4   Picket fence, top detail 226

8.5   An example of a new bollard fence in Nogales, on the
      Mexican side. It is built next to the existing older fence
      constructed with salvaged WWII corrugated metal used for
      construction of pontoon bridges (foreground, left) 227

8.6   Bollard Fence, top detail—on the San Luis/Yuma (AZ)-San
      Luis Rio, Mexico border 227

8.7   A U.S. Border Patrol Agent standing next to an 18–foot tall
      post-and-rail with wire mesh Pedestrian Fence, Santa Teresa
      port of entry, New Mexico 228

8.8   A Normandy-style vehicle fence near El Paso sector,
      New Mexico 229

8.9   A rabbit hole underneath the new bollard fence in
      Nogales-Nogales border on the Mexican side. Note the
      destroyed concrete base by border crossers 231

8.10 Blow-torched holes on the Mexican side of the old fence in
      Nogales-Nogales border, with the patched-up areas on the
      U.S. side 232

8.11 Status of completed Fence/Wall sections along the
      U.S.-Mexico border, December 2009 234

8.12 The no-man's land security buffer zone between the new
      border fence (forefront) and the old chain link fence that
      used to separate Friendship Park on the U.S. side from
      Tijuana, Mexico (seen in the background) 236

8.13 The San Diego-Tijuana border fence on the U.S.-side. Note
      the combination of virtual fence and the physical barrier,
      with sensors, cameras and stadium lights 238

8.14 The westernmost section of new picket fence and the patrol
      road on the Pacific Ocean separating San Diego from Tijuana
      (seen beyond the old border barrier in the background) as
      seen from the Friendship Park 239

8.15 Recorded migrant deaths along the Arizona-Mexico border,
      1999–2012 241

8.16 Crosses posted in memory of deceased border crossers on a
      section of the old border wall on the Mexican side,
      Nogales, Sonora 242

8.17 A close-up image of crosses with names of the deceased
      migrants, Border wall on the Mexican side, Nogales,
      Sonora 242
8.18 A fresh water plastic container slashed by local residents
      who oppose humanitarian help provided by volunteer
      groups, north of the U.S.-Mexican border near rural Campo,
      about 50 miles east of San Diego, CA 244
10.1 Israel's Separation Barrier between Rumana, in the West
      Bank (right) and Umm al-Fahem in Israel 299
10.2 Prefabricated reinforced concrete wall slabs waiting to be
      put in place in Jerusalem 300
10.3 The concrete Separation Wall and an Israeli Defense Force
      (IDF) watch tower on the Israeli side seen from the town
      of Qalqilya on the western edge of the West Bank occupied
      territories 301
11.1 The Berlin Wall's double-row cobble stone line-marker with
      the embedded signifier plaque near the Brandenburg Gate ... 327
11.2 The Berlin Wall Memorial on Bernauer Straße as seen from
      the observation platform across the street 329
11.3 The East Side Gallery Wall memorial along the Spree River ... 329
11.4 A 'Disneyesque' version of the Wall: Fake East German
      border agents stamping passports for tourists in front of the
      painted Berlin Wall slabs at Potsdamer Platz, 20109 330
11.5 Another 'Disneyesque' version of the Wall: A replica of the
      Allied guardhouse at Checkpoint Charlie on Friedrichstraße
      facing towards East Berlin, installed in 2000 330

Figures

2.1 Roman Empire at the end of Caesar's rule (44 BC) 25
2.2 Southern Scotland between the Forth-Clyde and Tyne-Solway
     Isthmuses (sites of Antonine and Hadrian Walls,
     respectively) 27
2.3 Map of Celtic Britain's Ethnic Tribes, 1st century BC 29
2.4 Original plan of Hadrian's Wall north of the Stanegate 33
2.5 A cross-sectional sketch of (from left to right) the ditch, the
     Wall and the Valllum 37

3.1   Sketch map of the Gorgan Wall, starting in Pishkamar
       mountains on the east and ending on the Caspian Sea coast
       on the West   54
3.2   The Boundaries of Parthian Empire and its vassals at the
       turn of 1st Century, AD   57
3.3   Approximate territorial boundaries of the Sassanid Persian
       Empire in AD 500   61
3.4   Location of the city of Merv   63
3.5   Main routes of the old Silk Road   64
3.6   Magnometer survey of Fort 4 revealing three rows of
       barrack-like structures and two entry gates   77
3.7   A conceptual partial map of the Gorgan Wall's hydraulic
       system N.E. of the city of Gonbad-e Kavus, illustrating the
       Chai Ghushan Kuchek Canal (top) that may have transferred
       water from the reservoir north of Garkaz earthen Dam to the
       ditch that ran parallel to the Wall on its north side   80
3.8   Plan of the Sadd-i Garkaz Dam near northeast end of the
       Gorgan Wall, with Gorgan River running through the washed
       out portion of the earthen dam   81
3.9   Contemporary flood-prone/risk areas in the Golestan
       Province   84
3.10 The Fertile Crescent, location of the Gorgan and Tamishe
       Walls, and the eastern entrance   88
4.1   Divided Germany, 1945   91
4.2   Unification and Creation of the German Empire, 1866–1871 ...   93
4.3   Emigration of East German residents to the West, 1950–1963   114
5.1   Berlin Map showing the Wall route separating Eastern
       (GDR) and Western sectors (FDR under American, British
       and French control), August 13, 1961 120
5.2   Map of Central Berlin, 1922. The Brandenburg Gate is on the
       west end of Unter den Linden Boulevard 123
5.3   Sketch of the expansion of border security system, ca. early
       1970s (note that the concrete wall on West Berlin side is still
       the third generation design) 137
5.4   A diagram of a heavily fortified inner German border
       (third generation) between West and East Germany, ca. 1984   140
5.5   Emigration from the GDR to the FRG, 1949–1989 144

6.1 Gender-specific spaces in a Muslim Magrebin rural-tribal culture 166

6.2 The veil (hijab) and its function in urban public spheres 167

6.3 Women wearing the *hijab* 171

7.1 The Mexican Cession of 1848 177

7.2 Annual Growth Rates of U.S. Gross Domestic Product and Maquiladora Employment, 1982–2002 193

7.3 Synchronization of Mexico's industrial production with that of the United States: quarterly changes in industrial production, January 2000–December 2007 194

7.4 Map of U.S.-Mexico Border States and Twin Sister Cities 196

7.5 Combined Trans-border Metropolitan Population of Major Twin Cities along the U.S.-Mexican Border Region, 2010 206

8.1 Proposed two-layer Fence/Wall along the U.S.-Mexican Border 219

8.2 Artist's Rendition of the Three-Fence Barrier System 221

8.3 Potential Long-Term SBInet Concept of Operations for the "Virtual Fence" project 223

9.1 Hypothetical Map of Biblical Boundaries of *Eretz Yisreal* 249

9.2 Sykes-Picot Agreement of 1916 255

9.3 The British Mandate 257

9.4 Peel Commission Partition Plan for Palestine, 1937 264

9.5 The United Nations' Partition Plan of 1947 268

10.1 The Original 1947 UN Plan and expanded, congruous Israeli territories at the conclusion of hostilities in 1949 274

10.2 Israel and Occupied territories since June 1967 278

10.3 Cantonization of the West Bank: Palestinian Bantustans under the Terms of Oslo II Agreements 284

10.4 Map of Bypass Roads in the West Bank and Their Connection to Israel's Highway Grid, 2012 287

10.5 Location of Jewish Settlements in Relation to the Final Status Map of the West Bank Presented by Israel at Camp David in 2001 289

10.6 The 1967 Allon Plan 291

10.7 Map of the West Bank Separation Barrier, 2007 295

10.8 Israel's Separation Barrier-a Typical Chain Link Fence 298

10.9 Map of the Separation Barrier surrounding the Town of Qalqilya in the Occupied West Bank 303

10.10 Location of Seam Zones 314

10.11   The Bunker State: Israel's militarized Barriers along Her
Borders, 2012 318

11.1   Conceptualizing Four Types of Imperial Wall 323

Tables

3.1   Hydrologic and Hydraulic Investigation of Chai-Ghushan
Kuchek Canal at the conjunction with Sadd-i Garkaz Dam   83

5.1   Basic Facts about the Wall 137

5.2   Occupational Breakdown of Refugee Movement in
Percentages (1952–1961) 142

6.1   Estimated French Muslim Population by the Region/Country
of Origin/Category, 2000 158

7.1   Variations in Periodization of Mexican Emigration Pull-Push
Cycles to the United States, 1900–2000 181

7.2   Periodization of Maquiladoras' Growth and Decline and
Total Work Force, 1964–2006 190

7.3   Population of U.S.-Mexico Border Twin Cities, 1930–2020
(projected) 198

8.1   The Offensive Border Strategy Timeline ("*Prevention Through
Deterrence*"), 1993–Present 215

8.2   Number of full-Time Border Agents Deployed along the
U.S.-Mexico Border, 1975–2005 217

8.3   Completed Border Fence by the end of 2008 230

9.1   Jewish Population and Jewish-Owned Land in Palestine,
1922 & 1944 259

9.2   Jewish and Non-Jewish Immigration to Palestine, 1932–1937   263

9.3   Membership Composition of UNSCOP's Two Subcommittees
and their Recommendations for Palestine's Future 266

10.1   Basic Employment Data on the West Bank and Gaza Strip,
1995–2002 309

FOREWORD

The 21st Century has been cast as the globalization century, in which all
the forces of global economic change developing during the 20th Century—from colonialism to liberation struggles to neo-colonialism; with
imperial, ideological and economic rivalries that produced two world
wars; from regional economic and political associations, trade agreements
and mutual defense arrangements like the European Union, NAFTA and
NATO, from the spread of global finance (IMF, World Bank), governance
(UN, WTO, ILO) and multinational corporations—have culminated into
an ever greater coordinated global political economy under the banner of
neo-liberalism.

   This is not a calm century, a century of shared prosperity and universal rights. Rather, what is emerging is a world of winners and losers, of
great prosperity in some countries (however narrowly experienced among
its population) and great deprivation in others. World wars have given
way to regional wars and unconventional wars, or to internal conflict
and chaos. Freely flowing capital and interlocking international finance
has created systems vulnerable to shocks in one country that destabilize
financial markets in the rest of the world. And with all this has come the
increasing tension of population flows as workers in poor countries seek
employment in richer countries. These are all stories well rehearsed in the
current literature, but worth revisiting often to remind us that the current
global economy is not the panacea proclaimed by the strongest supporters of globalization.

   The combination of greater austerity efforts due to the neoliberal
agenda, economic crisis, and an increasing sense of despair and chaos,
creates a climate in which immigrants have become the target of increasingly xenophobic publics worried about job loss associated (rightly or
wrongly) with these new arrivals. Apparently, the borderless economies
with freely moving capital do not bring with it borderless labor markets
and a free flow of workers. This "crisis" is most clearly manifest in the
former colonial and imperial centers of Europe and the United States,
whose populations increasingly displaced by the restructuring of production struggle with the immigrant flows from the global South. What were
once welcoming countries seeking to fill vacant positions in production
(Turks and Greeks coming to Germany, Commonwealth citizens flocking

to Great Britain, North Africans coming to France and Italy, Mexicans and Central Americans coming to the United States) are now at the forefront of efforts to stem the tide, expel those migrants living within their borders, and erect both legal and literal barriers.

In this expansive analysis of walls, Mohammad Chaichian revisits those barriers that separate societies and populations—whether literal or figurative—to explore the mechanisms, practices and consequences of history's effort to keep people apart, to keep out ideas, to protect privilege and wealth or to enforce its appropriation. He begins his analysis by reminding the reader that walls are not new inventions, and even great walls have failed. Perhaps the earliest and most famous was Hadrian's Wall, a symbol simultaneously of what Rome had conquered, and also what it could not conquer. From Rome's perspective behind the wall was "civilization" and the rule of empire, beyond the wall chaos and the barbarians who resist progress. By building the wall Hadrian sought to literally keep the barbarians away from the gates of Rome. As history showed us, the effort failed.

The Berlin Wall was another effort to keep populations apart, but unlike Hadrian's Wall, not to keep people out but to keep out ideas. Regardless of our own sense of which idea, which ideology, had greater merit, the Berlin Wall was a symbol of the refusal to allow ideologies to interact, and in so doing refused to allow citizens from one part of the world from freely moving to another. The demise of these walls foreshadows the reality that contemporary walls cannot survive, cannot achieve goals that attempt to hold back social change.

The second part of this work takes us from physical barriers to cultural symbols by exploring France's relationship to its non-Christian colonial and post-colonial subjects. Franz Fanon gave us a language with which to understand the psychological damage created on individuals from colonies when they abandon the symbols which defines them in an attempt to assimilate into the colonizer's society. For Fanon, cultural colonialism creates a disconnect between one's own core values and identity in the hopeless goal of identifying with another culture. The notion of "dominant" culture is just a rhetorical ruse to denigrate the culture of the oppressed. Chaichian's exploration of the role of the hijab and the conflict in France as it struggles against the formation of a Muslim identity, represents a cultural wall no less intrusive than the physical walls in history. Other example of walls that were not real walls was the Green Line separating Greeks and Turks in Cyprus, each side bearing grudges born of centuries-old colonial conflict.

Rarely a day goes by, and certainly fairly constantly during political seasons, when we are not reminded of the problems of immigrants and the desire to keep them out, or of the efforts at self-determination and the denial of human and civil rights—whether it be the wall between the US and Mexico, the wall separating Palestinian villagers from their fields and orchards, or the struggles in South Africa as it comes to terms with its apartheid legacy and the farce of the creation of "independent" Bantustans separating Whites from non-whites. Mohammad Chaichian's contribution to the literature on post-colonial struggles brings a clarity and incisive analysis to a seemingly intractable problem—social justice in a globalizing and neoliberal world.

David Fasenfest
Wayne State University

PREFACE

In the spring of 1991 I led a delegation of faculty to the People's Republic of China. The trip was organized as part of an educational exchange program between the university I was teaching at back then, and a business college in the city of Tianjin located about 137km (85 miles) southeast of Beijing on the Bohai Sea. While there, we traversed the country from Beijing all the way to the ancient city of Xian in central China, and of course we visited the Great Wall! We were taken to a section of the Wall in Badaling that runs through the Jundu Mountains northwest of Beijing. From our Chinese hosts' standpoint the Badaling Pass was understandably the most logical and practical spot for us (as tourists) to see the Wall, as it was only a short, easy 40-some miles bus ride from the Capital.

The Wall is a gigantic yet magnificent artifact—a historical testimony to Chinese people's resolve and creativity to design and construct protective barriers through large-scale mobilization of material and human resources in order to secure imperial territories. The Chinese wall has a long and tortured history. Contrary to popular perceptions of the Wall as being a one-piece, long and solid stone structure; it has been built in different times and in different parts of the Chinese imperial and dynastic territories as varied disjointed stretches of protective/defensive barriers mostly made of rammed-earth.[1] Except for a brief period during its early stages of development that parts of the Wall served as a primitive defensive barrier on the frontier (5th–3rd centuries, BC); various segments of the Wall have in most parts been built *within* the Chinese imperial territories and not on the imperial frontier lines. This was certainly the case during the long reign of the Han Dynasty (2nd century BC–3rd century AD) as well as the Ming Dynasty (14th–17th centuries AD), when the wall structure was overhauled and extensively renovated using more durable materials such as bricks, lime and stone.

Standing on the Wall on that sunny spring morning I marveled at this magnificent stone and mortar sculpture which like a giant serpent seemed to have organically grown out of a rough and rugged terrain to safeguard and protect the Chinese civilization from nomadic "barbarian" intrud-

---

[1] Rammed-earth is an ancient wall-building technique that utilizes a compressed damp mixture of clay, sand and gravel.

ers. Ironically, a historical survey of other macro-level walls erected by empires and contending political entities, some of which included in this book, reveals that the *civilized/barbarian* dichotomy has been a recurring theme in justifications for construction and maintenance of such large-scale structural barriers. Surely, the "barbarians" on the other side of these walls would have had the same vision—to consider themselves the "civilized" social entities vis-à-vis the "barbarians" who erected the walls; otherwise they would not have contemplated breaching the walls and barriers! At that moment, I also contemplated a much shorter modern counterpart in Berlin that was brought down merely eighteen months back, in November 1989.

To me, these two archetypes of ancient and modern walls signify the futility of such efforts to prevent regional migration and control population movements when competing and contending political economies begin to be intertwined and incorporated. Like Sisyphus, the Greek mythological character who was condemned to push a boulder up a mountain in perpetuity only to witness it in despair to roll back down again; wall builders in human history have also been engaged in exercises in futility. But unlike Sisyphus who eventually acknowledged the absurdity and futility of his task, wall builders have never come to that realization and have instead always stubbornly justified their rationale to erect these barriers.

Although I became interested in studying the historical reasons for rise and fall of imperial walls on that fateful spring day while standing on the Great Wall; it was not until 2008 that I could find both time and financial support to work on this project. This book is based on both an extensive research of available sources on the subject matter and my field research by visiting various wall sites, affiliated museums and archives, nearby cities and communities; as well as meeting with various individuals and agencies that in one way or another have been actively involved in the issues pertaining to borders, walls, and immigration issues.

This project has literally taken me to all corners of the globe. In 2009 I trekked 500 miles along the U.S.-Mexico border from the San Diego-Tijuana twin cities on the Wall's extreme western end on the Pacific Ocean to the twin cities of Nogales-Nogales in Arizona on the American and Mexican sides of the border fence/wall, respectively. I visited Berlin and what has remained of the Berlin Wall in the summer of 2010; and with the help of a German friend I was also able to trek 25 miles of the border region and see remnants of the notorious Death Strip and affiliated structures between West Berlin and former German Democratic Republic.

The following summer I managed to visit the entire length of the Roman Hadrian's Wall in northern England and visit associated archaeological sites and museums that provided me with a wealth of information. My final trip was to northeastern Iran in the summer of 2012, when I visited a hundred-kilometer stretch of the 196–kilometer long lesser known ancient Great Wall of Gorgan—also known as the 'Red Snake' due to the color of red baked clay bricks used in its construction. For logistical reasons I was unable to visit Israel and the occupied Palestine, and had to instead rely on available sources and research material to examine the separation barrier that the Israeli government has erected between the occupied West Bank Palestinian territories and Israel proper.

I begin the book with a search for conceptual tools and theoretical explanation of constructing barriers and walls within the context of colonial and imperial domination and control; and then present my case studies in three parts. I examine the defunct and dismantled ancient and modern walls in Part I—Hadrian's Wall in northern England and the *Red Snake* in northeastern Iran represent the former, and Berlin Wall the latter. Recognizing the fact that building walls is not exclusively the business of colonial powers and imperial entities, I bring an example of an ideological wall that is erected by the colonized as a defensive protective shield in Part II; using the case of Islamic *hijab* (veil) worn by Muslim immigrant women from northern Africa residing in France. I have devoted Part III to two contemporary and still evolving border walls/fences erected by the United States and Israel on the U.S.-Mexican border and between Israel proper and the occupied Palestine, respectively. Finally, although tentative, in the epilogue I propose a conceptual model that identifies several types of walls.

I am indebted to many institutions, colleagues and individuals who during the last five years have helped me to achieve the objectives of this ambitious project. I would like to thank Mount Mercy University's generous support through its Summer Faculty Scholarship Program that allowed me to research, write and travel to various sites of ancient and contemporary walls/barriers from 2009–2012. Furthermore, I am grateful for the University of Iowa's Obermann Center for Advanced Studies, particularly its director Dr. Teresa Mangum who enthusiastically supported my residency at the Center as a Research Fellow during my sabbatical leave in the spring 2012.

I would also like to thank those who have helped me with research and writing of this book: My book editor at Brill, Professor David Fasenfest

whose academic wisdom and insightful editorial suggestions have drastically transformed and definitely strengthened my manuscript; Brill's Assistant Editor Rosanna Woensdregt, who carefully reviewed the manuscript
and patiently worked with me to finalize the manuscript for production;
our dedicated librarians at Mount Mercy University without whose expert
help this project could not have been completed—Vicky Maloy who dili-
gently and meticulously edited the final manuscript and helped me to
see many inconsistencies; Marilyn Murphy who helped me solving many
technical problems I had with manuscript preparation, and Robyn Clark-
Bridges and Boyd Broughton who with light speed located and acquired
hard-to-find books and articles; my colleagues at the University of Iowa's
Obermann Center, Professors Kathleen Diffley, Till Heilmann, Rebekah
Koval, Ellen Lewin, Teresa Mangum, Kathy Schuh and H.S. Udaykumar
whose careful review and constructive criticisms of the theoretical chapter during our bi-weekly seminars helped me to revise and restructure it;
and finally my good friend and colleague Professor Ellen Lewin who gra-
ciously agreed to read the chapters on Israel's separation barrier despite
her very busy schedule and provided me with numerous helpful suggestions for revisions.

Last, but not least, during my field research and site visits many individuals, friends and agencies provided me with valuable data and material; and helped me to get to various wall/barrier sites that I could not visit
on my own. Along the U.S.-Mexico border, Enrique Morones of Border
Angels, Rosemary Johnston of the Interfaith Shelter Center, and the American Friends Service Committee in San Diego (CA); Proyecto San Pablo
in Calexico (CA), Chicanas por la Casa and several members of the City
Council in San Luis Rio Colorado (AZ), Poverty 24/6 and the Kino Initiative in Nogales (AZ), and the Humane Borders in Tucson (AZ) were of tre-
mendous help and support. In Berlin, Germany my good friend, Hartmut
Holthofer shared his recollection of living in the Cold War era Berlin and
took me for a tour of former East Berlin and rural border areas between
West Berlin and former East Germany where I could see some remnants
and relics of the defunct border wall/fence. While in the Golestan Province
in northeastern Iran, I had the pleasure of meeting Dr. Jebrail Nokandeh
and Hamid Omrani-Rekavandi of the Iran Cultural Heritage and Tourism
Organization (ICHTO) in Gorgan who helped me filling many information
gaps in my study of the ancient Wall of Gorgan; and organized visits to
several archaeological sites in the company of their colleague Bay Arteghi.
Although the book is the product of a collective effort, it goes without

saying that I am solely responsible for the presentation and interpretation of data.

A final note—I have excluded the Great Wall of China in my book by design, as I believe it has been widely and extensively studied, analyzed and also is better known (if not better understood) than the rest. The book is not exhaustive, and there is a long list of other equally significant historical walls and barriers that merit close scrutiny and analysis.

CHAPTER ONE

WALLS, BORDERS, AND IMPERIAL FORMATIONS:
IN SEARCH OF AN EXPLANATION

The history of constructing large-scale protective walls is as old as the history of settled human populations. All ancient cities and towns built the so-called "defensive" walls encircling the seats of government, temples and shrines, army barracks, the residences of the elite, and at times those of the ordinary inhabitants. Ancient Greeks built the first fortifications around their towns in the late 8th and early 7th centuries BC (Winter, 1971), at about the same time that archaeological excavations indicate the presence of defensive walls around the biblical town of Jericho in Palestine, or in present time occupied West Bank territories (Kenyon, 1970). But it would be too simplistic to argue that walls have always been built for defensive purposes. For one thing, with their highly guarded gates these walls also served to control in- and out-flow of townspeople and strangers. They were also an indication of the presence of social inequalities, a socially stratified community, and by default an implicit yet clear announcement about the presence of valuable objects and social surpluses that they were intended to guard. Erecting walls on one hand signifies power and the ability of those who build them to dominate, but at the same time represents the builders' insecurity and fear of the other (Marcuse, 1994: 43). In his attempt to make sense of the barriers, both physical and conceptual, that have divided populations along the U.S.-Mexican border and or in cities like Berlin, Belfast and Jerusalem, Marcuse (ibid., p. 41) uses *walls* as an ambiguous metaphor, with the most important being the ambiguity of purpose in building them, as:

> They have come to reflect, and to reinforce, hierarchies of wealth and power, divisions among people, among races, ethnic groups, and religions; hostilities, tensions, and fears. Their use has become aggressive as much as defensive; they have imposed the will of the powerful on the powerless as much as they have protected the powerless from superior force (p. 42).

Similar to the ruling elites who built defensive walls around ancient cities; imperial powers have often been preoccupied with constructing walls and barriers on a much larger scale. In contrast to an often too obvious and conventional explanation of the rationale and functional utility of erecting walls for defensive purposes around human settlements, macro-level walls erected to safeguard imperial territories and interests, both ancient and modern, are still shrouded in mystery as to their real *raison d'être*; in light of the fact that most of them have failed to serve the 'defensive' functions they were created for. The Great Wall of China in northern China (2nd century BC–3rd century AD), the Great Wall of Gorgan in northeastern Iran (3rd–5th century AD), and Hadrian's Wall in northern England (2nd century AD) are the best examples of ancient imperial walls. The Berlin Wall represents a short-lived barrier (1961–1989) whose demise ushered in the era of neo-liberal *Empire*. Although the book's focus is not on empires and the intricacies of imperial structures and functions and rather the logic and historical necessity of erecting walls and barriers at certain stages and phases of imperial rule, it is nonetheless important to have a working definition for the concept.

In their provocative book *Empire* Hardt and Negri (2000: xiv) point out that they are not using empire as a *metaphor*, but as a *concept* that requires theoretical explanation. This is also my approach in this book, but it goes without saying that in our search for theoretical explanations we shall not lose sight of the fact that the nature, structure, functions and reasons for the rise and fall of empires are historical variables. Thus, in spite of similarities each imperial entity has its own intrinsic and unique *raison d'être*. Empires predate capitalism, and their ancient forms in Persia, China, Macedonia or under the Roman rule were qualitatively different form each other and from their modern counterparts. While ancient and pre-capitalist empires were in large part supported and sustained by outright plunder or collections of taxes and tributes paid by subjects in the periphery to the metropolitan center; empires formed and sustained by an expanding capitalist economy have invested in the colonies, dominated their economic, cultural, and political institutions, and integrated their colonial holdings' political economy into a global system of capital accumulation (Parenti, 1995: 3).

Imperial formations always possess several inherent features. First, they are fragile multi-national/multi-ethnic entities held together by means of violent political structures; and challenges to empire either by rebellious subjugated entities within the empire or threats from without are always wrought with racial-ethnic discrimination. Imperial intentions therefore operate on cultural relativist terms, and in order to maintain control over imperial subjects they have to provide justification that they "stand for a higher degree of civilization" (Perreau-Saussine (2006: 280). Second, with their boundaries being in constant state of flux empires are inherently aggressive by nature (Hassig, 1994: 23–24), necessitating to always having a standing army of both offensive and defensive capabilities. Third, despite the claims by imperial entities in various historical periods empires are inherently anti-democratic, as they always expand by conquest of new territories and people without their consent. The earliest example of an empire allegedly established based on democratic principles is the Persian Empire during the rule of Emperor Cyrus (Kourush) the Great in 6th century BC. In a much celebrated human rights document, his ancient bill of rights which is inscribed on a baked clay cylinder credits Cyrus for freeing the Jewish residents of ancient Babylon in Mesopotamia and respecting their traditions, culture and freedom of religion. But claims to the famed emperor's alleged non-violent conquest of territories and fair treatment of his subjects are seriously questioned by some historians who argue that "conquering a huge empire in the ancient world did not come without a list of atrocities" (Tom Holland, cf. de Quetteville, 2008).[1] Similarly, in the contemporary period the American Empire's invasion and occupation of Iraq in 2003 that was also justified and promoted by the promise of establishing a true democracy in the occupied territories has not been a non-violent and peaceful process, to put it mildly.[2]

The advent of mercantile capitalism in the 15th century ushered in a new era of territorial expansion and new imperial formations, first by the Portuguese and later the Spaniards. Development of new social relations based on capitalist principles in the 17th and 18th centuries also led to the colonization of both "known' and 'recently known" territories at the time by emerging Dutch, British and French capitalist power houses in Europe. This was a new era that empires were formed by colonial expansion and domination dictated by the inner logic of capitalism. By 19th century there was no "unknown" territory left in the world from a European colonial viewpoint, and all regions of the world were identified and mapped. With the development of industrial capitalism in the later part of 19th century European colonialism entered a phase which historian Hobsbawm (1987) calls *The Age of Empire*, which is also the title of his book on this subject. It was during this period that the partition of the world and control of global economy by a handful of European states was almost complete, with its

---

[1] This is a revisionist interpretation of Cyrus's rule, as it is also celebrated by the United Nations as one of the earliest (non-Western) human rights documents. There are also Iranian proponents and defenders of the Persian Empire who defend its humanistic virtues (see Farrokh, n.d.).

[2] For a critical assessment of this position see Johnson (2006).

"most spectacular feature" being the "growing division of the globe into the strong and the weak, the 'advanced' and the 'backward'." Hobsbawm makes the point that in the late 19th century "emperors and empires were old, but imperialism was quite new" (ibid.: 59–60). On this point, alluding to negative connotations of the word "imperialism" even during the 19th century colonial period, in his study of the theories of imperialism Etherington (1984: 6) notes that while the British Empire was expanding beyond the British Isles and adding new overseas territories to its imperial possessions in the mid-1800s; the term "imperialism" still had a "sinister past bound up with strutting dictatorships, contempt for liberty and a lust for military glory." But in the 1890s some proponents of colonial expansion began to accept the label of "imperialist" and even "wear it as a badge of honor" (ibid.). The English economist John Hobson was one of the first to denounce the horrors of imperial army during the South African War of 1899–1902, for "burning civilian farms and putting women and children in stinking concentration camps" just because of the "self-interested manipulation of a little clique of capitalist investors" (Hobson, cf. Etherington, op. cit.).[3]

One of the first critical Marxist interpretations of imperialism was offered by Lenin (1968) who considered the turn of the 20th century phase of capitalist development as the new imperialism that led to territorial division of the world among a few European capitalist powers; who then established formal colonies, spheres of influence, and territories dependent on respective imperial centers. After much investigation, analysis and observation, as an activist-revolutionary thinker he came to the conclusion that not only the First World War was a predatory and annexationist imperialist war, but wars had also become a permanent feature of imperialism (see Etherington, 1984: 133–137). This new phase of colonial imperialism was distinctly different from previous imperial entities. First, unlike previous empires it relied on a single global economy that as Hobsbawm (1987: 62–66) explains progressively reached "into the most remote corners of the world," and created "a dense web of economic transactions, communications and movements of goods, money and people" that effectively linked the developed capitalist countries with each other

---

[3] Known as the Second Boer War (1899–1902), it was fought between two imperial rivals in South Africa, the British and the Afrikaan-speaking Dutch settlers who had established independent republics in the provinces of Transvaal and Orange Free State. The British eventually crushed the Boer resistance and annexed both republics to the British Empire's possessions in southern Africa. See also Hobson's classic work *Imperialism: A Study* (1902).

and with the less developed pre-capitalist territories and nations. Second, it relied on extraction of raw materials in the colonial territories, which were then exported to the imperial centers to be used in the production processes. In addition, the new imperialism was dependent on colonial expansion in order to open and establish new markets for products manufactured in the center.

The new age of imperialism impacted colonial subjects in ways that did not have a precedent in pre-capitalist empires. For instance, the economic and political dependencies created by a capitalist economy created a new class of indigenous elite that was trained and educated, often in the colonial metropolis which internalized cultural values of the empire and served their masters as local proxies of the empire. The new imperialist era was also justified based on racist ideology of the superiority of one race (white European) and domination over other races (darker skinned colonial subjects).

As I will make the case for the Roman Empire's presence in Britain in the following chapter, dichotomous divisions of imperial subjects into 'civilized' and 'barbarians' has been an ideological tool to govern and control empires from ancient times to the present. But Romans for example did not hold prejudicial thoughts similar to what that has evolved during colonial-imperial expansion period particularly in the 19th century. (see Salway, 1993). The modern concept of 'race' evolved and was perfected by the Europeans' colonial expansion, hand-in-hand with the new biological based social Darwinist ideas of racial superiority and inferiority in a new global theatre.[4] This was clearly manifested at the 1900 World Exposition (*Exposition Universelle*) held in Paris to showcase and celebrate the achievements of the past century. Hobsbawm (ibid.: 70–71) notes the novelty of fourteen "colonial pavilions" at the Expo that were extremely popular and "hitherto virtually unknown" to the European public, providing a detailed account of what they represented:

> British jubilees, royal funerals and coronations were all the more impressive because, like ancient Roman triumphs, they displayed submissive maharajahs in jeweled robes—freely loyal rather than captive. Military parades were all the more colourful because they contained turbaned Sikhs, moustached Rajputs, smiling and implacable Gurkas, Spahis and tall black Senegalese: the world of what was considered barbarism at the service of civilization. Even in Hapsburg Vienna, uninterested in overseas colonies, an Ashanti village magnetized the sightseers.

---

[4] For a discussion of the evolution of concept of race see Chaichian (2006, Introduction).

As the "world" and "colonial" expositions, showcases of imperial-colonial achievements grew in popularity particularly in the *age of Empire*, so were the "human zoos" that were displayed as (highly popular) tourist attractions. Also called "ethnological expositions" or "Negro Villages," human zoos were displays in natural settings that emphasized racial and cultural differences between white western-European ('civilized') nations and the rest of the world (darker skin populations), placing non-European people in a visual continuum between apes and those of European descents. In addition to the famous diorama, "Living in Madagascar," the 1900 Paris Expo also included pavilions and sections demonstrating the 'exotic' cultures and behaviors of non-European colonial subjects juxtaposed with those of the civilized world. A New York Times reporter's observation of the "Cairo Street" that displayed Egyptian street life at the 1900 Paris Expo is revealing:

> The Cairo donkey drivers have been reduced to a more quiescent mood, but owing to the change of surroundings, to the atmosphere perhaps, they certainly look more devilish than under the uniformly blue Cairo sky, with pyramids as a background. It is hard for them to be very reserved. For their very appearance with their daring patrons—for it does take a good deal of audacity to ride a donkey through the exhibition grounds—is a constant signal for wild applause. Half of these Arabs have to be imprisoned every night, and three were sent back to the Khédive yesterday. Like the dancers ambitiously called Almees, they are one of the great attractions, and Cairo Street is a swell resort and the proper place to be from 5 to 7 o'clock (New York Times, 1889) (see Photos 1.1 & 1.2).[5]

Social forces of global capitalist production along with its social relations have evolved dramatically and undergone several transformations since Lenin's time. We have witnessed an increasing concentration of capital in fewer hands and an increasing number of mergers that also have led to higher levels of monopolization; while at the same time production of goods and services have increasingly become decentralized at the global level through outsourcing and piece-work—or what David Harvey calls the *post-Fordist* phase of global capitalism (see Harvey, 1991). Imperial formations have also evolved accordingly, and here I will use one interpretation of the force behind present-time imperialism by Hardt and Negri (2000), or what they simply call *Empire* with a capital E. They note that

---

[5] Readers can still visit a revised, more subdued postmodern version of this colonial-imperial mentality on permanent display at Disney World's *Magic Kingdom* in Orlando, Florida!

Image source: http://www.loc.gov/pictures/resource/cph.3c06581/.

Photo 1.1 Girl riding donkey in front of the Pavilions of Morocco on "a street in Cairo," Paris Exposition, 1889.

Image source: http://www.loc.gov/pictures/resource/cph.3c09488/.

Photo 1.2 Three Arab men sitting in front of Kabyle house, Paris Exposition, 1889.

although this "postmodern" Empire is a uniquely evolved historical global entity, it has striking similarities to the model of imperial Rome that was explained by Polybius, a Greek historian in the 2nd century BC who conceptualized it as a complex structure based on a combination of three sources of power: monarchic, aristocratic and democratic. Thus they situate the new *Empire*'s structure within the context of a new world order:

> The Empire we find ourselves faced with today is also—mutatis mutandis—constituted by a functional equilibrium among these three forms of power: the monarchic unity of power and its global monopoly of force; aristocratic articulations through transnational corporations and nation-states; and democratic-representational *comitia*, presented again in the form of nation-states along with the various kinds of NGOs, media organizations, and other 'popular' organisms (ibid.: 314–315).

In his review of *Empire* Balakrishnan (2000: 144) inserts actual players in the above scenario, whereby the "U.S. nuclear supremacy represents the monarchical, the economic wealth of the G7 and transnational corporations the aristocratic, and the internet the democratic."[6]

Interestingly, and convincingly, Hardt and Negri argue that the *Empire* has a vast arsenal of "legitimate force" for imperial intervention, and that military intervention is but one tool, usually of the last resort. The other forms of intervention include juridical and moral, with the latter including the media, religious organizations and in their words, "the so-called" non-governmental organizations (NGOs). In particular, they consider some of the NGOs such as Amnesty International, OXFAM, or Médecins sans Frontièrs as 'moral" agents of the Empire at the global, regional or local levels:

> Such humanitarian NGOs are in effect (even if this runs counter to the intentions of the participants) some of the most powerful pacific weapons of the new world order—the charitable campaigns and the mendicant orders of Empire. These NGOs conduct 'just wars' without arms, without violence, without borders. Like the Dominicans in the late medieval period and the Jesuits at the dawn of modernity, these groups strive to identify universal needs and defend human rights. Through their language and their action they first define the enemy as privation (in the hope of preventing serious damages) and then recognize the enemy as sin (p. 36).

Elsewhere, I have taken a similar position and extensively discussed the role played by NGOs within the context of "civil societies" in various

---

6 With the inclusion of Russia in 1997 the G7 became known as the G8.

emerging nation-states which I consider as political and cultural "projects" that serve the interests of the new world order (or Hardt and Negri's *Empire*). Historically, the emergence and evolution of "civil society" as a concept goes hand in hand with the emergence and evolution of capitalist market economy and its domination over all other economic forms. Earlier definitions of civil society ranged from the notion of a *social sphere* in which citizens utilized to protect their property rights (Locke); the privileged classes guaranteed their rights to have economic, political, and cultural freedom (Hegel); and the bourgeoisie controlled the market and organized the production of commodities (Marx).[7]

Hardt and Negri (2000: xii–xiii) further contend that unlike previous imperial systems that were based on a secured flow of tribute from the peripheries to the center, the new Empire has no "territorial center of power" or fixed boundaries of barriers: "It is a *decentered* and *deterritorializing* apparatus of rule that progressively incorporates the entire global realm within its open, expanding frontiers. Empire manages hybrid identities, flexible hierarchies, and plural exchanges through modulating networks of command." In their analysis, the Empire's "hybrid identities" are not *people*—with homogeneous identities within the confines of nation-states, but rather *multitudes*, arguably the global working poor which "is not homogeneous or identical with itself and bears an indistinct, inclusive relation to those outside of it" (ibid.: 103). In their view the engine that drives the global capitalist development is the "deterritorializing desire of the multitude" that in their opinion needs to be constantly controlled by the capitalist system (p. 124). Although stripped of any social class position, as Balakrishnan (2000: 147) points out in his critique of *Empire*, the *multitude* is granted a new power within the new world order:

> Empire, seemingly in control everywhere, is unable to bridle the planetary flow of workers seeking jobs and a better life in rich countries. Reshaping social relations, everywhere, immigration on this scale reveals both the hostility of the multitude to the system of national borders and its tenacious desire for cosmopolitan freedom.

It is at this juncture that I depart from the postmodern depiction of *Empire* for two reasons. First, the new phase of global capitalist development is based on decentralization of production and consumption of goods on one hand and centralization of decision making and capital accumulation on the other. Although the former process gives some credence to horizontal

---

[7] See Chaichian (2003: 20).

'decentered' tendencies of the *Empire* such as the informal, non-binding cooperation among some members of the so-called G8 countries,[8] the latter still relies on a vertical hierarchy and the power of decision making being in the hands of certain governments, nation-states and their upper class operatives. As Balakrishnan (ibid.: 145) points out, although Hardt and Negri acknowledge the position of the United States at the top of global power structure, they nonetheless insist that the Empire operates without a center of decision making. It is true that the Empire at times conducts business from multiple centers, like the *Lernaean Hydra* in the Greek mythology—an ancient serpent-like water beast with multiple heads (Kerenyi 1959: p. 143), similar to mythical creature the Empire's multiple heads belong to a unified economic bulk (see Photo 1.3).[9] Ancient Greeks believed that one of Lernaean Hydra's heads was immortal, and even if it was cut off it would remain alive keeping the creature's terrorizing powers intact. In contemporary real-time politics this was the case when the so-called *coalition of the willing* led by the United States planned and executed invasion and occupation of Iraq in 2003.[10] While the coalition members left the conflict "theatre" one-by-one after the initial assault (mostly due to domestic pressures within their nation-states), the American forces still remained in Iraq pursuing the U.S.-specific set of goals and defined objectives in the conflict. Furthermore, in many instances individual sovereign nation-states with imperial intentions and ambitions still act on their own specific global interests—such as the American government's role and interest in Mexican economy and labor force since the early 20th century as demonstrated in the most recent examples of inter-state treaties such as NAFTA, trans-border economic activities such

---

[8] The G8 (Group of 8) is an informal and non-binding forum that is comprised of France, Germany, Italy, Japan, the United States, Canada and Russia. The leaders of these countries that were once the world's strongest economies gather at annual summits and discuss important issues affecting their economies. However, exclusion of China as the second strongest global economy which is predicted to soon surpass that of the United States and few other strong emerging economies including Brazil and India make a 'decentered' global economy proposition rather problematic.

[9] According to the myth, the Lernaean Hydra was killed by Hercules, the demigod son of Zeus. But as an expression of the hopelessness of fighting the beast, he found out that upon cutting off each head new heads grew back. Similar vicious, multi-headed snakes also exist in ancient Egyptian, Indian, Japanese and European mythologies.

[10] The *coalition of the willing* is a post-1990 term used mostly by the United States and her close allies to justify military interventions for the Empire that did not have global support, particularly when the United Nations Security Council members failed to agree on stationing a UN peacekeeping force in a given region or country. The infamous example is the American-led invasion of Iraq by "coalition forces" during George W. Bush's presidency that mainly comprised of the U.S., British and Australian forces.

Source: The York Project: *10.000 Meisterwerke der Malerei.* http://commons.wikimedia.org/
wiki/File:Hercules_and_the_Hydra_Lernaean_by_Gustave_Moreau.jpg

Photo 1.3 Hercules and the Lernaean Hydra.

as the maquiladora industries, and erection of U.S.-Mexico border wall/
fence to manage the flow of Mexican migrant workers.[11]

Second, Hardt and Negri's *multitude* may account for part of billions
of global work force, but they cannot substitute the majority of workers
who, although weakened by the forces of a neo-liberal global capitalism

---

[11] See chapter 7 for a detailed historical account of the U.S.-Mexican relations.

are still comprising a mighty fighting force within the context of nation-states' political economy. The new global reality of working conditions and environments that with no doubt has undermined the bargaining power of workers at the national levels is a direct outcome of neo-liberal economic policies promoted by the likes of Milton Friedman and crept to center stage in the 1970s as a response to a declining rate of profit and high levels of inflation within the capitalist world system. As Harvey (2006: 25–29) explains, these policies led to the emergence of "profoundly anti-democratic" neo-liberal states whose main mission is to establish "a good business climate" through extreme measures taken for privatization, deregulation, economic restructuring often leading to massive lay-offs, and facilitation of free movement of labor and capital at regional and global levels which are collectively known as 'flexible, just-in-time production and accumulation.'[12] Internally, neo-liberal states brutally repress and prevent all forms of workers' solidarity, while reducing the barriers to movement of capital across borders which are often promoted and protected by global capitalist monopolies.[13]

Furthermore, disintegration of the Soviet Union in the early 1990s as an *empire* in its own terms;[14] and increasing hegemony of global capitalism based on neo-liberal policies as the main political-economic force have effectively undermined the possibility of having successful insurgent movements that seek to establish independent and progressive national-ist regimes particularly in the so-called "developing" countries. The Soviet Union's sudden demise as the main ideological force behind centralized socialist governments allowed the West to promote the civil society proj-ects in both post-socialist and developing countries. One of the earliest ideologues of postmodern politics was Daniel Bell whose "post-industrial society" thesis popularized the assumption that industrial-capitalism is reaching its zenith whereby labor and capital will no longer be in conflict (Bell, 1974). It was within this context that Francis Fukuyama's "End of History" thesis (1992) found a receptive audience in the West and, in my opinion provided ideological support for the "civil society" as

---

[12] See also Harvey (1991).

[13] In her ground-breaking work *The Shock Doctrine* Naomi Klein (2007) provides numer-ous examples of neoliberal policies and interventions within confines of the American "Empire."

[14] Later in chapter 4 I will discuss in detail how in the aftermath of the 1917 October Revolution the newly established Soviet Union was destined to evolve as the first imperial socialist entity in the world on the ashes of former Tsarist Russian Empire.

a postmodern project. In brief, Fukuyama argued that liberal democracy had finally overcome all other ideologies, and has put an end to all ideological conflicts in the world. He concluded that Western liberal democracy has become a universally acceptable concept, one that all nations will move to embrace. Thus without addressing the "problematic" of developing nations' structural dependency on the West, or questioning the shortcomings of a corporate-dominated global capitalism and its ideological legitimacy, the post-Cold War advocates of the *new world order* argued that the globalized industrial-capitalist system is no longer threatened by alternative political and economic systems such as socialism:

> There will not be three "worlds" but only one world, a world in which countries at various levels of development interact in a multitude of diverse and mutually beneficial ways. The development model that largely prevailed from the 1950s to the 1980s and that was characterized by non-democratic, authoritarian *dirigisme*, and social engineering aimed at "modernization" has indeed been washed away by the tide of history (Madison, 1998: 188).

The above interpretation is also clearly echoed in Hardt and Negri's rendition of Empire's new global environment, whereby the boundaries of the earlier identified three worlds are blurred, and that their often overlapping identities make them indistinguishable from each other:

> [T]he spatial divisions of the three worlds (First, Second, and Third) have been scrambled so that we continually find the First World in the Third, Third in the First, and the Second almost nowhere at all. Capital seems to be faced with a smooth world—or really, a world defined by new complex regimes of differentiation and homogenization, deterritorialization and reterritorialization (2000: xiii).

I end my brief comparative survey of empires and imperial formations by identifying one main difference and one similarity between the old and new forms of empire. First, a significant point of departure for the new Empire under American hegemonic power from all other empires in the past, both ancient and colonial-capitalist, is the way it has skillfully substituted the real, identifiable national and local anti-imperialist entities with faceless, nationless individuals and enclaves that are situated outside the confines of "civilized," law abiding global community of nation-states. As a reflection of this new reality, the neo-liberal lexicon of the American Empire has accordingly and quite effectively substituted "insurgents" for "nationalists," and "terrorists" for "guerilla fighters." The creation of these fictitious individuals and groups who are considered as sworn enemies of the new world order, albeit with no demonstration of logical and explicable reasons, has justified the *Empire's* maintenance of what Hardt and Negri (2000: 18) rightly called a "permanent state of emergency and exception."

Second, we can find a common ground between the postmodern *Empire* and its ancient predecessors such as the Roman Empire, which as Hardt and Negri postulate is in fact a manifestation of their inherent contradictions that characterizes their "decadence and decline" from the early stages of imperial formation:

> Empire is emerging today as the center that supports the globalization of productive networks and casts its widely inclusive net to try to envelop all power relations within its world order—and yet at the same time it deploys a powerful police function against the new barbarians and the rebellious slaves who threaten its order (p. 38).

In their analysis, empires are sustained in a "permanent state of emergency and exception" that is justified by an appeal to all citizens and subjects under imperial jurisdiction to adhere to universal "essential values of justice" which in turn will legitimize the use of police force domestically and military intervention outside nation-state boundaries (p. 18).[15] On this point, using historian Charles Beard's famous phrase *"perpetual war for perpetual peace"* and in a book by the same title Vidal (2002) portrays the United States as a plutocracy that is run by and for the wealthy few, that is constantly engaged in wars of aggression to safeguard imperial holdings.[16]

---

[15] However, in their postmodern interpretation of *Empire* they categorically reject those who consider American global economic, political and military involvement as an indication that an American Empire is a reality:
> First of all, the coming Empire is not American and the United States is not its center. The fundamental principle of empire as we have described it throughout this book is that its power has no actual and localizable terrain or center. Imperial power is distributed in networks, through mobile and articulated mechanisms of control. This is not to say that the U.S. government and the U.S. territory are no different from any other: The United States certainly occupies a privileged position in the global segmentations and hierarchies of Empire (ibid.: 384).

Their rejection of the American Empire's reality is hardly tenable, and as Balakrishnan (2000: 147) points out, if we assume the contemporary global capitalist system as an *Empire*, this position is only tenable because of the "overwhelming concentration of financial, diplomatic, and military power in American hands."

[16] In his tribute to Charles Beard, Martin (1981) states that "'Perpetual war for perpetual peace' was an expression coined by Beard, to describe satirically the apparent objective of the world 'liberators' in fashioning their peculiar 'postwar world,' in which the United Nations Organization was presumed to be put into business largely to conduct military operations against any power 'threatening the peace'." Related to the American Empire's foreign policy and military interventions, Vidal's assertion is supported by the

Borders, Walls and Globalization

Walls and fortifications remained signature features of cities and towns at least in the context of central European history up until the end of the Thirty Years' War and the Treaty of Westphalia in 1648, when an emerging and evolving capitalist economy rendered these micro-level dynastic fortifications obsolete and instead necessitated creation of political borders to defend and safeguard the economic interests of nascent sovereign capitalist *nation-states* (Agnew, 1994; Jackson, 2000; Walker, 1993). By the late 19th and early 20th centuries the integrity of *nation-state* at the global level was then reinforced with international treaties that were based on three inviolable principles: (1) states were deemed responsible to formulate their domestic legal systems; (2) states had to respect other states' rights to also formulate their own domestic laws; and (3) all nation-states had to respect each other's territorial integrity (Elden, 2006: 11; Gregory, 2006: 422).

In analyzing the ethics of maintaining territorial borders within the context of international relations, Williams (2003: 39) makes the case that inter-state borders function as "fences between neighbors" while tolerating diversity of national identities. This argument implicitly characterizes international borders, once established, as being non-violent and peaceful by nature. But challenging this interpretation, Vaughn-Williams (2008: 325) makes the point that "borders between states are not necessarily limits on but rather markers and even upholders of violence in political life." In a similar fashion, Connolly (1995: 163) contends that "[political] boundaries form indispensable protections against violation and violence; but the divisions they sustain also carry cruelty and violence."

In his extensively discussed theorization of borders, Manuel Castells (1990, 2000) postulates that territorial nation-states and regional communities ('*a space of places*') are being replaced by the network society ('*a space of flows*')—the latter being the domain of capital, labor, information and business alliances. By definition, the constantly changing European Union can be considered as the "paradigm" of the network society, where "territorial borders are easily transcended by flows and mobilities which take place within globalized circuits of information and exchange" (Rumford, 2006; 155–156). Similarly, as I shall make the case later in the

---

U.S. involvement in Korea, Vietnam, Iran, Nicaragua, Grenada, former Yugoslavia, Iraq and Afghanistan in the post-WWII period.

book, the United States, Mexico and Canada have become a "network society" under the economic stipulations of the North American Free Trade Agreement (NAFTA). I shall also make the case that Israel proper and the occupied Palestinian territories comprise a "network society," both being part of a much more complex global network society that also includes the United States. However, I concur with Beck (2002: 25) who warns us about the inherent danger of taking "the metaphor of the *fluid* that flows" at its face value, as if capital, labor, information, etc. move across national boundaries at will without the presence of a center (or centers) of control:

> The very suggestiveness of the powerful metaphor of the 'fluid' begs the question of whether 'networks' and 'flows' as social processes can be so independent of national, transnational and political-economic structures that enable, channel and control the flows of people, things and ideas. In other words, there is a lack of institutional (power)-structures, sometimes even an anti-institutionalism involved in the powerful cultural research and theory about 'fluids' and 'mobility.'[17]

Furthermore, citing Sassen's seminal work in theorizing cities in the context of a globalized political economy (2000) Beck also alludes to two common "misunderstandings of globalization." First, globalization is not about globalization, rather, it is "about localization as well." In his words, "globalization happens not *out there*, but *in here*."[18] Second, globalization is not "an additive" to the reality of nation-state societies, rather, as a new paradigmatic "sociological imagination" it substitutes nation-states. This is what he terms "globalization from within" or "cosmopolitanization of nation-states" (Beck, 2002: 23, 2004: 143–166).[19] It derives from Sassen's assertion (2000: 145 ff.) which does not see the 'national' and the 'nonnational' as being mutually exclusive:

> ... one of the features of the current face of globalization is the fact that a process, which happens within a territory of sovereign state, does not necessarily mean that it is a national process. Conversely, the national (such as firms, capital, culture) may increasingly be located outside the national territory, for instance, in a foreign country or digital spaces. This localization of the global, or of the non-national, in national territories, and of the national

---

[17] See also Urry (2000).

[18] Emphasis is mine. Beck relates this definition to what Robertson calls 'glocalization' (1992).

[19] Beck defines 'cosmopolitanization' as "*internal* globalization, globalization *from within* the national societies" (ibid.: 17).

outside national territories, undermined a key duality running through many of the methods and conceptual frameworks prevalent in social sciences, that the national and the non-national are mutually exclusive.[20]

The new phase of globalization which coincides with proliferation of neo-liberal economic policies since the 1970s can be described as the end of national boundaries and emergence of regional and global economic power houses that operate based on four principles: 1) emergence of capital markets and trans-border capital movement and investment; 2) establishment of new types of industry that rely on the mobility of capital, labor and information—all controlled by transnational corporations; 3) development of information technology that facilitates decentralization of production processes; and 4) promotion of global individual consumers who look for higher quality products with the lowest possible prices (Ohmae, 1995: 2–5). To facilitate this process, powerful state and quasi-governmental institutions such as central banks, the International Monetary Fund (IMF) and the World Trade Organization (WTO) are also established (Stiglitz, 2002: 10–13; Harvey, 2006: 27).

Empires and imperial formations are intrinsically intertwined with and benefit from the new phase of globalization, and both are violent by nature. But postmodern and neo-liberal interpretations of globalization in particular tend to portray it as a peaceful process of *transformation* of an evolving market economy. In his review of various theories of globalization Brar (2005: 147) explains how this new global reality is presented and justified for the *multitude*:

> *Transformationism* makes globalization appear less threatening, perhaps even reassuring, to the 'losers.' They could find in it openings for their own betterment. Since the world is not merely integrating but also fragmenting, there should be no real basis for the fear that the local and the national will get subordinated to the global. Rather, the three would continue to constantly interact as before (emphasis mine).

As Brar (ibid.) points out, there is an ideological objective to conceal the aggressive and violent nature of globalization; as otherwise "it could provoke the 'losers' of globalization into organizing a revolt against the 'winners'."

The preceding discussion as to the conceptual notion of globalization is a theoretical prerequisite in conceptualizing imperial borders and border

---

[20] For a detailed account of Sassen's views see her conversation with Nicholas Gane (Gane, 2004: 125–142).

formations. For one thing, borders no longer define boundaries between two nation-states, or demarcate the outer limits of a nation. Rather, in this light the borders can as well be mobile, meaning depending on their functionality they may be located *outside* or *within* a social-territorial entity (i.e., Castells' 'network society').[21] Related to the former case, since 2004 the British immigration agents have set up border checkpoints in the cities of Lille, Calais and Paris in France to examine the documents of those intending to travel to the UK; and in the latter case in the aftermath of a series of bombings in London in 2005 internet café users in Italy were required to "produce their passports before being granted access to communication networks" (Rumford, 2006: 157–58). This is what Beck (2002: 19) calls *"pluralization of nation-state borders"* which he defines as "the implosion of the dualism between the national and the international." Also, as I will make the case for North African migrants mostly from Algeria and Morocco who reside and live in France, they use Islamic/tribal veil (*"hijab"*) to cover women—the *essence and cultural core* of immigrant populations, in order to shield their communities from Western cultural onslaughts, or *globalization from within*. Finally, cosmopolitanism means "having 'roots' and 'wings' at the same time" (Beck, ibid.), and as Rumford (2006: 163) points out this global reality also means that borders and mobilities are intricate components of a unified entity:

> A globalizing world is a world of networks, flows and mobility; it is also a world of borders. It can be argued that cosmopolitanism is best understood as an orientation to the world which entails the constant negotiation and crossing of borders. A cosmopolitan is not only a citizen of the world, someone who embraces multiculturalism, or even a 'frequent flyer.' A cosmopolitan lives in and across borders.

In his discussion of a resurgence of border fortifications in the aftermath of the fall of the Berlin Wall Davis (2005: 88–89) distinguishes between walls and fences that demarcate "internal borders" even in many developing ("Third World") countries such as those between India and Bhutan in Asia, Botswana and Zimbabwe in Africa, Costa Rica and Nicaragua in Central America—and the "Great Wall of Capital" that "brutally separates a few dozen rich countries from the earth's poor majority." In his opinion the latter's proliferation contradicts the premises of "physical and

---

[21] On this issue see also Balibar (2004) and his discussion of the new reality of the European Union, whereby the continent has witnessed a major shift in the relationship between borders and territorial identities.

virtual-electronic mobility" in an era of globalization dominated by neo-liberal capitalism. But as I shall explain in the following chapters these "Great Walls of Capital," such as the wall/fence along the U.S.-Mexico border or the wall/fence built by Israel around the occupied West Bank and Gaza Strip in Palestine are not separating the rich from the poor, but rather regulating the population flow in an already integrated political economies of their respective empires. Thus globalization calls into question the conventional concept of nation-states' sovereignty and facilitates the operation of empires at regional and global levels.

PART ONE

THE IMPERIAL WALLS THAT ARE NO LONGER AROUND

HADRIAN'S WALL: AN ILL-FATED STRATEGY FOR TRIBAL MANAGEMENT IN ROMAN BRITAIN

Britain first came into contact with the Romans when, in an unsuccessful attempt, Julius Caesar and a small contingent of troops crossed the ocean and invaded the island in 55 BC. At the time, German territories north of Gaul and the British Isles were beyond Roman control on the northern and western frontiers (see Figure 2.1). The timing of invasion (late summer) and the size of the accompanying army (about 10,000) suggest that this was only meant to be a reconnaissance expedition. Caesar returned in the following year landing on the southeastern shores better prepared and with a much larger military force. The British tribes gathered their forces under the leadership of Cassivellaunus, king of the Catuvellauni, the most influential and powerful tribe in southern Britain, and confronted the Roman army (Salway, 1981: 25–33). Although Caesar eventually succeeded in winning the submission of British tribes, for practical reasons he decided to delineate Gaul's western shores as the Empire's northwestern boundaries. Salway (2002: 15) considers the Emperor's decision to be mainly based on a calculated cost-benefit analysis:

> Like all cross-Channel invasions, not least the D-Day landings of 1944, the risk factor was very high, even for so formidable a general as Caesar. Whilst he was not accorded an appropriate celebration in Rome, he cannot have been unpleased with the outcome of his expeditions to what even in the days of the Claudian conquest, nearly a century later, was widely regarded as an island 'outside the limits of the known world.'

New evidence indicates that Caesar's successful invasion in 54 BC and appointment of some tribal leaders as client kings facilitated cross-Channel trade between Roman traders and British merchants.[1] However, for nearly a century after Caesar's invasion Britain remained outside Roman Empire's orbit until Emperor Claudius and his army invaded the island again in AD 43—the year considered by most historians of Roman

---

[1] Salway (2002: 16) makes this point by providing examples of artifacts that are exhibited in a collection of Iron Age and Romano-British antiquities in the British Museum since 1997.

colonial intentions in Britain as a historic watershed. Between the last third of the first century and the early years of second the conquest of Britain was complete (Salway, 1993: 116). From then on Britain was incorporated into the imperial holdings and for the next four centuries was ruled as a Roman province.

When in 117 AD Hadrian succeeded Trajan as the new Roman Emperor, he inherited an empire that faced trouble on both eastern and northern frontiers. Historians often portray Trajan and Hadrian in different lights in terms of their personalities, worldviews, and imperial ambitions. For instance, one scholar of Roman Britain offers the following comparison:

> Yet, a provincial like Trajan, Hadrian was a very different person. The former had seemed a personification of all the old Roman virtues: a deliberately modest style of life, a devotion to the ancient ideals of the family, a grandeur in his public works essentially based on utility, and *a conviction that the glory of Rome was best served in the extension of the empire by wars of conquest*. Hadrian shared Trajan's devotion to duty, his incorruptibility, and his scale of vision but *he broke away completely from the ideal of military glory by conquest*. His personal tastes were for Greek culture, his character complex (Salway, 1981: 169–70) (emphasis mine).

Facing social upheavals and rebellion in the eastern empire Hadrian ordered his troops to completely evacuate from untenable provinces of Mesopotamia, Assyria, and Greater Armenia (Opper, 2008; 64–66). On the western front, except for northern Britain and southern Scotland as early as AD 60 most parts of the island in the south and east have been pacified and did not require massive concentration of Roman troops (Salway, 1993: 79). By 85 AD all of Wales, northern England and southern Scotland were "brought into the province" and under Roman control. Yet by 86 AD the reigning Emperor Domitian had to withdraw one of the four Roman legions stationed in Britain to the Balkans in order to confront the threat from Dacians on the Danube, which weakened the Roman occupation forces' ability to effectively keep the territories north of the Tyne-Solway line in check (Breeze and Dobson, 1976; 16).[2] Thus Hadrian also had to find a solution for serious challenges posed to the Roman occupation by tribes particularly in the northern frontier of Tyne-Solway in southern Scotland—not a welcoming news for the new Emperor, as the northern frontier was once beyond the Forth-Clyde isthmus in Scottish highlands.

---

[2] An Indo-European population, the Dacians were ancient inhabitants of Dacia—an area that includes present-time Moldova and Romania, as well as parts of eastern Ukraine and Serbia, Poland, Slovakia, and northern Bulgaria.

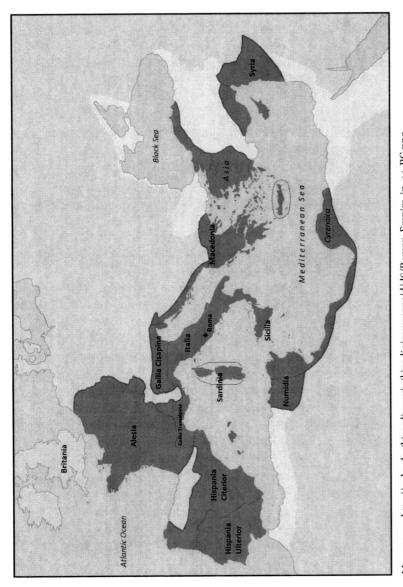

Map source: http://upload.wikimedia.org/wikipedia/commons/d/d6/Roman_Empire_in_44_BC.png

Figure 2.1 Roman Empire at the end of Caesar's rule (44 BC).

Hadrian's solution to secure Rome's imperial holdings in Britain was simple yet ambitious:

> He planned to build a massive wall, fronted by a wide ditch, stretching from coast to coast, just beyond existing chain of forts. Castles situated at every mile along its length would guard gates opening to the north and south. *Anyone could enter or leave the Roman province at any of 80 such crossing points—but only on Rome's say-so and under its direct scrutiny. The wall was to be not a military line, but a supremely efficient frontier control system* (Martin, 2003: 29–30) (emphasis mine).

Archaeologists and historians of the Romans' presence in Britain have extensively and meticulously written about Hadrian's Wall. Most accounts of the events that led to the planning and construction of the Wall begin by the infamous quote from Hadrian's fourth-century biographer who recounted Hadrian's journey to Britain in 122 AD, where "he set many things right and—he was the first to do so—erected a wall along a length of eighty miles, which was to separate the barbarians and Romans" (cf. Birley, 1997; 123) (see Figure 2.2).

But who exactly were these "barbarians" who inhabited territories north of the Wall that had to be kept in check by the Romans? In general, the Greco-Roman chroniclers at the time have portrayed Britain and Ireland as primitive societies of "barbarians." But using archaeological evidence, Salway (2002: 12) provides examples of the presence in the British Isles of a rather "highly complex and sophisticated system of tribal societies" that although were mostly illiterate, they were anything but primitive (see Figure 3).[3] At the time of the Roman conquest Britain was run by Celtic tribal societies, each with their own territories and hierarchical social structure comprised of petty kings, noble warriors, skilled craftsmen, and peasants (Todd, 1999: 18). The Roman Britain's northern territory was populated by the Brigantes, probably the most populous of all British tribes. Their territory stretched from southern Lancashire to as far as north of the Tyne-Solway line, the site of future Hadrian's Wall (Scullard, 1979: 35). The Brigantes were not nomadic, but settled pastoralists who also cultivated limited tracts of arable lands (Todd, 1981: 41). Further north, between the Tyne-Solway and Forth-Clyde isthmuses lived four tribes (the Novante, the Damnonii, the Selgovae, and the Votadini), and as settled

---

[3] Examples include monumental architecture such as the Stonehenge erected during the 4th and 3rd millennia BC, the use of wheeled vehicles for "well over a thousand years," and coins from late 2nd and 1st centuries BC (ibid.). For a comprehensive account of British tribes see Miles (2005).

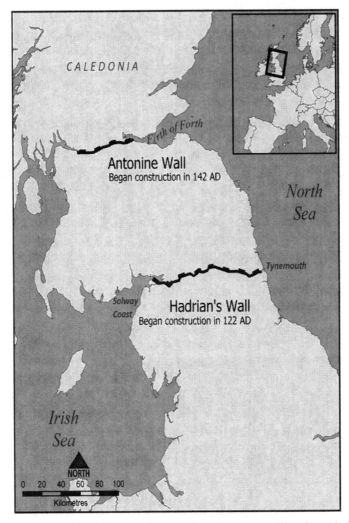

Source: Map courtesy of Norman Einstein, http://commons.wikimedia.org/wiki/File: Hadrians_Wall_map.png

Figure 2.2 Southern Scotland between the Forth-Clyde and Tyne-Solway Isthmuses (sites of Antonine and Hadrian Walls, respectively)

agriculturalists they were more advanced than the Brigantes in terms of social organization (Scullard, 1979: 35). Most data on the northern tribes are sketchy, and there are discrepancies among scholars. For example, Salway (1981: 46) contends that "the state of development" for the four tribes residing in territories north of the Brigantes (north of the future

Hadrian's Wall) was "... in some ways parallel to that of the Brigantes—a basically Bronze Age culture with some Iron Age features, notably, in the Scottish case, hill-forts."[4]

North of the Forth-Clyde isthmus lied Caledonia, or *terra incognito* as far as the Romans were concerned, where eleven tribes resided. Foremost amongst these were the *Caledones* or *Caledonii*, yet the Romans indiscriminately used this name for all the tribes living in northern Scotland.[5] In all likelihood these tribes were hunter-gatherers or nomadic populations who, according to Roman historian Dio Cassius, "lived in tents, naked and unshod;" and survived "off their flocks, wild game and certain fruits." (cf. Scullard, 1979: 35) (see Figure 2.3).

Although partially speculative, the available information and scholarship indicate the presence of a rather diverse composition of tribal groups who operated at different levels of socio-economic development within their loosely defined territories.[6] But the Roman colonial/imperial culture indiscriminately labeled all who were outside the empire's boundaries as "barbarians" who presented real or perceived threat to imperial interests. They borrowed the word from ancient Greeks who coined the term for those who did not speak Greek, an onomatopoeic representation of the babble ('bar bar bar') of non-Greek speakers (Divine, 1969: 10; Ferris, 2000: 3). This stereotypical representation played a significant role in shaping the Roman identity, allowing them to separate themselves from those uncivil alien barbarians who were "close to nature," wore "strange clothing," lived differently, and displayed irrational and "aberrant behavior" (Burns, 2003: 5). More specifically, barbarians allegedly lacked what the Roman society and culture stood for—civility, high moral values, advanced technology, and law and order (Millett, 1990: 20). The dichotomous distinction between the barbarian (uncivil) and Roman (civilized) also provided a justification for subjugation of populations and nations that suited Roman imperial appetite:

---

[4] Used in archaeological literature, hill-forts refer to earthworks that are used in fortified settlements, taking advantage of a rise in elevation for defensive purposes.

[5] Most information about the names and locations of the tribes living north of the Tyne-Solway isthmus at the time of the Roman invasion depends primarily upon two sources, Ptolemy's *Geography* and Tacitus's *Agricola*; two highly unreliable sources, as neither of the two ever set foot on Britain or Scotland (see Mann and Breeze, 1987).

[6] For a more detailed account of Britain's Celtic tribes see Todd (1999: 19–42). Moffat (2005: 225–284) also provides a comprehensive historical narrative for Caledonia and its inhabitants.

Image source: Map courtesy of University of North Carolina at Chapel Hill, http://www.unc .edu/celtic/catalogue/boudica/map.html (copyright granted from UNC).

Figure 2.3 Map of Celtic Britain's Ethnic Tribes, 1st century BC.

It had suited Roman moralists to see the barbarian as the noble savage, struggling to save his native virtues against the corruption of Roman civilization... Overall, however, Roman attitudes to the barbarians were still based on the assumptions that they were both a menace to be guarded against and fair game for generals ambitious to make their names and fortunes. This was to remain the dominant approach of Rome to her barbarian neighbors, long after the realities of power had decisively changed (Salway, 1981: 240).

There is an interesting nuance in chronicling the Romans' presence in Britain. In his account of Rome's attempts to assimilate the British subjects, or their 'Romanization' Salway (1993: 337) contends that Romans did not hold any prejudicial thoughts and beliefs "in the modern sense" of racial/ethnic notions of differences and superiority or inferiority, and that "there was nothing immutable" in their assessment of "a man's worth":

Hence they assumed that anyone, or almost anyone, could absorb Roman culture and manners, even as they themselves (despite the protests of moralists and conservatives) borrowed extensively from other cultures, especially in the fields of art and religion. They had a keen sense of class and an enormous pride in their family histories, but on the whole they treated a man on the basis of what he was now rather than on the background from which he had come, though they were not above making fun of the nouveau riches.

Certainly there is an element of truth in the above assessment, to infer that the Romans were perhaps ancient precursors to modern multiculturalists on their own terms. Yet promotion of multiculturalism for the benefit of the empire was based on the tacit acknowledgement of Rome's moral and cultural superiority over all others. Similar to its modern counterparts such as the United States, assimilation of imperial subjects to the dominant culture and ethos was the prerequisite for subjects' transition from backwardness ('barbarity') to development ('civility').

When in AD 122 Hadrian landed in Britain most of island's southern and central parts were 'Romanized.'[7] One main tool for Romanization was the ability of Britons to speak (as well as read and write) Latin in order to be fully participating in the affairs of the Empire—Latin was the language of law, public administration, as well as the military. Thus "men of influence"

---

[7] My my objective here is not to examine the long history of Romans' presence in Britain, rather, historical conditions and socio-political factors that led to the building of Hadrian's Wall. Other scholars have accomplished this task more eloquently and in full detail. For an account of "Romanization" of Britain see Salway (1993: 337–367). Also, for detailed accounts of Roman Britain see Frere (1987), Mattingly (2006), Salway (1993, 1981), and Scullard (1979).

and their families were pressured to speak Latin and adopt the dominant Roman culture and way of life throughout the empire:

> It was as these leading provincial families came to identify themselves with Roman political and social culture, and to strive with one another within its terms, that the Romanization of the provinces that we can recognize archaeologically followed. The merging of these people with the Roman official classes, military and civil, and the creation of a unified substructure of urban society to serve this establishment were the mainsprings of the provincial cities now developing, which in turn influenced the economies and expectations of the countryside around them (Salway, 1993: 79).

Yet colonizing entities, the Romans included, have always used derogatory terms for those subjected to their domination as a psychological and ideological tool to justify their imperial intentions in front of their subjects and reduce the guilt of occupation within the rank and file of their occupying armies. For example, Miles (2005: 121) describes the way in which one of the documents found by archaeologists in Vindolanda, a garrison fort built prior to the construction of Hadrian's Wall along the Stanegate ("stone road" in old English) military road refers to native British subjects under occupation in such terms:[8]

> Among the Vindolanda documents there are no accounts of battles, or even skirmishes with local tribesmen. One memorandum refers disparagingly to the 'Brittunculi', which we can translate as 'the little Brits' or 'wretched Britons'. This might be a contemptuous reference to hostile local tribesmen or alternatively, to a recruiting officer's low opinion of native conscripts. *By AD 100 British soldiers were serving overseas in the Roman army. Nevertheless, the stalwarts of Imperial Rome dismiss their new subjects with the casual slang of colonial troops of any age* (Miles, 2005: 121) (emphasis mine).

Geopolitics of Hadrian's Wall

Due to a sketchy documentation of events at the time, little is known about the nature of unrest during Hadrian's early years in northern Britain. But there are all indications that he had to settle for designation of the Tyne-Solway isthmus as the northern-most British frontier, as "his inclinations were to conserve rather than expand, and so he chose to improve the existing frontier on the Tyne-Solway line rather than conquer the whole

---

[8] Stanegate was a military road built by the Romans prior to the construction of Hadrian's Wall.

of the island of Britain or move forward to the much shorter Forth-Clyde isthmus" further north (Breeze and Dobson, 1976: 29). The Tyne-Solway line had already been established as a de facto frontier before Hadrian's time; where the Stanegate military road was built connecting two Roman forts in Corbridge in the east and Carlisle in the west—guarding and securing two river crossings along the Tyne-Solway line. Forts were also built at a day's marching intervals along the Stanegate to allow a safe movement of troops and needed supplies. Building the Wall along the Stanegate seems to have been the most logical plan, with the former securing the northern frontier and the latter providing logistical support for soldiers who guarded the wall and the frontier.[9] Thus during his visit to Britain in AD 122 Hadrian considered strengthening the northern frontier by constructing a wall from Newcastle upon Tyne on the North Sea Coast in the east to Bowness-on-Solway on the Solway Firth in the west, a stretch of 76 Roman miles (a little more than 70 British miles) (see Figure 2.4).

The Wall's Architecture

By AD 128, six years after Hadrian's visit to Britain the Wall was almost complete. Due to several revisions the completed wall varied in its dimensions, about 15 to 20 Roman feet high (Roman foot = eleven inches) above the ground and 6 to 10 feet wide, possibly with 6 feet high parapets at the top of the wall. Archaeological traces of the wall reveal that the eastern stretch of the wall from Newcastle to the crossing of the River Irthing near Carlisle was built of stone, with remaining 31 miles of the western stretch being initially constructed of turf.[10] The wall's path took advantage of topography so that Roman soldiers could have a commanding view of the territories north of the wall, such as the central section where it climbed the ridges of a chain of north-facing volcanic crags known as the Whin Sill (Johnson, 2004: 6; Wilkes, 2005: 5).[11] On the north side of the wall ran a V-shaped ditch, about 27 feet wide and 10 feet deep except in places like the Whin Sill "where the terrain rendered it superfluous" (Breeze and Dobson, 1976: 30). This was obviously a *defensive* design aimed at securing the wall from possible unhindered approaches from the north, giving the

---

[9] For a detailed discussion of Stanegate's origins and development see Breeze and Dobson (1976: 20–27).

[10] This was due to inadequate supplies of limestone.

[11] The Whin Sill in Northumberland is a narrow ridge of hard dolerite rock.

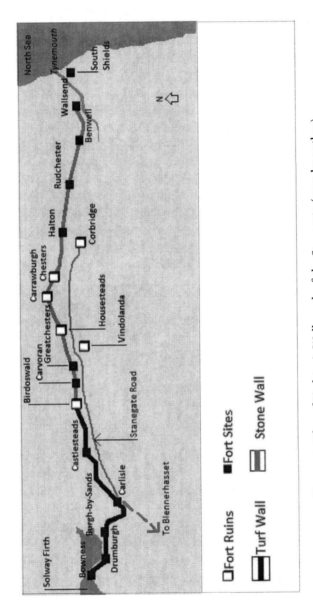

Figure 2.4 Plan of Hadrian's Wall north of the Stanegate (map by author).

soldiers who guarded the wall a superior strategic position in quelling the advancing forces.

Thus, an enemy who was attacking at an inland location would be confronted by a formidable barricade that reached about 31 feet from the bottom of the ditch to the top of the parapet wall and stretched as far as the eye could see in both directions.[12] Fortified gateways were also built along the Wall at one Roman mile intervals, thus commonly known as "milecastles," with the Wall serving as its northern defensive structure. Each milecastle housed a small contingent of troops and in most cases provided crossing points with gates on both the north and south sides. But the Wall's original plan was rather mechanical, as by spacing milecastles in regular intervals it did not seem to have taken "any peculiarities of the terrain" into consideration (Opper, 2008; 80). For instance, the milecastle in Cawfields is situated in a territory that makes it impossible for troops and particularly wheeled traffic to go through the gates in either direction (Johnson 2004: 46, 50; see Photo 2.1). Breeze and Dobson (1976: 38) also question the "lavish" provision of so many gates at the milecastles and turrets and the Wall's simplistic design:

> Lavish is the word, for there is a clear overprovision of gates and there is something artificial about their regular, even over-regular, spacing which led to milecastles and turrets being built in ludicrous positions on a steep hillside or with an almost precipitous drop immediately outside the north gate. *This smacks of over-systematic planning, probably done at some distance, presumably by Hadrian himself, with little attention to local geography* (emphasis mine).

There were also two turrets between milecastles built at roughly one-third of a Roman mile apart that apparently functioned as observation towers. The turrets most likely functioned as signal stations, an important component of the Roman military strategy from which "messages could be transmitted by semaphore or fire signals" (Frere, 1987: 215). They also served as surveillance towers so that "attempts at unauthorized crossing of the barrier by raiding parties and the like could be foreseen and prevented" (Breeze and Dobson (1976: 37). The Wall's original plan only provided limited capacity and space for each milecastle that was large enough to house at the most about 50 or 60 soldiers who were charged with guarding the frontier wall, while the majority of the troops were accommodated in forts and fortlets built along the Stanegate from Corbridge to

---

[12] Time-Life Books (1994: 121).

Photo 2.1 Milecastle 39 in Cawfields (foreground) and Hadrian's Wall on the Great Whin Sill (left) looking East. Photo courtesy of Adam Cuerden.

Carlisle (Forde-Johnston, 1978: 46). This arrangement was modified at a later point, probably around AD 126, to build forts along the Wall itself or closely associated with it. Archaeological evidence indicates that at least 16 forts were constructed in this fashion.

In addition to the defensive ditch that stretched the entire length of the wall on its north side, another east-west earthwork known as the *Vallum* was constructed south of the wall.[13] Breeze and Dobson (1976: 49–50) contend that the Vallum was constructed at about the same time the decision was made to construct the forts along the wall. The Vallum's design consisted of a "... flat-bottomed ditch 20 feet wide and 10 deep with two mounds, 20 feet wide, one on either side, set back 30 feet from the lip of the ditch" (see Figure 2.5). As is illustrated in Figure 2.6, the Vallum provided a crude east-west track for movement of troops just south of the wall, with the Stanegate serving as the main east-west military road. But it appears that the main purpose of the Vallum was to function as a low-maintenance physical barrier to restrict access to the wall from the south (Johnson, 2004: 58). This is based on the fact that "internal resistance to the construction of the Wall was unexpectedly fierce; and that there had been a miscalculation of the reaction by the Brigantes [Celtic tribes residing mostly south of Wall] to their contacts with the north being cut off" (ibid.: 59). Although speculative, this seems to be a sound argument, as tribes have always relied on freedom of movement within their own territories and to other tribal areas; a cultural, economic and political necessity that is at odds with artificially created boundaries and barriers such as Hadrian's Wall that cut right through tribal lands and territories. Although not defended militarily, the Vallum kept any population movement from south to north in check, allowing Roman troops stationed at the Wall to focus on territories north of the Wall (ibid.). Martin (2003: 31) provides a more plausible explanation for Vallum's function, that "it delineated an official military zone—the equivalent of a "Government Property—Keep Out" notice in a form no illiterate tribesmen could fail to understand." After all, similar to other colonial situations the Roman army was an occupying force and despite the relative calm south of the Wall it was regarded as such by the populace in Britain's occupied territories. The Vallum's other function was "to seal off the Brigantes (the main tribe in northern Britain) from their potential allies beyond the Wall" (Todd, 199: 124). More importantly, the Vallum's design contributed to a more efficient passage

---

[13] This is a misnomer, as the word *vallum* was actually the Roman term for the wall.

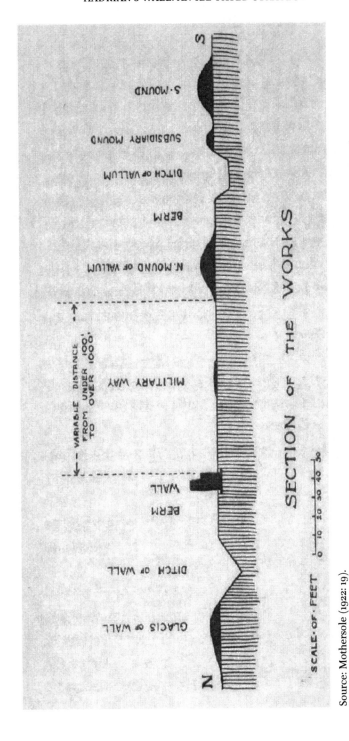

Source: Mothersole (1922: 19).

Figure 2.5 A cross-sectional sketch of (from left to right) the ditch, the Wall and the Valllum.

Photo 2.2 The Vallum crossing over the ditch at Benwell (near Newcastle) looking east with the fort on the left (photo by author).

of the population through the Wall's gates both north- and south-bound:
while originally there were more than seventy crossing points at the Wall,
the Vallum reduced them to about fifteen and thereby effectively increasing the Roman army's ability to control the movement of people" (Breeze
and Dobson, 1976: 51) (see Photo 2.2). Most of the work on the Wall and
the frontier was completed by the end of second decade in the second
century. Mattingly (2006: 157) sums up the "total building requirements"
of the Wall and the frontier during the AD 122–128 period:

> 20 forts (including outposts), 100 milecastles/fortlets, 200 turrets and tow-
> ers, 1 million m³ of stone wall and 800,000 m³ of turf wall, removal of over
> 5 million m³ of material from the ditch and Vallum. This was one of the great
> engineering projects of the ancient world. It is estimated that a workforce of
> 15,000–20,000 men completed the bulk of this work in about ten years.

The Wall started at Wallsend in the east near the North Sea and stopped
at Bowness on the Solway Firth in the west. But as Forde-Johnston (1978:
55) points out, the greatest danger for any linear defense system such as
the Hadrian's Wall is "that of being by-passed." This was particularly the
case for a forty miles stretch of the Cumbrian coast along Solway Firth
towards southwest Scotland, where the Roman frontier's security could
be easily breached by Scottish tribes' potential infiltration. Thus Hadrian

established a system of defenses similar to the Wall on the Cumbrian coast with some modifications—here the shoreline as a natural barrier was substituted for the wall while fortlets replaced milecastles at one-mile intervals with watch towers (similar to turrets along the Wall) being placed in one-third of the mile intervals. Estimates for the number of troops that guarded the frontier at the Wall vary, but there is a consensus that there were about 10,000 troops and cavalry when the forts and milecastles along the Wall were at full capacity. Frere (1987: 117–118) estimates that about 1,000 cavalry (*alae*) were stationed on "either flank" of the Wall (at Benwell and Chesters forts on the east and Stanwix on the west); as well as about 500 troops in each of the sixteen forts along the Wall (see Figure 2.5).

Hadrian's long rule ended in 138 AD. He was succeeded by his adopted son Antoninus Pius. Facing the Senate's displeasure with his predecessor's passive policies on the British frontiers, within a year Antoninus abandoned Hadrian's Wall and marched north, establishing instead the Forth-Clyde isthmus in central Scotland 100 miles farther north as the new frontier by building the Antonine Wall. Built of turf (instead of stone) the new wall extended for 40 Roman miles (58 km). Once completed, it comprised of a series of forts and milecastles attached to the Wall (fortlets) and some argue that for the duration of its operation it was more intensely used and guarded by the Roman army than the Hadrian's Wall (Johnson, 2004: 60). But it too was abandoned upon Pius' death in 163, with the frontier once again being pulled back to Hadrian's Wall.

Upon Hadrian's Wall's reoccupation in the mid-160s, the entire complex underwent a complete repair and renovation with the milecastles being replaced and the barracks and the turrets repaired and rebuilt (Breeze and Dobson, 1976: 124–125). Based on scant evidence, however, the Wall's integrity seems to have been compromised when in the early 180s Scottish tribes north of the frontier crossed the Wall and several forts were either destroyed or badly damaged.[14] By the turn of the 3rd century AD the Wall demarcated the Empire's "lasting frontier" under Emperor Severus' rule, which in turn led to a limited growth of settlements along the Wall that catered to the troops and those who crossed the frontier. Two such settlements evolved and functioned as full-sized towns—Corbridge (or Corsopitum) strategically located on the River Tyne on the Wall's eastern end,

---

[14] The affected forts included the ones at Halton Chesters, Rudchester, and Corbridge (Breeze and Dobson, 1976: 128).

and Carlisle near Stanwix, located at the confluence of the rivers Eden, Caldew and Petteril on the West. These two were the largest forts along the Wall where the western routes between Britain and Scotland crossed the Wall barrier line. But these settlements never grew beyond the limits and characteristics associated with garrison towns (Salway, 1993: 134; Wilkes, 2005: 8) (see Photo 2.3).

This strongly suggests that the Wall was not the Empire's 'frontier,' as it would have led to the establishment of permanent settlements on both sides of the wall for economic reasons. Rather, it was an artificial barrier constructed right in the midst of the already existing inhabited territories populated by various tribal and rural communities. Breeze and Dobson (1976: 231) provide the following scenario for the fate of the disintegrating Roman army's troops stationed at the Wall:

> The soldiers stationed on Hadrian's Wall were not withdrawn. They no doubt stayed where they were, *for they were local recruits, probably from the civil settlements outside the fort or a nearby farm, and many of the soldiers had families in the houses beyond the fort walls.* Some more adventurous soldiers may have joined the bands of brigands which were ever a prey on settled life, others the mercenary armies which became such a feature of fifth century life. *The more home loving, or simply the lazy, stayed where they had always lived* (emphasis mine).

In the last decade of the 3rd century the *Picts* nation, a coalition of Caledonian and several other tribes north of Forth and Clyde isthmus in Scotland challenged the Roman army, a prelude to the latter's declining ability to defend imperial interests on the British front and the Wall's subsequent gradual decline during the 4th century. There is inconclusive evidence suggesting the Wall was still occupied by Roman troops toward the end of 4th century. By 410, when the Roman rule in Britain ended, the Wall had ceased to function as a barrier.

Why Did Hadrian Build the Wall?

Johnson (2004: 5) contends that the Wall "….ought to be counted as one of the wonders of the ancient world." But there is no consensus on the rationale for its construction. These range from serving as a defensive barrier against the "barbarians" from the north, to being a regulating and monitoring mechanism for the movement of population, or simply a symbolic monument to demonstrate the power and military might of the Roman Empire in the far-away frontiers in an occupied territory.

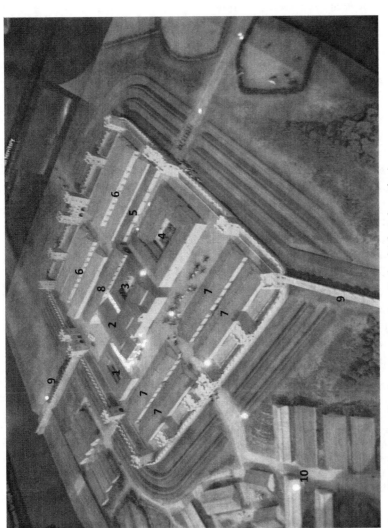

Source: The Museum at Segedunum, northeastern England (photo by author).

Legend: 1) hospital, 2) granaries, 3) headquarters building, 4) commanding officer's house, 5) workshop, 6) infantry barracks, 7) cavalry barracks, 8) forehall, 9) the Wall, and 10) attached settlement south of the Wall.

Photo 2.3 A reconstructed model of the Segedunum Roman Fort and a settlement south of Hadrian's Wall at the eastern end of Hadrian's Wall ca. 200 AD. Reportedly, the fort was garrisoned by a cohort of 480 infantry and 120 cavalry.

I will make the case that it is a fair assessment to consider all of the above to be true, but not all of them carry an equal weight as for the Wall's *raison d'être*.

The Wall as a Military Defensive Structure

As I stated earlier, based on a fourth-century biographer's statement Hadrian built the Wall apparently to confront and repel the Scottish tribes in northern Britain, or the "barbarians." The fact that the Wall was built mainly by Roman troops is an indication that its path and the surrounding areas on both sides were hostile territories. The Wall's design was definitely based on a military strategic planning. For instance, digging the ditch north of the Wall testifies to the presence of a defensive planning strategy on the planners' agenda. But the Wall's design and scale, its capacity to utilize troops for such a purpose, and its strategic location do not fully support this proposition. In addition, the Roman troops were trained to confront the enemy in open fields rather than engage them from a distance, such as the wall top (Breeze and Dobson, 1976: 39). Thus in all likelihood they would have been more effective while operating out on the north side of the Wall by "patrolling and neutralizing military threats at an early stage" (Todd, 1999; 126). Also, there were no provisions for the use of artillery either on the wall top or at the turrets. In his book of historical fantasy *Puck of Pook's Hill* published in 1908 Rudyard Kipling, the British novelist and an ardent supporter of Western imperial excursions provides an imagined description of the Wall's structure as explained by Parnesius, a fictitious 4th century Roman soldier stationed at the Wall:

> Along the top are towers with guard-houses, small towers, between. Even on the narrowest part of it three men with shields can walk abreast, from guard-house to guard-house. A little curtain wall, no higher than a man's neck, runs along the top of the thick wall, so that from a distance you see the helmets of the sentries sliding back and forth like beads. Thirty feet high is the Wall, and on the Picts' side, the North, is a ditch, strewn with blades of old swords and spear-heads, set in wood, and tyres of wheels joined by chain.[15]

However, there is no evidence that the Wall's top functioned as a fighting platform for Roman soldiers, nor could its width permit three armored soldiers "walk abreast." For example, if we assume the existence of the

---

[15] Excerpt from the story "On the Great Wall" by Kipling (1906: 153).

parapet, of about two feet wide, then the wall top's width would have varied between 4 to 8 feet, leaving little room to pass behind a fighting soldier, bring reinforcements or remove the wounded, as the milecastles and turrets were about 540 yards apart. One of the earliest and most comprehensive arguments made in discounting the Wall's military value is that of Collingwood (1921: 5) who questioned British writer Rudyard Kipling's fictionalized story of the Wall in which he imagines Roman archers fighting the "barbarians" and repelling the invaders from the wall top, with catapults and ballistae installed on tower tops and finds such reality as the least pragmatic and feasible from a military standpoint:

> The auxiliaries were armed with the ordinary Roman fashion, with the pilum and gladius; and though a heavy throwing-spear like the pilum would be useful to throw off a wall at a Caledonian, each man was only issued with two of them, and their use was to give a kind of 'preparation' for a charge with the short sword. A man on the top of the Roman Wall who had thrown his two pila and was armed with nothing but a short sword would be simply out of action; there would be nothing further for him to do while the enemy began at their leisure to prepare their works for a breach or escalade.[16]

Standing on the top of the Wall remains in Housesteads on a chilly, rainy August day, and trying to put myself in a Roman soldier's shoes I could easily and practically conclude the absurdity of Kipling's fantastic imagination in most segments of the Wall (See Photo 2.4). Furthermore, except in the central region where the Wall was built on the crags it could be easily scaled by an advancing force determined to breach the defensive line. But there is no documented evidence indicating that the Wall has ever been stormed by "barbarian" troops during the times it was guarded by the Roman army. Supporting Collingwood, Johnson (1999: 53) also concludes that "the picture of scaling ladders and defensive alarms, with Roman troops responding to a sizeable attack on the barrier is probably fiction."

The preceding account adds credence to another argument that the Wall structure and the Vallum instead created a relatively safe and protected military zone for the stationed Roman army in a hostile environment, threatened not only by unconquered Caledonians in the north outside Roman territorial control but also by British tribes who resided south of the wall within the occupied territories. Thus as Mattingly (2006: 158)

---

[16] The pilum was a heavy javelin, about 6–7 feet long, commonly used by the Roman army. "*Gladius*" is the Latin word for the sword.

Photo 2.4 Author standing on the Wall's remains in Housesteads next to the Fort facing east, summer 2011. As can be seen, the presence of a hypothetical two feet-wide parapet at the top of the Wall would have left not much room for a soldier to maneuver (the partially seen stone wall on the right is part of the fort structure).

observes, the Wall and the Vallum formed a "controlled cordon" with the crossings over the Vallum on the south and northern gates at the mile-castles and forts on the north for population movement. The secured zone between the Wall and the Vallum also served as a training field for Roman troops. This allowed the Roman army units "to segregate themselves from civilians and to use the zone between the two barriers for grazing military pack animals and cavalry horses." This suggests that Roman soldiers in most cases had to live in isolation even from the subjects who lived within the Roman British territories. This is a sad commentary on the long pres-ence of the Romans in the area during which they failed to gain the trust of the British inhabitants and always remained as an occupying force.

In *The Puck of Pook's Hill* Rudyard Kipling also fantasized about the Wall frontier's glorious past as explained by the Roman soldier Parnesius:

> Just when you think you are at the world's end, you see a smoke from East to West as far as the eye can turn, and then, under it, also as far as the eye can stretch, houses and temples, shops and theatres, barracks and granaries, trickling along like dice behind—always behind—one long, low, rising and falling, and hiding and showing line of towers. And that is the Wall![17]

But in my field observations along the Wall's remains in summer 2011 I could not escape the fact that the Wall was built in a desolate fron-tier. One of the sites that I visited was the Wall and milecastle remains at Cawfields, on a rainy and windy day in mid-August. The steep land-scape from the foot of the hill to the Wall and milecastle location was immensely beautiful and picturesque yet desolate, challenging and unin-habited—there the visitor has to navigate through fresh cow dung dotting a landscape that once symbolized imperial Rome's futile quest for glory (see Photos 2.5 & 2.6). On my way to the site I also drove on what is now called the "military road," a narrow, paved rural road partially built on the path of the old "Stanegate," the east-west Roman military supply road. As I was enjoying the spectacular landscape and scenery while driving on this rarely-traveled rural road I tried to imagine how the Roman cav-alry felt two millennia back while traversing northern England territories. Kipling's fantasized image of the Wall through the lens of his protagonist Parnesius seemed to be far removed from the reality.

---

[17] As told in the story "On the Great Wall" by Kipling (1906: 153).

Photo 2.5 Author standing on top of the Wall's remains facing east next to the Cawfields milecastle, summer 2011. Note the Vallum line running parallel to the Wall on the top right corner (photo by author).

Photo 2.6 Sheep grazing at Housesteads Roman Fort along Hadrian's Wall, summer 2011 (photo by author).

The Wall and the Vallum as a Means to Control Population
Movement and Flow

The tribal nature of British population on both sides of the Wall required
the fluidity of spaces and environments utilized by various tribes—an
undeniable anthropological reality of this particular political economy at
the time that was effectively disrupted and cut in two pieces by this artificial barrier. Like many other walls, this linear barrier was surely designed
to allow population movement through its numerous gates at milecastles
and turrets across the frontier lines, albeit under Rome's tight control
(Todd, 1999: 125). In fact, the gates were so numerous that travelers only
had to walk less than half-a-mile in order to reach one. But as Breeze
and Dobson (1976: 38) point out, the gates also allowed troops to conduct
"the more humdrum day-to-day patrolling" as well as the maintenance
and repair of the Wall and the ditch. This dual purpose of the wall as a
defensive barrier and a controller of population flow is characteristic of
similar walls and fences built and erected in more recent periods, such
as the Berlin Wall or the Wall-fence along the U.S.-Mexico border. With
its ditch on the north side, the Wall reminded those beyond the frontier
who were found on the Roman side that they "could not plead ignorance
or innocent intentions," if they attempted to cross it "otherwise than at
the authorized and controlled gateways" (Collingwood, 1921: 7–8). Similarly the Vallum and the Wall were a constant reminder to the population
residing in the southern territories that they were under Roman occupation and control, and that their northward passage through the gates had
to be approved by Roman agents:

> Civilians, whether merchants, local farmers moving their cattle and sheep or
> simply local people visiting relatives on the other side of the Wall, would be
> allowed through the gateways, though only presumably when they had sat-
> isfied the guards of their peaceable intentions and on payment of customs
> dues (Breeze and Dobson, 1976: 37).

The Wall as a Symbol of Imperial Might

In addition to its functional purposes in deterring undesirable advances
by the adversarial northern tribes and controlling the population flow
through its gates, many scholars of the Wall also consider it as a symbol of the Roman Empire's military might in a faraway place such as the
northern British frontiers. An indication of the Wall designers' intentions
to represent it as a symbol of Roman imperial power was that the grey
stones used in its building were painted white on both sides so that the
immense barrier that stretched from coast to coast would stand out:

The [W]all was originally white. Traces of white rendering have been found and it seems that when the masons had completed the stonework they covered it with a lime-based plaster thickened with hemp. It helped make the walls waterproof and kept out the damp, but more than that, it meant that the gleaming ramparts could be seen from many miles away on either side as they snaked along the ridge north of the Stanegate. Rome had divided the island and the barbarians were to be left in no doubt about the magnitude of the power of the Empire (Moffat, 2005: 275).

Ancient monuments of such magnitude required powerful centralized states that could mobilize large contingents of workers and provide funds and resources to accomplish such tasks (Wells, 2005). Thus by building the Wall Hadrian intended not only to impress upon the entire populations within Roman imperial territories and those outside its boundaries, but also "to show the Brigantes, Selgovae and Novante, and the peoples to the north of them, how spectacularly Rome could exercise its power" (Moffat, 2005: 275). Seen from the eyes of tribal people from both sides of the barrier in 2nd century Britain, a combination of the Wall with its northern ditch and the Vallum must have been a spectacular representation of the immense capabilities of an occupying force, both economically and militarily, to construct and maintain a monument of such magnitude as far as the eye could see.

Hadrian's Wall: Beginning of the End?

From a theoretical standpoint building walls and fortifications can be considered as an indication of declining power and authority and inability to manage existing social conflicts between the dominator/colonizer and the dominated/colonized. At about the same time that Hadrian's Wall was built, Rome established another fortified barrier and demarcation line known as the *Limes* in Europe that connected the Roman frontier on the middle Rhine and upper Danube Rivers. The *Limes* consisted of fortresses for legions, extensive turf walls in certain parts, as well as a system of roads for the rapid transit of troops.[18] As an indication of imperial decay, from about mid-3rd century onwards massive walls and fortifications were constructed to protect Roman forts and towns due to threats posed

---

[18] The *Limes* extended for about 342 miles and once fully developed consisted of "a palisade of oak trunks on the outside, then a ditch some 8 m wide and 2.5 m deep, followed by an earth bank over 2 m high, then a road, along which watch towers stood" (Wells, 2005: 21).

by the Frankish invaders who crossed the *Limes* in southern Germany and devastated Gaul.

The highly centralized and top-down nature of the Roman imperial administration also forced newly seated emperors, some of them still at the mercy of the Roman Senate's approval, to lead symbolic military excursions or build impressive monuments in order to establish themselves as powerful leaders of the Empire. In this light, Hadrian's Wall might be taken as an early indication of Rome's declining power on the British front. The Wall was also Hadrian's personal project, symbolically legitimizing his authority and that of the empire in northern British territories. After all that has been said it is safe to conclude that the Wall's *raison d'être* included a combination of all three factors discussed above, as is explained by Mattingly (2006: 158):

> In sum, Hadrian's Wall was probably several things: a huge symbol of power that functioned as an effective deterrent to native aggression and facilitated customs control and frontier supervision. Most importantly, as originally designed, it did not entirely differentiate between Britons to north or south—both groups appear to have been considered as potential enemies, requiring intimidation and military supervision.

Most historical accounts of the rise and fall of the Roman Empire have adopted an uncritical approach, as there is a general tendency to chronicle the events by identifying with the "Roman cause," by glorifying the emperors and imperial conquests and almost completely downplaying the plight of the conquered populations. This uncritical, celebratory recognition of a nation's subordination to Rome's imperial rule is still manifested in many museums and exhibits along the Wall, from Newcastle to Carlisle. For instance, the Toulie House Museum and Art Gallery in Carlisle has an impressive collection of Roman artifacts on display; so is the British Museum in London. In his critical account of the Romans' presence in Scotland Moffat (2005: 225–26) makes note of this tendency:

> There are many other, less blatant examples of this sort of thing to be found in the literature dealing with the north [Scotland] in the period from AD 43 to 410, and the cumulative effect is extraordinary. Rarely has an invasion by foreign armies and all its attendant waste and slaughter been so eagerly celebrated by the descendants of the peoples, indeed the 'barbarians,' who suffered it. The historical fact is that the Romans were, as usual, utterly ruthless in pursuit of their own interests, occasionally adopting genocide as imperial policy, ordering their soldiers to kill on sight any man, woman or child they came upon while campaigning in the north.

Similar to other colonial situations certain parts of the colonized population in Britain accepted the Romans' presence and domination as a practical matter and not as a matter of principle. Yet in spite of all the pro-colonial narratives that praise the glory of Roman Empire and its conduct in the occupied territories, similar to other colonial situations the majority of the subjects did not easily accept the occupiers' legitimacy and presence:

> The evidence for pro-Roman attitudes can at least be described as opportunistic or pragmatic. Rome played an increasingly central role in the lives of the peoples of south-eastern Britain, but that does not mean that the British leaders were reconciled to eventual Roman take-over. People who might be conceived of as pro-Roman from their consumption of Roman goods (Italian wine, olive oil, metal tableware, medical tools, toilet utensils, and board games) did so primarily as part of a new formulation of power and status within their own societies.... This close contact with Rome did not necessarily predispose the British peoples as a whole to submit to military incorporation; rather it had the potential to make them more determined opponents of renewed invasion (Mattingly, 2006: 84).

Hadrian's era marked a turning point in the Roman Empire's fortunes, and at least for almost three quarters of a century changed the dynamics of managing the empire. For one thing, despite occasional excursions and attempts to expand or subdue the rebellious contingents outside imperial boundaries the empire remained within its existing borders. This was mainly due to a strategic shift in managing the Empire from an offensive to a defensive stance which was initiated by Hadrian. The relative stagnation of the Empire can as well be interpreted as the beginning of the end, but it can also be construed as a positive peace initiative policy:

> Looked at from the long perspective of history, it is sometimes argued that the loss of dynamism involved in the conversion from offence to defense was the first sign of 'decadence' in the empire. Nevertheless the immediate effect was three quarters of a century of peace in most corners of the empire, and the consequent development of its general prosperity and its institutions to their highest peak (Salway, 1981: 170).

But Salway (ibid.) quickly adds that the relative peace during the second century AD should not be taken as a sign that "there was any change of heart among the Romans on their nation's role in the world"; as Rome continued to pursue its colonial policies of domination and subjugation of population using its military might both within and outside the Empire's boundaries. Related to Britain, Divine (1969: 9–10) makes the case that the

Roman conquest and occupation of the island for more than four centuries was "intrinsically a failure" for four reasons:

> The continuing necessity throughout the occupation to maintain an excessive garrison for the defence of Britain. The permanent military requirement of the Wall itself. The exorbitant cost of the military structure in relation to the resources of a relatively unproductive province. And, finally, the inability of Romanization to establish—and ultimately leave behind it—an enduring social structure for the island Province.[19]

---

[19] However, he acknowledges the fact that many historians have arrived to a conclusion more favorable to the Romans.

CHAPTER THREE

RED SNAKE: THE MYSTERIOUS GREAT WALL OF GORGAN, IRAN

By the early 5th century Hadrian's Wall in northern England was being rendered obsolete due to Rome's diminishing power and military capability to prevent the Wall being overrun by Caledonian tribes from the north. But at about the same time period another long wall was being erected allegedly for defensive purposes by the Sassanids at the helm of the contending Persian Empire in the east. This was the Great Wall of Gorgan located in northeastern Persian (Iranian) territories south of the border with present time Turkmenistan. In an introduction to a report on a joint Iranian-British project to excavate and survey portions of the Gorgan Wall Omrani Rekavandi et al. (2008: 13) boast of its scale and historical siginificance, and at the same time are puzzled by its relative obscurity compared to other ancient barriers:

> It is longer than Hadrian's Wall and Antonine Wall taken together. It is over a thousnad years older than the Great Wall of China as we know it today. It is of more solid construction than its ancient Chinese counterparts. It is the greatest monument of its kind between central Europe and China and it may be the longest brick, or stone, wall ever built in the ancient world- and yet few have ever heard of it.

The 195 kilometer-long wall runs east-west from Pishkamar Mountains at the junction of the Alburz and Kopet Dagh mountains all the way to the south-eastern corner of Caspian Sea coast north of the town of Gumishan in Iran's Golestan Province, where according to Howard-Johnston (2006: 192) "its western extremity was probably destryoed when it was submerged under the Caspian, during the last high-water phase in the eighteenth-nineteenth centuries." (see Figure 3.1). This lesser-known and studied ancient wall has many names: the *'Red Snake'* ('Qizil Alan' in Turkeman language) because of the red-colored brick used for its construction[1];

---

[1] Cf. Arne (1945: 7).

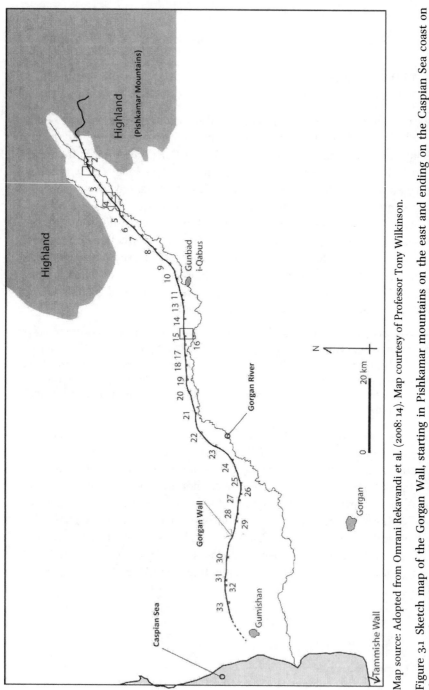

Map source: Adopted from Omrani Rekavandi et al. (2008: 14). Map courtesy of Professor Tony Wilkinson.

Figure 3.1 Sketch map of the Gorgan Wall, starting in Pishkamar mountains on the east and ending on the Caspian Sea coast on the West. The Wall runs almost parallel to Gorgan River with similar origination and destination points (numbers refer to fort locations).

'Sadd-i Iskandar' ('Alexander's Barrier'),[2] 'Sadd-i Piruz' ('Barrier of Peroz'),
and 'Sadd-i Anushiravan' ('Khusrau I's Barrier').[3]

Kiani (1982a: 73) makes the point that attributing the Wall to Alexander is "of more recent date" and has nothing to do with "Alexander of the Macedon." Rather, he speculates that "it may be owed indeed to popular interest in [10th century Iranian poet] Firdawsī's Persian hero, Iskandar" [in his epic book Shahnameh (Book of Kings)]. On this note, more recent writings have also made similar assertions as to the Wall's construction date and imperial sponsors. For example, Pirnya (1934: 172) attributes the Wall's construction to the Sassanian Emperor Peroz "in order to block intrusions by nomadic Hephthalites from the north"; while Daryaee (2008: 39) considers Xusrō I,[4] another Sassanian king as the mastermind behind the Gorgan Wall and three other defensive wall projects in order to protect the Sassanid Empire from four directions:

> One was built in the northeast, along the Gurgān plain to defend against the Hephthalites, one in the northwest at the Caucasus along with fortification at Daniel (qal' at Bāb al-Lān), one in the southeast, and one in the southwest called the 'wall of the Arabs' (wār ī tāzigān).[5]

Khosrau I is regarded by historians as "a great builder" who established new towns; rejuvenated agricultural production in war-torn rural areas by rebuilding irrigation systems and canals. Reportedly, he "built strong fortifications at the passes and placed subject tribes in carefully chosen towns on the frontiers, so that they could act as guardians of the state against invaders."[6] Due to the immensity of the Gorgan Wall as an imperial public-works project it is more plausible to consider it as a 6th century undertaking, given Khosrau I's superior administrative and organizational skills as well as his longer reign period compared with that of Peroz (48 years vs. 25, respectively).

---

[2] The Arabic noun "Sadd" has multiple meanings—dam, dike, barrier and obstacle. The noun's Farsi (Persian) version simply means "dam," thus as I will make the case later increasing the possibility that the Red Snake could have functioned as an imperial irrigation system in the region.

[3] According to Kiani (1982: 73) the 13th century historian Ibn Isfandiyār attributes the barrier to King Firüz (Peroz); while the 16th century Sīyaqī Nizām identifies Anüshirvān (or Khosrau I) as the builder.

[4] Khosrau I, also known as Anushiravan in Persian, literally meaning "with immortal soul".

[5] Darial is also known as "Derbent" or "Darband."

[6] See Iran Chamber Society (n.d.).

Kiani (1982a: 73) credits "the first extensive description of the Wall" to archaeologist Lester Thompson , who in 1938 provided a detailed account of the Wall.[7] Two years later, Eric Schmidt (1940: 55) detected and observed the ancient wall's extensive path by flying over Iran and taking aerial photographs of Iranian landscape. He estimated the Wall's construction date to be anywhere from 4th century BC (Macedonian conquest of Persia) to the Arab conquests in 7th century AD. The first extensive fieldwork on the Wall and creation of detailed maps was however carried out in 1976 by Iranian archaeologist Dr. Kiani himself. He established a more precise, if not completely accurate, time period for the Wall's construction, as well as its architectural style and the size of standardized bricks used in the Wall complex (Kiani, 1982a: 76–77; 1982b: 37–38). He attributed the Wall's construction to the Parthian period (mid-3rd century BC to 224–28 AD), and its probable restoration during the Sassanid era (3rd–7th centuries AD). Kiani made this determination due to the Caspian Sea's high water levels particularly "from AD 300 onwards," that in his opinion "would have made it physically impossible to extend the Wall to its present western limits [on Caspian Sea's eastern shores]" (Kiani, 1982a: 78). The origins of Parthians can be traced back to the Parni, one of the three east Iranian nomadic tribes of the Dahae Confederacy who resided in the Ochus River valley (present-time Amu Darya) in Central Asia. But as Bivar (2002) points out, since the Parthians came from the steppe region northeast of the Wall they "would not have needed fortifications against it." In fact, most of the threats to Parthian control came from the west, such as the Seleucids who were kept at bay west of the Euphrates; and the Scythians (in parts of present-time India) from the east (see Figure 3.2).

From then on studies of the Wall adopted Kiani's chronology until a joint fieldwork project carried out in 2005 by two teams—one from the Iranian Cultural Heritage and Tourism Organization (ICHTO) of Golestan Province (where the Wall is located), and the other from the University of Edinburgh in England who established a new timeline. Using modern archaeological techniques including "geophysical survey, landscape survey, radiocarbon and optically stimulated luminescence dating," the joint-team concluded that the Wall was built during the Sassanid King Peroz (459–484 AD) or a later 5th century period; or "at the very latest, early 6th century" (Nokandeh et al, 2008: 124; 163). They also rule out the possibility that the Wall was built in "two or more phases of construction" due to

---

[7] See Thompson (1938: 196–200).

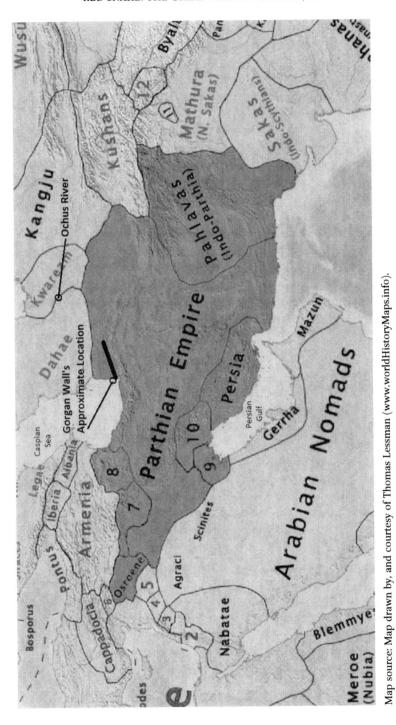

Map source: Map drawn by, and courtesy of Thomas Lessman (www.worldHistoryMaps.info).

Figure 3.2 The Approximate Boundaries of Parthian Persian Empire and its vassals at the turn of 1st Century, AD.

the "striking similarity in the architecture of the Wall and the rectangular brick kilns in the easternmost section and near Gonbad-e Kavus" (ibid: 162). In their 2008 follow-up study, the ICHTO-University of Edinburgh team members confidently reiterated that the "OSL and radiocarbon samples demonstrated conclusively" that the Gorgan Wall "had been built in the 5th, or possibly 6th century AD" (Omrani Rekavandi et al., 2008). The team's confidence in determining the historical timeline for the Wall's structure is also supported by the fact that various Sassanid administrations, particularly the one during Emperor Khosrau I's reign (531–579 AD) had undertaken public work mega-projects that also included erecting defensive walls and building moats in Mesopotamia, the Caucasus and in the north-east; as well as establishing settler colonies along the barriers to defend the Empire on the frontiers (Ghodrat-Dizaji, 2011: 316–317).[8] However, there exist some methodological problems in the joint-team's rather extensive study of the Wall segments and estimate of the time period during which it was constructed and maintained. For instance, Eduljie (n.d.) makes note that they have made the above conclusion based on the age of some limited brick samples taken from the Wall, and further questions the validity of their findings:

> We do not know how the archaeologists managed to make their sampling (out of the millions of bricks used to construct the Wall) statistically significant enough to produce such certainty. Even if the sampling was executed in a manner to give statistically significant results, the authors may have the data to conclude that the brick samples date back to Sassanian times, but we see no data to support the date for the construction of the Wall itself.

Considering legitimate criticism of Kiani's timeline for the Wall's construction (absence of any reason to build a defensive barrier during the Parthians' reign), and in the absence of any other competing and more compelling archaeological studies of the Wall except for the one by the ICHTO-University of Edinburg team, in this chapter I will tentatively adopt the latter team's conclusions and reconstruct the 5th–6th century AD historical timeline and possible rationales for the Wall's construction and functions. This I will try to achieve by examining the Wall complex within the context of Sassanian Persian Empire's geopolitics related to its northern and northeastern neighbors and rival powers.

---

[8] Also see Frye, 1977; Harmatta, 1996; and Mahamedi, 2004.

Was the Red Snake a Defensive Wall?

For more than four centuries, from 224 to 651 AD the ancient Sassanid Persian Empire encompassed a vast territory that included present time Iran, Iraq, Afghanistan, the Caucasus (Armenia, Georgia, Azerbaijan and Daghestan), eastern Syria, southwestern Central Asia and parts of Pakistan, the persian Gulf region and parts of the Arabian Peninsula, Egypt and East Africa. Suceeding the Parthians, the Sassanid Empire was one of the great powers of late antiquity and the most significant power in southwest Asia. It was also the last Persian Empire that challenged the Roman and Eastern Roman empires during one of Iran's most important historical periods, until the emerging Islamic Empire defeated it (Khaleghi-Motlagh, 1996). From the outset the Sassanids had to deal with the Romans and their constant threat on the Persian Empire's northwestern and western boundaries; an ongoing conflict that lasted for four centuries and was only ended with the Arab-Islamic conquest of Iran in the early 7th century.

On another front, between the 4th and 6th centuries AD four major political entities, namely, Kushans, Chionites, Kidarites, and Hephthalites occupied and ruled vast Central Asian territories east and northeast of the Sassanid Empire. The strongest of the four, the Hephthalites, also widely known as the "white Huns" established a powerful empire in a territory that included all or parts of present time nations of Turkmenistan, Tajikistan, Uzbekistan, Kazakhstan, Afghanistan, Pakistan and India (see Figure 3.3).[9] But Dignas and Winter (2007: 97–98) contend the Empire was situated in the "so-called 'Scythian Mesopotamia,' between Amu-Darya and Syr-Darya (Jeyhoun and Seyhoun Rivers); and the 6th century Byzantine historian Procopius of Caesarea makes the case that although "the Ephthalites are of the stock of the Huns," they did not "mingle with any of the Huns known to us."[10] Procopius further provides the following description for the Ephthalites not as nomadic populations always on the move, but rather as a settled population:

---

[9] The term "Hephthalite" is Greek, but they are also referred to as "Ephthalita" (Syriac), "Hephtal" (Persian), "Hayatela" (Arabic), "Huna" (Indian), and "Ye-da" (Chinese) (see Kurbanov, 2010: 2; Bivar, 2003). Most Persian/Iranian sources use the Arabic term "Hayatela."

[10] The Huns were pastoral nomadic populations that migrated from east of the Volga River to the southeastern areas of the Caucasus region west of the Caspian Sea around 150 AD (Gymrya, 1995: 9).

[T]hey are not nomads like other Hunnic peoples, but for a long period have been established in a goodly land. As a result of this they have never made any incursion into the Roman territory except in company with the Median army.... [I]t is also true that their manner of living is unlike that of their kinsmen, *nor do they live a savage life as they do*; but they are ruled by one king, and *since they possess a lawful constitution, they observe right and justice in their dealings both with one another and with their neighbors, in no degree less than the Romans and the Persians* (Procupius, 1914: III, 2–8) (emphasis mine).[11]

De La Vaissière (2007: 123), quoting observations of Menander, a guards-man at a Hephtalite king's court probably toward the end of 5th century AD also confirms Procopius' assertion, that the Hephthalites were not nomadic and lived and ruled in the cities. Here is Menander's account of a conversation that took place between the Hephthalite emperor and one ambassador from Sogdia:

> To a Sogdian ambassador, after the conquest of the Hephtalite Empire by the Turks, the emperor asked: 'you have, therefore, made all the power of the Ephthalites subject to you?' 'Completely,' replied the envoys. The Emperor then asked, 'Do the Ephthalites live in cities or villages?' The envoys: 'My Lord, that people lives in cities.' 'Then,' said the Emperor, 'it is clear that you have become master of these cities.' 'Indeed,' said the envoys." (Menander, 1987: 17).

The Sassanid Empire's eastern territories were under control up until the early 5th century AD, when the Hephthalites, an emerging Central Asian regional power posed a serious security threat to the Empire's territorial integrity that lasted for over a century. Most studies of the Gorgan Wall's historical chronology and its *raison d'être* have adopted an as yet unsubstantiated narrative and hypothesis that the Wall was built as a defensive barrier to prevent the Hephtalite forces' incursion into Persia from northern territories east of the Caspian Sea in present-time Turkmenistan (see for example, Pirnyia, 1934; Nokandeh et al., 2006; Omrani Rekavandi et al., 2008; Masoudian et al., 2011, Ghodrat-Dizaji, 2011; Mashkour, 2011; and Charlseworth, 1995). Although the Hephthalites' incursions into Persian territories during the 5th century AD cannot be disputed, as I will discuss below the tenability of above-mentioned adopted hypothesis can be contested mainly for one possibility: the direction of Hephthalites' incursions into Persian territories was east-west rather than north-south (see Figure 3.3).

---

[11] Here, Procopius follows the dominant dichotomous customary definition within the Roman culture that depicted nomadic populations as "savages" and "barbarians," and the settled agrarian populations who lived in the cities within the Empire's confines as "civilized."

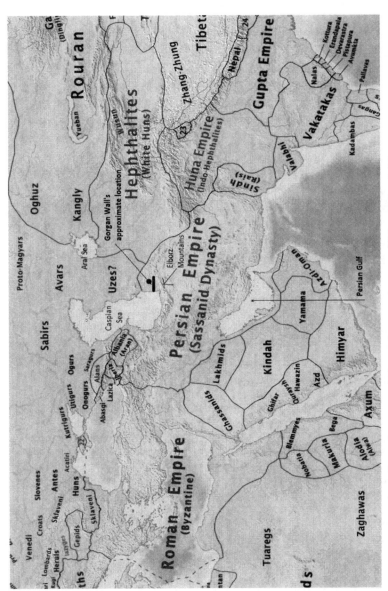

Map Source: Map drawn by, and courtesy of Thomas Lessman (www.worldHistoryMaps.info).

Figure 3.3 Approximate territorial boundaries of the Sassanid Persian Empire in AD 500 with the Hephthalite Khanate and the Eastern Roman Empire on its eastern and western boundaries, respectively. Note the location of Gorgan Wall related to the Hephthalite territories.

The first encounter between the Hephthalites and the Sassanids allegedly took place in 425 AD during which the latter's army led by Emperor Bahram V defeated the Hephthalites near the city of Merv and forced them to retreat east of the Oxus River ("Jeyhoun" in Persian) (Pirnya, 1934: 68; Razi, 1968: 68).[12] The ancient city of Merv ('Marv' in Persian) was a major administrative, military and commercial center of regional trade during both Parthian and Sassanian empires. It lays on the Murghab River Delta located in southeastern present-time Turkmenistan between Kopeh Dagh Mountains (Iran's extreme northeastern boundaries with Turkmenistan) and Amu Darya (Oxus) River in present-time Uzbekistan. Merv was on one of the main east-west routes of the ancient Silk Road that handled long-distance trade between China and Europe; as well as "an important departure point for the 180 km [106 miles] journey across desert northwest to ancient Amul (today Turkmenabad) located on the banks of the Amu Darya River."[13] Since the city of Merv was located southeast of the Gorgan Wall, from a military logistical view point it was the most logical route the Hephthalites and other invading forces could have utilized to encroach on the Persian imperial territories (see Figures 3.4 and 3.5).

The Hephthalites later defeated the Sassanids in two decisive battles that took place during the reign of Emperor Peroz (459–484 AD).[14] According to Procopius (1914: III, 8–13) during the first encounter the advancing Hephthalite army had entered the Persian territories, but when confronted with the Sassanid forces they "made it appear to their enemy that they had turned to flight because they were wholly terrified by this attack." Procopius continues the narrative and describes this move as a calculated retreat to trap the enemy forces:

> They [the Hephthalites] retired with all speed to a place which was shut in every side by precipitous mountains, and abundantly screened by a close forest of wide-spreading trees. Now, as one advanced between the mountains to a great distance, a broad way appeared in the valley, extending apparently to an indefinite distance, but at the end it had no outlet at all, but terminated in the very midst of the circle of mountains (ibid.).

Apparently fooled by this strategic enemy retreat, Peroz and his army were lured into the mountain impasse; and once deep inside the "greater

---

[12] According to Pirnya (ibid.) the Hephthalite king ("Khaghan") was killed in the battle and the Sassanid army returned home with huge war booty. The defeat was reportedly so decisive that the Hephthalites did not dare attack Iran until Bahram's death in 438 AD.

[13] See Eduljee (n.d.b.).

[14] See Pirnya (1934: 170–173).

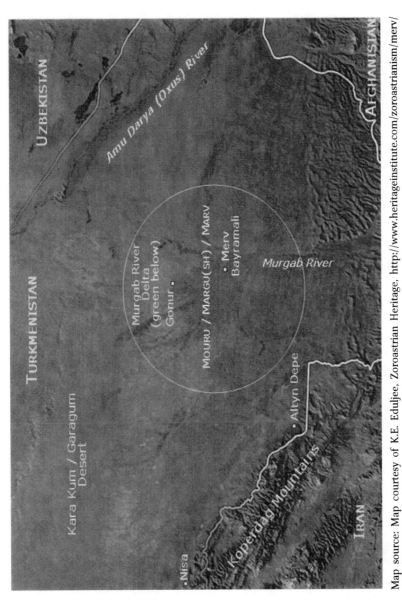

Figure 3.4 Location of the city of Merv.

Map source: Map courtesy of K.E. Eduljee, Zoroastrian Heritage, http://www.heritageinstitute.com/zoroastrianism/merv/merv.htm

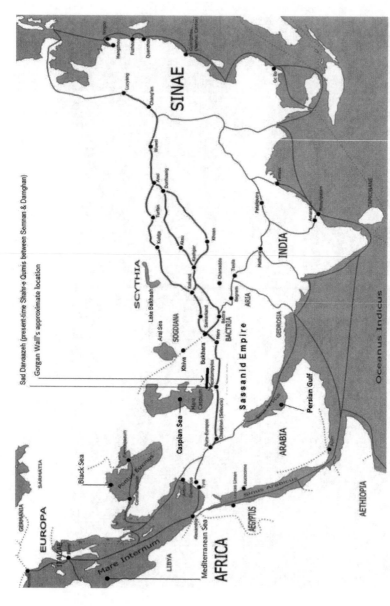

Map source: Original map courtesy of Ancient Encyclopedia History, http://www.ancient.eu.com/image/146/.

Figure 3.5 Main routes of the old Silk Road (map reconstructed by Author).

part" of the mountain path the Hephthalite army managed to close the escape route behind the enemy lines. Procopius writes that Peroz was then forced to accept a peace treaty by consenting to "prostrate himself" before the Hephthalite king Khoshnavāz as his master, and giving pledges "that they would never again take the field against the nation of Hephthalites" (ibid.). Procopius' account of the location where this battle took place is more compatible with the mountainous region that lies between Iran and Afghanistan, and not the steppes that separate Iran from Turkmenistan. If this were the case, then we can question the Gorgan Wall's military significance as a defensive barrier at the time.

The humiliated and disgraced Peroz later waged the second war and allegedly marched toward the city of Balkh (Bactria) with five hundred elephants marching in front of his army (Pirnya, 1934: 172).[15] The decisive battle according to Procopius took place in 483 AD near the ancient city of Gorgo in the vicinity of present city of Gunbad-i Qabus located in the Golestan Province in Iran. Back then, Gorgo was within Hephthalite territory and lied "on the extreme [eastern] Persian frontier."[16] Again, the Hephthalite king Khoshnavāz played another military trick by marking off "a tract of very great extent" and digging a wide, deep trench. He then allegedly built a narrow passage over the trench made of reeds and concealed them with dirt, wide enough for the passage of ten horsemen. Forced to cross the trench over the narrow passage, the Sassanian army allegedly "fell into the trench, every man of them, not alone the first but also those who followed in the rear" and reportedly Emperor Peroz was also killed in this battle (Procopius, 1914: III, 10–16). In their account of the battle, Dignas and Winter (2007: 98) note that "peroz met his death in what is now Afghanistan," again, an indication that the Hephthalites incursions into Persian territories took place from the east and not as commonly noted by many from the steppes north of the Gorgan Wall in present-time Turkmenistan.

---

[15] The west-east direction of this offensive is another indication that the Hephthalites were a threat from Persian Empire's eastern borders and not from the north (see Figure 3.6).

[16] However, Procopius is not specific about the date, and the given year (483 AD) is noted in Pirnya (1934: 172). The ancient city of Gorgo is usually referred to as being the medieval "Jorjān" near the present-time city of Gunbad-e Qābus. "Jorjān" is probably the Arabized version of "Gorgan," but ancient Jorjan should not be mistaken for the city of Astarabad further west between Gunbad-e Qābus and the Caspian Sea that its name was changed to Gorgan in the early 20th century.

The detailed narratives provided by Procopius in his *Book of Wars* at times read like well-crafted fables. Referring to Procopius and other historical accounts Pirnya (1934: 172) also provides a detailed narrative of both wars, but he too nonetheless considers them as "contradictory" and "more like fairy tales." But quoting Veh (1970: 459), Dignas and Winter (2007: 97) contend that Procopius' account of the Hephthalites "is trustworthy and based on good sources." In later periods successive Sassanid emperors after Peroz had to at times pay tribute to the Hephthalites in order to avoid the latter army's encroachments. According to Bivar (2003), "it was only with the rebuilding of Sassanian power under Khosrow I Anoširvăn, between AD 558 and 561, when the Persians acted in concert with the newly arrived Turkish horde under their Khăgăn Sinjibu, ... that the two powers were finally able to crush the Hephthalites in an epic battle near Bukhara, dividing their territories along the line of the Oxus (Amu Darya)."[17]

At this juncture it is only fair to conclude that both the historical narratives pertaining threats posed by tribal and settled populations who resided in the territories northeast of the Sassanid Empire; and determination of the Gorgan Wall's construction date(s) and its builders' actual intentions are at best tentative. Yet notwithstanding the shortcomings, based on preceding discussion I will adopt the late 5th to mid-6th century AD time-period as the period in which the need for erecting the Wall became an urgent undertaking by the Sassanid administrators, whatever its purpose and functions might have been.

The Wall's Architecture[18]

At this juncture I can make one observation regarding the Gorgan Wall's geographic location: similar to other ancient barriers such as Hadrian's Wall, the *Red Snake* was not constructed on the Sassanid Empire's northern frontiers. Rather, it was built well within the territories that were

---

[17] Khăgăn Sinjibu (alsko known as "Dizabul" or "Silzibul") ruled over the vast Turkish Empire northeast of the Hephthalite territories, commonly known as the "Khanate of the Juan-Juan" which became an independent and powerful nomadic confederation in the early 5th century. They ruled over eastern Turkestan and present-time territories of Mongolia and Manchuria until their decline toward the end of 5th century.

[18] The following section is based on historical documentation/archival research; and my field observations on the Wall's path during a trip to northeastern Iranian province of Golestan in summer 2012.

under imperial control and domination either during the Parthian or Sassanian periods. In fact, the Atrak River that flowed east-west from the highlands to the Caspian Sea further north could have served as a more logical natural barrier against possible incursions and raids from northern territories with the Wall being erected on its north side (see Figures 3.2 and 3.3). Kiani's concluding remarks in his book *Parthian Sites in Hyrcania* (1982b: 76) also support the above proposition:

> The fertility of the land, especially between the rivers Atrak and Gurgan, made it a desirable region to live in from the prehistoric period, and traces of occupation were found by the survey dating back to the fifth Millennium BC.

The Wall and the Ditch

Although little has remained from the Wall, the linear mound-like impressions of the Wall ruins and forts are visible in aerial photographs and maps. The approximately 195 kilometer-long east-west wall runs almost parallel to the Gorgan River, and in most sections "through a landscape of windblown loess."[19] The Wall starts in Pishkamar Mountains in the eastern highlands, skirts north of the city of Gunbad-e Qabus, and continues westward to the Gorgan Plain lowlands on the eastern shores of the Caspian Sea north of the city of Gumishan (see Figure 3.1). Based on his field observations in 1938, Thompson (cf. Kiani, 1982a: 73) noted "a low regular mound from one to four meters in height, about four times as broad as it was high, which stretched from 'under the Caspian Sea near Gumish Tepe' to 'the perpendicular cliffs of the Pishkamīn [sic] ridge, 100 miles (160 km.) to the east'."[20]

Thompson's estimate of the Wall's width seems to be exaggerated, as in few excavated sections the brick Wall is around two meters wide (6–7 feet) comprised of five rows of baked bricks (see Photo 3.1). But in one section, on the northeast corner of Fort 13 the Wall's width is about 10 meters (33 feet), that according to one report suggests the Wall in this section "reached greater height and was provided with a broad walkway, capable of being manned by substantial number of soldiers" (Nokandeh et al., 2006: 138). Furthermore, based on their archaeological excavations the ICHTO-University of Edinburg team make a speculative conclusion that the wall was constructed of millions of standard-size fired square

---

[19] Loess is a highly porous sediment formed by the accumulation of windblown silt comprised of clay, sand and silt, all loosely cemented together by calcium carbonate.

[20] It should be 'Pishkamar' and not 'Pishkamin.'

bricks made of loess, 40 centimeters in diameter on the Wall's eastern stretch and 37 centimeters in the western sections; with a thickness ranging from 8–11 centimeters (Omrani Rekavandi et al., 2008: 14).[21] But in his earlier excavations in and around forts 11, 12 and 13 Kiani (1982a: 75) made a less glorious observation of the Wall and material used in its construction:

> Trenches B and C consisted of trial tests made directly on the line of the Wall. In Trench B we could do little more than document the scale of damage that had been done by local farmers digging for bricks. But in Trench C more interesting evidence came to light. *We came down on two parallel rows of standard, well-laid, baked bricks with a filling of broken bricks placed between them. In short, the Wall proves not to have been built of standard brick courses throughout; instead, as other exposed sections show, fillings of broken brick and sometimes even plain earth were employed on occasion* (emphasis mine).

The on-site evidence led Kiani (ibid.: 77) to conclude that "the varied standards of construction, especially the use of almost any material that could be pressed into service, would suggest an element of haste in the original programme of the work." However, more than two decades later the ICHTO-University of Edinburg team reported that the standardized bricks that were used in the Wall's construction were produced on an industrial scale in several thousand brick kilns that line up south of the Wall in 4–100 meters intervals (Omrani Rekavandi et al., 2008: 14; see Photo 3.2). Again, this seems rather an exaggeration of the total number of kilns along the Wall's path, and in light of a limited scope of archaeological excavations the exact figure remains to be determined. In contrast, in his earlier excavations of few sections of the Wall and the nearby kilns, Kiani (1982a: 75) was more careful in not making an overstatement:

> Given the huge number of baked bricks that went into the construction of the Wall, we can assume that many such kilns must have been erected to the south of the Wall, both near the individual forts and at intermediate points between the forts.

The kilns also appear to have been designed and built based on identical blueprints, as is evidenced by archaeological surveys of two kilns, one excavated in 2005 on the "easternmost known point in the foot hills of the Elburz Mountains" about "13–20 meters away from the Wall," and another excavated earlier in the 1970s by another team "over 60 kilometers

---

[21] Based on his excavations in the 1970s Kiani (1982a: 75) also mentions that "the standard brick size throughout the length of the barrier is close to 40 × 40 × 10 cm."

Photo 3.1 A profile of the brick Wall excavated in 2005 with an approximate height of 1.47 meters (Rekavandi et al., 2008: 13). In most areas the bricks have been rubbed out. Image courtesy of Professor Eberhard Sauer.

Photo 3.2 A view of a section of the 2 meter-wide brick Wall (lower left) and one of the kilns (center right) located south of the barrier in Qara Deeb (Omrani Rekavandi et al., 2008: 15). Image courtesy of Professor Eberhard Sauer.

further west and also next to the Wall" (ibid.: 15). Since either due to natural erosion, ploughing the land for cultivation, or removal of bricks by locals for other construction purposes most sections of the Wall are completely in ruins, the Wall's height has not been accurately determined (See Photos 3.3–3.5). But in one excavated section the Wall remains reach the height of 1.47 meters (5 feet) (see Photo 3.1). In the absence of clear evidence it cannot be determined whether the Wall was wide enough to be walked on the top, or the existence of a parapet on the Wall's top edge for defensive purposes.

Furthermore, similar to Hadrian's Wall, a ditch 6–8 meters wide (20–27 feet) in most parts and 5 meters deep (16 feet) runs along the Wall on its north side or (the assumed "enemy territory") presumably for defensive purposes, as is indicated in most studies of the *Red Snake* (Nokandeh et al., 2006: 128). But citing archaeologist Thompson's observation in the 1930s, Kiani (1982a: 75) points out that as a matter of simple design principle in constructing a barrier the ditch may have served another functional purpose since "the excavated earth from the defensive ditch must have provided the material required by the [Wall's] brick makers" as well. In certain segments such as in the vicinity of fort 9 the ditch is 30 meters wide (100 feet) at the top, and no less than 6.54 meter (21 feet) deep (ibid: 141, 144) (see Photo 3.6).

The Forts

Again, similar to Hadrian's Wall a chain of forts, thirty six of them identified so far, are abutting the Wall or in some cases located in its close vicinity either to its north or south (Kiani, 1982a: 16; 1982b: 73–74; and Nokandeh et al., 2006: 121) (see Figure 3.1). Out of the thirty six known fort sites seven have been partially surveyed and excavated:

> Fort #1 (initially by Kiani, 1982a and 1982b; with a follow-up by Nokandeh et al., 2006)
> Forts #4 and 9 (Nokandeh et al., 2006; Omrani Rekavandi et al., 2008)
> Fort #10 (Amin pour, 2005)
> Forts #12 and 13 (initially by Kiani, 1982a; with a follow-up by Nokandeh et al., 2006)
> Fort #16 (Omrani Rekavandi et al., 2008)

The square-shaped forts are irregular in shape and size, are spaced out at various intervals of between 10 and 50 kilometers (6 to 31 miles), and come in different sizes. For instance, Schweitzer (cf. Arne, 1945: 10) recorded two fort types measuring 80 × 80m. and 160 × 160 m.; while Kiani (1982a: 75)

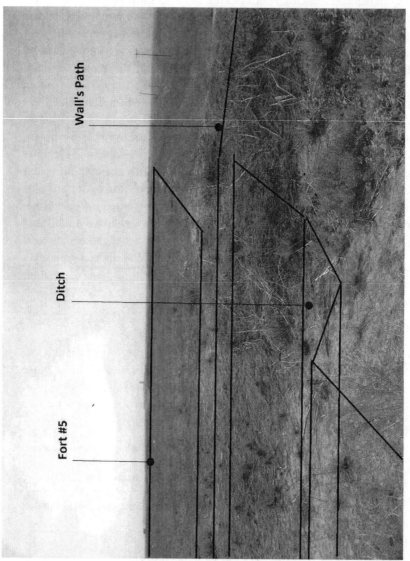

Photo 3.3 Conceptualization of the ditch, the Gorgan Wall, and Fort # 5 facing south. All that is left is a mound-like impression of this 196 kilometer-long ancient structure (photo by author, August 2012).

Photo 3.4 Bricks salvaged from the Gorgan Wall used in construction of this house (top portion) in the village of Tamar Qara Quzli, northeast of the town of Kalaleh, Golestan Province (photo by author, August 2012).

Photo 3.5 Two more houses built by bricks salvaged from the Gorgan Wall in the village of Tamar Qara Quzli, northeast of the town of Kalaleh, Golestan Province (photo by author, August 2012).

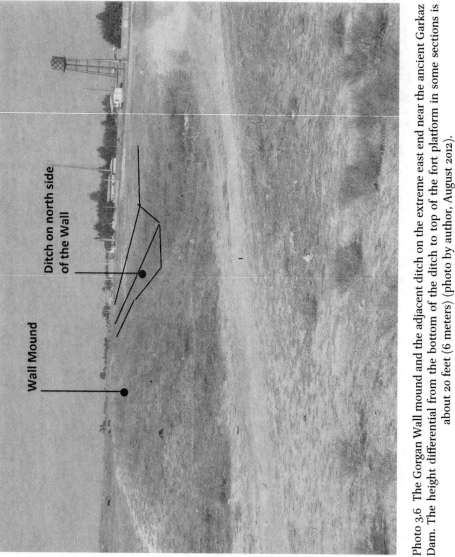

Photo 3.6 The Gorgan Wall mound and the adjacent ditch on the extreme east end near the ancient Garkaz Dam. The height differential from the bottom of the ditch to top of the fort platform in some sections is about 20 feet (6 meters) (photo by author, August 2012).

and his team also recorded "one or more forts" measuring 120 × 120 m., 150 × 150 m., 200 × 200 m., 300 × 60 m., and 400 × 100 m. Kiani (ibid.: 76) reports that in one excavated site in 1975 the remains of the fort wall still stood "up to 3.70 m. in height," and the main construction material were 50 × 50 × 10–11 centimeter mud-bricks. Similar to the Wall's rather make-shift construction the use of mud-bricks in the construction of forts can be an indication of the builders' intention to erect a structure with a lim-ited life-span. In their excavations of selected fort and "associated surface surveys" Kiani and his team (ibid.) also found "large quantities of pottery," some belonged to the Parthian and others to the Sassanian periods. How-ever, in light of limited excavated sample sites and absence of substantial archaeological finds all the interpretations provided by various archaeo-logical teams and surveys are at best tentative, requiring further extensive excavations of additional fort sites and examination of historical facts.

One common feature of the forts' design is their rectangular shape with 90 degree angled corners, in contrast to rounded corners of Roman forts. Fort 1, for example, located on the extreme eastern end of the Wall near Pishkamar Mountains abuts the Wall, with one possible entry gate on the south-southeast facing side of the fort; and probably a central road that ran perpendicular to the Wall throughout the fort's interior. Fort #1's total area from the outer edges of its walls is about 3.9 ha. (205 × 182–199 meters) (Nokandeh et al., 2006: 127).[22] Based on geophysical surveys by Kiani (1982b: 19–21) and their own investigations Nokandeh et al. (2006: 126–27) do not find strong evidence of the presence of permanent, sturdy non-defensive structures inside Fort 1, leading them to conclude that uti-lization of "yurt and sturdy tents" by fort inhabitants was a "possibility." However, they found it "improbable" that the fort to have been occupied on a long-term basis, thus they most likely were occupied for short-term defensive purposes only. In addition, there are indications that the fort was surrounded by a ditch on all sides, and in parts the bottom of the ditch was 7 meters below the fort platform level.

Magnetometer surveys of Fort #4 in 2005 by Omrani Rekavandi et al. (2008: 17–18) suggest the presence of a gate on the fort's NE-NW wall that opened to the presumed enemy-side territory, across from the fort's main entry gate on its SE-SW facing wall.[23] Based on their surveys Nokandeh et al.

---

[22] An earlier survey by Kiani (1982b: 15) estimated the fort's area to be around 4.8 ha. (240 × 200 meters).

[23] For their complete and most recent report on the Gorgan Wall see Sauer et al. (2013).

(2006: 128) furthermore conclude that "if there was just a single gate and none on the enemy-side [on the wall portion that comprised the N-NE side of the fort facing north], then this would suggest that the Wall was intended to function as a barrier rather than a permeable line of control.[24] In addition, the survey revealed the presence of three 228 meters-long barrack-like structures inside the fort that covers an area of about 5.5 ha. Based on satellite images the team has also concluded that the presence of permanent structures, most likely army barracks, was the rule in many other forts rather than an exceptional anomaly (see Figure 3.6).[25] However, in his earlier excavations in the 1970s, particularly related to Fort No. 12, Kiani (1982b: 21) was less certain of the fort's military functions:

> It was unfortunate that the excavations did not, as had been hoped—if not expected, uncover any military construction in this fort. We hope that further investigation and excavations in other forts will lead in the future to the discovery of such construction.

Finally, the "quantity of pottery and animal bones" excavated and recovered from two sample trenches on site and radiocarbon dating tests led the team to also conclude that the fort "bustled with life" and most likely "remained occupied until at least the first half of the 7th century" (ibid.).

There exist some anomalies in the fort locations and their proximity to other forts. First, geophysical surveys at Fort #16 have revealed the presence of brick kilns underneath the fort, an indication that it was built and added to the chain of forts at a later date (ibid.: 19). Second, forts 11, 12 and 13 are clustered together with "little more than a kilometer" apart, also suggesting that they might have been built in "more than one phase" (Nokandeh et al., 2006: 163). Third, Fort #3 on the eastern end of the Gorgan Plain is not attached to the Wall and is located about 500 meters further south on the foothills of the Pishkamar Mountains. Finally, in their excavations and field observations Kiani and his team (1982b: 39–43) surveyed ten forts on both sides of the Wall.[26] Of note, is Qaleh Qarniareq (also known as 'Qizlar Qaleh') located 15 km. northwest of present-time city of Gorgan and north of the Wall near Fort No. 29. Kiani (ibid.: 40)

---

[24] In the absence of extensive excavation and survey of the majority of forts, this could be an exception rather than the rule, increasing the plausibility that the Wall mostly functioned as a 'barrier.'

[25] Similarly, in the absence of any viable evidence this should be considered merely as a 'speculation' rather than a definite 'conclusion.'

[26] In nine of the fort sites (qaleh) the excavated pottery remains date from prehistoric to Sassanid/pre-Islamic periods (ibid.).

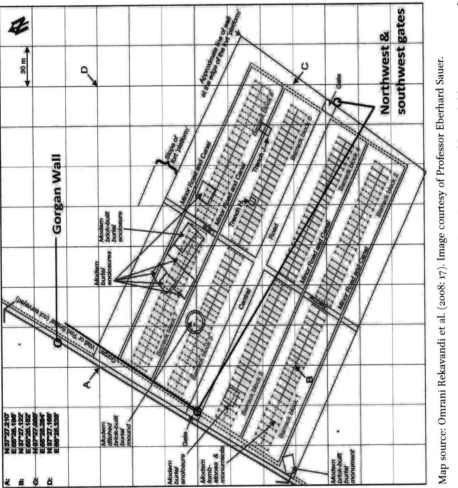

Map source: Omrani Rekavandi et al. (2008: 17). Image courtesy of Professor Eberhard Sauer.

Figure 3.6 Magnometer survey of Fort 4 revealing three rows of barrack-like structures and two entry gates.

describes Qaleh Qarniareq as an oblong/square-shaped citadel "rising 15 m. above the level of the plain" and measuring 200 m. × 200 m. (ibid.: see Figure 8a, Appendix). But in their site observations Nokandeh et al. (2006; 147) estimate the fort and the surrounding extensive settlement to cover about 70 ha. and "extend over an area of approximately 1,110 m. E-W by 700 m. N-S," with its eastern and western-facing walls extended southward to join the main Gorgan barrier (Nokandeh et al., 2006: 147–49). In his earlier investigations in the 1970s Kiani (1982b) also identified "several large sites of Partho-Sassanian date" to the Wall's north well beyond the Wall's presumed protective zone. The last two cases indicate the presence of relative security (or absence of any threats) north of the Wall, as otherwise Qaleh Qarniareq and the surrounding settlements, for instance, would have been susceptible to enemy raids from the north. This once again raises more questions about the viability of the assertions that the Wall was erected merely as a defensive barrier to fend off northern invaders.[27]

The Wall's Associated Hydraulic Structures and Functions

Most studies of the Gorgan Wall are based on a generally accepted assumption that the Wall's main function was to protect the fertile Gorgan plains to its south from hostile nomadic attacks from the steppes to its north. But conspicuously, the Wall and the ditch follow "a curvilinear path down the hydraulic grade of the [Gorgan] plain" and run east-west parallel to the Gorgan River's downstream flow and with a remarkably calculated and steady gradient all the way to the Caspian Sea shore lines (Nokandeh et al., 2006: 147). Thus, instead of building the Wall in straight lines that would have made it a more effective defensive barrier; or like Hadrian's Wall that took advantage of higher elevation routes to increase its defensive capabilities, the *Red Snake* was built to run parallel to a river in relatively low-laying areas. This has led the archaeologists to hypothesize that the ditch on the Wall's south side served both as a defensive barrier and an irrigation canal. In particular, a team led by Nokandeh (1999: 171–72) observed three cross canals that run between the Gorgan River valley and the Wall, namely, Chai Ghushan Kuchek, Aghabad, and Sarl-i-Maktoom (see Figure 3.7 and Photo 3.7). Later, in 2005 they made a more careful observation of these canals:

---

[27] However, the settlements were reportedly not inhabited on a continuous basis.

....each canal was followed on foot to ascertain the relationship of the
canal[s] to the river itself, and each could be seen to lead approximately
from the edge of the river valley towards the Gorgan Wall, where in each
case the canal flowed through what appears to have been a deliberately constructed gap in the Wall to merge into the ditch located on the north side of
the Wall (Nokandeh et al., 2006: 138).

Of particular significance, is that the eastern end of Chai-Ghushan Kuchek
Canal terminates at the top of a massive earthen dam, *Sadd-i Garkaz*, 700
meters long and 20 meters deep (67 feet), with a yet-to-determine construction time-period.[28] On its western end, at some point in time about
300 meters of the earthen dam has been breached by the Gorgan River
(see Figure 3.8 and Photo 3.8). Nokandeh et al. (2006: 141) hypothesize
that the Sadd-i Garkaz Dam has been constructed presumably to block
the course of the Gorgan River "thereby impounding a reservoir upstream
so that the water was able to reach the level of the Chai-Ghushan Kuchek
Canal"; which then directed the reservoir water to the ditch north of the
Gorgan Wall. However, they conclude that in the absence of "any significant sedimentation upstream of the dam" this massive structure "must
have been breached in antiquity, presumably after a relatively brief period
of use." Furthermore, even if there are no indications that the other two
canals (namely, Agahabd and Sarl-i Maktoom) were connected to similar earthen dams downstream, they do not rule out such possibility, as
they contend similar to Sadd-i Garkaz the "powerful flow of the Gorgan
River" could have easily washed them away (ibid). The team concluded
that if this were the case, it is unlikely the three earthen dams to have
been contemporary structures since they "used water from the same river"
(ibid.: 145).

Based on the earlier evidence produced by Kiani (1982b) and their own
field observations, Nokendaeh et al. (2006: 148) do not rule out the possibility that the ditch north of the Wall could have functioned as a conduit "to
supply water for irrigation downstream." However, based on the accumu-
lated sediments in the ditch they conclude that the water's flow rate was
"sluggish" and that "the entire system can [sic] only have functioned when
the reservoir(s) were full." Earlier, Kiani (1982a: 77) casts doubt about the
possibility of "outer ditch" north of the Wall to have been "a continuous
feature throughout the length of the Wall. Thus in their follow-up study

---

[28] Nokandeh et al. (2006: 141) report that "fragments of fired brick, of similar type to
those used in the construction of the Gorgan Wall, were found in base of the dam fill near
where the eroded face of the dam had been cut by the river...."

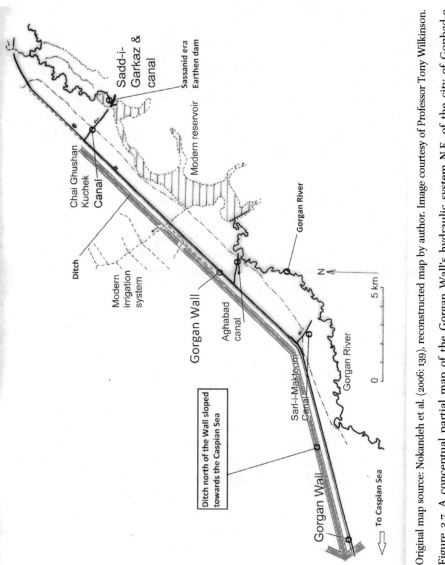

Original map source: Nokandeh et al. (2006: 139), reconstructed map by author. Image courtesy of Professor Tony Wilkinson.

Figure 3.7 A conceptual partial map of the Gorgan Wall's hydraulic system N.E. of the city of Gonbad-e Kavus, illustrating the Chai *Ghushan Kuchek Canal* (top) that may have transferred water from the reservoir north of Garkaz earthen Dam to the ditch that ran parallel to the Wall on its north side.

Photo 3.7 A view of Chai-Ghushan Kuchek Canal, facing northwest towards the Wall (photo by author, August 2012).

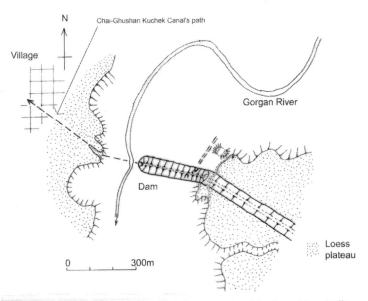

Map source: Nokandeh et al. (2006: 140). Image courtesy of Professor Tony Wilkinson.

Figure 3.8 Plan of the Sadd-i Garkaz Dam near northeast end of the Gorgan Wall, with Gorgan River running through the washed out portion of the earthen dam. The northwest arrow running through the village is the path of the ancient *Chai-Guchan Kuchek Canal* that directed the reservoir water toward the ditch on the Wall's north side.

Photo 3.8 Author standing on the Sadd-I Garkaz Dam facing east. The 300 meters-long washed-out portion of the earthen dam is visible in the center, with the slow-flowing Gorgan River running through during dry summer season (Photo by author, August 2012).

the ICHTO-University of Edinburg team speculate that the ditch provided water at least for the brick kiln's operations during the Wall's construction phases (Omrani et al., 2008: 21). In light of Sadd-i Garkaz's apparent short-lived functionality, this is the most plausible explanation for the link between the Wall on one hand, and the water reservoir and the Gorgan River via the three east-west canals on the other. But the ditch's irregular width and its discontinuation in certain segments raise more questions as to its original purpose and function. One possibility is that diversion of water from the reservoir to the ditch behind the Wall via the Chai-Ghushan Kuchek Canal hydraulic network was designed as a flood control system in the region. In fact, a contemporary flood map of Golestan Province indicates that the Wall/ditch closely trails on the northern boundaries of the flood plain areas, especially in the eastern sections where the cultivated lands are more prone to flooding (see Figure 3.9). In their brief examination of the functionality of Chai-Ghushan Kuchek Canal as a flood channel that could have diverted water from Sadd-i Garkaz Dam to the ditch behind the Wall, Masoudian et al. (2011: 100–102) conclude that the

Table 3.1. Hydrologic and Hydraulic Investigation of Chai-Ghushan Kuchek Canal at the conjunction with Sadd-i Garkaz Dam

Flood Return Period (Year)	Calculated flow Depth (m)
Mean base flow	0.25
2	2.27
10	4.12
25	5.00
50	Out of canal capacity
100	Out of canal capacity
500	Out of canal capacity

Source: Table constructed based on information in Masoudian et al. (2011: 101).

canal's average width and depth (11–12 meters by 3–5 meters, respectively) was adequate to handle up to 25–year flood levels (see Table 3.1).[29]

However, they calculate at most times the mean base water flow during the Sassanid era would have been too shallow, around 0.2 meter deep. They conclude that Gorgan River could not have possibly supplied enough discharge at the reservoir to generate the 5–7 meters depth needed for the ditch north of the Wall to function as a defensive moat. In his earlier excavations Kiani (1982a: 75) also implicitly ruled out the defensive significance of the ditch to function as a moat, as his team found "the remains of an extended burial" in one of the excavated sites where they also found "two Grey Ware jars and two Grey Ware cups" belonging to the Parthian and Sassanian periods, respectively.

Since the Wall is built at a safe distance from Gorgan River's flood plain, it is logical therefore to assume that if not all, but good number of forts along the Wall could have served as high, dry and safe places of refuge for the rural population and their livestock during the flooding seasons. First, site surveys by Kiani (1982b) indicate that a number of forts had been built on a plateau and above and beyond even the 25 year flood level of 5.00 meters. In their excavations in and around Fort 9, Nokandeh et al. (2006: 144) also conclude that "the overall difference in elevation between the preserved fort platform and the bottom of the ditch.... was no less

---

[29] Flooding is still a constant threat to the livelihood of rural and urban residents of the Gorgan River valley. For example, during 2001–2002 heavy rainfall in the east province around the Gorgan River catchment basin caused flooding that killed more than 200 people, with an estimated monetary loss of about $30,000,000 (Fars Foundation, n.d.). This was in spite of the presence of a network of modern water control reservoirs and irrigation systems.

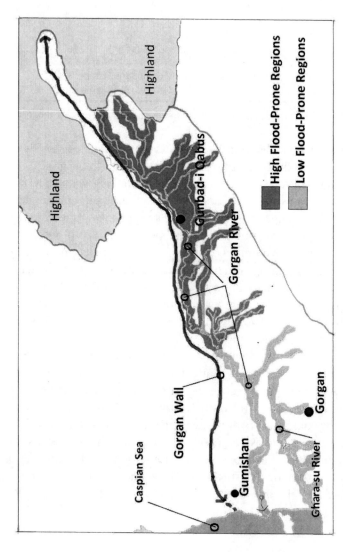

Source for flood-prone risk regions: Fars Foundation, http://www.iran.farsfoundation.net/en/golestan.html?start=12.

Figure 3.9 Contemporary flood-prone/risk areas in the Golestan Province (map by author).

than 6.54 m." Second, as I stated earlier the rather large and varied sizes of the fort platforms could be an indication of the need to provide adequate space to accommodate and protect varied local populations and their livestock during emergency situations such as seasonal flooding and raids by invading armies. From a military standpoint these super-sized forts along the Wall would have been hard (and costly) to maintain, guard and defend on a long-term basis; and in light of the Sassanid builders' expertise and their knowledge of the Roman architecture and design principles (their main imperial rival), smaller and more standardized forts would have made more sense for defensive purposes.[30]

The Red Snake as a Yet Unsolved Enigma

In his review of archaeological field work carried out related to the Sassanian period's large-scale monuments and buildings Huff (1986) acknowledges the presence of a "considerable regional heterogeneity of material culture" within the Sassanian Empire, particularly "in the southwestern and northwestern provinces, marked by rock carvings and stone architecture."[31] However, in central and eastern provinces there is a change in the "scenery" of large-scale projects, whereby "ashlar as building material disappears, even stone-mortar masonry becomes rarer and mud-brick ones more frequent." But this brief narrative partially explains the less-than-glorious nature of what little has remained of the Gorgan Wall complex. In particular, the forts' irregular shapes; the varied standards and rather rudimentary methods of construction of both the Wall and the forts; the tentative nature of buildings; and the haste with which this mega-structure has been constructed—all are indications that this extensive public works project was not undertaken to build long-lasting structures on one hand, and to project glory in the eyes of the subjects and contending imperial forces alike on the other. Rather, it most likely was built in response to local leaders and associated subjects' needs possibly during a brief historical period.

---

[30] Pirnya (1934: 156) notes that the Sassanid Emperor Shahpour, who reigned from 241–271 AD, utilized Roman slaves and engineers in order to build the Shadravan Dam, a magnificent engineering feat over Karun River in the city of Shushtar in southwestern Iran.

[31] For instance, the Palace of Ardeshir I in Firuzabad, Fars Province; and Takht-e Soleyman in northwestern Iran are two examples of such structures.

As I have argued earlier, in the absence of any threats from territories north of the Gorgan Wall, and the fact that the Sassanid Empire's
main contenders came from the northeastern and eastern territories one
wonders what could have possibly been the rationale to build the barrier.
'Gorgān' or Latin 'Hyrcania' (The present-time Golestan Province) is comprised of two distinct climatic zones: the rainforest of the Alborz northern
slopes and the fertile Gorgān plain situated between the eastern shores
of the Caspian Sea, the Alborz foothills in the south, and desert steppe
further north.[32] But it is also the easternmost culmination of a long stretch
of a *fertile crescent* that is squeezed between the Caspian Sea and Alborz
Mountains and extends all the way to Azerbaijan to the west. Not only
the Gorgān Plain was the bread basket of the Sassanids in the Empire's
eastern region, it also was the gateway to the western fertile lands of
Tabaristān and thus a highly valued region of interest for invading tribal
contingents and armies of the eastern and northeastern neighbors. Since
Gorgan was sealed by the Alborz Mountain range on the south, the only
possible access to this region from the east (Khurasan Province) and the
city of Merv region from the northeast was through an east-west passage
(from present-time city of Bojnoord) that winds up and down between
Kopeh Dagh and Alborz Mountains on its north and south, respectively.[33]
Charlseworth (1987: 160) describes in detail the landscape of the Wall's
"east end" northeast of the city of Gunbad-i-Qabus:

> In this area, the terrain traversed by the Wall can be divided into the follow-
> ing, very distinct, zones: to the south rear the wooded peaks of the elburz
> mountains. Proceeding from south northwards from the Elburz, one first
> encounters the foothills.... The foothills in turn give way to a wide belt of
> fertile farmland, crossed by numerous small rivers meandering from the
> Elburz to the river Gurgān, which meanders alng the bottom of the chan-
> nel. A short distance to the north lies the Wall itself, with its associated forts
> built against its southern side, and the ditch on the northern side.

In the absence of any convincing historical documentation about threats
from nomadic tribes north of the Gorgan Wall, it would be plausible to
make the proposition that the Wall was constructed as a physical barrier to trap the invading tribes and armies between this barrier on the

---

[32] 'Hyrcania' is the Greek name for this region which in old Persian was called 'Verkăna.'
literally meaning 'land of the wolves.'
[33] Today the passage is an uphill winding road that connects the Khurasan Province to
the Fertile Crescent. The other route would have been from south-east, from the direction
of city of Sabzevar.

north (the Wall) and Alborz Mountains on the south, once they entered the Gorgan Plain from the east. Furthermore, excavation of a 10.3 km. long (about 6.5 miles) *Wall of Tamishe* and its associated fortifications in 1964 that runs from the southeast corner of the Caspian Sea into the foothills of Alborz Mountains adds more credence to this scenario (Bivar and Fehérvári, 1966).[34] As is illustrated in Figure 3.10, once the advancing enemy or invading forces had entered the Gorgan Plain from the east, they would have been literally trapped within a triangular-shaped enclosure: the Gorgan Wall to the north, the Tamishe Wall to the west, and Alborz Mountains to the south (see Figure 3.10). Since the Sassanid armies heavily relied on their highly mobile and versatile "anti-nomad" cavalry, they could be stationed in a number of forts along the Wall, but not necessarily on those abutting it, to launch their attacks against invading forces (Howard-Johnston, 2006: 195). Certainly, the barrier and the ditch to its north could have been breached in certain, less protected areas, but their most likely function was to create a physical obstacle once the invaders were on the Wall's south side. Farrokh (2009) provides the following hypothetical narrative for the Sassanid army's fighting strategy in the region that is also applicable to the above-mentioned scenario:

> The system of castles [forts] was developed by the Sassanians into a system of fluid defense. This meant that the Gorgan Wall was not part of a purely static system of defense. The main emphasis was in a system of fluid defense-attack system. This entailed holding off potential invaders along the line and in the event of a breakthrough, the Sassanian high command would first observe the strength and direction of the invading forces. Then the elite Sassanian cavalry (the *Savaran*) would be deployed out of the castles [forts] closest to the invading force. *The invaders would then be trapped behind Iranian lines with the Gorgan Wall to their north and the Savaran attacking at their van and flankes. It was essentially this system of defense that allowed Sassanian Persia to defeat the menacing Hun-Hephthalite invasions of the 6th–7th centuries A.D.* (emphasis mine).

Howrad-Johnston (ibid.) offers an alternative scenario for the Sassanian army's defense of northeastern frontiers—that of a centrally psitioned base that allowed the cavalry to "move at speed" in order to intercept and stop the invading force regardless of their point(s) of entry:

---

[34] Bivar and Fehérvári (ibid.: 47) estimate that the Tamishe Wall is a 6th century AD structure that was constructed by similar material used in the Gorgan Wall. Based on a survey of the Tamishe Wall's remains undertaken in 2001, Nokandeh et al. (2006: 151–152) report that "the wall was faced with a single row of bricks on either side, while the core consisted of earth."

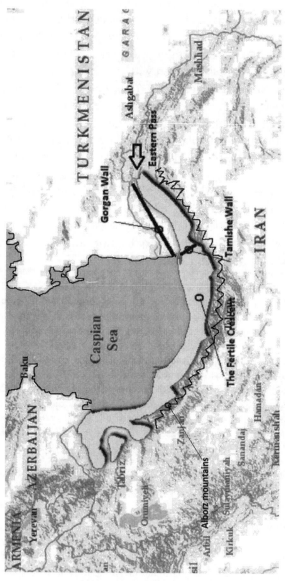

Background Map courtesy of the World Wildlife Fund (with permission) http://www.eoearth.org/article/Caspian_Hyrcanian_mixed_forests.

Figure 3.10 The Fertile Crescent, location of the Gorgan and Tamishe Walls, and the eastern entrance.

The base from which they watched over the safety of the whole of Iran, ready to strike at nomad invaders in highlands or open plains along the length of the eastern frontier, is surely to be identified with Nev-Shāpūr (Nishapūr), founded by Shāpūr I as the capital of Khurāsān.

The Wall was built at a time of the Sassanid Empire's plunge into a period of uncertainty and territorial disputes. As I discussed earlier in the chapter, with the Hephthalites creating a formidable empire east of the Persian Empire's frontiers during the 5th century, the Sassanians were forced to pay tribute to their eastern neighbors. For a brief period during Khosrau I's reign in the 6th century AD the Sassanid Empire regained its glory by defeating the Hephthalies. This is also the most plausible period during which the Gorgan Wall could have been constructed. Similar to other imperial mega-projects, erecting the Gorgan Wall complex was an immense undertaking that required an administrative body capable of securing financial resources, as well as recruiting and supervising a sizable labor force. In the aftermath of Khosrau I's death the ensued internal revolts led to the disintegration of the Sassanian Empire and its eventual defeat by the invading Muslim Arab forces in 642 AD. This might have also been the period that the Wall complex fell into disrepair, leading to its gradual disintegration and eventual demise.

CHAPTER FOUR

CLASH OF EMPIRES: PRELUDE TO THE BERLIN WALL

In the early morning of Sunday August 13, 1961 residents of Berlin woke up, bewildered and surprised, to see the western sectors of their city, which had been occupied for sixteen years by the United States, Britain, and France, being cut off by barbed wire from the Soviet-occupied eastern sector, all under the supervision of the East German government. Pavements and street car tracks were torn up and in a week parts of the initial wall were built using cinder blocks, replacing the barbed wires. The original makeshift walls were then replaced by more permanent concrete walls and fortifications that extended for twenty eight miles along the East and West Berlin boundaries. This was followed by another seventy five miles of border fortification and barricades that also sealed off West Berlin from East German territory. For the next twenty eight years friends and family members were separated from each other and Berlin's streets, subways, sewers and phone lines were cut or blocked, disrupting the services for what in many ways used to be a functioning if not unified metropolis. The border closure and construction of the physical barrier was denounced by the West German government as the "wall of shame" (Klausmeier and Schmidt, 2004: 12). But for the East German communist authorities the Berlin Wall was a defensive barrier, both physical and ideological, which they considered as an "anti-fascist protection wall" (*antifaschistischer schutzwall*) being erected to protect East German citizens from enemies of socialism (Taylor, 2006: 262; Wyden, 1989: 608).

At the time of the Berlin Wall's erection in 1961 Germany was already a divided country. Following Adolf Hitler's defeat in 1945, the invasion of Germany by the four allied nations (United States, Soviet Union, Britain and France); carved both Germany and Berlin into four occupied zones and sectors, respectively. However, the Berlin Wall finalized the political division of Germany as well as Western and Eastern Europe (See Figure 4.1).

Construction of the Berlin Wall did not happen overnight. Rather, it was the culmination of a series of historical, political, and economic events that were related to colonial rivalries among European nations in the late 19th and early 20th centuries; as well as to the increasing involvement of

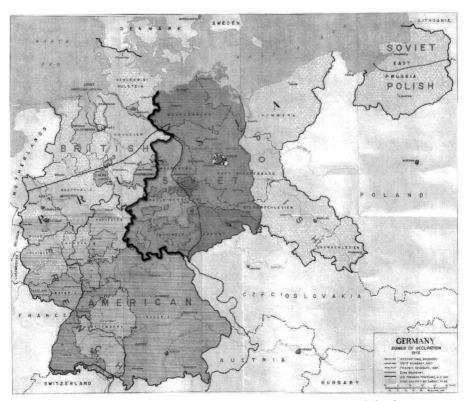

Map source: http://en.wikipedia.org/wiki/File:Germany_occupation_zones_with_border.jpg

Figure 4.1 Divided Germany, 1945.

the United States in empire building and its desire for global domination in the 1930s. Even a cursory review of most of the literature published by Western scholars and investigators will indicate that the majority of reports and analyses consider East Germany as a totalitarian communist dictatorship while West Germany is presented as the beacon of Western democracy and freedom. But what is often overlooked and discounted, is that both Germanys were occupied and under colonial domination, rendering the efforts to establish a viable capitalist democracy in West Germany and a democratic socialist nation in East Germany unrealistic and impossible. Finally, even though the Wall was constructed and maintained by the German Democratic Republic (GDR) for twenty eight years under the Soviet Union's tutelage, it should be considered a "German project" that also had the support of part of the East German population. Thus in order to appreciate the Berlin Wall's historical *raison d'être* a survey of modern Germany's presence and involvement in continental and global affairs is in order.

The Rise and Fall of the German Empire

Up until the mid-19th century the German-speaking territories in Europe were comprised of several hundred independent cities, towns and municipalities; kingdoms and fiefdoms; and duchies and bishoprics. Two loosely defined and fluid political entities competed to control the territories: the Protestant and more industrialized Prussian kingdoms in the north and east; and the Catholic, agrarian Austria in the south and west. Germany's assent to nationhood and formation of a German national identity was facilitated by Prussia's military victories against Austria (1866) and France (1870) under the leadership of Chancellor Otto von Bismarck, which paved the way for German unification and emergence of the German Empire (Second Reich) in 1871 (see Figure 4.2). The new Germany became the hotbed of rival political movements, from Marxist internationalism to social democracy and right-wing ultranationalist tendencies.

In particular, from 1875 onward the Social Democratic Party (SPD) became the strong voice of the German working class which, due to the nation's rapid industrialization was increasing in numbers and influencing many social policies. Eventually the right wing nationalist political forces succeeded in suppressing the SPD and the left; and by the 1890s German politics were dominated by the former, paving the way for an

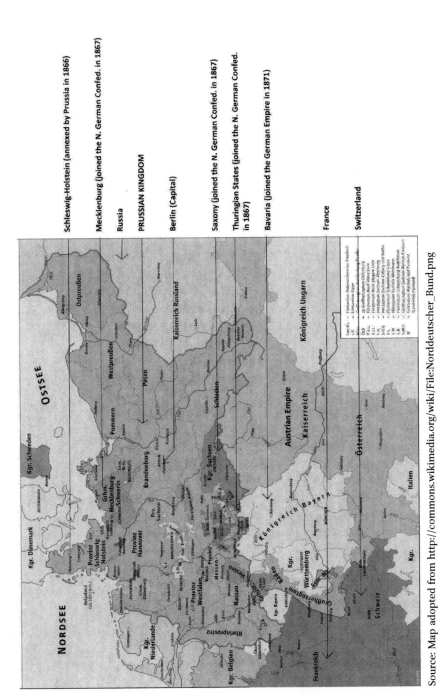

Figure 4.2 Unification and Creation of the German Empire, 1866–1871.

Source: Map adopted from http://commons.wikimedia.org/wiki/File:Norddeutscher_Bund.png

authoritarian government with expansionist overseas policies and colonial interests.

Germany was a latecomer to colonial rivalries of 19th century Europe, particularly when compared with Britain and France. However, by the turn of the 20th century it held colonial territories in Africa, Asia and the Pacific almost "five times the size of the fatherland" (Spiegel Online, 2007). Germany's expansionism however was not supported by all Germans particularly social democrats and socialists, who right before the start of the First World War had the support of almost 35 percent of the population (Taylor, 2006: 22). This is an important historical fact and an indication that progressive and socialist ideals are deeply rooted in German modern history, and that the establishment of the German Democratic Republic (GDR) in the aftermath of WWII was not a mere anomaly. Nonetheless, it was the persuasive power of ultra-nationalist right wing majority faction that pushed Germany into the First World War which led to Germany's humiliating defeat and loss of colonial holdings and finalized the division of colonial territories among major colonial powers of the time.

The War also led to the demise of the Second Reich and the monarchy on one hand and increased the popularity of the pacifist wing of the Social Democratic Party (SPD) as well as the far left on the other, leading to the establishment of the Weimar Republic in 1919. Although short lived, the Weimar Republic ushered in a period of liberal democracy that allowed political participation within a multi-party system—this in spite of the debilitating outcomes of the Treaty of Versailles that led to financial bankruptcy of the state.[1] Of note, is the founding of the Communist Party of Germany (KPD) by Walter Ulbricht in 1920, which had risen "out of the ruins of the Spartakist movement," (Taylor, 2007: 24). Known as the Spartakist League during the war years, this anti-war group on the far left followed the lead of Vladimir Ilyich Ulyanov (Lenin) who successfully led the Russian Revolution and ended the Tsarist rule in 1917. The KPD under Ulbricht's leadership strictly adhered to Marxist-Leninist ideals of international communism under the newly established Soviet Union's

---

[1] Signed in 28 June 1919 between Germany and the Allied Powers, the Versailles Treaty forced Germany to disarm, cede both parts of German territories and colonial holdings, accept responsibility for inciting the war, and pay war reparations. The monetary reparations were substantially reduced under the Dawes and Young Plans in 1924 and 1929, respectively; and completely forgiven by 1932. None the less, the Treaty's outcomes led to political, economic, and social instability, paving the way for power grab by the National Socialist Party during the 1932–33 period (for a complete itemized text of the Versailles Treaty see the following web page: http://net.lib.byu.edu/~rdh7/wwi/versailles.html).

leadership; and it was Ulbricht who thirty years later established and ruled the German Democratic Republic (GDR).

Germany's short-lived post-war experimentation with social democracy under the Weimar government was marred by hyperinflation and extreme devaluation of its currency. Yet by the mid-1920s the government was able to stabilize the currency and return German economy to normalcy. However, ripple effects of the Great Depression in the late 1920s dashed any hopes for economic recovery; and a persisting sense of national humiliation and defeat caused by the signing of the Versailles Treaty continued to flame ultranationalist and conservative sentiments. In this context, the rise of the far right National Socialist Party (NSDAP) and Adolf Hitler to power should be considered as the outcome of both domestic and international developments.[2] This is reflected in the NSDAP's popularity among the populace. For instance, in the 1928 German parliamentary election, just a year before the Great Depression, the Nazi Party was able to secure only a dozen seats in the Reichstag, or a meager 2.5 percent of the vote. But as Taylor (2007: 28) points out, this was drastically changed in the aftermath of the Great depression and during the last few democratic elections before WWII:

> The depression hit skilled working-class and white-collar workers especially hard. The political extremes began to recruit successfully. In September 1930, the Nazis won 107 seats to the KPD's 77; in July 1932, 230 to 89; in November 1932, 196 to 100. Almost half the deputies in the Reichstag represented parties that rejected parliamentary democracy.

Meantime, in the last democratic election in November 1932 the Social Democrats (SPD) also secured 20.4 percent of the votes or 121 seats in the Reichstag, preventing the NSDAP to gain a majority (Administration of the German Bundestag, 2006). Not having a majority vote in the Reichstag, and after being elected as the Chancellor in 1933 Hitler quickly moved to ban the communists and KDP from German politics, thus preventing a KDP-SPD coalition in the Reichstag and reducing the Reichstag to an emasculated parliamentary machine that was subordinate to Hitler's plans and the Third Reich's cabinet. The Reichstag's legislative power was further undermined by the passage of *the Law to Remove the Distress of the People and the State* known as "The Enabling Act" which was presented to the public as an emergency measure and only for four years, to become

---

[2] The *National Socialist German Workers' Party* (NSDAP) is commonly known in English as the *Nazi Party*.

void by 1937. In brief, the act empowered the Reich Chancellor and his cabinet to enact laws without the approval by the Reichstag and implement them in a matter of days. Article 2 of the Enabling Act indicates "the national laws enacted by the Reich Cabinet may deviate from the Constitution as long as they do not affect the position of the Reichstag and the Reichsrat."[3] Article 4 also stipulated that the Reich Cabinet could negotiate treaties with foreign countries without a need for parliamentary approval. Thus in spite of strong popular support for social democratic principles, both liberal and left, for more than a decade Germany experienced a one-party dictatorship of the NSDAP that took the nation to another war of aggression of international magnitude that once again decimated German economy and caused much death and destruction. The fact that the *Enabling Act* was passed by a majority vote in the Reichstag is also an indication of the fact that NSDAP and Hitler's demand for unlimited authority were most likely supported by a significant portion of the German society.[4] Although like any other regime the popularity pendulum oscillated depending on events and government actions, it is important to establish the fact that the German people were not a faceless apolitical mass. Rather, they continued to espouse political tendencies from extreme right to the extreme left throughout the brief period of the Third Reich's grip on power. It was under these fluctuating and dynamic political conditions that Germans reached the final and decisive moments of the Second World War.

Germany's fate was already sealed long before the end of WWII by the Allied forces. After a late entry in joining the war efforts, in early 1943 the U.S. President Franklin Delano Roosevelt made a public statement at the Casablanca Conference that the main objective of the war was Germany's unconditional surrender. Later, in 1944 the three leading Allies,

---

[3] Source of English translation: Law to Remove the Distress of the People and the Reich (Enabling Act); reprinted in U.S. Department of State, Division of European Affairs (1943: Appendix, Document 11, pp.217–218. See also http://www.germanhistorydocs.ghi-dc.org/ sub_document.cfm?document_id=1496. The Reichstag refers to Germanys' general assembly, with its members directly elected by the people. The Reichsrat was the second German assembly with its members appointed by regional governments.

[4] It is not difficult to find statements by admirers of Hitler who lay claim on the Nazi Party's popularity and public support. But a rare observation by Willy Brandt, an active member of the Social Democratic Party and future mayor of West Berlin is worthy of note. While in exile in Norway, in 1936 he visited Berlin on an intelligence mission and "experienced a shocking realization" that the Third Reich and Nazism was firmly in control and that "Hitler had Germany—and most of its people's allegiance—firmly in his grip" (cf. Taylor, 2007: 95. For the original source see Merseburger, 2004: 18ff.).

the Soviet Union, the United States, and Great Britain made an agreement in the *Protocol on Zones of Occupation and Administration of Germany and Greater Berlin* to establish three occupation zones in Germany. While the agreement finalized boundaries for Soviet Union's East German territories and north-eastern Berlin, those for the other two Allies remained undefined.[5] Germany's unconditional surrender on May 8, 1945 and detention of the remaining members of the Reich government in Schleswig-Holstein ended the NASDAP's imperial ambitions. The 1944 protocol was amended twice (in November 1944 and July 1945) which finalized zones of occupation both in Germany and Greater Berlin for each of the four occupying forces (see Figure 4.1).[6]

Preparing Germans for Occupation, 1945–1947

Our examination of historical conditions under which the Berlin Wall was built in 1961 has to take into consideration that Germany and Berlin's division into Eastern and Western territories and its maintenance until 1990 all took place under military occupation. Both liberal and conservative interpretations of post-WWII Germany have equally portrayed Western Germany as a "democratic" entity while East Germany was being brutalized by a totalitarian undemocratic political machine. But even without further documentation a logical conclusion can be drawn here, that historical circumstances under occupation were not conducive for development of viable democracies neither in the East nor West. This is a proposition worthy of further investigation and analysis.

During the war years the Allied forces approached Germany with a clear policy of non-compromise with the Nazi regime out of the "moral outrage and disgust aroused by German aggression and atrocities" (Hartenian, 1987: 146). With the terms of occupation already in place after the Casablanca Conference, the Commanders-in-Chief of the three main Allied countries plus France formed a *Control Council* and took over the government power in the occupied Germany.[7] In a joint statement the

---

5 Protocol on Zones of Occupation and the Administration of the "Greater Berlin" Area (September 12, 1944); reprinted in *Documents on Germany* (1959: 1–3).
6 For a text of the July 1945 protocol visit the following web page: http://www.german historydocs.ghi-dc.org/sub_document.cfm?document_id=2293.
7 The 1944 protocol was later amended in the summer of 1945 to add France as the fourth occupying power both in Germany and Berlin.

occupying countries outlined the terms of occupation and control for
both Germany (1) and Berlin (2):

> (1) In the period when *Germany* is carrying out the basic requirements of
> unconditional surrender, supreme authority in Germany will be exercised,
> on instructions from their Governments, by the British, United States, Soviet
> and French Commanders-in-Chief, each in his own zone of occupation, and
> also jointly, in matters affecting Germany as a whole. The four Command-
> ers-in-Chief will together constitute the Control Council. Each Commander-
> in-Chief will be assisted by a Political Adviser.

> (2) The administration of the *"Greater Berlin"* area will be directed by an
> Inter-Allied Governing Authority, which will operate under the general
> direction of the Control Council, and will consist of four Commandants,
> each of whom will serve in rotation as Chief Commandant. They will be
> assisted by a technical staff which will supervise and control the activities
> of the local German organs (Italics by author).[8]

Thus the 'liberators' of Germany immediately established themselves also
as 'occupiers,' an oxymoron by definition that defied the innate logic of
liberation. The immediate task for the *Control Council* then was to demili-
tarize Germany and dismantle its corporate industrial economy on one
hand and introduce democracy by ridding the nation from Nazism and
Nazi sympathizers on the other. Whereas prior to occupation the military
objectives of complete destruction of Nazism and unconditional surrender of its army were supported by the Allied forces' Psychological Warfare Division (PWD); after Germany's defeat a new propaganda machine,
namely, the Information Control Division (ICD) replaced PWD.[9] The ICD's
first propaganda policy was Directive No. 1 which laid out the terms of
occupation and reeducation of the German population. Hartenian (1987:
147) summarizes the Directive's main objectives:

> In order to "deepen the mood of passive acquiescence and acceptance of
> orders" all output was to bear the "hallmark of a command," all informa-
> tion was to be given "coldly and objectively," and a sense of distance was to

---

[8] Source for both statements: Statement by the Governments of the United Kingdom,
the United States of America, the Union of Soviet Socialist Republics and the Provisional
Government of the French Republic on Control Machinery in Germany (June 5, 1945), in
Selected Documents on Germany and the Question of Berlin, 1944–1961. London, HMSO, 1961,
Cmnd. 1552, 43–44; reprinted in C.C. Schweitzer et al., eds., *Politics and Government in
Germany, 1944–1994. Basic Documents*. Providence, RI, and Oxford, UK: Berghahn Books,
1995, pp. 8–9. http://www.germanhistorydocs.ghi-dc.org/sub_document. cfm?document_
id=2298.

[9] ICD was eventually incorporated into the Office of Military Government United
States or OMGUS for short.

be "deliberately cultivated." The first step of reeducation was to be limited to the strict presentation of "irrefutable facts" which, it was stated, would "stimulate a sense of Germany's war guilt and of collective guilt for such crimes as the concentration camps."

In a cover letter accompanying the Directive No. 1 and sent by the ICD Director General Robert McClure to Chief of Staff, he commented that the rather cold and impersonal nature of the directive held all Germans responsible for the Nazi era, and was meant to emphasize Anglo-American "hatred and contempt for German practices" (Mcclure, cf. Hartenian, 1987: 150 fn. 4). This blanket policy statement that assumed Germans to be a faceless, homogeneous population that lacked political plurality or intellectual sophistication in understanding Germany's past history or the Allied forces' occupation objectives was of course far from reality. In the words of one ICD historian:

> Collective guilt was never accepted. The efforts on our part "to arouse a sense of collective responsibility" for the Nazi crimes, in the words of Brig. Gen. Robert A. McClure, head of the American Military Government's information and cultural program, "never took place" (Norman, 1946: 14–15).

A similar set of policies for denazification, reeducation, and promulgation of a collective guilt for the Third Reich's actions were adopted by the Soviets and their communist allies in the Soviet occupation zone in the initial postwar period (from May to September 1945). For example, in June 1945 the KPD declared that "the German people carry a decisive portion of the guilt and co-responsibility for the war and its results" (Vogt, 2000: 254). In 1946 the American Military Government (AMG) eventually abandoned the "collective guilt" policy and replaced it by a new directive emphasizing that although "most Germans still have to bear a share of the responsibility for Nazism and aggression," the German people's guilt nonetheless had to be "presented in terms of cause and consequence" in order to make a distinction between "active guilt of the criminal" and "passive guilt of the population as a whole" (Hartenian: 1987: 154–55). This opened the door to include some Germans in the ICD's reeducation and democratization efforts still under the AMG's control of the occupied territories. Thereafter a carefully selected group of anti-Nazi Germans were given the responsibility of reeducating the populace using the mass media. "Democratization" implied being inclusive, but the AMG clearly preferred centrists and "did not want to flood the new German media with leftists" (ibid., 157–58). Furthermore, Germans were not allowed to express any partisan views under AMG's rule, as from the early days of the occupation the Directive No. 1 made it clear that citizens had to "follow the orders":

> No line will be taken, either on the issue of good vs. bad Germans, or on the claims of rival German political groups. *The only distinction* which overt allied information services may recognize at this phase *is between those Germans who carry out orders and those who do not* (Italics the author's own) (cf. Hartenian, ibid.: 152).

The Soviets also had their own propaganda machine both during the last year of the war and after Germany's unconditional surrender in May 1945 during the occupation years. The task of preparing Germans for the Soviet occupation was assigned to the Seventh Section, the propaganda and counter-propaganda arm of the Red Army's Main Political Administration (GlavPURKKA). In the aftermath of German assault on the "Homeland" until late 1944 the Seventh Section's main task was to spread a message about a Free Germany that will rise out of the ashes of the Nazi regime among German soldiers (*Wehrmacht*), who were fighting on the front or being held in the POW camps. A radio broadcast and a newspaper run by pro-Soviet German communists aided promotion of Free Germany plan. However, it appears that either out of sympathy or fear of retribution the German citizens initiated little resistance to Nazism and Hitler's rule.[10] The Seventh Section's role in the Soviet zone of occupation shifted from promotion of Free Germany which was no longer an issue, to a propaganda campaign to "convince the Germans to submit to the occupation regime and to remind them that the Soviets had honorable intentions regarding the unity and integrity of Germany."[11] As I discussed earlier, for a brief period the Soviets also tried to submit the Germans' conscience to bear and accept their "collective guilt" for atrocities committed during the Nazi regime. The Soviet Military Administration in Germany (SVAG) had an advantage over AMG in that it could rely on the members of the German Communist Party (KPD), many of whom were brought back to Germany after years of exile in the Soviet Union during Hitler's rule. Similar to its American counterpart SVAG also extensively utilized the media to advance its propaganda campaign during occupation years. In particular, the Seventh Section sponsored publication of several German-language newspapers including the *Täglische Rundschau* (Daily View) and

---

[10] See Naimark, 1995: 16–18.
[11] Ibid., p. 18.

Berliner Zeitung (Berlin Newspaper).[12] But the often-overlooked aspect of the Soviet Union's ability to advance its objectives in the occupied Germany is the nature and extent of violence exerted on Germans that terrorized the populace and helped the occupiers to control them. Historical accounts of the advancing Soviet Army's atrocities, once it marched into German territory, indicate excesses of brutality particularly against German women, destruction of property, and looting. Red Army soldiers were allegedly often encouraged to take revenge on what German soldiers did to their country during Hitler's earlier offensive; and there was even a "booklet of revenge" that urged them to kill Germans and reminded them "...of the need to repay the Germans for their evil."[13] Similar to the AMG but with a more blunt approach SVAG also issued directives on how to confront and treat German subjects. On the eve of crossing the borders into East Prussia the final directive advised soldiers that

> On German soil there is only one master—the Soviet soldier, that he is both the judge and the punisher for the torments of his fathers and mothers, for the destroyed cities and villages... 'Remember your friends are not here, there is the next of kin of the killers and oppressors' (Pirogov, cf. Naimark, 1995: 72, fn. 15).

But probably the most violent aspect of the occupying Soviet army's behavior was the extent of violence against women, as countless number of women regardless of their age were raped during the first year of occupation, particularly during the spring and summer of 1945.[14] Biddiscombe (2001: 611) makes the case that "wartime rape is the ultimate metaphor for military victory." Naimark (1995: Chapter 2) goes into detail on the nature of rape during the Soviet onslaught and occupation of Germany. Citing several German sources and eyewitness reports he provides an account of rape incidents that was repeated all over the Soviet occupied zone, particularly in Berlin:

> It was not untypical for Soviet troops to rape every female over the age of twelve or thirteen in a village, killing many in the process; to pillage the houses for food, alcohol, and loot; and to leave the village in flames. The

---

[12] Ibid., p. 19.
[13] Ibid., p. 72.
[14] It is hard to come up with exact figures and the extent of rape by the Soviet soldiers. But using several sources on this topic Biddiscombe (2001: 614) puts the number around 2 million.

reports of women subjected to gang rapes and ghastly nightly rapes are far too numerous to be considered isolated incidents.[15]

The violent nature of the Soviet Army's actions toward Germans both during the war and post-war occupation periods seems to have served to pacify the vanquished populace, who were thrown into a long period of submissiveness mostly because of their fear that any resistance and violent reaction to the occupiers would have been dealt with more violence.[16] But in spite of Germans' deeply rooted hatred against the Soviet presence, there are also accounts of "acts of kindness" by Russian soldiers towards the populace. In his analysis of the Soviet Army's use of violence as means of social control Slaveski (2008: 391) provides an account of this paradoxical reality during the last days of the war, when

> ...Soviet forces assumed the role of government in areas under their control, unexpectedly providing basic food and medical services essential to the occupied population's survival. For many Germans suffering from wartime depression, material shortage and widespread disease, it made little sense to react violently against this emerging occupation regime, no matter how vicious the provocation of its soldiers.

Naimark (1995: 75) also discusses similar sentiments during the occupation by providing several accounts of statements made by German citizens and local authorities who describe Soviet soldiers' dichotomous "good-evil" behavioral patterns; as for example "how they could give their last piece of bread to German children" on one hand, and how they could "...attack unaccompanied women or girls to rob them and to rape them" on the other. The tragic incidents of rape in occupied Germany are also documented in the occupied zones under the Western Allies' control. Although less severe, "considerable spate of raping" is documented in Western Germany by advancing American and French armies particularly during April and May 1945 (Biddiscombe, 2001: 614). Citing several sources, Biddiscombe (ibid., fn. 27) reports that "by April 1945, 500 rape

---

[15] Naimark, 1995: 72–73).
[16] Biddiscombe (1998: 269–70) cites an example of such case during war years when Germany was still under the Nazi rule:
> During a Soviet raid on the Breslau suburb of Elfenhagen, which typically degenerated into a binge of rape and pillage, an outraged German civilian was barely prevented from tossing a hand grenade at Soviet troops. At the last moment, local women convinced him that such an attack would result in retaliation causing the death of every inhabitant of the village.

cases per week were being reported to the Judge Advocate General of American forces in Europe.

During the occupation period incidents of extreme violence toward German women in the three-powers West German zone were rare. However, fraternization of the occupying army members with German women, particularly by American soldiers was widespread; leading to the emergence of anti-fraternization movement which ironically targeted mostly German women who fraternized with the American military personnel and not the soldiers.[17]Among the three Western occupying forces the American personnel were more attractive to German women since they projected an image of wartime affluence and luxury, whose needs were reportedly "met by an excellent system of commissaries, sports facilities and entertainment."[18] This "luxury living" further isolated American soldiers from German people who were living amidst ruined cities and extreme poverty, which in turn contributed to the former group's feeling of superiority over the natives. When combined with a male chauvinist attitude of considering women as property particularly under occupation, the American Army personnel developed a mentality that German women are a "war booty" whose main function is to satisfy their sexual needs.

By all accounts, German people's lives under the Nazi rule may have been far less than desirable, but evidence suggests that it was a peculiar historical period that evolved out of Germany's experimentation with democratic processes and institutions since the establishment of the Second Reich in the late 19th century. But Germany's post-WWII reality took shape during a transitional period under the four foreign powers' occupation. In particular, regardless of differences or similarities between American and Soviet colonial policies and occupation strategies it is fair to postulate that formation of the two German states took shape under occupation; a historical condition that is never conducive for nourishing and promoting genuine democracies.

Emergence of the Two Germanys under Occupation, 1947–1949

By early 1947 there was a distinct shift in AMG's propaganda objectives in Germany, from reeducating the public about the evils of the Nazi regime

---

[17] For an interesting and detailed examination of the anti-fraternization movement see Biddiscombe (2001).

[18] Ibid., p. 616.

to confronting the Soviet Union's ideological and political presence in the Soviet occupation zone. However, this was a subtle campaign that still operated within the context of the four powers *Control Council* that did not challenge the Soviet Union as an occupying force. The first phase of anticommunist propaganda campaign was launched after the U.S. President Harry Truman made his landmark containment policy speech in March 1947 which became known as the *Truman Doctrine*. In his speech Truman identified two distinct "ways of life" in the world for all nations to choose, particularly those devastated by war or emerging out of the past colonial experience:

> One way of life is based upon the will of the majority, and is distinguished by free institutions, representative government, free elections, guarantees of individual liberty, freedom of speech and religion, and freedom from political oppression. The second way of life is based upon the will of a minority forcibly imposed upon the majority. It relies upon terror and oppression, a controlled press and radio, fixed elections, and suppression of personal freedoms (parts of Truman's speech, cf. Jones, 1974: 143).

This simplistic, ahistorical and distorted comparison of Western capitalist and collectivist socialist democracies was meant to undermine the legitimacy of the Soviet Union as the main force in the socialist camp at the time in order to curb its expansionist colonial ambitions. However, this had to be done not by directly attacking the communist camp through military action; but by assisting countries that were on shaky economic grounds or susceptible to radical revolutionary ideas that pushed them toward the Soviet camp. Truman's immediate economic help plan submitted to the Congress for approval was limited to Greece and Turkey only. But the American containment policy was reinforced three months later, when in his commencement speech at Harvard University the U.S. secretary of State George Marshall invited the war-torn European nations to launch a joint economic recovery plan with American assistance and supervision. He warned Europeans that post-war economic plight amidst much destruction in Europe has left many countries on the verge of political and financial collapse, making them vulnerable to communist ideas and the Soviet Union's interference and domination. Thereafter the United States and European countries drafted the four-year Economic Recovery Program (ERP) of grants and loans to be provided and directed under the newly created Economic Cooperation Administration (ECA). The Marshall Plan clearly was subversive in its intent, as it also aimed at helping Eastern European countries that were in the Soviet Union's influence zone. Although the plan did not explicitly exclude the Soviet participation, in the aftermath of Truman's speech it was viewed by the Soviets as an offensive anti-communist plan aimed at keeping the socialist camp weak and underdeveloped:

> Russia also read an integrated plan as a return to the status quo ante bellum; that is, Western Europe would be the industrial center and Eastern Europe the supplier of raw materials, especially grain and coal. The Russians feared this subordination of the agricultural East of the industrial West (Paterson, 1974: 169).[19]

The Truman Doctrine and the Marshall Plan solidified the Cold War era's uncompromising two-camp positions, which particularly sealed the fate of Germany by being divided into the Western (American) and Eastern (Soviet) zones of ideological, economic, and political influence. Conventional views and interpretations of the origins of the Cold War often see it simply as the American reaction to the Soviet Union's expansionist policies and actions. However, in their assessment of the Cold War history Cox and Kennedy-Pipe (2005: 102) conclude that "it was American policies as much as (and perhaps more than) Soviet actions that finally led to the division of Europe and thus to the Cold War itself." This is also the position taken by this author in analyzing the historical roots of the building of the Wall.

By the end of 1947 the ICD's anticommunist propaganda became increasingly overt in the aftermath of Truman Doctrine and implementation of the Marshall Plan. The campaign's tone also became more negative and explicit by emphasizing the evils and disadvantages of the communist system while at the same time it "positively" indicated the advantages of "true democracy," a theme that was spelled out by the Truman Doctrine (Hartenian, 1987: 171). The ICD's anticommunist ideological campaign was complemented with implementation of a drastic economic measure by the Western occupying powers on June 18, 1948, when the Americans, the British and the French military governments introduced the new DeutscheMark and withdrew the Reichsmark (the existing

---

[19] Paterson (ibid., p. 174) also makes the case that substantial part of the U.S. financial aid to European countries was diverted to their colonial holdings to expand extraction processing of raw materials for Europe's industrial development. The U.S. also benefited from importing raw materials from European colonies. Thus contrary to the Marshall Plan's stated objective of promoting peace and stability in the world, the plan supported the exploitation of colonial subjects, which in turn contributed to social and political unrest in the peripheries.

currency in all four occupied zones) from their respective zones of influence. In brief, they

> ...issued everyone in their zone with 40 new DeutscheMarks (D-Marks), with another 20 due shortly, in exchange for 60 old marks...the new D-Marks were put into circulation elsewhere at the rate of between 10:1 and 15:1 to the Reichsmark depending on the type of currency and debt held (Taylor, 2007: 53).

Clearly in blatant violation of the 1945 Potsdam agreement, this bold action increased Germans' purchasing power in the Western zones while drastically reducing the buying power of those under the Soviet control in the Eastern zone. It was particularly detrimental to East Berlin residents, as they no longer could take advantage of West Berlin's quality goods and services.[20] But the bombshell that put an end to any possibility of reinstating a unified Germany was dropped in July 1948, when the Western military governors of the three occupied zones asked their respective ministers-president (heads of state government) to set up the West German state by convening a constituent assembly and reviewing state boundaries. Obviously this task had to be accomplished within the confines of the occupation statute set forth at the Potsdam meeting, which envisioned a decentralized political structure in a demilitarized Germany.

The three Western occupying powers held different positions on Germany's future. The French favored a political future only in the framework of the states (*Länder*). The British espoused a demilitarized, economically unified Germany under the four-power control. The U.S. position was more in favor of allowing Germans design their government while the four-power agreements would guarantee demilitarization and disarmament of Germany for at least twenty-five years (Hahn, 1995: 10–12). On the other hand, the Soviets advocated a unified Germany with a strong central government, with anticipation that it will join the Soviet-socialist camp. But the Cold War policies of the four occupying powers practically put an end to prospects of a unified Germany for a foreseeable future.

By April 1949 the three military governors of the Western zones and members of the newly established West German Parliamentary Council (*Parlamentarischer Rat*) came to an agreement on the constitution of the new West German state, or what is commonly known as the *Basic Law*. Soon after, on May 23 1949 the Federal Republic of Germany (FGR)

---

[20] In retaliation, the Soviets staged the infamous blockade of West Berlin that lasted for eight months. For a detailed account of the Berlin blockade See Taylor (2007: 53–59).

became a reality in the three western occupied zones, with the university city of Bonn becoming its provisional government seat. Forced to make a move, the Soviet Union held elections in its zone of occupation in order to elect members of the new *People's Congress*. The 2000-member body then selected 300 members to serve on the *People's Council* in order to draft and ratify the new constitution for the German Democratic Republic (GDR). Thus the die was cast for a divided Germany under close U.S. and Soviet control.

Hans Simons who served as the liaison officer of the AMG to the German parliamentary council considered both constitutions for East and West Germany as being exceptional cases, as in his words they were "made primarily for international purposes (Simons, 1951: 14). Conscious of this public perception, after finalizing the *Basic Law* document members of the West German Parliamentary Council declared that they "were guided by their decisions by German considerations and free from foreign influence" (cf. Hahn, 1995: 7). But Hahn (ibid.) questions their claims by arguing that "it does not seem plausible that victors would have allowed the vanquished Germans, whose experience with democracy had been brief and disastrous, complete freedom in drafting a constitution." The main flaw in the writing of the Basic Law lies in its deliberate language regarding the function of the armed forces, which was an imposition by the military governors of the occupying forces to cut the wings of future German expansionist ambitions. For instance, Article 87a, Section 1 clearly indicates that "the Federation shall establish Armed Forces for purposes of defense" only, and Section 3 in more detail clarifies the army's tasks and responsibilities "during a state of defense or a state of tension" by only authorizing them to "protect civilian property and to perform traffic control functions to the extent necessary to accomplish their defense mission."[21] In contrast, the 1949 Constitution of the GDR imposed no limitations on the nature of the armed forces and instead pledged to respect international law regarding other nations and people's right to self-determination. For instance, Article 5 affirms that "no citizen may participate in belligerent actions designed to oppress any people."[22] Interestingly, both constitu-

---

[21] Basic Law for the Federal Republic of Germany, http://www.iuscomp.org/gla/statutes/ GG.htm#87a accessed 8-3-2010. This provision was somewhat changed after German reunification in the 1990s, and allowed German armed forces to defend the nation even outside its political boundaries.

[22] Constitution of the German Democratic Republic, October 7, 1949, reprinted in Snyder (1958: 540–541).

tions delineated the basic premises of political structure and the workings of its institutions based on respect for individual and human rights, but one within the context of Western liberal bourgeois democracy and the other based on social democratic principles of building a workers' state. Both constitutions also made provisions for a pluralist political system. The GDR Constitution was not specific about political parties. Rather, it called them "associations," which had to meet the following criteria:

> Nominations for the People's Chamber may be made only by those associations which, pursuant to their statutes, aim to bring about the democratic organization of public and social life in the entire Republic and which maintain an organization throughout the territory of the Republic.[23]

But GFR's Constitution clearly recognized political parties and their role in the "formation of the political will of the people," yet also deemed certain parties which "seek to undermine or abolish the free democratic basic order or to endanger the existence of the Federal Republic of Germany" as unconstitutional.[24] The two constitutional documents were products of Germans' past political participation history. As a reaction to their negative experiences under the one-party Nazi rule, in the immediate aftermath of the surrender there was a rush toward maximizing political participation that was also sanctioned by the four occupying powers. As early as June 1945 all anti-fascist parties were allowed to function in the Soviet occupation zone. In particular, the German Communist Party (KPD) was revived by veteran communists such as Walter Ulbricht and Wilhelm Pieck who had just returned from exile in the Soviet Union. But at the time the Proclamation by the Central Committee of the German Communist Party (KPD) had a deliberate mild and non-antagonistic language that hailed the Allied forces' victory over Hitler's "barbarism," which fought for "the cause of justice, freedom, and progress."[25] By July, 1945 the Unity Front of the Anti-Fascist Democratic Parties was formed in the four zones under occupation. It comprised representatives from the Liberal Party (LDPD), the Christian Democratic Union (CDU), the Communist Party (SPD) and

[23] Constitution of the German Democratic Republic, Article 13, http://www.ena.lu accessed 8-3-2010.

[24] Basic Law for the Federal Republic of Germany, Article 21, http://www.iuscomp.org/gla/statutes/GG.htm#87a,accessed 8-3-2010.

[25] Aufruf des Zentralkomitees vom 11. Juni 1945 [Proclamation by the Central Committee, June 11, 1945], reprinted in Ossip Kurt Flechtheim, *Die Parteien der Bundesrepublik Deutschland* [*The Parties of the Federal Republic of Germany*]. Hamburg, 1973, pp. 292–99. Text translated by Thomas Dunlap, http://www.germanhistorydocs.ghi-dc.org/docpage.cfm?docpage_id=3253 accessed 8-2-2010.

the KPD; with the latter having "the ear of the all-powerful SMA [Soviet Military Administration]."[26] Later, in April 1946 the KPD and SPD in the soviet occupation zone merged and formed the Socialist Unity Party of Germany (SED) which by the early 1949 evolved into a Leninist-Stalinist party with a centralized leadership structure.[27]

In the western occupation zones all political parties were initially allowed to participate in the political processes. The two major parties were the Christian Democratic Union (CDU) and the Socialist Democratic Party (SPD). The CDU was founded by former members of the bourgeois liberal Catholic Center Party which after the formation of GFR eventually became the dominant political force in West Germany.[28] But despite its popularity among German voters, the SPD eventually lost ground to CDU in the 1953 and 1957 elections. Of note is an appeal by the Socialist Democratic Party (SPD) that advocated establishment of a parliamentary democracy that will support extensive nationalization in the context of a socialist economy.[29] The KPD was also allowed to Participate in West German politics. But in 1951 the Federal Government submitted a petition to the Federal Constitutional Court requesting a ban on KPD's political activities. The FCC eventually issued a verdict in 1956 that considered KPD's political objectives "unconstitutional" and put an end to its political presence in West Germany.[30] German politics after the establishment of the GFR and GDR were influenced by past historical experiences yet with no doubt played by German political actors. Each of the two German nations set foot on a different path for social and economic development, but they both entered this new era under military rule and terms set forth by the four occupying powers. The East-West divide soon morphed into a long, fierce ideological and military conflict between two contending imperial powers, namely, the Soviet Union and the United States, which lasted for four decades.

---

[26] Taylor, 2006: 43.
[27] See "From the Resolution of the 1st Party Conference: the SED becomes a 'party of the new type'" (January 28, 1949), in Thomaneck (1989: 47–49).
[28] Mitchell (1995: 279).
[29] Aufruf vom 15. Juni 1945 zum Neuaufbau der Organisation [Call to Rebuild the Party Organization, June 15, 1945]; reprinted in Flechtheim (1973: 212–215).
[30] Pfeiffer and Strickert (1957: 225–227).

Post-War Dependent Development of a Divided and Occupied Germany

The post-war invasion and occupation of Germany by the Allied forces, its division into Eastern and Western zones of influence, and the eventual creation of the two Germanys set the stage that led to the dependent development of both half-nations and the eventual demise of the German Democratic Republic. Through this period in history people in both Germanys yearned for a unified nation, albeit each seeing it through their own political kaleidoscope that was designed by these two emerging imperial powers. By the early 1950s the developments on the Asian front and the Korean conflict intensified the Cold War tensions between the United States and the Soviet Union. The war time "alliance of convenience" between Western powers and the Soviet Union that led to the Third Reich's defeat was replaced by their mutual distrust and ideological rivalry.

On the German front, the Western powers began to consider the incorporation of a rejuvenated West German defensive military into a unified European army that would block Soviet influence and the spread of communism; thus abandoning the original goal of a demilitarized Germany.[31] The Soviet Union was alarmed by the possibility of such an agreement, and in March 1952, two months before the signing of the European Defense Community (EDC), tried to block West Germany's incorporation into EDC. In what is known as Joseph Stalin's "first note" the Soviet Foreign Ministry delivered a copy of the German peace treaty to the American Embassy. After a rather detailed explanation of the history of East-West relations since the 1944 Potsdam Agreement, the document proposed the establishment of a unified Germany as "an independent peace-loving state", contingent upon the complete withdrawal of the four-powers' armed forces from Germany (including Berlin) and the liquidation of all foreign bases; a guarantee of individual rights and "free activity" of all political parties; and establishment of a "defensive" national German armed forces. However, the proposal signified that the unified Germany should obligate itself "not to enter into any kind of coalition or military alliance directed against any power which took part with its armed forces in the

---

[31] Western Declaration on Germany, the European Defense Community, and Berlin (May 27, 1952); reprinted in *Documents on Germany* (1959: 102–103). http://www.germanhistory docs.ghi-dc.org/sub_document.cfm?document_id=3036&language=english, accessed 8-4-2010.

war against Germany."[32] Not trusting the Soviets and Stalin's proposal for a unified Germany the United States quickly responded by affirming the Western powers' commitment to a future unified Germany. However, it turned down Stalin's proposal by arguing that it was an inherently flawed proposition:

> [T]he United States Government also observes that the Soviet Government now considers that the peace treaty should provide for the formation of German national land, air, and sea forces, while at the same time imposing limitations on Germany's freedom to enter into association with other countries. The United States Government considers that such provisions would be a step backwards and might jeopardize the emergency in Europe of a new era in which international relations would be based on cooperation and not on rivalry and distrust. Being convinced of the need of a policy of European unity, the United States Government is giving its full support to plans designed to secure the participation of Germany in a purely defensive European community which will preserve freedom, prevent aggression, and preclude the revival of militarism.[33]

Stalin's proposal was worthy of a more serious consideration by the West, in that it was a clear departure from the Soviet Union's past colonial and expansionist practices. The Soviet proposal to create a neutral Germany nonetheless was an implicit last minute effort to block West Germany's entrance into the EDC or any other future military alliance with the Western block. Rejection of the Soviet proposal by the American government and its Western allies is also an indication that out of fear of the possibility of a left-leaning socialist victory, there was no intention on their part to leave Germany and allow Germans to freely choose their future form of government. Two months later the three Western occupying powers signed the EDC Treaty, but its implementation required ratification by the three nations. At the end, the EDC Treaty had to be abandoned after the French National Assembly rejected it.[34]

Western powers' negative reaction to Stalin's peace initiative was a prelude to further separation and increasing distance between the two Germanys. Although under the original 1944 Potsdam Agreement the four

---

[32] Note from the Soviet Foreign Ministry to the American Embassy, Enclosing a Draft for a German Peace Treaty, March 10, 1952; reprinted in *Documents on Germany* (1959: 85–87).

[33] Note from the American Embassy in Moscow to the Soviet Foreign Ministry, Regarding the Soviet Draft of a German Peace Treaty, March 25, 1952; reprinted in *Documents on Germany* (1959: 87–88).

[34] Declaration on Germany, the European Defense Community and Berlin (op. cit.).

powers had agreed to guarantee the free movement of people and goods across zones of occupation and influence, East German authorities under direct instructions by Stalin began to strengthen the security of the border between East and West Germany:

> A no man's land five kilometers wide was cleared. In 'night and fog' actions planned by the *Stasi*, thousands of people living near the border were removed at short notice from their homes. The authorities concentrated on 'unreliable' types such as known anti-Communists, those with close Western contacts, or farmers known to oppose collectivized agriculture. Towns and villages were split in two, families often divided. Barbed wire was laid down along its entire length, and secondary and local roads leading to the border were ripped up in order to prevent access (Taylor, 2006: 76).[35]

The border closure coincided with the signing of the "Germany Treaty" that paved the way for West Germany's admittance into the anti-Soviet alliance. Soon after, in June 1952 the SED and Walter Ulbricht announced at the second party conference that East Germany's second five-year plan would concentrate on "building socialism," modeled after the Soviet Union's Stalinist-Communist state. This included large-scale development of heavy industries, further collectivization of agriculture, higher taxes and increased pressure on those who were not in support of such drastic measures (Mueller, 1999: 713). In particular, faced with a drop in workers' productivity in the GDR's manufacturing sector the Ulbricht government blamed the "subversive" elements who were corrupted by the capitalist culture of the West, and raised the work norms by ten percent without any increase in workers' wages. This state directive was issued at a time that workers' standard of living was also deteriorating, and a combination of social and economic discontent led to the June 16, 1953 workers uprising in East Berlin. The crisis began when the construction workers who were working on the mega-project of the high-rise residential complex in Stalin-Alee marched through East Berlin streets to protest the government's order to increase their productivity without a raise.[36] By the end of the day street demonstrations and riots got out of hand, leading to the declaration of a state of emergency by the Soviet Military Administration. By June 17 the rioting crowds in Berlin and many other East German

---

[35] 'Night and fog' refers to illicit actions taken by the *Stasi* or Staatssicherheitddienst (the East German Ministry of State Security) against East German population.

[36] Built by the GDR government in the 1950s in East Berlin's Mitte District, Stalin-Alee is a two kilometer-long monumental boulevard that characterizes Soviet style socialist classicist architecture and urban planning. Its name was later changed to Karl-Marx-Alee.

towns and villages were eventually brought under control with the help of Soviet tanks and military, with many protesters and bystanders being brutally beaten, and some fatally shot.[37] The GDR government issued a statement blaming the riots on outside fascist influences and the enemies of the socialist state:

> Measures taken by the government of the German Democratic Republic to improve the situation of the population have been answered by fascist and other reactionary elements in West Berlin with provocations and serious disruptions to order in the democratic sector of Berlin. These provocations are intended to impede the unification of Germany...The unrest that ensued is the work of *agents provocateurs* and fascist agents of foreign powers and their accomplices from German capitalist monopolies. These forces are dissatisfied with the democratic power in the German Democratic Republic, which is organizing improvements in the situation of the population.[38]

The SED's new socialist initiative and the brutal suppression of June 16–17 uprising intensified tensions among East German residents, leading to an unprecedented massive exodus to the West (Taylor, 2006: 77).[39] With the closure of the border between East and West Germany in 1952 the only available route for dissident East Germans to escape or emigrate to the West was the still porous border between East and West Berlin. Ulbricht and his supporters within East German government were cognizant of this fact and were in favor of sealing the border between East and West Berlin as well; a plan that also had Stalin's implicit support. However, after his sudden death in 1953 the new Soviet leadership sought to take a more conciliatory position toward the West by suggesting "the problem of population loss from the GDR should be solved not by shutting the people in but by making their life better" (ibid., 79). In fact, sealing the border between East and West Germany did not put a dent in the flow of East German emigrants and refugees, and as data in Figure 4.3 indicate the number of refugees increased from 1952 to 1957. In particular, in the aftermath of the June 1953 workers' uprising around 300,000 East Germans fled to the West, comprising the highest number of emigrants since the establishment of the GDR in 1949.

---

[37] It is not clear how many people were killed during the two-day uprising, but the estimates range from 55 to 125 dead. see *Tote des 17. Juni 1953*.

[38] Statement by the Government of the GDR (June 17, 1953), *Neues Deutschland* (June 18, 1953); reprinted in Beate von Oppen (1955: 590).

[39] For a detailed narrative of the June 1953 uprising see Taylor (ibid., pp. 79–87).

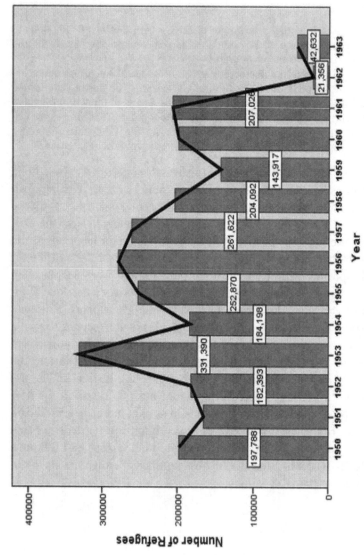

Source: Bundesministerium für gesamtdeutsche Frage [Federal Ministry for All-German Affairs], ed., *SBZ von A bis Z* [*Soviet Occupation Zone from A to Z*]. Bonn, 1965, p. 133.

Figure 4:3 Emigration of East German Residents to the West, 1950–1963 (chart by author).

West Germany's integration into the NATO Pact in May 1955 put the final nail in the German unification coffin. The Soviets reacted immediately by establishing the Eastern Bloc's defense shield through the formation of the Warsaw Pact and inclusion of East Germany in that alliance.[40] From then on the Soviet Union explicitly expressed its interest and concerns about both GDR's internal security as well as the role it played in the European theatre of the Cold War years. In his famous November 1958 speech, the Soviet Premier Nikita Khrushchev directly accused Western powers of rearming West Germany in violation of the terms of the Potsdam Agreement, and also abusing their privileges in West Berlin in order to undermine GDR's socialist economy. This was followed by a note delivered to the governments of the three Western allies by the Soviet foreign ministry in November 1958, known as the *"Berlin Ultimatum,"* in which Khrushchev demanded that West Berlin be demilitarized and declared a "free city" within six months. The note accused Western powers of being increasingly "influenced by forces obsessed with hatred for Socialist and Communist ideas," sentiments which were concealed during the war years for pragmatic political reasons. Khrushchev also criticized the West of undermining unification goals as set forth in Potsdam in 1944, and thus forfeiting "their rights to maintain a presence in [West] Berlin." The message concluded that "it might be possible to agree that the territory of the free city [West Berlin] be demilitarized and that no armed forces be contained therein." The message ended by indicating that a free city with its own government and economy will certainly be "a definite sacrifice on the part of the GDR for the sake of strengthening peace in Europe."[41] In a press conference after the delivery of the *Berlin Ultimatum* Khrushchev warned that the Western powers' refusal will leave no other option for him than to "unilaterally sign a treaty with the GDR and turn over all control of access to Berlin to the East Germans." But faced with a long, painful period of non-response and stone-walling by the West, Khrushchev later backtracked and "simply pretended that there had never been an ultimatum."[42]

---

[40] Officiated on May 14, 1955, the Warsaw Pact or the "treaty of mutual defense, friendship, Cooperation and assistance" was an association of eight Eastern Bloc countries with the Soviet Union.

[41] For the complete text of the *Berlin Ultimatum* see Note from the Soviet Foreign Ministry to the American Ambassador at Moscow (Thompson), Regarding Berlin (November 27, 1958); reprinted in *Documents on Germany* (1959: 317–331).

[42] Taylor (2006: 104–105).

An interesting aspect of the political process that eventually led to the erection of the Wall is that it increasingly became an East German project that was not always envisioned or supported by the Soviet Union. For example, during his historic trip to the United States in September 1959, in a joint-communiqué Soviet Premier Khrushchev and the U.S. President Eisenhower stated that "all international disputes should be settled through negotiations and not by force." This signaled an implicit departure from Khrushchev's 1958 *Berlin Ultimatum*," raising hopes that some form of agreement could be negotiated about Berlin's future.[43] In his analysis of the Cold War politics that led to the building of the Wall Taylor (2006: 127) contends that Khrushchev was "on a tightrope" and faced a dilemma in bringing about a satisfactory resolution for the Berlin crisis:

> If he was not aggressive enough, the West would sit tight and wait for the GDR (and possibly the East Bloc in general) to fall apart. If he pushed too hard, however, he might provoke a counter-reaction, in the shape of Western military and economic sanctions against the East. Such sanctions would seriously harm the economies of the Warsaw Pact countries in general and East Germany in particular.

In the aftermath of the failed U-2 spy flight mission over the Soviet Union, the follow-up Paris summit in spring of 1960 was a failure on the Berlin question. Although border closure between the two Berlins was not discussed at the Paris summit, Khrushchev apparently gave the green light to Ulbricht to "start exploring military options to stop the refugee flow, including the closing of the sector border.[44] Unknown to the West, during the same period the GDR Premier Ulbricht expressed his concern about the "Berlin hole" that was draining East Germany of its people and resources and a need to find a remedy:

> In this political and economic struggle against our republic West Berlin plays the role of the channel with whose help this trade in people is practiced, and through which also food and other materials flow out of our republic. West Berlin is therefore a big hole in the middle of our republic, which costs us more than a billion marks each year.[45]

Later, in June 1961 Premier Khrushchev reissued his threat of striking a separate peace treaty deal with East Germany with a deadline of December 31, 1961 if an agreement is not reached on Berlin's future; and further

---

[43] Roberts (1959).
[44] Mathias Uhl (2003), cf. Taylor (2006: 126).
[45] Harrison (2003: 169f).

threatened to end the four-power agreements that guaranteed American, British, and French access rights to West Berlin. The three powers did not heed and declared that unilateral treaties could not abrogate their rights in West Berlin. The Kennedy administration's reaction to Khrushchev's rather blunt threat was also equally aggressive, and in his July 25, 1961 address to the American people, President Kennedy emphasized the possibility of military action to defend the U.S. rights in Berlin:

> So long as the communists insist that they are preparing to end by themselves unilaterally our rights in West Berlin and our commitments to its people, we must be prepared to defend those rights and those commitments. We will at times be ready to talk, if talk will help. But we must also be ready to resist with force, if force is used upon us. Either one alone would fail. Together, they can serve the cause of freedom and peace.[46]

The same day the President announced a request to the Congress for an additional $3.25 billion for military spending to increase the Army's strength from 875,000 to one million, and to prepare the nation for the possibility of a nuclear face-off with the Soviet Union. At the time of Kennedy's speech John J. McCloy, his chief disarmament negotiator happened to be in Moscow, when he was suddenly summoned to Khrushchev's Black Sea vacation dacha, whereby the Soviet Premier discussed the U.S. administration's latest move. A week later at the Warsaw Pact summit conference in Moscow Khrushchev recounted his conversation with McCloy: "Please tell your president we accept his ultimatum and his terms and will respond in kind. . . . We will meet war with war . . . .," and if Kennedy started a war, he would be the "last president of the United States."[47] By then East German leaders were set on giving their go ahead to border closure, and on August 7, 1961 Ulbricht informed members of the GDR Politburo of its imminence. Thus began the quiet behind the scenes preparations for border closure, which was code-named "*Operation Rose*": moving the needed material, equipment, and both the military and civilian work force closer to the border line and accomplishing the task without raising the public's suspicion of what lies ahead.[48] Even the thousands of East German police units and 'factory fighting groups' on

[46] *The Cold War in History.* John F. Kennedy Presidential Library and Museum. http://www.jfklibrary.org/Historical+ Resources/JFK+in+History/The+Cold+War+in+Berlin.htm, accessed 8-6-2010.

[47] Khrushchev, cf. Taubman (2004: 501–502).

[48] For an interesting narrative of the planning and execution of *Operation Rose* see Taylor (2005: 155–163).

the standby alert were kept in the dark, and were informed only five hours before the border sealing operation was launched on Sunday, August 13 at one a.m. Taylor (2006: 162) provides some of the details of the logistics and objectives of *Operation Rose* that had to be accomplished in that short time period:

> Sentries were placed at two-meter intervals along the entire Berlin sector border to prevent escapes, while border troops, factory paramilitaries and construction units barricaded the streets by means of barbed wire, tank traps and improvised concrete bolsters. Street lights were turned off, masking the nature of the operation.

Considering the time limitations for completing the job under the guise of the night in order to have Berlin citizens waking up and facing a *fait accompli*, what lay ahead of the task force was even more daunting:

> Sixty-eight of 81 crossing points were to be barricaded. All 193 streets that straddled the border would be closed. And then there were the transport systems. Twelve underground (U-Bahn) and surface (S-Bahn) city railway lines were to be blocked off at the sector borders. Dozens of stations on or near the border were to be closed and sealed. The police, including the *Trapos*, had charge of that. The most challenging task was at the busy FriedrichStraße station complex, favoured route for refugees, where U-Bahn, S-Bahn and international passenger trains all stopped on the east bank of the Landwehr Canal, just meters from West Berlin.[49]

The closure of this border separated the German people for 28 years from each other. This action was not the inevitable result of the close of war, but rather one that was a consequence of nearly a decade of escalation. The wall that divided Germany hindered and weakened its place in the political stage in the global power struggles for years to come.

---

[49] *Trapo* is the nickname for The "Transportpolizei" (Transport Police) in the German Democratic Republic. After the Wall's construction, however, only seven of the former 80 checkpoints on the city's internal border between East and West Berlin remained in place. One checkpoint was reserved for foreign nationals, the infamous "Checkpoint Charlie"; two were reserved for the FDR citizens, and four were designated for West Berlin residents. West Berliners could still travel to West Germany via road, railway and canals uninterrupted through the four checkpoints indicated on the map.

CHAPTER FIVE

BUILD THE WALL: THE TWO GERMAN ECONOMIES ARE NOW UNITED!

By daybreak on Sunday August 13, 1961 what many Germans considered as an improbable possibility, that is, to cut a city of about four million in two and seal the crossing lines was a reality. Bewildered and surprised, Berlin residents woke up to the new reality of a divided city that for the next twenty-eight years separated friends and families who happened to reside on either side of the sealed border between East and West Berlin. From the East German leaders' vintage point *Operation Rose* was a success in that it accomplished the task without firing a shot or resorting to violence; other than the clearly violent action taken against Berlin residents as the wall effectively divided loved ones from each other.

The date and time for accomplishing the task were "obviously chosen to give the operation the maximum degree of surprise and to minimize the possibility of prompt and effective counteraction from the West."[1] However, the border closure between Berlin's eastern and western sectors was without doubt a defensive military operation that was carried out by the GDR's militarized police force and backed up by the Soviet Union's military command stationed in Germany. The U.S. Department of State estimated that two infantry divisions and one armored division were involved in sealing the border, a military presence that was "fully adequate both to quell any attempts at outbreaks by the East German population and to discourage any possible Western ideas of counteraction" (see Figure 5.1 and Photos 5.1 and 5.2).[2]

The Wall effectively gave the East Germans the heart and soul of old historic Berlin, although it was in ruins. This is a less explored and discussed issue in the Berlin Wall literature, probably because its admittance by the West would have delivered their adversary on the East a victory. In contrast, what became West Berlin after the border closure was in fact the westward expansion and growth of Berlin beyond its western gates since the early 20th century, such as the infamous Brandenburg Gate or

---

[1] Slusser (1973: 129).
[2] Cf. Slusser, ibid., p. 131.

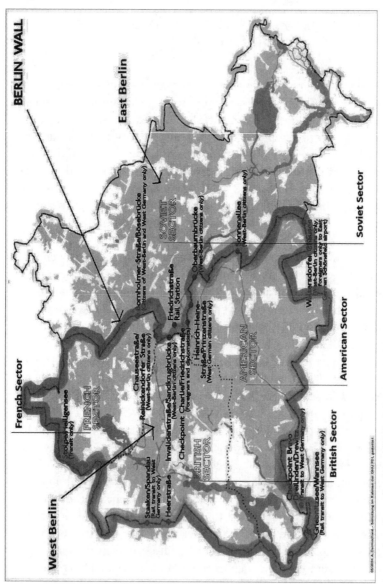

Source: http://en.wikipedia.org/wiki/File:Karte_berliner_mauer_en.jpg

Figure 5.1 Berlin Map Showing the Wall Route Separating Eastern (GDR) and Western Sectors (FDR under American, British and French control), 1961–1989.

Photo courtesy of U.S. Government's Archives (USA.GOV) http://blogs.archives.gov/prologue/
wp-content/uploads/Berlin-Wall-baby.jpg.

Photo 5.1 A Berlin family separated by the newly laid out barbed wire on the corner of Bernauer and Schweder Straße, August 1961. The scene beyond the barbed
wire is the new West Berlin.

the gate at Potsdamer Platz. East Berlin was the city proper, old and somewhat poor and yet carrying a heavy historic and cultural load; while West
Berlin was the suburbs with newer buildings and bigger lots. In a prologue
to his study of Berlin in the 1920s Friedrich (1972: 8–9) describes old Berlin
and its historic buildings in a rather nostalgic way:

> Berlin evolved, over the years, along an east-west axis. At the center of this
> axis, there was, and still is, the Brandenburg Gate, a gigantic neo-Grecian por-
> tal, supported by twelve Doric columns, sixty-five feet high, and surmounted
> by a sculpture of four horses drawing the chariot of the Goddess of Victory.
> To the east of this gate, along the broad expanse of Unter den Linden, the
> Kaisers built the solemn buildings of official Berlin—the square, massive,
> pillared edifices of the Reichschancellery, the opera, the state library, the
> university, the arsenal, the cathedral, and finally the Royal Palace. Beyond
> that lay the cluttered alleys of the old city, that original island in the middle
> of the Spree River, and then row on row of the glum stucco tenements that
> housed the city's workers (see Figure 5.2 and Photos 5.3–5.4).

He further describes the area west of the Brandenburg Gate which became
part of West Berlin where Unter den Linden turns into the Charlottenburger Chaussee that runs through the lush wooded Tiergarten, on to the

Photo courtesy of the German Federal Archive, http://en.wikipedia.org/wiki/File:Bundesarchiv_Bild_183-
85458-0002,_Berlin,_Mauerbau,_Kampfgruppen_am_Brandenburger_Tor.jpg

Photo 5.2 Armed East German Combat Groups of the Working Class (*Kampfgruppen der Arbei-
terklasse*) with water cannons behind them are deployed west of the Brandenburg Gate to secure
the border between West and East Berlin, August 13, 1961.

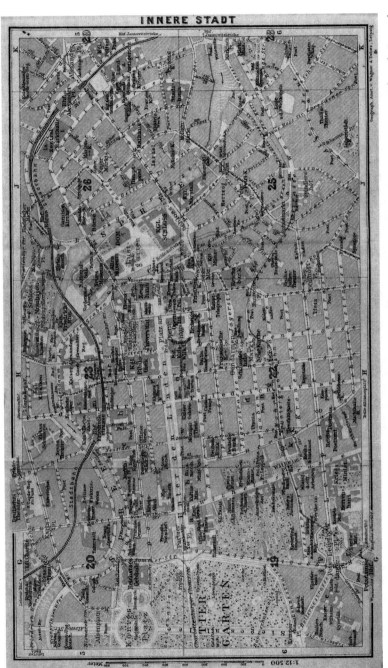

Source: Baedeker, Karl. 1910. *Northern Germany as far as the Bavarian and Austrian Frontiers; Handbook for Travelers*, p. 9. Fifteenth Revised Edition. Leipzig. Karl Baedeker; New York, Charles Scribner's Sons.

Map source: http://mapas.owje.com/maps/10167_berlin-inner-town-map-germany-1910.html.

Figure 5.2 Map of Central Berlin, 1910. The Brandenburg Gate is on the west end of Unter den Linden Boulevard (center left) which runs between an artery of Spree River (east) and the Tier Garten (west).

Source: Photograph by Willian Vandivert, http://www.geolocation.ws/v/P/72818780/aerial-
view-of-the-brandenburg-gate-in/en

Photo 5.3 Aerial view of East Berlin under Soviet control in the aftermath of
Allied bombing, July 1945 (historic Brandenburg Gate is in the forefront with
Unter den Linden Boulevard running eastward behind its gates). The photograph
is taken from West Berlin side.

Photograph by Robert Knudsen, the John F. Kennedy Presidential Library and Museum, Boston. http://www.jfklibrary.org/Asset-Viewer/K_R3l2jkWo61dm2h_3icTg.aspx.

Photo 5.4 Berlin Wall blocking the historic Brandenburg Gate, 1963. President John F. Kennedy on a platform overlooking the Berlin Wall at the Brandenburg Gate during his visit to West Berlin. Unter den Linden Boulevard runs eastward behind the Brandenburg Gate, so is the historic East Berlin.

Kurfürstendamm commercial district, and "out to the new villas of the rich in Grunewald."[3] Friedrich then makes his own observation of post-Wall Berlin's social geography as it looked in the early 1970s, that things had remained "much the same—slums and official buildings in the Communist East, parks and department stores in the West."[4] Nonetheless, he concludes that "Berlin today (West Berlin, specifically) has become a sad and stoical city. Its neon lights no longer look so brightly attractive as they once did; its economy depends on outside subsidies; its population is old and growing older; and there is a pervading smell of sewers overflowing beneath the esplanades."[5]

In his book *City Divided: Berlin 1955* Butler (1955: 57) also affirms centrality of eastern districts, particularly Mitte, for the vitality of Berlin's urban life in pre-Wall era. In describing the commercial district of Berlin's western sectors in the 1950s, particularly the Kurfürstendamm that became the main commercial thoroughfare in West Berlin, Butler notes of its decline and status as perceived by Berlin residents:

> Twenty years ago [1930s] it was an important street, a street of fine shops, restaurants, theatres, and cinemas, but it was not *the* important street of Berlin. Old residents spoke rather contemptuously of the "West End"; the heart of Berlin did not beat here. It beat in Unter den Linden, in the banking and business quarter around the BehrensStraße nearby, in the Government offices which lined the WilhelmStraße, in the newspaper offices of the ZimmerStraße [all situated in what later became East Berlin]. The Kurfürstendamm was new even by Berlin standards, brash, and rather vulgar.

With *Operation Rose* in progress, the East German government also launched a political campaign to convince Germans who resided on both sides of the border of the legitimacy of its actions. This objective was accomplished by issuing two documents—one was a joint declaration of the governments of the Warsaw Treaty members, and the other by the GDR's Council of Ministers. The first document affirmed the urgency to sign a peace treaty for Berlin's future but also stated the need to take action against the West German government's "militarist and revanchist policies" that were threatening the socio-economic security of the GDR and other

---

[3] After the June 1953 riots in GDR Cahrlottenburger Chaussee's name was changed to "Straße des 17 Juni" by the FDR government.

[4] Op. cit.

[5] Ibid., p. 7.

Warsaw Pact member nations. Thus according to this document the War-saw Pact members made an appeal to the GDR's People's Chamber, the government and all workers to take measures that will stop "diversionist activities against the socialist countries," including placement of "reliable guards and effective controls" around West Berlin.[6] The GDR government document was meant to be read as a response to the Warsaw Pact declaration document. First, it reiterated the imminent threat of the West German government's plan that intended "to incorporate the whole of Germany into the Western military bloc of NATO, and to extend the militarists' rule of the Federal Republic to the German Democratic Republic." This, concluded the statement, required the establishment of "the forms of control which are customary on the frontier of every sovereign state."[7] The statement also made it clear that except for Western *provocateurs*,' the new border control regulations will still allow West Germans to enter East Berlin by showing their identity cards, but that GDR citizens will be required to get special permission to enter West Berlin.[8]

Western powers' reaction to the border closure was rather slow and belated. President Kennedy was not informed of the new developments until Sunday afternoon, August 13. The American government reacted with caution and its released statement was intended to play down the border closure's significance. Thus after condemning the action as being in direct violation of the four-power agreement, the official State Department statement simply indicated that the event would not affect the Allied long-standing position on West Berlin, and that they will register their protest through appropriate channels.[9] This reluctance to react harshly and with resolve reflected a dangerous dilemma on the U.S. part in that the Soviet Union's support of the border closure was a justified action under the post-war four-power agreements; as the latter was considered as a 'legal' occupier of East Germany. On the other hand, using military force in order to prevent the Wall's construction was a military suicide for the United States, as it would have risked "a crushing response from the overwhelming superior Soviet forces in and around East Berlin," as well as "the possibility of an even more devastating general military counteraction."[10]

---

[6] Warsaw Pact Declaration, cf. Slusser (1973: 129–130).
[7] GDR statement, ibid., p. 130.
[8] Ibid., p. 131.
[9] See Taylor (2006: 205–206).
[10] Slusser (1973: 135).

The Kennedy administration was also somewhat relieved, as the walling-up effectively averted an American-Soviet military confrontation over the East German refugee crisis.[11]

The official three-power Western Allies' formal protest was even slower, as it was declared four days later. They called the August 13 border-sealing operation a flagrant and serious violation of the four-power agreements on Berlin's status, and rejected the Soviet's claim that Berlin's eastern sector was part of the GDR territory. Thus they challenged the GDR's military control of East Berlin which was still 'legally' under Soviet occupation.[12] For internal political reasons the West German government's response was also cautiously diplomatic primarily because of the upcoming national elections in September 1961, as any miscalculated move by Chancellor Adenauer would have jeopardized continuation of his coalition government. Instead, it was West Berlin's mayor Willy Brandt, his challenger in the next election who on Sunday afternoon addressed the West Berlin city parliament and harshly criticized the border closure. He referred to the "powers of darkness" that have created "the barrier fence of a concentration camp" and requested a strong Allied response, the United States in particular, so that the Soviets and the GDR government know "the West means business."[13] Faced with West Berlin citizens' serious discontent with the three-powers' indecisiveness in protesting against a divided Berlin, President Kennedy eventually dispatched Vice President Johnson to Berlin; and ordered a battle group comprised of 1,500 men to depart for West Berlin from their base near Frankfurt. This required the passage of a convoy of 491 military vehicles through East German territory, to which East German authorities showed little resistance. Despite a brief military standoff between the American and Soviet forces from across the new inner city border, the American show of force was meant to please West Germans, and West Berlin residents in particular; and to dispel their dissatisfaction with American government's lack of resolve. Thus the surreal border fence erected on the fateful early morning of August 13th became a historical reality, and for the next twenty eight years gradually evolved into a formidable defensive wall. Meantime, the two "Berlins" also evolved as two completely separate urban entities, each based on a distinctly different socio-economic, political, and ideological prescription.

---

[11]   Schick (1971: 166).
[12]   Slusser (1973: 137–138).
[13]   For a narrative of Wily Brandt's response see Taylor (2006: 218–219).

The Wall's Architecture

When on Sunday morning, August 13, 1961 the Berlin residents woke up to witness their city being divided by a crudely laid out barbed-wire fence with concrete posts, they saw no "walls" and no indications of the presence of a well-designed and durable barrier between Berlin's western and eastern sectors. In general, the barbed-wire fence is considered as the "first generation" of the wall in most studies. But in fact it was a hastily constructed barrier that only served a political objective, to convey to the West (and West Berlin residents) that East Germans meant business. As for its function as a security barrier to prevent border-crossing it proved to be far from satisfactory, and thus only lasted for few days.

In less than a week after August 13, the East Germans began to build what generally became known as the "second generation" of the Wall. By all accounts, the second generation of the roughly two meters high Wall was an improvisation evident by its crude form, absence of a clear blueprint, carelessness of its construction, and the haphazard way it navigated Berlin's urban landscape. Klausmeier and Schmidt (2004: 15) provide a detailed description of the way it was built:

> It was constructed from large square breeze block elements originally developed and produced for residential architecture.... On top of the large block elements, two to four layers of smaller breeze blocks were laid; these supported long concrete beams into which iron railings had been set. These railings, often Y-shaped, angled the barbed wire between them towards the East as well as towards the West, thus rendering it difficult to scale from either side (see Photo 5.5).

The second generation of the Wall naturally proved to be more effective than the initial barbed-wire fence, yet it was not full-proof, particularly against escape attempts that used heavy trucks.[14] During the first year, several GDR citizens managed to make successful escapes, and 77 border guards also managed to cross the line in 1962. Part of the problem for the Wall's inadequate security was related to the fact that border guards were under the Interior Ministry's command and did not have adequate training and discipline; and not all of them had the conviction that "border violators [should be] captured as enemies at all costs, and if necessary

---

[14] The Wall at this stage consisted of "12 km of wall, 137 km of barbed wire fortifications (made up of 8,000–10,000 km of hardened wire) and 450,000–500,000 square meters of no-man's-land" (Rühle and Holzweißig, 1988: 145–47).

Source: http://www.jfklibrary.org/Asset-Viewer/Archives/JFKWHP-KN-C29210.aspx.

Photo 5.5 The Wall, second generation: President John F. Kennedy views the Berlin Wall from an elevated platform at Checkpoint Charlie. Cement slabs and cinder blocks replaced the original barbed wire, but in order to increase security the barbed wire was then installed on the top of the low-height wall, late August 1961. Photo credit: Robert Knudsen, JFK Presidential Library & Museum.

exterminated." This was corrected in 1962 by putting the border guard units under the Ministry for National Defense's command (*Ministerium für Nationale Verteidigung*), thus transforming the border operations into a full-fledged military operation.[15] In conjunction with this shift in operation from about 1965 onwards the third generation of the wall that was an improvement in terms of design, construction, and higher levels of impenetrability gradually replaced the second generation. The new design "consisted of fairly narrow concrete slabs inserted horizontally between H-sectioned posts of reinforced concrete; and was later topped by lengths of concrete sewer pipe rendering it virtually impossible to scale" (see Photo 5.6). This ended a period of building the wall in "makeshift fashion," and the GDR government began mass production of border wall elements, including the watch towers.[16]

In time, the third generation of the Wall also proved to have defects and weak spots, and from mid-1970s it was replaced by the infamous fourth generation wall (*"Stutzwandelement UL 12.11"*), commonly known to its builders as *Grenzmauer 75* (Border Wall '75). This last generation was the product of a long process of testing and research aimed at finding a practical and effective design. The main component of the Wall was an L-shaped pre-fabricated concrete slab 3.6 meters high (11.81 ft.) and 1.2 meters wide (3.937 ft.) used by East German farmers "as walls for storing liquid manure."[17] To make it harder for escapees to climb the Wall, it was then topped off by "a smooth asbestos-concrete pipe 40 centimeters in diameter" with a section cut out so that it can be mounted on the slabs (see Photos 5.7–5.9).[18] In all, 45000 concrete slabs were used to erect 54 kilometers (34 miles) of the Wall at a total cost of about $3,638,000. The fourth generation Wall lasted until it was dismantled in 1989, and had certain advantages over the previous generation:

> It needed no foundations, it was far stronger and it was practically impossible to break with a vehicle. Furthermore, the 'fourth generation' Wall offered a smooth and clean face towards West Berlin; an aspect of some significance to the GDR rulers, who, from the 1970s, were becoming more and more interested in public appearance of their state which they did not want to see compromised by the obvious brutality of the border fortifications.[19]

---

[15] An estimated 50,000 border troops were involved in securing the East-West Berlin and German border lines. See Hertle (2008: 93, 97).

[16] Klausmeier and Schmidt (2004: 15–16).

[17] Hertle, ibid., p. 94.

[18] The Cold War Museum, *Berlin Time-Line 1945–1990*, http://www.coldwar.org/articles/60s/BerlinWallTimeLine.asp, accessed 5-4-2012.

[19] Klausmeier and Schmidt (2004: 16–17).

Photo 5.6 The Wall, third generation: Remains of the Wall on the right, in St. Hedwig Cemetery on Liesen Straße, 2010 (photo by author).

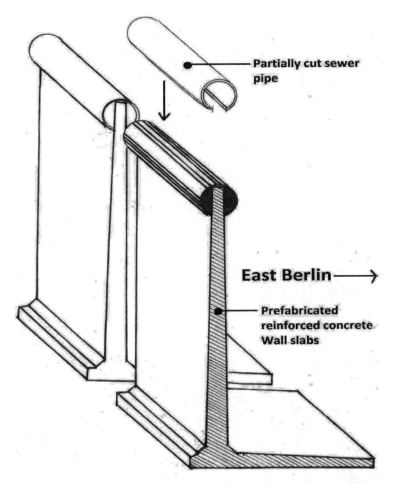

Source: Document VS-Nr. H095 931, 2.Ausf. (cf.http://www.dailysoft.com/berlinwall/history/facts_02.htm).

Photo 5.7 Fourth generation Berlin Wall concrete slabs, detail (sketch by author).

Photo 5.8 The removed concrete sewer pipes on display at the Bernauer Straße Wall Museum, 2010. The pipes were partially cut to fit on the top of concrete Wall slabs (photo by author).

Photo 5.9 The Wall's Fourth Generation (1975–1989): Deteriorated pre-fabricated reinforced concrete slabs with semi-circular sewer pipes mounted on the top seen from West Berlin side on Bernauer Straße, 2010 (photo by author).

Although done in poor political taste, the fourth generation Wall succeeded in achieving the above objective. That is, unless they could stand
on observation platforms or peek from higher floor levels in buildings
adjacent to the Wall, West Berlin residents could only see its "smooth
and clean face" that often concealed the extensive layout of defensive
tools and obstacles on the other side that made the border barrier system
almost impregnable. Hertle (2008: 96) provides a detailed description of
how the barrier system commonly known in the West as the "death strip"
functioned:

> From east to west, the death strip, between 15 and more than 150 meters in
> width, begins with a two-to-three-meter-high so-called "hinterland" barrier,
> the wall or fence nearest to East Berlin territory. An electrified signal fence,
> a good two meters high, follows at a short distance. This "contact fence" is
> equipped with several rows of wires that are live and send out acoustic and/
> or optical signals. The more technically developed versions of this fence, like
> the "Grenzsignal- und Sperrzaun II", are driven fifty centimeters deep into
> the soil to make it more difficult to crawl underneath. In the modern fence
> systems, the alarm triggered is a silent one; while escapees think they are
> still safe, they have already been located by the command centre for that
> segment of the border (see Figure 5.3).

This expansive physical barrier system that in its varied forms ran for
96 miles required a 50,000-strong militarized border patrol troops that
were trained and instructed to "arrest or exterminate' border violators (see
Table 5.1). In parts of the border considered as "high risk," both between
East and West Berlin and East Germany and West Berlin, dog runs (*Ketten-
laufanlagen*) were also installed consisting of a suspended wire up to 100
meters long (330 ft) that ran parallel to the electric signal fence, to which
dogs were chained.[20] Right before its demise in November 1989 the core
of this border military force, the *Central Border Command*, was comprised
of 11,000 soldiers and officers equipped with "2,295 vehicles, 10,726 sub-
machine guns, 600 light and heavy machine guns, 2,753 pistols, 29 border
security boats and 992 tracker and guard dogs."[21]

Without a doubt, securing the border was a violent military operation
against unarmed GDR citizens and anyone who dared to challenge the
system. Up until few months before the very end, border troops were
ordered to 'shoot to kill" escapees. This resulted in a total of 134 fatalities in the Wall's twenty eight years' existence including 99 GDR citizens,

---

[20] Rottman (2008: 25).
[21] Hertle (2008: 99).

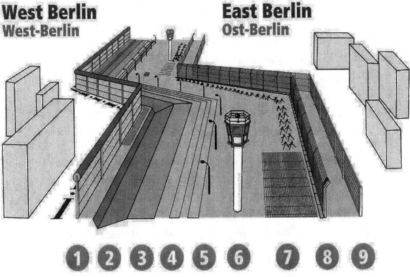

West Berlin
West-Berlin

East Berlin
Ost-Berlin

Source: http://en.wikipedia.org/wiki/File:Structure_of_Berlin_Wall.svg

Legend: 1. Concrete wall with piping at the top, with West Berlin on the left; 2. Anti-vehicle obstacle; 3. Raked strip to detect footprints; 4. Border patrol road; 5. Floodlights; 6. Observation tower; 7. Anti-vehicle obstacles; 8. Electric signal fence; and (in certain sections) spiked gratings nicknamed "Stalin's lawn" (in the foreground) to prevent human escapes; and 9. Hinterland fence.

Figure 5.3 Sketch of the expansion of border security system, ca. early 1970s (note that the concrete wall on West Berlin side is still the third generation design).

Table 5.1. Basic Facts about the Wall

Border crossings between the GDR and West Berlin (roads/railway)	6
Fourth generation concrete slab wall (3.6m/11.81 ft. high)	106 km/66 miles
Wire mesh fencing	66.5 km/41 miles
Observation towers	302
Bunkers	20
Dog runs	259
Anti-vehicle trenches	105.5 km/62 miles
Contact or signal fences	127.5 km/75 miles
Border patrol roads	124.3 km/73 miles

Sources: http://www.dailysoft.com/berlinwall/history/facts_01.htm; http://www.berlin.de/mauer/zahlen_fakten/index.en.html#numbers.

27 "non-escapees" from both sides who had fatal accidents at the border, and 8 GDR border soldiers who were killed while on duty.[22]

Erection of the Berlin Wall and its significance for Germany's East-West divide seems to have been exaggerated and fantasized by the media and popular culture as the only physical barrier which prevented the unification of the two Germanys—hence the often-quoted statement by the U.S. President Ronald Reagan "Mr. Gorbachev, tear down this wall!" in 1987.[23] But as I stated earlier the Wall was the culmination of border fortifications as a defensive measure by the GDR government that began in the 1940s. Definitely, this was a defensive system that was directed inward and against the GDR's population. It was also a unique defensive installation because the GDR shared a border "with a neighboring, more affluent state with a population of the same ethnic origin" (Mueller, 1999: 700). Emigration from the Soviet-controlled zone of German territories in the east to the western zones began in late 1945, but the Allied forces controlled it. From 1947 onward, the Soviets imposed stricter border control measures to prevent the east-west exodus of Germans. Border security measures were stepped up from both sides after the unilateral declaration of the Federal Republic of Germany (FGR) by the Allied forces in 1949 and subsequent declaration of the GDR by the Soviet Union. However, the inner border between East and West Germany was relatively porous. For example, between 1949 and 1952, when the GDR boosted border security in order to prevent illegal crossings, an estimated 675,000 people managed to escape to West Germany (Berdahi, 1999: 144; Cramer, 2008: 15) (see Figure 5.4). Similar to the Berlin Wall the inner border fortification between the two Germanys also had its own metamorphosis. The first generation of the inner border security barrier was a crudely constructed single-row barbed-wire fence, about 1.2–2.5 meters high (Rottman, 2008: 16). This was replaced by a stronger, double-row fence, with watchtowers along the border in the late 1950s. Similar to the Berlin Wall's evolution, construction of the third generation border fence system began in 1967 and improvements continued well into the 1980s. A total of 1,289 kilometers of fences and supporting structures were constructed along the entire inner border (see Photos 5.10–5.11). In describing the immense amount of

---

[22] Ibid., p. 104. Fearing isolation and under international pressure, on April 3, 1989 the GDR leader Erich Honecker issued an order that put a halt to shooting "border violators."

[23] Ronald Reagan's concluding remarks during his June 12, 1987 speech in front of the Brandenburg Gate in West Berlin.

land required for the security fence Rottman (2008; 20–21) provides the
following comparison:

> The third-generation border retained the 5 km restricted zone, wider or nar-
> rower in some areas, running the entire length of the border. This requires
> a considerable area, approximately 6,900km², although portions of it were
> still used for grazing and agriculture, and contained some villages. For com-
> parison, today's reunited Berlin covers 890km², greater London 1,706 km²,
> and Los Angeles 1,215 km². *Together these three major cities would fill just
> over half of the land occupied by the restricted zone, a considerable sacrifice
> for a country slightly smaller than the state of Kentucky, but over four times
> the population* (emphasis mine).

Was the Wall a Sign of East Germany's Weakness?

In her analysis of the Berlin Wall's significance in defining the nature of
East-West détente, Harrison (2003: 5) points out that on one hand the
Wall's construction signaled the GDR's "external strength" to close the
border around West Berlin and fortify the inner German border in that
it withstood the Western threat; yet it was also an indication of its "fun-
damental internal weakness" in its inability to stop the outflow of East
German citizens on the other. In all, between 1949 and August 1961, when
the border between East and West Berlin was sealed, around 2.7 million
people left the GDR. A closer look at the status of the East German refugee
population reveals that more than one-third were skilled industrial and
technical workers, with another 6–7 percent being agricultural workers
(see Table 5.2). These workers emigrated as families, taking with them
their school-age children; and reportedly between 1949 and 1961 "East Germany lost around a sixth of its population.[24]

With no doubt this mass emigration of the mostly young and skilled
East Germans contributed to the country's "brain drain," an undesirable
and dangerous trend for the GDR's socialist nation-building efforts. However, using internal documents of the East German Ministry of State Security or *Stasi*, Maddrell (2009) argues that another main concern was that
the open borders subjected the GDR to massive espionage and subversive
actions orchestrated in the Western-occupied zones. He further argues
that the open border between East and West Berlin yielded "four benefits"
for the Western secret services and agencies.

---

[24] Taylor (2006: 100).

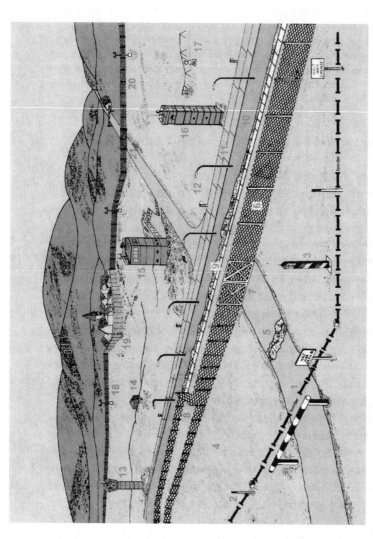

Source: Stacy, William E. 1984. *"US Army Border Operations in Germany."* US Army Military History Office. http://en.wikipedia.org/wiki/File:System_of_gdr_border_fortification.jpg. http://www.history.army.mil/documents/BorderOps/ch6.htm#fi2.

1. Border 2. Border markers (on the West German side) 3.border marker pole with diagonal black, red, and yellow stripes (on the East German side) 4. Security zone 5. Anti-vehicle ditch 6 metal-mesh fence 7. Gate 8. Mined area between the two fences 9. Anti-vehicle ditch 10. Flood-lit strip 11. Border guard patrol road 12. Open green territory 13, 15 & 16. Guard towers 14. Observation bunker 17. Dog run 18. Signal fence 21. Gate 22. Check point deep in East German territory.

Figure 5.4 A diagram of a heavily fortified inner German border (third generation) between West and East Germany, ca. 1984.

Source: http://en.wikipedia.org/wiki/File:Inner_german_border_1st_generation.jpg

Photo 5.10   Inner German border with a control strip (first generation, 1952–early 1960s).

Source: Image courtesy of Andrew Eick, http://www.flickr.com/photos/andreweick/335746066/ http://en.wikipedia.org/wiki/File:East_German_border_1962.jpg.

Photo 5.11   Inner German border, second generation (1962).

Table 5.2 Occupational Breakdown of Refugee Movement in Percentages
(1952–1961)

Occupational Category	1952–1957	1958	1959	1960	First six months of 1961
Crop production and animal husbandry	7.6	4.5	5.0	7.4	6.1
Industry and manufacturing	20.7	19.3	20.1	21.3	22.3
Technical fields	1.9	2.1	2.4	2.6	2.9
Trade and Commerce	11.8	11.8	12.0	11.8	12.0
Household work, medical services, personal hygiene	4.9	5.8	5.3	4.8	4.7
Law and administration	2.9	4.4	3.8	3.5	3.3
Intellectual and artistic fields	1.5	2.6	2.0	1.9	1.6
Employed persons with unspecified occupations	11.0	10.0	10.1	7.4	8.9
Employed persons in total	62.3	60.5	60.7	60.7	61.8
Pensioners and Retirees	4.4	6.8	10.3	7.6	8.4
Stay-at-home wives	11.9	11.3	10.3	10.5	9.4
Children and pupils (grades K-12)	21.0	20.2	17.7	20.4	19.5
University-level students	0.4	1.2	1.0	0.8	0.9
Total	100.0	100.0	100.0	100.0	100.0

Source: Table constructed based on information in *Der Bau der Mauer durch Berlin* [*The Building of the Wall through Berlin*], edited by the Federal Ministry for Inter-German Relations. Bonn, 1984, p. 16. http://germanhistorydocs.ghi-dc.org/sub_document.cfm?document_id=3512 , accessed 8-5-2010.

First, it allowed East Germans to leave GDR either for good as refugees, or as visitors for few days to shop or visit friends and relatives. Either way, it made East Germans susceptible to Western cultural influence. Nevertheless, refugees in particular were excellent sources of information and intelligence for the West, as "once in West Berlin they were interrogated and asked to name people still in East Germany, usually colleagues at work or friends, who would be willing to cooperate with Western intelligence." This proved to be an effective means of recruiting informants from the Eastern zone. Second, open border allowed the recruited informants to freely travel to West Berlin and deliver their information to their "controller." Third, open border in Berlin allowed Western intelligence agencies "to inspire the defection of people who were of value to the Communist regimes of the Bloc." In particular, skilled workers and state employees in important positions were lured by offers of jobs and resettlement in the West if defected. This Policy served two purposes: it drained the GDR of its skilled and educated workers, but more importantly, it served to delegitimize the state and the socialist system it espoused. Finally, West German anti-Communist organizations often funded by Western intelligence agencies could freely visit East Berlin and spread their anti-regime and anti-socialist propaganda through their contacts.[25]

Unlike capitalism that often thrives and expands best when the economy is less planned and regulated, socialist economies are projects that require meticulous short- and long-term planning in order for them to survive and succeed. Maddrell's analysis above helps us to appreciate the rationale for building the Wall from East Germans' perspective, that it was simply a *defensive wall* erected to protect them from non-military but equally hideous intrusive and subversive actions from the West. In addition, I consider the construction of the Berlin Wall and fortification of West Berlin's borders with the GDR as both the GDR's (and Soviet Union's) realization that West Berlin will remain as a Western urban enclave protected by the Allied occupation forces; and that it was the final phase of Germany's division into two territories occupied by rival imperial powers.

Most of the literature about the Soviet Union and GDR's decisions to close the borders between East and West Germany in 1952, and later in 1961 between East and West Berlin by building the Wall, present the issue as a matter of the system's stability to prevent increasing outflow of refugees to the West.[26] This seems to be a plausible proposition, as installation of highly militarized border fortifications along the GDR's western borders with West Germany followed by the Berlin Wall's construction were very effective in stemming the emigration flows. Based on one estimate there was a ten-fold decrease in the average annual out-migration before and after 1961, from 210,000 to 21,000, respectively (see Figure 5.5).

Although as I discussed earlier the East German government eventually assumed the Wall's ownership, its long-term sustenance depended on economic, political and ideological strength of the GDR's sponsor, namely, the Soviet Union. Like in all colonial situations, the first signs of an empire's weakness are manifested in the inability of imperial center to provide the needed economic and political support for its client colonial entities in the periphery—an implicit indication that things are not going

---

[25] See Maddrell (2009: 2–3). Enticing and luring individuals from "the other side of the fence" has been a long-standing practice by the American administrations that has continued to the present time. Maddrell (op. cit.) states that "Declassified US Government records on the Truman Administration's psychological warfare program confirm that inducing the defection of valuable people was seen as a useful means of reducing Communist control of the Bloc."

[26] See, for example, Harrison (2003).

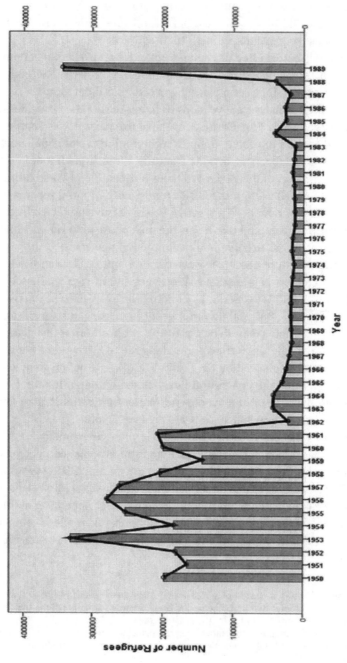

Sources: Figure 4.3 and Matthias Judt, ed., *DDR-Geschichte in Dokumenten [GDR History in Documents]*. Berlin, 1997, pp. 545–46.

Figure 5.5 Emigration from the GDR to the FRG, 1949–1989 (chart by author).

well in the center either. In fact, in his memoirs the last Soviet General Secretary Mikhail Gorbachev later recounted that when he came to power in 1985 "he was immediately faced with an avalanche of problems"; from an stagnating economy and aging industry, to expensive commitments throughout the empire from Eastern Europe to Cuba, but particularly the Soviet Union's increasingly unpopular occupation of Afghanistan. But probably the one main factor that bankrupted the Soviet economy was the Cold War era's arms race with the United States, its arch-rival imperial power—while the American military buildup was a profitable capitalist enterprise, that of the Soviets was a state-run entity which was a heavy burden on an already failing socialist economy which by the 1980s consumed "upwards of one-third the state's budget" (Engel, 2009: 20).[27]

If not worse, the GDR's state of the economy in the 1980s was not any better than that of the Soviet Empire. In contrast to the 1960s and 1970s when East Germany was a successful exporter and had a relatively healthy economy, in the 1980s "the story had in fact been one of steady decline and increasing indebtedness" and the state was on the verge of bankruptcy (Taylor, 2006: 409). To make the matters worse, Soviet leaders also indicated that they would scale down the delivery of cheap oil and raise foreign trade tariffs to world market levels within the Eastern Bloc countries (Dennis, 2000: 264 f.). Less than two weeks before the fall of the Wall the East German Politburo members reviewed a highly secret "Report on the Economic Situation of the GDR with Consequences" which concluded that the country was a wreck, and in the words of a historian it "was approaching bankruptcy like a horse galloping towards a cliff":

> More than half of all industrial facilities were effectively classified as scrap. 53.8 percent of all machines were write-offs, only reparable at a cost that could simply not be justified. Half the transport infrastructure was in a state of decay. Productivity was around 40 percent behind the West's. State indebtedness had risen from 12 billion marks in 1970 to 123 billion in 1988. Direct debts to capitalist states and banks had increased during that period from 2 billion to 49 billion West marks (Taylor, 2006: 414–415).

In addition to the economic crises in the center and periphery, an equally significant factor was Gorbachev's ascendance to power which

---

[27] Although the Soviet Union was admittedly an arms merchant in its own terms, the military industries drained state coffers due to the public ownership and socialist nature of the economy. Thus in order to compete with the American military buildup the Soviets had to drastically cut back expenses in other areas, including the empire's peripheries.

represented a younger and more open-minded generation of communist leaders in the Soviet Union. For instance, his admission of systemic flaws which required adherence to principles of comprehensive restructuring ('*perestroika*') and openness ('*glasnost*') opened up the door for further reforms in the peripheries. The first Eastern Bloc country that was taken over by reform-minded communists was Hungary. The new reformist government made a surprise announcement in May 1989 that it would dismantle its fortified border fences with Austria. Since East Germans could freely travel to Hungary via Czechoslovakia, by early July 1989 more than 25,000 East Germans had defected to Austria. Others went to the neighboring socialist countries and headed for West German embassies in Prague and Budapest, for instance, and sought refuge there. The final straw was Gorbachev's repudiation of the Soviet Union's iron fist policy of military intervention within the Warsaw Pact countries to quell unrest and dissent by force, or the so-called "Brezhnev Doctrine."[28] This drastic change in policy left the socialist client states within the Eastern Bloc out in the cold to fend off political dissent and social unrest on their own. It was within this climate of economic and political uncertainties that right after the opening of the Hungary-Austria border that local elections were held in East Germany, which as was expected government-endorsed candidates received 99 percent of the votes. Allegation of election fraud set the tone for public mobilization not only in Berlin but also in other major cities throughout the GDR. Young East Germans' presence in the protest movement was conspicuous, who also made the majority of refugees in Prague, Budapest and elsewhere. As one historian of the Wall explains, they were "children of the Wall *par excellence*" (Taylor, 2006: 406). A combination of above-mentioned factors also explains the surprisingly non-violent nature of the Wall's downfall. In the words of Engel (2009: 17), on November 9, 1989 "the once unthinkable occurred: The Berlin Wall fell, not to a conquering army, but to the regime's own citizens."[29] Thus, the

---

[28] The Warsaw Pact, or more accurately the Warsaw Treaty Organization of Friendship, Cooperation, and Mutual Assistance was initially comprised of eight nations: Albania, Bulgaria, Czechoslovakia, GDR, Hungary, Romania, and the Soviet Union. The Warsaw Pact was a Soviet military response to the integration of West Germany into NATO in 1955. Leonid Brezhnev was the General Secretary of the Central Committee of the Communist Party from 1964 to 1982.

[29] My objective here is to sketch a brief historical account of the Wall's downfall. For an interesting and detailed narrative of the wall's history and its final days see *Chronic der Mauer*, http://www.chronik-der-mauer.de/index.php/ de/Start/Index/id/652147. Hans-Hermann Hertle's illustrated book (2008) also chronicles the Wall's evolution and demise. For a historical account of the Wall see Taylor (2006). Maksimychev (1988) who was the

opening of several checkpoints along the Berlin Wall in the late hours of November 9 was only a symbolic culmination of a long episode of ideological standoff between two imperial entities.

Concluding Remarks

In his study of post-Wall East German society, McAdams (1985) identifies three approaches that have examined the Wall—"historical" studies that focus on "the day-to-day events leading up to and following its construction"; studies that focus on the Wall's significance to ward off a potentially dangerous confrontation between the two superpowers; and finally those analyses that consider the Wall's construction as the main factor for "de-escalation of conflict and tempering of Cold War hostilities."[30] In this and previous chapter I have mainly taken the historical approach to chronicle the events that led to the Wall's erection in 1961. But by briefly outlining socio-economic and political factors that contributed to its demise I have also concluded that a critical examination of the Wall has to appreciate the historical reality of the two Germanys under occupation. Furthermore, the Wall was built as a *defensive wall* to protect the East German socialist system, albeit imperfect and repressive, from outside forces and a superpower (the United States) that embodied an expansionist global capitalist economy. However, I have also argued that building socialism (as a social project) under the duress of Soviet occupation and external existential threats by the Western powers was a highly improbable possibility. One would wonder what would have been the outcomes of socialist experiments in the Soviet Union, the Eastern Bloc, Cuba, Vietnam, and elsewhere; had they not been under constant threat of violence, military interventions, and outright economic sanctions by the contending empires and nations within the global capitalist camp.

A final note on the significance of the Wall for the Soviet Empire and the GDR—As Igor Maksimychev, the Minister-Counselor of the Soviet Embassy in the GDR during the fall of the Berlin Wall has noted, prior to the Gorbachev era's *perestroika* "the Soviet attitude to the Wall was

---

minister-Counselor of the UUSR Embassy in GDR in 1989 also provides an intriguing narrative of the politics of the Wall's fall from the perspective of the Soviet Union and GDR leaders.

[30] McAdams (1985: 9–10).

basically unconnected with any ideological dogmas"; and Soviet officials sought to avoid "the Wall theme" if possible:

> All insiders knew perfectly well that the Wall was just a least-evil solution–nothing to write home about. It was clear to Moscow for quite a while that the Wall problem would have to be addressed in earnest at some stage, if the policy of détente was to succeed after all. To be sure, it wouldn't be soon, and some acceptable terms would have to be negotiated with the FRG. But here you inevitably ran into an obstacle; the Honecker-led GDR leadership was totally blind to changes in the world, including the socialist community, and unwilling to modify even some of their habitual attitudes.

Even after the Wall's fall the post-*perestroika* Soviet leaders did not seem to be overly concerned about the consequences, and as Engel (2009: 70) notes the Soviet Politburo "did not even bother to meet right after the Wall fell." Thus "the Wall was not the logical and predictable product of some grand design or elaborate scheme, but rather an initially desperate act, *a sign of gross weakness and not strength.*"[31] In fact, this is the common characteristic of all defensive walls that have been erected during different historical periods. Finally, construction of the Berlin Wall was also a "formative experience" for the GDR ruling elite both in term of its ideological and political symbolism that marked their "first opportunity to establish their authority on a lasting basis;" as well as the initial tentativeness of its design and its historical evolution during the next three decades.[32] Be it the theoretical shortsightedness of Gorbachev and his Kremlin colleagues, or their preoccupation with the Soviet Union's domestic problems, dismantling of the Wall and eventual unification of the two Germanys turned out to be too costly. Eventually, collapse of the Eastern European imperial holdings led to the Soviet Union's collapse as well.

---

[31] Ibid., p. 10.
[32] McAdams, op. cit.

PART TWO

ANTI-IMPERIALIST WALLS

DISMANTLING THE DEFENSIVE WALL OF THE COLONIZED: BANNING THE ISLAMIC VEIL (*HIJAB*) IN FRENCH SCHOOLS[1]

On October 22, 1989 thousands of French Muslims staged a demonstration in Paris in support of three Muslim students who were expelled from the Gabriel-Havez secondary school in the Creil municipality. The students' only crime was that they wore headscarves while attending school in defiance of the French Education Minister's decree that banned wearing any "ostentatious religious insignia" (Seljuq, 1997; Kaitlin, 2007). Two political events make the year 1989 particularly significant related to the headscarf controversy: The Iranian leader Ayatollah Khomeini's religious decree (fatwa) that was in fact a death sentence for the British writer Salman Rushdie on the occasion of publishing his novel *Satanic Verses*; and the Algerian Muslim militants' killing of several French residents that rekindled a debate on Islam's alleged violent nature (McGillion, 2004). Later in the 1990s, the Gulf War and its aftermath exacerbated the situation not only in France but all over Europe (Seljuq, 1997). In this highly charged and tense political environment the French public and the media interpreted the wearing of headscarves by French Muslim students as a religious-political statement in defiance of the French principles of separation of church and state. Furthermore, opponents of the headscarf also argued that the Muslim girls were co-opted by Muslim fundamentalist groups who intended to advance their militant political agenda in France (Begag and Chaouits, 1990).

The headscarf controversy continued in the 1990s amid public demonstrations and law suits. In 1996, the matter appeared to be settled, as an appeal court in the city of Nancy in two separate cases ruled in favor of seven female Muslim students of North African origin, ordering the French government to pay compensation to one student and allow the other six to return to school while wearing the headscarf. But their victory was short-lived, as public opposition to this alleged "Islamic militancy" continued and forced the French government in July 2003 to set up a

---

[1] This is a revised and expanded version of an earlier article that was published as a chapter in Dello Buono and Fassenfest (2010).

special investigation commission on religion. Headed by Bernard Staci, the commission heard hundreds of witnesses and published its report in late 2003; recommending twenty three measures to guarantee both the state's neutrality on religion and the equality of religious faiths. In addition to proposed legislation to clarify acceptable religious garb in school, the report also recommended addition of Muslim and Jewish holidays (*Eid-al-Adha* and *Yum Kippur*, respectively) as public holidays; instruction of "religious facts;" teaching "non-state" languages such as Kurdish and Berber in addition to state languages like Arabic or Turkish; and the rehabilitation of "urban ghettoes" where most French Muslim immigrants resided.

Acting on the Staci Commission's recommendations in late 2003 the then French President Jacques Chirac proposed a law for constitutional review which was subsequently passed in early 2004 by the French National Assembly by a large majority. But ironically, the proposed law only focused on legislation against "ostentatious religious signs and dresses" which according to the Ministry of Education "whose wearing in public schools leads to the immediate recognition of the wearer's religious belonging, which is to say the Islamic veil, whatever name one calls it, the Jewish Kippa, or a cross of massive dimensions." Yet despite the claim for the law's universality, it clearly focused on the *hijab* or the head covering worn by Muslim women (Silverstein, 2004). The initial law banning conspicuous religious symbols in schools became effective in September 2004. But despite divided public opinion its enforcement was rather uneventful. According to one survey taken before the law's passage in February 2004, the law was favored by 69 percent of the population while 29 percent opposed it. Among the French Muslims, 42 percent were supportive of the law while 53 percent opposed it (Anon, 2004). Even among the French Muslim female population 49 percent supported it while 43 percent opposed the law. In all, once the law was enforced in schools about 240 female students attended school wearing the headscarf, and reportedly 170 students later accepted to remove it and the rest had undergone "conciliation procedures" (Müller, 2005).

France is home to the largest Muslim population in Europe outside Turkey, which in 2000 was estimated to be about five million or 8.3 percent of the population (Silverstein, 2004: 3). However, according to an opinion poll taken after September 11, 2001 only about 30 percent of France's heterogeneous Muslim community described themselves as "practicing Muslims;" and the majority of them, or about 58 percent were non-practicing Muslims who can better be described as French persons of Muslim origin (Sondage IFOP, 2001). This might be an explanation for an absence of mass protest after the law's passage. In the absence of an all-out protest against the 2004 law among France's Muslim population and the prevalence of the more "moderate" French Muslim citizens and residents, it is more accurate to define them as a population that consider their faith as an Islamic version of "civil religion," a term coined by the American sociologist Robert Bellah in the late 1960s (Bellah, 1967).

The insignificant and rather low numbers of violations did not deter the French government to finalize the imposition of the *hijab* ban on its Muslim citizens. Eventually, in 2010 the upper house of the French Parliament overwhelmingly passed the legislation that forbade public wearing of garments covering the face, including *burqa* which is a "full body veil with mesh over the eyes," and "*niqab*" that like *burqa* completely covers the face but "leaves an unobstructed opening for the eyes." The law became effective in April 2011, but reportedly this is applicable only to an estimated 2,000 Muslim women in France. Women who violate the law will be subjected to a €310 ($400) fine; and anyone who forces women to cover their faces in public will be also fined a steep €30,000 ($39,600) and face up to one year in prison (Archick et al., 2011: 13). The law had the strong backing of France's former conservative President Nicolas Sarkozy who was desperate to win conservatives' support ahead of 2012 presidential election. Notwithstanding the law's passage and the right wing's support, Sarkozy eventually lost the election to the socialist candidate François Hollande in May 2012.

In the aftermath of the passage of the *hijab* ban opinion polls in France indicated that about 70 percent of citizens believe French Muslims have neither assimilated to French secular values nor integrated well into the French society. In addition, the percentage of French citizens who believe Islam is not compatible with western values has been on the rise, from 12 percent in 1994 to 31 percent in 2011 (Le Bars, 2011). This demographic reality provides a context within which we can appreciate the rather harsh reaction by the French government in dealing with the Islamic headscarf. In a search for answers, we need to examine two issues: France's colonial excursions and imperial ambitions in the Muslim world particularly in North Africa; and the socio-economic status of Muslim immigrants who have settled in French territories due to colonization, and more recently globalization.

The French Colonial Presence in North Africa

Prior to the invasion of Egypt in 1798, Napoleon Bonaparte told his soldiers that they were about to be "engaged in a conquest whose consequences will be incalculable" (Hermassi, 1987: 33). What distinguished the French colonial expedition in Egypt from other European colonizers' conquests, was a group of French scientists who accompanied Bonaparte in an apparent attempt to learn about the history, language and culture of the people who were about to be subjugated. Some have considered this new approach as an indication of Bonaparte's keen interest in, and adherence to one of the main principles of the Enlightenment by acknowledging the common people's basic human and legal rights vis-à-vis the arbitrary power of the dictators and the European aristocracy (Youssef, 1998). But other observers have interpreted it as "propaganda" to cover up the true imperialist intentions of the French in their overseas ventures (Cole, 2007). In general, the European expansion led to the emergence of an ideology rooted in the paternalistic belief that colonialists had a responsibility to govern and take care of their subjects who allegedly were incapable of doing so on their own. While the Anglo-Saxon colonialists justified their imperial intentions by promoting the "white man's burden," the French colonizers were prone to see themselves as being on a mission to conquer and civilize the colonized people ('la mission civilisatrice'). Thus while the British were more interested to rule over and control their colonial subjects without forcing them to assimilate to the British way of life, the French did not vie for multiculturalism and considered the French culture to be superior to all other cultures in the colonies which made it necessary and a "noble" objective to impose it on the colonized (Nasr, 1999: 560–61; Lewis, 1980: 338).

During the 19th century France colonized Algeria, Tunisia, and Morocco in north-west Africa, or what is collectively known as the "Maghreb."[2] While Tunisia and Morocco were decolonized relatively peacefully in 1956, the Algerians had to fight a bloody war to finally rid themselves from 130 years of brutal French colonial rule in 1962. In general, the Muslim "Magrebin" proved to be a tough challenge to French colonial ambitions, as they fiercely resented and resisted colonial domination which the French attributed to Islam and its theological doctrine that allegedly condones violence. The French of Algerian origin are the most prominent

---

[2] The Arabic word *maghreb* means "place where the sun sets", or simply the west.

population within the context of French colonial history. For instance, Algeria was France's major "settler colony" to which French citizens and their European allies migrated, expropriated land from the indigenous population, and effectively destroyed Algeria's agrarian and nomadic economic, political and social structures (MacMaster, 1997). This led to massive displacement and emigration of Algeria's indigenous population, mostly in search of employment. Since Algerian colonial subjects were considered as French nationals prior to Algeria's independence from France in 1962, those Algerian migrant workers who went to France did not see themselves as leaving one country to enter another but rather considered themselves as French citizens entitled to full economic, political and legal rights. However, the French government simply considered them as colonial subjects who were in France as temporary migrant workers.

The post-independence Algerian governments under two leaders, Ahmed Ben Bella and Houari Boumediene were highly critical of this stark reality: they considered perpetuation of their citizens' stay in France a product of neo-colonialism that continued to exploit Algerians even after independence, while France benefited from a supply of cheap migrant labor (House, 2006).[3] The turbulent and bloody history of the French colonial presence and their eventual defeat in Algeria has subjected immigrants of Algerian origin to a harsher treatment in France. According to Naravane (2005) a considerable number of French citizens still feel that "Algeria was a part of France and should never have been granted independence"; consider continued presence of Algerians and other immigrants of North African origin as "adding insult to injury"; and as a consequence "cannot let go of sentiments of racial and colonial superiority."

France's presence and involvement in colonial and post-colonial Algeria led to polarization and radicalization of Algerians both in their home country and in France. During the war of independence most Algerians sympathized with the National Liberation Front (FLN, *Front de Libération Nationale*), a coalition of several nationalist parties and groups that led the war for independence against France. In contrast, the French of Algerian origin played a decisive role in the Algerian war of independence by siding with the pro-France resistance movement during the 1954–1962 period. Since the French ruled Algeria as a settler colony, no Algerian comprador bourgeoisie class in its classic form was created. As a result,

---

[3] Ahmed Ben Bella and Houari Boumediene held office from 1962–1965 and 1965–1978, respectively.

unlike in other revolutionary situations such as the Iranian revolution in 1979 where the members of the ruling class emigrated or simply fled (both before and after the revolution) out of fear of persecution by the revolutionaries, there was no exodus of Algerian upper class after the French defeat and withdrawal in 1962.

Historically speaking, the Algerian mercenaries were the first significant group of Muslim immigrants who settled in France after Algeria's independence. They are known as the *harkis*, Algerian soldiers who fought along with the French colonial army to suppress the Algerian revolution, and were relocated and settled in France after 1962 to avoid reprisal and persecution by the triumphant Algerian resistance army (Haddad, 1999: 604). According to one estimate, there were about 450,000 *harkis* in France mostly of lower class origins, the majority of whom being born and socialized in that country (Seljuq, 1997). Once in France the *harkis* were "parked in unspeakable, filthy, crowded concentration camps for many long years and never benefited from any government aid—a nice reward for their sacrifice for France, of which they were, after all, legally citizens." The *harkis'* horrible treatment by the French government added them to the rank and file of other immigrants of Algerian origin who considered themselves second-class citizens after Algeria's war of independence (Ireland, 2005).

French Republicanism and the Problematic "Collective Identity"

France has always promoted "French Republicanism" that is based on individualism and full assimilation of all individuals who have made a political choice of becoming a "French citizen." Urban riots during the first decade of the new Millennium and the *hijab* controversy have led some to question the practicality of Republican ideals, yet other alternative models such as the Anglo-Saxon/American doctrine of multiculturalism have not gained official support in France.[4] Those opposed to multiculturalism often argue that allowing various ethnic groups and nationalities to express their "cultural particularities" such as religious symbols will lead to the "fragmentation of society into several separate communities," which in turn will ruin "the unity of the nation" (Kastoryano, 2006).

---

[4] In late 2005 a series of riots mostly by youths of French-*Maghrebin* origins erupted, first in the suburbs of Paris and later in other major French cities. Riots were triggered by the deaths of two teenagers in Clichy-sous-Bois, a poor housing project in a northeastern Paris banlieue (suburb).

The opposition to wearing religious symbols in schools is based on a French law passed in 1905 that recognizes complete separation of church and state and prohibits the latter from funding or supporting any religion. The French term *"laïcité"* which sometimes is erroneously translated as "secularism," in essence means creating a balance between public order and religious freedom. Related to educational institutions, the 1905 law enforced *laïcité* in schools in order to prevent the anti-democratic influences of Catholicism and the Catholic Church (Vaiss, 2004: 2). Keeping schools as "religion free zones" therefore lies at the heart of the French idea of citizenship, and schools that are funded and operated by national or local governments are prohibited from endorsing any religious doctrine (Astier, 2004).

Furthermore, the French government does not have any officially sanctioned racial, ethnic, or religious group classification, and only recognizes individuals as citizens who in turn should pledge allegiance to the Republic. More specifically, the concept of "minority" does not have any relevance to French social relations, as the official policy is to legally and socially unify the population in accordance with the constitutional definition of the French Republic as "one and indivisible" (Open Society Institute, 2002: 71). In addition, France does not recognize rights of groups, and under the constitutional principles of *"läicité"* only individual rights are recognized (Haut Conseil à l'Intégration, 2000). In the context of the European Union, France has signed but not ratified the European Charter of Regional Minority Languages (ECRML), nor has she signed the Framework Convention for the Protection of National Minorities (FCNM) (Open Society Institute, 2002: 72). This is highly problematic for religious groups and immigrant populations who are subjected to overt and covert forms of prejudice and discrimination and yet have no legal and political recourse to address their concerns.

Muslim Immigrants in France

French Muslims come from diverse ethnic and national backgrounds, but in the absence of any official recognition of immigrants' ethnic and religious identity they are all lumped together and recognized as "French Muslims." Being Muslim within the French context of *"läicité"* means being the "other" vis-à-vis the *"Français de souche"* (French by extraction) (Hervieu-Leger, 2000: 80). Since the French census enumerators do not ask about religion or ethnic origin, there are no accurate statistics on French

Table 6.1 Estimated French Muslim Population by the Region/Country of Origin/Category, 2000

Origin/Category	Population
Algeria	1,550,000
Morocco	1,000,000
Tunisia	350,000
Turkey	315,000
Arab Middle East	100,000
Sub-Saharan Africa	250,000
Converts	40,000
Asylum seekers and Undocumented	350,000
Asia	100,000
Other	100,000
Total	4,155,000

Source: Haut Conseil a L'Integration (2000: 26).

Muslims and their ethnic/national origins. Estimates for the French Muslim immigrant population range anywhere from 3 to 6 million, but one official estimate in 2000 put the total number at 4,145,000 of which about 3 million were from the Maghreb (The French High Council of Integration, 2000, Table 6.1).[5] The most recent government data indicate that in 2004 there were five to six million Muslims in France or about 8–9.6 percent of total population, of which 70 percent have come from the Maghreb (NISES, 2004).[6] France's involvement in Algeria is of particular interest for this study, as the French were not only after economic gains but also total integration of Algeria and its subjects into the French political economy.

France's Constitution considers everyone to be "French," and at least on paper it follows a color-blind policy leaving no room for affirmative action programs. Yet there is a consensus that discrimination based on religion, race or national/ethnic origin is prevalent and a fact of life in France, particularly related to the French Muslim populations (Mattack,

---

[5] The *Maghreb* defines most of the northwest region in Africa between the Mediterranean Sea and the Atlas Mountains; and includes Tunisia, Algeria, Morocco, Libya and Mauritania.

[6] However, there are noticeable discrepancies in the estimated numbers of French Muslims. For example, in its projection of Europe's Muslim populations the Pew Forum on Religion and Public Life (2011) reports France's Muslim population in 2010 around 4.7 million, which is "expected to climb to 6.9 million" by 2030.

2005). In the absence of affirmative action policies to support immigrant families; presence of a subtle but persistent racism; disdain for the Muslim *Maghrebi* migrant workers and their families; and a *de facto* segregation of migrant workers in suburban working class neighborhoods around factories in French cities has led to a deterioration of quality of life and housing conditions for many of the French residents of *Maghrebi* origin. The majority of Muslim immigrants left their homelands for France due to the latter country's need for cheap labor during several crucial periods; such as in 1919 when 119,000 Algerians came to France to work in factories, and many others after WWII who were needed to work in jobs left vacant by war casualties (Killian and Johnson, 2006: 62). The majority of earlier immigrants were single men or men who left their families behind, with inadequate housing and accommodations made available to them. This prompted the French government in the 1950s to build hostels mainly designed to house single men.

The economic recession of the mid-1970s forced the French government to temporarily suspend entry of foreign workers; yet another change in immigration policy facilitated the migrant workers' reunification with their families. This led to the so-called 'feminization of foreign population' (*feminization de la population*) from the late 1970s onward (Lequin, 1992). To bring one's family, the policy required migrant workers to prove that they have adequate funds and salaries to support their families, and lodging large enough to house them. Although many workers did not qualify, their spouses often arrived with tourist visas but then extended their stay without obtaining legal permits (Killian and Johnson, 2006: 63). During a three decade period after WWII, known as *"les trente glorieuses"* (30 glorious years of prosperity) both the older generation *Maghrebin* and their French-born off-springs were warehoused in high-rise low-income housing structures (HLM, or "Habitation à Loyer Modéré"). In contrast to the American public housing projects that were mostly situated in inner cities, these large-scale housing structures were built in the suburbs of major French cities like Paris, Lyon, Toulouse, Lille and Nice, where most factories and industries were also situated. This effectively segregated the *Maghrebi* workers and their families in urban peripheries (*"les banlieues"*) where there were little or no provisions for shopping or leisure activities.[7]

---

[7] The phrase *les banlieues* (literally the 'suburbs') is used as a euphemism to describe low-income housing projects, mostly dilapidated and in a state of disrepair, in which mainly the French of foreign descent or immigrants are housed.

Ireland (2005) vividly describes the present living conditions in the French HLMs:

> Now 30, 40, and 50 years old, these high-rise human warehouses in the isolated suburbs are today run-down, dilapidated, sinister places, with broken elevators that remain un-repaired, heating systems left dysfunctional in winter, dirt and dog-shit in the hallways, broken windows, and few commercial amenities—shopping for bare necessities is often quite limited and difficult, while entertainment and recreational facilities for youth are truncated and totally inadequate when they're not non-existent.

In her discussion of the roots of urban riots in 2005, Cesari (2005) argues that spatial segregation of the *Maghrebin* in post-colonial France and the tension between the "poor suburbs" (the periphery) and French metropolises (the center) is at the core of any discourse about the merits of the French Republican ideals. In general, there is a prevalent opinion among the ghettoized and marginalized Muslim immigrants that there is a "conscious or unconscious national consensus in France to keep immigrants depressed so that they will always be around to do the dirty, low paid jobs that the French disdain" (Ibid.). This is supported by different studies and official statistics indicating that French Muslim immigrants from the Maghreb have historically had a much lower socio-economic status compared with the rest of the population. Home ownership rates among various immigrant populations are usually considered as indices of their economic well-being and integration into the host society; and the *Maghrebin* fare poorly. For instance, in 1992 French families of North African origin had a much lower rate of home ownership (10 percent) compared with French citizens and other immigrant populations (56 and 22 percent, respectively) (Kastenbaum and Vermesesee, 1996; 44). The findings of another study of immigrants in France indicated that the *Maghrebin* occupied the lowest levels of the social structure by mainly holding manual jobs in factories and construction sector, were poorly educated, and had a much higher rate of unemployment compared with the general French population (Tribalat, 1995, 1996). A slow economic growth in France and across Europe in the new Millennium has further perpetuated the plight of *Maghrebi* workers and their families, as by 2005 the unemployment rate for those under 25 was 50 percent compared with 22 percent for the country (Matlack, 2005).

Social Spheres and the Maghrebi *Muslim Identity:*
A New Frontier for Anti-colonial Resistance

Similar to the American "melting pot" approach, the assimilationist perspective espoused by supporters of French Republicanism assumes integration and cultural adjustment is a necessity for immigrant populations in order to survive in the host culture. Studies of identity formation increasingly emphasize its interactive nature in a process of negotiation with other identities. For instance, Hall (1996: 4–5) argues that identities are constructed "through the relations to the other, the relation to what it is not, to precisely what it lacks, to what has been called its *constitutive* outside that the 'positive' meanings of any term—and thus its 'identity'—can be constructed." Identity formation and its maintenance is often stronger among the groups that have unequal access to a society's social, cultural, political, and economic spheres. On the other hand, those who support the totalizing power of the French Republic, both French and assimilated immigrants, tend to resist and resent such identity formations. In addition, several studies indicate to the differences of identity formation processes among the first- and second generation immigrant populations (Chaichian, 1997, 2008; Portes and Borocz, 1989). Related to the French case, the period between 1975 and 1985 was a transitional period during which a new political discourse emerged when both the government officials and the media identified and recognized the "second-generation" French of *Maghrebi* origin in general and of Algerian origin in particular. Commonly known as the *"Beur"* (Arab) and born in France, they were the sons and daughters of the *Maghrebi* immigrants; and even if they were not immigrants per se they were born into the involuntary status of being a *Maghrebi* with French citizenship. In relative terms, compared to their first generation immigrant parents they were better adjusted in society, yet they did not get fully accepted and embraced by the French public:

> Access to French nationality for Maghrebian youth...involves Frenchmen granting to the children of the ex-colonized what was, formerly, the colonizers' exclusive privilege. Frenchmen returning to France from Algeria (*pied-noirs*), Algerians who deliberately chose France (*harkis*) and a considerable number of other Frenchmen accept with difficulty [that] the offspring of the formerly colonized, who refused to belong to the French Empire, now call for French nationality after their parents fought against colonial France. An unresolved historical argument, a feeling that immigrants' membership in the nation is fraudulent, the general feeling that young people with migrant origin reject French civilization by their ostentatious adhesion to

Islam—all this generates discomfort, which deepens insofar as it has never been classified or publicly discussed (Khosrokhavar, 1997: 37–38).

Segregation, discrimination, and subhuman conditions in the suburban ghettoes led to the mobilization of the *Beur* as a new political force who in 1983 organized a march from Lyon's suburban high rise (*Les Minguettes*) to Paris, and demanded to be recognized as French like everyone else (*"comme les autres"*). Elia (1997: 47) observes that while their parents emigrated to France with the dream and illusion of a better life, the *Beur* generation has to deal with a tense reality of a day-to-day life of

> ...[C]ommuting between a Muslim, Arabi-speaking home when tradition up-holding parents reminisce about North Africa as they prepare *cous cous* and *meschwi*, and the streets of the only city they know, the French metropolis with its corner bistros, its secular culture, and the growing racism of Jean-Marie le Pen supporters and Neo-Nazi skinheads.

France's resistance to the French Muslim identity has also taken place within a highly gendered post-colonial discourse. On one hand, young Algerian males are stereotyped as dangerous Islamic fundamentalists, juvenile delinquents and criminals who allegedly refuse to integrate and obey the French civic laws (House, 2006; Geesey, 1995: 139); while young women of Algerian origin are represented as passive and submissive, "barriers to assimilation," and yet prone to integration and assimilation into secular French society due to their subordinate status within the *Maghrebi* male dominant culture on the other. Thus the French *Maghrebi* women "are alternately seen as potential agents of integration or victims of Islamic fundamentalist agendas" (Geesey, 1995: 137). The conservative assimilationist camp in France also holds the position that the *Maghrebi* Muslim women who are subordinate to men will assimilate easier than men, since the latter "stand to lose a significant amount of control over female family members" if the former choose to do so by integrating into modern French society (Schnapper, 1991: 173). As Abdelkarim-Chikh (cf. Geesey, 1995: 144) argues, the characterization of *Maghrebi* women, particularly those married to non-Muslims, as willing agents of assimilation is rooted in the colonial ideology held by French Orientalists who "shed crocodile tears" over women's oppressive conditions both in colonized Algeria and in contemporary post-colonial French society. However, she further characterizes the position as "narcissistic satisfaction evoking a symbolic abduction, or better yet, proof of self-admiration of one's own values, in which the abducted woman is a consenting accomplice" (Abdelkrim-Chikh, 1990: 241). The French assimilationist approach is also problematic, by not only overlooking the significant role Islamic cultural values play in the lives of *Maghrebi* immigrants; but also as Maillard (2005: 71) points out, by its utter disregard of stark "anthropological" differences between the French and Algerian social systems:

> The anthropological Algerian system—Arab and Kabyle[8]—was the opposite of the French egalitarian nuclear system in colonial Algeria. Communitarian, patrilineal, and endogamous, it implied a confinement of women incompatible with French customs, whether these were rooted in the central egalitarian and nuclear family pattern or in the peripheral stock-family pattern. The anti-individualism of the Algerian anthropological system added to the conflict between France and Algeria. Its preference for endogamy a priori discouraged any matrimonial exchanges between the colonizer and the colonized. For the French bilateral and exogamous anthropological system, the endogamous patrilineal model was unacceptable. Conversely, French mores with independent and equal women represented barbarism in the Arab eye.

Hijab as the Last Defensive Tool of the Colonized: Soft as a Cloth, Tough as a Wall!

There is a general consensus that in pre-Islamic empires in what is now known as the "Middle East," the urban male elite veiled and secluded women (wives, relatives and concubines) in the private sphere (palaces and residential compounds). But despite the prevalence of a patriarchal culture in rural areas and particularly within nomadic societies there was little or no seclusion or veiling of women in the public sphere, as they had to work in the fields and take part in communal and public affairs (Keddie, 2002, cf. Bayes and Tohidi: 27–28). Later on, Islamic ethos reportedly condoned the veil (*hijab*) in urban settings so that enslaved and free women could be clearly distinguished. In his biographies of the Prophet's female companions the 9th century Muslim scholar Ibn Sa'ad (cf. Mernissi, 1991: 186) provides the justification for *hijab*, that "God ordered women to change their clothing to distinguish it from that of slaves and to do this by covering themselves with their *hijab* [cloak]." Mernissi (ibid.: 187) concludes that "[T]he female Muslim population would henceforth be divided by a *hijab* into two categories: free [veiled] women against whom

---

[8] The Kabyles are tribal people who live in the highlands of the Atlas Mountains in northeastern Algeria on the Mediterranean Sea. The term Kabyle is a truncated form of the original Arabic word "Al Qabayel" which literally means "tribes." The kabyles are predominantly Sunni-Muslim and speak *Kabyle* which is a *Berber language* mainly spoken by tribal people in Algeria, Morocco, Mali and Libya (see Brett and Fentress, 1997).

violence is forbidden, and [unveiled] women slaves toward whom *ta'arrud* [aggression] is permitted."

Lapidus (1988: 557) argues that Muslim societies and communities have responded to the external challenges posed by colonial domination and "modernization," or introduction of capitalist relations of production and its socio-cultural ethos in two distinct cultural ways. One response according to Lapidus is "retrogressive," espoused by both rural/tribal populations and urban residents of rural/tribal origins whose economic and political *modi operandi* are undeniably affected by colonization and globalization; yet their social and cultural lives are still ruled by pre-capitalist and corresponding traditional Islamic values. A second and seemingly "progressive" response from a portion of urban population that is more modern and tuned to the language of a dependent capitalist economy. The latter includes the urban intelligentsia, the educated middle class, the military top brass, technocrats both in the government and the emerging private sector, and members of the landowning and upper class families who are more secular and less governed by the Islamic traditional (pre-capitalist) culture.

Related to the former tendency, and in the context of post-colonial French society, what the popular media often overlook in their reporting and analysis is the rural and tribal origins of the predominant majority of the French *Maghrebin*. In her examination of the status of North African female immigrants in France Geesey (1995: 140) recognizes this reality and contends that most studies focus on their most observable differences from the rest of the French society such as "illiteracy, modest or Islamic dress, rural origins, higher birth rates, poverty and physical seclusion." However, most interpretations gloss over the immigrants' rural, and particularly tribal cultural backgrounds, and instead quickly move to criticize the restrictions placed on women based on alleged Islamic teachings, without acknowledging the fact that Islamic movement had strong roots in an already existing tribal political economy, culture, and lifestyle. There are no official statistics on the *Maghrebin's* rural or tribal origins. But Chaker (2006: 3) estimates the number of immigrants in France who speak Berber (language of the *Maghrebins* with tribal roots, or the *Kabyle*) being close to 1,500,000 of which 1,000,000 are Algerians and 500,000 are of Moroccan origin.[9] This indicates that almost two-thirds of French Muslims of Algerian origins come from tribal areas.

---

[9] "Berber" is a derogatory term used by European colonizers in reference to all languages spoken in North Africa. As I discussed in chapter 2, the origins of the term go back

The Algerian Kabyle also come from a long tradition of fighting colonial domination, a historical reality that has certainly affected their identity both as Algerians and immigrants/ citizens in France. It is within this historical context of colonial and post-colonial realities that one has to see the link between Islamic and tribal cultures, particularly related to the meaning and utility of the *hijab* for Muslim women. Some studies of the *Maghrebi* women in France have made note of "negative pressure put on female family members who seek changes in their traditional lifestyle and status, even by relatives who are still living in their home country" (Taboada-Leonetti and Levy, 1978: 168–178). Thus Muslim women are discouraged from adopting "foreign ways" that go against their traditions, out of fear of being ridiculed and censured by family members and neighbors (Geesey, 1995: 144).

Muslims in general and Arab-Muslim societies in particular depend on a "bipolar" and seemingly harmonious and productive social order that creates two strictly separate, gender-specific spheres—women belong to and are in control of the interior of the home (private sphere) and men are in charge of the exterior world (public sphere) (see Bouhdiba, 1975: 43). The strict division of male and female spheres of Maghrebi communities in France closely mirrors that of Arab and Kabyle communities in the Maghreb (North Africa). Applying the French anthropologist Pierre Bourdieu's analysis, in his study of gender relations in 20th century Algeria Knauss (1987: 4–5) explains in detail the rigid sexual segregation, stratification and patriarchal notion of "male honor" particularly among the Kabyle, the Algerians of tribal origin. Bourdieu (1979: 121–122) depicts a typical gender division among the tribal people:

> The opposition between the inside and the outside is expressed correctly in the sharp division between the women's sphere—the home and its garden...a closed, secret, protected space, away from intrusions and public gaze—and the men's space—the place of assembly, the mosque, the cafe, the fields and the market.

Algerians have an expression that demarcates this gender-based social-spatial division: "*Que la femme fasse le cous cous, et nous la politique*" (let women make the couscous, and we will take care of politics) (Knauss, 1987: 5). In Kabyle tribal culture the men are also expected to protect

---

to the ancient Greeks who labeled all non-Greek languages as "bar-bar," or a collection of nonsensical syllables.

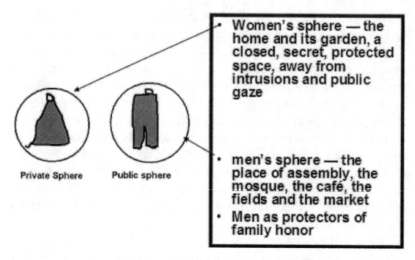

Figure 6.1 Gender-specific spaces in a Muslim Magrebin rural-tribal culture.

women and the intimacy of the family (private sphere) while girls are socialized to expect to be protected by men (see Figure 6.1).

Outside the home, women in most Muslim tribal cultures, including the Kabyle, are not protected by the veil, but by an elaborate system of masculine and feminine pathways and public accommodations that effectively keep men and women separate. As Bourdieu (1979: 122) explains, it is "in the urban world where men's space and women's space overlap" that female intimacy is "safeguarded by confinement and the wearing of the veil." Thus the veil becomes a protective tool for tribal men who have to confront other men, strangers who may not necessarily belong to their own tribe. The evolution of the veil's symbolic meaning therefore has its roots in the gendered cultures of tribal rural and urban communities. In her book *The Veil and the Male Elite*, Mernissi (1991: 85–6) provides a narrative of the Muslim Prophet Mohammad's wedding night to one of his wives, Zaynab, and explains in detail the rationale for the descent of the verse of the *veil* (curtain in Arabic) in the Qur'an and the fact that it was "not to put a barrier between a man and a woman, but rather between two men:

> The Prophet had just got married and was impatient to be alone with his new wife, his cousin Zaynab. He was not able to get rid of a small group of tactless guests who remained lost in conversation. The veil was God's answer to a community with boorish manners whose lack of delicacy offended a Prophet whose politeness bordered on timidity.

Thus the Prophet reportedly draws a curtain "between himself and the man who was at the entrance of his nuptial chamber" as a symbolic act to demarcate boundaries between the public (urban Medina) and private (family, tribe, blood relatives) spheres. Led by men of tribal origin, the Islamic movement facilitated transition of the Arab tribes from pastoral-nomads to rural and urban settlers. In chronicling the first year of the Prophet and the entourage that emigrated with him from Mecca to Medina, Watt (1961: 93–101) explains how Medina's new community constitution was written in order to accommodate about nine different tribal clans who were residing in the agricultural urban oasis of Medina. Thus related to the origins of *hijab*, the Prophet's reaction reflects the mentality of an urbanized tribal man who is challenged by the newly emerging impersonal and individualistic urban culture in the city of Medina; and the *hijab* was symbolically used to separate tribal men and protect their honor (women) from strangers in the city (see Figure 6.2).

Although patriarchal in nature, here a "free woman" is perceived as residing within the confines of her tribal protection; and in a different fashion modern interpretations of the *hijab* by both male and female proponents of its utility for Muslim women also refer to it as a liberating tool, particularly in a Western consumerist culture that objectifies women and reduces them to sex objects. Mernissi (1991: 93) further argues that the concept of the word *hijab* has three interwoven dimensions:

> The first dimension is a visual one: to hide something from sight...the second dimension is spatial: to separate, to mark a border, to establish a

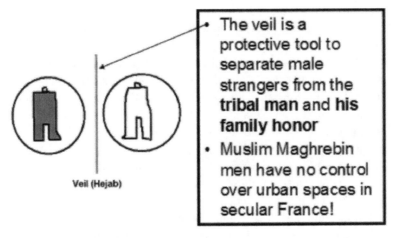

Figure 6.2 The veil (*hijab*) and its function in urban public spheres.

threshold. And finally, the third dimension is ethical: it belongs to the realm of the forbidden.

It is the *hijab*'s third dimension, namely, the ethical that is imperative to the tribal culture of male honor that the Kabyle also prescribe to. Bourdieu (1979: 123) describes how the male members of the Kabyle are socialized to protect not only their women, but also the whole sphere of intimacy including internal family and tribal dissentions and shortcomings from strangers. Clearly, all aspects of the Kabyle's cherished tribal culture are violated within the post-colonial French social context. First, the *Maghrebi* men are disenfranchised, discriminated against and forced to live in dilapidated housing and to take low paying jobs. They are also effectively cut off from the French political process: they no longer have any control over the public sphere and its associated politics in post-colonial France as they did back in their homeland. Second, women who joined their male relatives in the 1970s, as well as their French-born female off spring (*Beur*) are forced to live in the public housing complexes in the *banlieues* where there are no protective measures to keep their private spheres separate from the public sphere. This also exerts pressure on *Maghrebi* men who are expected to protect their women and their homes (private sphere) from strangers.

Conclusion

Similar to Judaism, Islam is both a religion and a way of life and a cultural practice that extends to all spheres for individuals living in Muslim communities. Both Islam and Judaism are also characterized by *orthopraxy*, or their dedication to correct practices as dictated by each faith (Denny, 1985: 43). Thus religious belonging and upbringing is an inseparable part of a Muslim society's inherited culture. Although in different ways, the "headscarf controversy" in France reflects on the significance of Islamic cultural values for both older generations and the *Beur* (Babes, 1997). As a consequence, regardless of one's level of adherence to Islamic theology Islamic culture continues to remain a strong component of one's identity. There are indications that the percentage of "practicing" Muslims in France has been on the rise since the late 1980s. But findings of a 2001 survey indicated that only 36 percent of French Muslims declared themselves "believing and practicing." The survey also indicated that among the upper-middle class French Muslims practicing families are more numerous than non-practicing ones (Open Society Institute, 2002: 76). As

Hervieu-Leger (2000: 80) explains, Islamic values for French Muslims are "the only cultural and symbolic good that they can specifically assert vis-à-vis the *Français de souche* ('French by extraction') which enables them, at the same time, to transform exclusion into a voluntarily assured difference." This voluntary assumption of differences between a French Muslim of *Maghrebi* origin and a person of French extraction is indicative of an identity that has emerged in France as a reaction to the government's policy of total cultural and political domination in post-colonial France.

The resurgence of the *hijab* at the end of the 20th century in many Muslim countries and in post-colonial situations signifies a new era when Muslim societies and populations have not only lost their economic and political independence, but are also on the verge of losing their cultural identity. In this context, new emerging social realities of globalized communities such as in France have forced Muslim immigrant populations to use the *hijab* as a conceptual defensive wall to protect their indigenous cultural reality in hostile, urban environments. First, Muslim women's interaction with employers, teachers, and strangers in general exposes them to the nuances of a secular urban environment influenced by the Western cultural values of a globalized economy. Second, in a rural-tribal cultural context where men and women are expected to uphold endogamous marriages, women are exposed to the "stranger male" residents in the urban public sphere and have a chance to meet and marry outside their real or perceived "tribes." This clearly poses a threat to the integrity of pre-capitalist notions of 'family' and 'community.' Third, being themselves subdued by a globalized political economy and continuously exploited in the post-colonial metropolis, men of rural-tribal origins use the *hijab* as the last available cultural tool at their disposal to protect their shattered honor and violated private sphere from a hostile and domineering public sphere that continues to colonize them and their families.

We can make a parallel historical analysis in the context of Muslim societies' anti-colonial and anti-imperialist struggles—that of the *hijab* controversy in the Islamic Republic of Iran. In the absence of any laws to mandate the *hijab* prior to the 1979 revolution and despite modernizing efforts of the Shah's *ancien régime* many women were veiled. In fact, except for the modern middle class and affluent urban residents, both female and male, who considered the *hijab* as backward and old-fashioned; a vast majority of women in working class urban communities, small towns and rural areas as well as those associated with the religious and bazaar communities wore the *hijab* in public places (Azari, cf.

Bullock, 2003: 90). Thus the Islamic government's mandatory *hijab* laws and regulations after the revolution even up to the present time are not aimed at *all* women. Rather, they are meant for women who according to proponents of the *hijab* had been allegedly "intoxicated" and influenced by the decadent values of the Western culture (see Figure 6.3).

Similar to the argument set forth by Ibn Sa'ad in my earlier argument (cf. Mernissi, 1991: 186), Muslim revolutionaries and even some secular supporters of the revolution perceived unveiled women (*bihijab*) as modern slaves of an invading and dominating Western culture, while wearing the *hijab* signified women's freedom. This was echoed in the arguments set forth even by factions of Iranian left and secular activists who supported the revolution during the early years of revolution—they questioned the legitimacy of claims by middle- and upper-class women that equated *hijab* with enslavement of women by arguing "[I]f affluent women are fighting for 'women's freedom,' does that not mean that the whole problem is a hoax?" (Shahidian, 2002a: 22). On the surface, one might find the above position incompatible with seemingly progressive socialist theories that espouse gender equality. However, Moghissi (1994: 102) observes that a vast majority of the Iranian left and secular activists "came from lower or middle urban traditional petty bourgeois families, where the hold of Shiite [Islamic] morality was strongest, was a determining factor in the left's approach to the 'women's question'."

The confinement of Muslim women by Muslim men in France can be seen as a solution for a crisis of global magnitude. As Mernissi (1991: 99) argues, "protecting women from change by veiling them and shutting them out of the world has echoes of closing the community to protect it from the West." In his critique of the way the French model of integration has handled the *hijab* issue Maillard (2005: 78) sides with French Muslim women and their right to decide on their own:

> Invoking the very principles of religious freedom and individual rights, consistent with liberty and equality in a republic, the Muslim girls—whether they are sincere or manipulated—challenge the democratic state. As long as they can claim that their decision to wear the veil is theirs and has not been imposed upon them by their fathers or brothers, the Muslim girls have a point when they ask as individual citizens for the right to dress as they wish. If secularism were strong enough, no law would be needed to strengthen it.

In brief, the French government's handling of the *hijab* controversy and eventual banning of the headscarf in French schools is a clear example of using Muslim immigrant women's bodies as a cultural and ideological

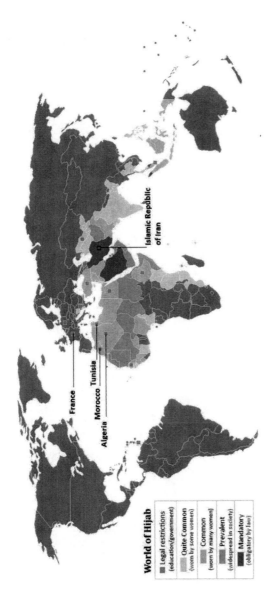

Original map source: http://en.wikipedia.org/wiki/File:Hijab_worldz.png.

Figure 6.3 Women wearing the *hijab*: commonly worn by many women in Morocco, Algeria, and Tunisia; and mandatory for Iranian women.

battleground to subject the Muslim immigrant population to total submission to France's post-colonial interests. In contrast, in light of *Maghrebin's* total economic dependence on the host country, the Muslim communities' pressure on women to wear the *hijab* in public is their last remaining defensive cultural tool against invasive forces of globalization in the context of the French society. Indeed, the Islamic *hijab* is a defensive curtain, though soft as a cloth, yet, as tough and strong as a wall, raised against the totalizing forces of globailization.

PART THREE

NEO-COLONIAL WALLS

AN EMPIRE IN THE MAKING: AMERICAN COLONIAL INTERESTS SOUTH OF THE BORDER

In November 2005 the U.S. Department of Homeland Security announced that it would launch the *Secure Border Initiative* (SBI) in order to secure the U.S.-Mexico border by drastically reducing illegal cross border immigration from Mexico.[1] The magnitude of this multi-year, multi-billion dollar undertaking was unprecedented in the context of American immigration control policies and procedures. As of January 2010 more than 643 miles of a planned 670 mile-long border fence along the 2000-mile border had been completed.[2] The crucial questions to ask is why did it take 150 years for the American government to come up with a serious plan to construct a border fence/wall between the two countries; and *similar to other border walls and fences was this one meant not to seal the border, but rather to more effectively regulate the population flow between the two nations?* From our brief historical journey and inquiries about the failed and dismantled ancient and contemporary walls in previous chapters we may infer that in a not-so-distant future a similar fate may await the U.S.-Mexican wall project as well. However, in order to understand the Wall advocates' rationale in supporting such an immense undertaking, both in terms of costs and human resources, in this chapter I sketch historical origins of the U.S.-Mexican relations that has culminated in the construction of what is dubbed as "the Great Wall of Mexico."

The genesis of U.S.-Mexican relations and territorial disputes can be traced back to the early 19th century, when after Mexico's independence from Spain in 1821 the Mexican territories stretched as far north as the present time state of Colorado. In order to prevent raids by Native American tribes and promote development in the sparsely populated Northern

---

[1] The U.S. Department of Homeland Security (DHS) was created by the U.S. government in the aftermath of September 11, 2001 attacks with the primary task of protecting the United States from terrorist attacks. The DHS is in fact the military arm of the U.S. government in the civilian sphere.

[2] I will discuss the design and construction of the fence in more detail in the following chapter. For a summary of the fence history and status visit the following web page: http://www.globalsecurity.org/ security/systems/mexico-wall.htm.

provinces, the Mexican government liberalized immigration policies to encourage immigration from American territories. This was in fact an extension of Spain's colonization law that was implemented right before the Mexican independence, allowing colonists from American territories to settle in the newly created state of *Coahuila y Tejas*, or what later became Texas. By 1834 an estimated 30,000 Anglophone settlers from American territories were settled in *Coahuila y Tejas* state. In contrast, Mexicans living in the state at the time were only numbered about 7,800 (Manchaca, 2001: 164–72). Soon the invited guests expressed their desire to establish an independent state outside Mexico's federal system. The events leading to the war between Mexico and the Anglo residents of *Coahuila y Tejas* eventually led to the creation of independent state of Texas in 1836. At the time, the United States' nascent capitalist economy had a need to move westward for its expansion and have access to raw materials; and the newly independent nation of Mexico stood on her way. The American government's colonial interests in acquiring territories in northwest Mexico and its desire for the annexation of Texas to American territories in 1845 was the beginning of a long and enduring animosity between the two nations. Not only did the Mexican Congress not recognize an independent Texas, the Mexican government also warned the Americans that annexation of Texas would mean declaration of war against Mexico. The subsequent Mexican-American war of 1846–48 proved disastrous for Mexico, leading to the loss of almost half of Mexican territories under the Guadalupe Hidalgo Treaty (Chance, 1991: 241). The treaty gave the United States an undisputed control over Texas, and Mexico was forced to cede 500,000 square miles that included the present-day states of California, Nevada, Utah, as well as parts of Arizona, Colorado, New Mexico and Wyoming (See Figure 7.1).

The U.S. aggression against Mexico and the subsequent occupation of more than half of the latter's territory took place within the context of economic and political demands of an emerging colonial power; and the invasion of Texas and subsequent war of 1845–48 has to be understood in this light (Acuña, 1981: 11). As Van Alstyne (1974: 106) puts it, by the 1840s the Pacific Coast "belonged to the commercial empire that the United States was already building in that Ocean." The invasion and conquest of Mexico was also justified by the Anglo-American conviction that the nation was chosen by God to be the custodian of democracy and Christianity, and that they were predestined "to spread its principles"; assume ownership and control "all of the land from ocean to ocean and pole to pole"; and to liberate the less fortunate and less developed Mexicans (Acuña,

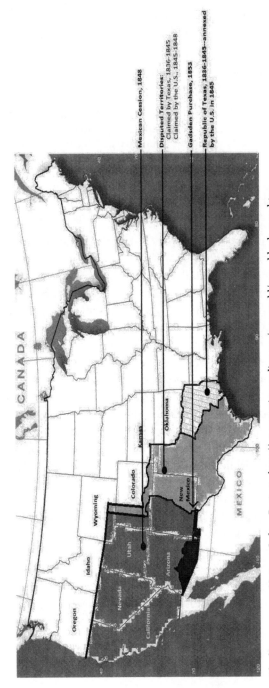

Mexican Cession, 1848

Disputed Territories:
Claimed by Texas, 1836–1845
Claimed by the U.S. 1845–1848

Gadsden Purchase, 1853

Republic of Texas, 1836–1845—annexed
by the U.S. in 1845

Blank map source: Nations Online Project, http://www.nationsonline.org/oneworld/usa_blank_map.htm

Figure 7.1 The Mexican Cession of 1848 (map by author).

1981: 11–13). In his essay *"We are all Israelis"* Lubin (2008) finds parallel historical trajectories that have led to the construction of Israel's separation barrier around the occupied Palestinian territories and the U.S.-Mexico border fence/wall erected by the American government. Looking back, he considers the year 1848 as a "watershed year" in the U.S. territorial expansion and development of colonial rule over Mexico:

> Having annexed half of Mexico in the Treaty of Guadalupe Hidalgo and doubling the geographic size of the nation, the United States realized what its leaders figured as its manifest destiny. The acquisition of northern Mexico raised new questions about who was an American as hundreds of thousands of Mexican nationals entered the body politic of the U.S. nation-state. Although the Treaty of Guadalupe Hidalgo extended citizenship to Mexico's colonized subjects, in reality, the United States was uneasy with the status of Mexicans within its borders and precluded full equality (p. 674).

The belief in "manifest destiny" was also deeply rooted in a racist ideology of the superiority of Anglo-Americans over Mexicans that has continued to influence popular beliefs and culture to the present time. In the context of colonial/imperialist ideology Mexican subjects for American colonialists represented the "barbarians," who were being treated similar to the northern English and Scottish tribal populations under the Roman occupation. This may explain why the occupation and conquest of Mexican territories and subjugation of its people was accomplished by overt acts of terror, murder, and disregard for civilian life, property, and dignity.[3]

Prior to 1848 there were about 25,000 Mexicans and 46,000 Native Americans in the areas that later became California, Arizona, New Mexico, and Texas. Once the new border boundaries were established, those Mexican subjects who remained north of the new boundary were given two options: stay and be granted rights of American citizenship, or move south. Approximately, three thousand Mexicans from New Mexico and Texas moved south, to the Mexican provinces of Chihuahua and Tamaulipas, respectively; and the rest who were either "unable or unwilling to move remained in their homes, placing their future in the hands of the U.S. government and those European Americans who migrated into the Southwest (Martinez, 2001: 3–5). But the new Mexican-descent population soon lost its numerical majority status to European-American settlers who flooded southwestern states in waves, and by the early 20th century

---

[3] Acuña (1981: 14–17) provides eye witness accounts of American soldiers' (both enlisted and volunteer) atrocities toward Mexican subjects particularly during the 1845–48 period.

Mexican-Americans comprised only about 7–10 percent of the Southwest's population (op. cit., 7). Major settlement nodes and population concentrations in 19th century southwestern annexed territories were in localities such as San Francisco, Los Angeles, San Diego, Tucson, Albuquerque, El Paso and San Antonio. These later became key urban centers and metropolitan areas in the Southwest.

Migration of Mexicans to the United States

The U.S.-Mexican relations since the former nation's annexation of Texas in the 1840s have been based on domination and exploitation. The American interest in Mexico was not grounded on a desire to establish a relationship based on mutual respect between two neighbors of equal status. Rather, it was part of an expansionist foreign policy that pertained all of Central and South American territories. Yet despite the presence and prevalence of a racist and prejudiced anti-Mexican sentiment in the United States, from the outset the two nations' inter-related economies provided a context for Mexican subjects' northward migration.

From a historical perspective three simultaneous processes of social and economic development in Mexico and the United States set the stage for migratory patterns in the second half of the 19th century. First, the Mexican government began an extensive plan of expanding the railroad networks that also involved foreign capital and technology. But during the Juarez and de Tejada administrations (1867–72 and 1872–76, respectively) the railroad line did not extend north to border out of the fear that they might be used by the Americans for military purposes. However, their successor, Porfirio Diaz advocated a liberal open door policy aimed at bringing the U.S.-Mexican economies closer by facilitating American investment in Mexico. Second, Diaz's industrialization programs and his simultaneous efforts to undermine and dismantle feudal relations in the countryside uprooted peasants (*peones*) from Mexican plantations and agricultural estates (*haciendas*)—either because of them being replaced by mechanized agriculture, or their realization that working on railroad construction sites (both in Mexico and the United States) and the booming mines of northern Mexico was more lucrative than the countryside (Acuña, 1981: 124–25; Gonzalez and Fernandez, 2003: 37).[4] Finally, President

---

[4] According to one estimate, Mexican workers were paid 75¢/day in the north compared to 25¢ in the interior (Cardoso, 1974: 23).

Diaz's open-door policy allowed unrestricted foreign capital investment in Mexico, particularly American, which effectively destabilized Mexican economy and ensured supply of cheap labor and raw materials for industrial and agricultural operations in the American Southwest. These developments took place with the building of 15,000 miles of railroad in Mexico between 1880 and 1910, mostly running north and south (Cumberland, 1968: 216); while At the same time, the United States developed its own railroad network in the Southwest reaching border cities of Yuma, Arizona in 1877; Denig, New Mexico; and El Paso, Texas in 1881 (Gonzalez and Fernandez, 2003: 37). As a consequence, Mexican workers mostly of rural origins "traveled long distances into the interior of the United States, thereby pioneering new migration corridors for the waves of immigrants who would follow in later decades (Martinez, 2001: 25). Based on some estimates in the last decade of 19th century about 77,000 Mexicans entered the United States as contract laborers, being transported by over 2,000 railroad cars (Cardoso, 1974: 57; and Alba, 1967: 106).

Mexican migration to the United States has been an ongoing process following the colonial war of 1846–1848. From 1853, when after the Gadsden Purchase the U.S.-Mexico borders were finalized; to the passage of the Secure Fence Act in 2006, the reasons for and intensity of Mexican subjects' migration to the northern neighbor have varied. The two nations' political and economic developments in the second half of 19th century set the stage for subsequent waves of south-north migration and population movements in the following century. Despite theoretical differences among scholars of Mexican-U.S immigration history, a survey of historical periodization of migration cycles indicates their consensus on identifying four distinct periods during the 20th century (see Table 7.1).

I. *The Era of Enganche*

Under Diaz administration (1876–1910) Mexico witnessed a period of economic development heavily dependent on foreign capital. This proved to be devastating for more than 90 percent of peasants who lost their lands to large-scale mechanized farming or their rights to work on communal lands that for centuries had been held by rural towns and indigenous villages (Gonzalez and Fernandez, 2003: 39; Massey et al., 2002: 29). The *Era of Enganche* (literally translated as "hook," but more politely as "indentured" workers) lasted for about three decades (1900–1930). By 1910, when Mexico entered almost a decade of revolutionary period, foreign capital

Table 7.1 Variations in Periodization of Mexican Emigration Pull-Push Cycles to the United States, 1900–2000

Mexico's Emigration Cycles to the United States		
1850–1900: Steady Flow		
Martinez (2001: chapter 2)	Massey et al. (2002: chapter 3)	Acuna (1981: chapter 6)
1900–1930: upsurge and restrictions	1900–1929: The era of Enganche	1900–1920: Nativist reaction to Mexican migration
		1920–1930: The restrictionist movement
1930–1940: Pressure and repatriation	1929–1941: The era of deportations	1930–1940: The Nativist fever and deportation of the Chicano
1940–1965: Resurgence	1942–1964: The Bracero era	1945–1965: The Bracero Program
1965–2000; Expansive immigration and renewed restrictionism	1965–1985: The era of undocumented migration	
	1986–2000: The great divide	

was in control of two-thirds of all corporations and more than 90 percent of mining, oil, agriculture, and industries of which 38 percent were owned by American investors alone (Baird and McCaughan, cf. Acuña, 1981: 126).[5] The revolution gave peasants and indigenous populations more control and power over the Mexican political economy. But the initial turmoil and disruption triggered a wave of immigration to the United States, when from 1910 to 1920 about 200,000 Mexicans emigrated (McCaa, cf. Massey et al., 2002: 30). The majority of immigrants came from rural, lower class backgrounds. But the revolution also forced many middle- and upper-class Mexicans who were either affiliated with the *ancien régime* or

---

[5] The British owned 29 percent and the French another 27 percent (ibid.).

were negatively affected by economic recession in Mexico to head north (Acuña, 1981: 128).

North of the border, the United States' entry into the World War I theatre caused an acute labor shortage that prompted the American government to further support and encourage entry of Mexican immigrants to the country. For example, in his 1916 report the Commissioner General of Immigration argued for the need to relaxing immigration laws particularly related to Mexico, due to "a general revival of industrial activity throughout the Southwest, and even in regions more remote from the border," that had a demand for unskilled labor (U.S. Department of Labor, 1916: 397). As a consequence of developments and policies in both countries, in the first three decades of the 20th century 728,000 Mexicans emigrated legally to the United States, compared with only 13,000 who did so from 1850 to 1900 (Massey et al., 2002: 31).

Similar to other colonial situations, economic exploitation of the Mexican workers by American employers was justified by the presumed cultural and racial superiority of the latter group. In his study of Mexican workers in the United States Clark (1908: 471, 496) explains the plight of Mexican workers who were transported by train in locked and guarded cars to designated work sites in the American Southwest, and the prevalent stereotypes that depicted Mexicans as docile but physically weak, irregular and indolent workers who were willing to work for very low wages.[6] In general, anti-immigrant sentiments during the last decade of 19th and early 20 centuries largely focused on people from eastern and southern Europe and Asia, while Mexican immigrants remained mostly invisible in the public's eyes. As Reisler (1976: 155) points out, "most Americans remained unaware of this new immigrant invasion since Mexicans were confined predominantly to the Southwest and hidden from sight in the boxcars, tents, and shacks of railroad and migrant farm labor camps." But as Mexican immigration grew and immigrants moved further north and into urban areas, a racist and nativist backlash emerged across the nation in the 1920s. Anti-Mexican immigration proponents demanded implementation of a vigorous quota policy for Mexican immigrants, arguing that

> Mexican labor displaced Anglo native workers and kept wages low; the economic benefits derived from a cheap labor force was a short-term gain

---

[6] As a sense of déjà vu, ironically similar situation still exists today after a century since Clark's report was published.

and a long-term cost; and the Mexican nationals posed a social threat to the 'white race' because Mexicans were *mestizos*, i.e., miscegenated, thus inferior. These views were, in turn, supported by allegedly 'objective scientific studies,' which rationalized the racist belief common to many whites (Gomez-Quiñones and Maciel, 1998: 37).

II. *The Era of Deportations*

The second period (1929–1941) started with the catastrophic collapse of stock market prices on the New York Stock Exchange in 1929 which plunged the United States and most of the industrialized nations into a decade-long depression. A deepening crisis and rising unemployment rates emboldened nativists and restrictionists to push for immigration quotas and even deportation of immigrants, particularly of Mexican origin.[7] The nativist sentiments were also supported by President Hoover who referred to Mexican immigrants as "foreigners," "foreign workers," and particularly "illegal aliens" and used them as scapegoats to be blamed for America's economic crisis. Thus began waves of mass deportations of Mexicans, many of them U.S. citizens or U.S.-born children of immigrant parents who were sent back to Mexico. Based on one estimate, during the 1931–34 years alone between 300,000 to half-a-million Mexicans were deported back to Mexico (Acuña, 1981: 138). Another estimate puts the total number of Mexicans who were either deported or left the United States on their own volition during the 1930s as being between half-a-million and one million (Billington, 1956: 1). By 1931, the deportation campaign had spread nationwide, and there were reports of disproportionate number of Mexicans being deported from Illinois, Michigan, Indiana, and Ohio.

South of the border, the administration of President Lázaro Cárdenas encouraged return of immigrants home during the 1930s by intensifying land redistribution programs. As a result, "some 45 million acres of land were confiscated from hacienda owners and given to local communities for allocation to agrarian families, thus creating a new class of small farmers that ultimately came to control half of Mexico's arable land" (Massey et al., 2002: 34). By waiving customs regulations the Mexican government also allowed migrants to bring home personal belongings and occupational tools with them. But despite government's good intentions the returning

---

[7] For an account of anti-immigrant sentiments during this period see for example Martinez (2001: 29–33); Acuña (1981: 136–42); and in particular Rodriguez (2007: chapter 7).

migrants did not have adequate savings to even survive the trip back home; were not welcomed by their compatriots who considered them as Americanized (*agringados*); and most of the government-sponsored agricultural colonies "languished because of remote locations, poor soil, water shortages, inadequate startup funds, insufficient support mechanisms, and unfavorable markets for the crops" (Martinez, 2001: 31–32).

III. *The Bracero Era*

President Franklin Delano Roosevelt's aggressive government interventionist New Deal Program in the 1930s was an attempt to take the American economy out of depression through deficit spending and direct government investment in key sectors of the economy. The New Deal Program was followed by what is dubbed as *The Bracero Era* (1942–1965), when the American involvement in the WW II war efforts in 1941 set the stage for economic recovery particularly through utilization of industries for war-time production. With the enactment of military conscription and further involvement of the U.S. military the industrial and agricultural sectors faced serious labor shortages. Labor shortages were particularly acute in the agriculture sector, as between 1939 and 1943 the U.S. had lost 2.8 million farm workers (Foley, 1997: 205). While women were mobilized by an extensive government propaganda campaign (known as "Rosie the Riveter") to replace absent male workers in industries, Mexican workers once again became desirable to work in the fields so that there would be no disruptions in food supplies. Related to the latter group, in 1942 the Roosevelt administration negotiated an agreement with the Mexican government so that the United States government would recruit and transport male contract workers from Mexico for the duration of the war period and return them back home at the end of their contract period. Known officially as the *Mexican Farm Labor Supply Program* and informally as the *Bracero Program*, it recruited 168,000 braceros during 1942–45, or the first three years of the contract period (Massey et al., 2002: 36).[8] But persisting labor shortages forced the government to extend the Bracero Program on a yearly basis through the late 1940s. Pressed by growers in the Southwestern states in 1951 the Congress passed the Public Law 78, giving the program a permanent status basis which allowed its

---

[8] Derived from Spanish word *brazo* meaning "arm," the term "bracero" is loosely translated as "farmhand."

continuation for another thirteen years (Calavita, 1992). Although the Bracero Program was designed to be based on mutual agreement between the two governments, it was nonetheless controlled unilaterally by the U.S. government effectively denying Mexican counterparts any leverage to protect Mexican workers. Of note was the U.S. government's refusal to grant Mexican workers "guarantees concerning hours, conditions of housing, healthcare, sanitation facilities, transportation, a minimum wage of thirty cents per hour, and repatriation" (McCain, 1981: 49). Acuña (1981: 146) provides an explanation of this situation and the ways Mexican workers were exploited and abused both by the U.S. government and their employers north of the border:

> The U.S. government functioned as a labor contractor at taxpayers' expense, assuring nativists that workers would return to Mexico after they finished picking the crops. Growers did not have to worry about labor disputes. The *braceros* were used to glut the labor market to depress wages and were also used as strikebreakers. The U.S. government fully cooperated with growers, *allocating insufficient funds to the border patrol, insuring a constant supply of undocumented laborers* (emphasis mine).

Under pressure by growers, particularly in Texas, the U.S. government literally opened the border and allowed the influx of undocumented migrant workers into the Southwest while still managing the Bracero Program. As a result, the number of undocumented workers apprehended by immigration officials increased from 69,000 in 1945 to 883,000 in 1950 (Massey et al., 2002: 36). This was the most bizarre aspect of dealing with Mexican migrant workers, as their arrest was not intended to send them back to Mexico, but to satisfy the growers' demand in the Southwest who were desperate and eager to hire them. Calvita (cf. Massey et al., 2002: 37) explains the paradoxical nature of the U.S. immigration policy and the Bracero Program:

> At one point the INS was raiding agricultural fields in the southwestern United States, arresting undocumented workers, transporting them back to the border, and deporting them into the waiting arms of officials from the U.S. Department of Labor, who promptly processed them as braceros and re-transported them back to the very fields where they had been arrested in the first place!

Although less intense, the recession following the Korean War in the early 1950s and the public paranoia resulting from McCarthy era once again ignited the anti-foreigner and anti-immigrant sentiments. Faced with public pressure to control the border on one hand and the growers' demand for more migrant workers on the other, in 1954 the INS officially institutionalized its past practices during the Bracero Program by Launching "Operation Wetback." A derogatory term used for undocumented or "illegal alien" Mexican workers, "wetbacks" were Mexican immigrants who entered Texas from Mexico by crossing the Rio Grande River and allegedly got their backs wet by swimming or walking across. Using border patrol agents, the INS militarized immigration control along the U.S.-Mexico border, and conducted aggressive raids and dragnets that resulted in massive apprehension of undocumented border crossers. Thus during 1954 more than 1 million migrants were apprehended by the INS while at the same time numbers of visas issued for bracero workers more than doubled. As a consequence, during the 1955–1960 period between 400,000 and 450,000 braceros entered the United States. It appears that Operation Wetback to have been more a political tactic to silence nativist and anti-immigrant public than a serious program to control immigration, as the number of immigrants apprehended by INS border agents actually plummeted from its peak in 1954 to about 100,000/year during the 1955–1964 period (Massey et al., 2002: 37).

The Bracero Program was initiated by the U.S. government at a time when social and economic conditions in Mexico were also conducive for such an agreement between the two nations. First, between 1940 and 1950 there was a dramatic increase in Mexico's population, rising to over 25 million or a staggering increase of 30.8 percent in just a decade (Dirección General de Estadística, 1954: 34). But in the same period Mexico was confronted with the limitation of available cultivable land of about 7–10 percent instead of possible 20 percent, which resulted in a crop yield far below the population needs and exacerbated by a severe draught in northern Mexico in 1948 (Tannenbaum, 1950: 183). Second, Mexico was experiencing an economic crisis of its own with high unemployment rates and severe inflation which in turn encouraged both legal and illegal immigration into the United States particularly from rural provinces (Garcia, 1980: 5). Third, while dramatic wage differentials for Mexican laborers in Mexico and the United States were a strong incentive for Mexican workers to migrate north of the border, they also contributed to a decline in the purchasing power of the Mexican currency (Peso) that in turn contributed to inflation. For example, during the late 1940s and early 1950s agricultural laborers' wage in Mexico ranged from $0.38 to $0.69 per day, compared with $0.25 to $0.50 per hour in the United States (Tomasek, 1957: 199). However, as Garcia (1980: 58) has documented, during the 1950s and 1960s "revenues from tourism, border transactions, and bracero

remittances helped reduce Mexico's trade deficit with the United States."
For instance, from 1954 to 1964 bracero remittances comprised 1.37 percent of Mexico's national income on average (op. cit., table 6, p. 59).
The Bracero Program proved to be beneficial to Mexican economy, and
despite its discriminatory and abusive practices against migrant workers
the Mexican government allowed its continuation through 1964 in order
to help an ailing economy that was heavily dependent on that of its northern neighbor.

The Bracero Program was officially ended by the U.S. Department of
Labor in December 1964. It seems to be a consensus among historians
and scholars that the one factor in particular that contributed to the program's demise was the advent of the civil rights movement in the 1960s.
For one thing, during the civil rights era Mexican Americans emerged as
loyal allies to African Americans in a nationwide campaign to end racial
segregation and ensure equal rights for all Americans. Martin (2003)
argues that the 1960 CBS documentary *"Harvest of Shame"* convinced the
Kennedy administration that braceros were negatively affecting working conditions and wage levels of American farm workers. In fact, after
more than two decades of Bracero Program's operation a new generation
of Mexican migrant population had emerged that became more familiar
with the nuances of American labor market than those in their homeland (Massey et al., 2002: 42).[9] Furthermore, years of debate on the racist
"national-origins" immigration laws passed in the 1920s that discriminated
against immigrants originating in eastern and southern Europe, Africa,
and Asia led to the passage of the landmark immigration laws in 1965. In
the aftermath of the Bracero Program the new quota system eventually
allowed a per-country quota of 26,000 immigrants across the board that
included those from Mexico as well. Also, the increasing power and rise
to prominence of the United Farm Workers Union (UFW) transformed
utilization of agricultural migrant workers under the leadership of Cézar
Chavéz (Greigo, 1996).[10] Ending the Bracero Program and implement-
ing stringent rules in admitting legal immigrants after the passage of the
1965 immigration law led to introduction of labor-saving mechanization

---

[9] Broadcast on Thanksgiving day in 1960, this CBS News production presented a vivid
portrayal of the plight of Mexican migrant farm workers in the United States by document-
ing their harsh living conditions, endless travels to find jobs and work, low wages, and poor
opportunities for their children. See *Harvest of Shame 50 Years Later*, http://www.cbsnews
.com/2100-18563_162-7087361.html.

[10] For a detailed account of Chavez's role and influence in the Chicano movement and
organizing migrant farm workers see for example, Rodriguez (2007; chapter 8).

in the agricultural sector in the 1960s, effectively helping growers in certain sectors to reduce the number of farm workers by almost 90 percent (Martin, 2003).

By the end of the Bracero Program, the economies of the United States and Mexico had reached a level of integration and interdependence where they could no longer function independent of each other unless the former could find a substitute for Mexican migrant labor and the latter could create new jobs to accommodate its growing labor force. Despite Mexico's nationalization policies that were implemented in the 1930s, by 1960 the American-based corporations had a tight grip on Mexico's energy-related industries and utility companies (Acuña, 1981: 164–65). This increasing power and the role played by multinational corporations during the 1960s changed the dynamics of production and consumption both in the United States and dependent satellite economies such as Mexico. In addition, the newly independent Third World nations in the post-colonial era not only provided multinational corporations with new opportunities for investment, but also offered an abundant supply of cheap labor.

IV. *The Era of Off-shore Production (Maquiladora Industries)*

In order to strengthen Mexico's internal markets in 1961 the Mexican government implemented the *National Border Industrialization Program* (BIP) to attract foreign investors to the border region. Modeled after the production-sharing program in Portugal, the BIP treated each factory as a single "foreign processing zone," allowing the plant to import to Mexico all machinery, equipment and raw material duty free (Sandoval, 2003: 4–5). The BIP's objectives were to "create jobs, to attract capital, to introduce modern methods of manufacturing in assembling, processing and exporting, and to increase consumption of Mexican raw materials" (Acuña, 1981: 166). This ushered in the fourth period of utilization of Mexican labor, both in Mexico and the United States in the context of American colonial (imperial) interests that has continued to the present time.

The era of off-shore capitalist production in Mexico dates back to the early 1960s, when in 1964 the Johnson administration dismantled the Bracero Program which in turn plunged Mexico into a deep social and economic crisis. The crisis was particularly acute in the border regions that were plagued by high rates of poverty and unemployment. In response to Mexico's high unemployment levels and under the BIP guidelines, in the same year the *Maquiladora Program* was initiated whereby foreign corporations were encouraged to open satellite manufacturing plants in Mexico using low-cost, cheap Mexican workers.[11] Under BIP provisions foreign corporations were exempt from all corporate taxes, but had to re-export finished goods out of Mexico. The only tax paid by them was on the value added to the final product in Mexico, which was an insignificant part of product's total value (Buie, 2008: 3).

The Maquiladora Program was a "Godsend" gift for American corpora-tions at a time when they were facing restructuring amid falling profit rates, and increasing pressure by the labor unions demanding that they should be included in any future negotiations involving the recruitment and hiring of migrant workers. Now, American corporations were able to enjoy Mexican cheap labor south of the border without having to cope with unions and organized labor's costly demands (Kopinak, 1996: 8). The U.S. investment in Mexico during the 1960s was more than $1 billion, and multinational corporations such as Del Monte and General Foods con-trolled processing and marketing of a variety of food products in Mexico and many other central and south American countries.

The maquiladora industries have experienced several distinct periods of growth and decline in conjunction with the two nations' political econo-mies since their inception in the 1960s up to the time the border wall con-struction was approved by the Congress in 2005 (see Table 7.2).[12] During the first decade of their operation in the 1960s the maquiladoras did not pick their workers from the Braceros as the Mexican government expected and anticipated. Rather, in search of the cheapest labor the maquiladoras employed mostly young female workers, a common practice by corpo-rations operating in export-processing zones in other parts of the globe as well. The economic recession of the mid-1970s in the U.S. negatively affected the maquiladoras as they experienced a period of decline both in the work force and output. In order to encourage foreign investors to

---

[11] The origins of the term *maquiladora* goes back to colonial Mexico and the word *maquila*, which was the charge millers collected for processing grain (Sandoval, 2003: 4). In practice, the modern meaning of the word *maquiladora* became to be known as "its use to designate any partial activity in an industrial process, such as assembly or packing affected by a party other than the original manufacturer" (Angulo P., 1990: 139).

[12] My objective here is not to study the maquiladora industries in depth, as it is already done by other scholars and observers (see for example Kopinak, 1996; Fatemi, 1990; and GAO, 2003). Rather, I intend to demonstrate their significance for the incorporation of the U.S. and Mexican economies in general, and economic development of the U.S.-Mexican border region in particular.

sustain their operations the Mexican government further relaxed investment limit laws in order to allow up to 100 percent of maquiladora ownership by foreign investors compared with the previous limit of 49 percent;
and lowered standards and requirements for working conditions in the
maquiladora industries. Thus in synch with the economic recovery in the
late 1970s and early 1980s in the United States the maquiladoras also experienced a period of growth.

Table 7.2 Periodization of Maquiladoras' Growth and Decline and Total Work
Force, 1964–2006

Period	Major Developments	Growth/ Decline	Total # Employed
1965–1974	Initial installation & consolidation of maquiladoras – Maquiladoras did not hire Braceros – Preferred hiring young female workers	Initial growth period	75,974 (1974)
1974–1976	Economic recession in the U.S. & deregulation of maquiladoras – Labor militancy in Mexico discouraged U.S. investors – Exemption of maquiladoras from Mexican federal labor law requirements	Decline (32,000 jobs lost in 1974)	67,214 (1975)
1977–1982	Shift from import-substitution to export-led development in Mexico – Devaluation of the Peso	Growth (13% annual growth 1977–1980)	119,546 (1980)
1983–1989	Economic liberalization pressured by the International Monetary Fund (IMF) – Mexico's debt crisis – IMF's push for more capital-intensive maquiladoras with fewer workers – Continued devaluation of the Peso led to cheaper labor & increased # of maquiladora plants and workers Mexico joins GATT (1985) and eliminates protectionist policies and lowers tariffs	High growth (19.2% annual growth)	217,544 (1985)

Table 7.2 (*cont.*)

Period	Major Developments	Growth/ Decline	Total # Employed
1990–1994	Deceleration and Consolidation – Strong Peso – Mexico signs a free trade agreement with Chile (1992) – Mexico joins the Asia-Pacific Economic Cooperation (1993) – Mexico finalizes NAFTA agreement with the U.S. & Canada (1994) – Devaluation of the Peso by 60% (December 1994)	Decline and then gradual growth (6.3% annual growth rate)	424,652 (1990)
1995–2000	Post-NAFTA growth – Expansion of maquiladora operations – Maquiladoras become Mexico's top foreign exchange generator	Steady Growth (11.0% annual growth rate for 1995–2001 period)	822,036 (1997) 1,347,803 (2000)
2001–2004	The China factor – China is admitted to the World Trade Organization (WTO) (2001) – China becomes the major locale for outsourcing and offshore production	Decline An overall 28% decrease in work force	800,291 (Oct. 2002)
2005–2006	Steady growth and comeback – Maquiladoras boost Mexico's manufacturing output	Growth 14% increase in Maquiladoras output	1,170,962 (Dec. 2006)

Source: Table constructed based on information in Kopinak (1996: 7–12), Cañas & Coronado (2002), GAO (2003: 69–70), and Gonzalez and Fernandez (2003: 59).

The joint efforts by the U.S. and Mexican governments were a boost to the maquiladoras, which experienced an unusually high annual growth rate of almost 20 percent during the 1983–89 period. The most significant event during this period was the Mexican government's decision in 1985 to join the General Agreement on Tariffs and Trade (GATT) which effectively ended almost half-a-century of government protection of domestic industries and ushered in the era of imposed neo-liberal policies on the

Mexican economy.[13] Despite fierce opposition by Mexican industrialists and trade unions, under the GATT terms the government had to lower tariffs on imported goods, thus opening the Mexican market to cheaper products manufactured elsewhere (The Age, 1985: 29). At the same time the Mexican Peso continued to lose its value while the International Monetary Fund (IMF) put pressure on the Mexican government to vie for economic liberalization. Although at a slower pace, in the early 1990s the maquiladoras continued to grow due to a stronger peso. But the finalization of the North American Free Trade Agreement (NAFTA) with the U.S. and Canada in 1994 and the Mexican government's decision to once again devalue the Peso by more than 60 percent gave a boost to the maquiladoras. By 2001 the maquiladora industries became the top foreign exchange generator surpassing the oil industry, as its products comprised about 50 percent of total exports (Cañas and Coronado, 2002: 33).[14]

The two nations' economies were integrated to the extent that their cyclical market fluctuations seemed to have the same tempo. For instance for more than two decades during the 1980–2002 period the annual growth rates of the U.S. Gross Domestic Product (GDP) and employment in Mexico's maquiladora industries have been almost identical (see Figure 7.2). More specifically, as Buie (2008: 4–5) has documented, when in 2001 the U.S. economy began to slip into a severe recession that crippled the manufacturing sector, Mexico's counterpart also "slid into a sympathetic downturn as well" (see Figure 7.3). This period was also coincided with China's membership in the World Trade Organization (WTO) and subsequent emergence as the new provider of low-cost, labor-intensive manufacturing goods for global markets. As a consequence, between 2001 and 2004 the number of maquiladora plants fell by 28 percent and their labor force also shrank by 25 percent (ibid.).[15] Since more than 75 percent of all maquiladora workers and employees operated in the five Mexican border region states—Baja California, Sonora, Chihuahua, Coahuila, and

---

[13] Imposition of neoliberal economic policies in developing countries usually requires putting limits on subsidies, removing fixed exchange rates, opening up domestic markets to trade and limiting protectionist measures, and privatizing state-owned businesses and deregulating the economy.

[14] According to Canas and Coronado (ibid., Figure 7.3), during the last two decades of the 20th century the top four foreign exchange generators of Mexico were the maquiladoras, oil industries, remittances from Mexican workers in the U.S., and tourism, respectively.

[15] By the end of 2006 there were 2,062 maquiladoras along the U.S.-Mexico border employing 905, 097 workers.

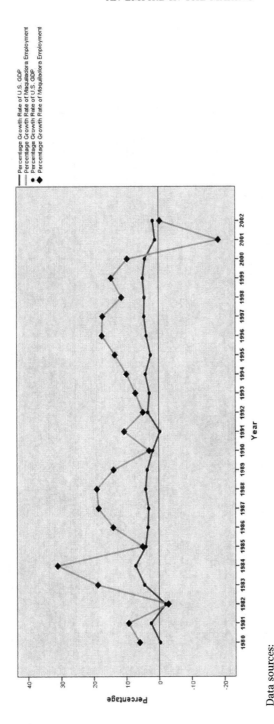

Data sources:

For U.S. GDP Annual Growth Rate (%): the World Bank, http://data.worldbank.org/indicator/NY.GDP.MKTP.KD.ZG?page=2

For Maquiladora employment rates:

1980–1990 data: http://www.nber.org/papers/w5400.reftxt, Table 4

1991–2002 data: Mendoza, Jorge Eduardo. 2009. *Developing the U.S.-Mexico Region for a Prosperous and Secure Relationship*, p. 15, http://www.bakerinstitute.org/publications/LAI-pub-BorderSecMendoza-041509.pdf

Figure 7.2 Annual Growth Rates of U.S. Gross Domestic Product and Maquiladora Employment, 1982–2002 (chart by author).

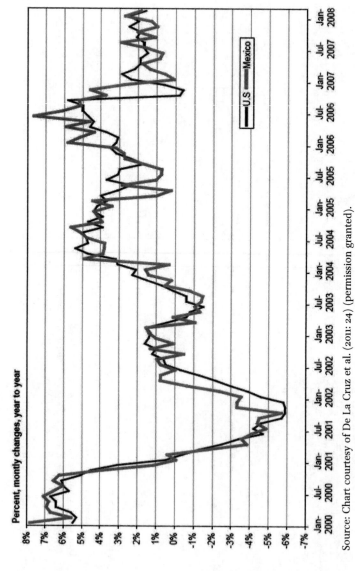

Source: Chart courtesy of De La Cruz et al. (2011: 24) (permission granted).

Figure 7.3 Synchronization of Mexico's industrial production with that of the United States: quarterly changes in industrial production, 2000–2008.

Tamaulipas, any changes in employment inevitably affected the intensity of cross-border migration as well (GAO, 2003: 11; Comité Fronterizo de Obrera, 2007).

Maquiladoras, NAFTA, and the Evolution of Twin Cities along the U.S.-Mexico Border

Mexico shares 1,969 miles (3,169 km) of border with its northern neighbor that traverses four southwestern U.S. states and six northern states in Mexico. It extends from the twin cities of Matamoros, Tamaulipas and Brownsville, Texas in the east where the Rio Bravo (Rio Grande in U.S. lexicon) empties in the Gulf of Mexico; and continues westward to Tijuana, Baja California, and San Diego, California by the Pacific Ocean. The border region expands 62 miles (100 km) on either side of the international boundary and contains fourteen twin cities which by 2015 its projected population will surpass fifteen million (*State of the Border Region 2010*, 2011).

To Spanish colonialists the vast expanses of hot and arid Sonoran and Chihuahuan deserts that are now part of the border region had little value in terms of prospects for an acceptable return for their colonial investments, thus they labeled the region "el despoblado," or the uninhabited place (Kaye, 1994: 79). By 1850 some of the original Spanish colonial settlements like San Diego in present-time California, el Paso del Norte in the Mexican province of Chihuahua (present-day Ciudad Juarez), and Laredo in the state of Texas were sizeable border towns (Martinez, 2001: 6). Other urban centers evolved around border military outposts and forts, such as Brownsville in Texas. With finalization of the U.S.-Mexico border in the early 1850s paired cities on either side of the border gradually evolved. In some instances the city north of the border has maintained its original name while the twin sister city south of the border has added the adjective "new," such as Laredo (Texas) and Nuevo Laredo (Tamaulipas). The twin cities of Nogales/Nogales in Arizona and Sonora have maintained their unity at least in name, and some others have chosen a composite name that signifies the states/countries they are located in and share border with, such as Calexico in California and Mexicali in Baja California, Mexico (Massey et al., 2002: 25) (see Figure 7.4).

Most border cities on the Mexico side are home to hundreds of maquiladora industries. In theory the maquiladoras were originally conceptualized as "twin plants" comprised of two factories, each on one side of

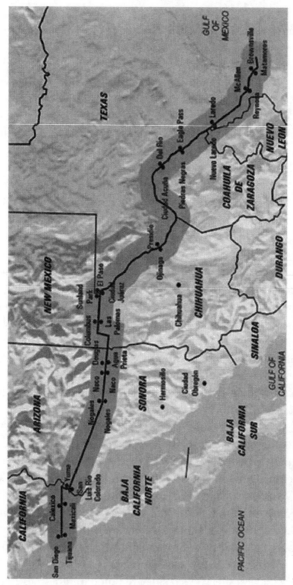

http://www.epa.gov/region9/annualreport/07/images/mexico-us-border.jpg
U.S. Government Archives (USA.GOV).

Figure 7.4 Map of U.S.-Mexico Border States and Twin Sister Cities.

the U.S.-Mexico border. According to this scheme the main product components would be produced in capital-intensive plants on the U.S. side,
which would then be shipped to the labor-intensive maquiladora plants
on the Mexican side for final assembly. But in practice the capital-intensive plants on the American side never materialized and instead corporate management offices and distribution warehouses were located on the
U.S. side (Sklair, 1989: 48). Also, border twin cities' did not evolve based on
an even pattern of urban growth; and with the exception of Tijuana, cities on the Mexican side of the border have a larger population than their
U.S. counterparts (Herzog, 1990: 48–49; Geo-Mexico, 2010). In their historical data analysis of the growth rates for major twin cities in the border
region Pick, Viswanathan and Hettrick (2001: 570) demonstrate that since
1930 the majority of cities on the Mexican side have had annual growth
rates almost double those of their twin sister cities on the U.S. side
(see Table 7.3).

In his study of the border region's growth Kaye (1994: 79–80) identifies several factors that have contributed to this lop-sided uneven urban
development—the Mexican government's "apprehension of further U.S.
expansion" in the southwest in the aftermath the former's defeat in 1848;
sustained high fertility rates throughout Mexico; and in the last three
decades implementation of the North American Free Trade Agreement
((NAFTA) and the growth of the maquiladora industries. Arguably, the
border twin cities' phenomenal growth can be mainly attributed to the
maquiladora industries. For instance, "the number of workers in border
maquiladoras increased by 75% between 1994 and 1998 as compared to
only 14% in the period 1989–1993 (Clement et al., 1999: 58).

In another study Dillman (1983) examines the border region's urban
growth patterns and demonstrates that while the U.S. side has had a
higher rate of poverty than the rest of the country, the Mexican border
region has been "better off than Mexico as a whole" (cf. Pick, Viswanathan
and Hettrick, 2001: 570). Thus on one hand Mexico's border region has
served as a magnet for domestic in-migration largely because of employment opportunities offered by the maquiladora industries; and a "holding
zone for migration into the U.S." on the other (ibid., p. 571). The built-up
urban areas of these twin cities also have a distinct spatial feature—the
cities south of the border tend to gravitate toward their counterparts on
the American side while the latter's pattern of urban growth indicate a
certain degree of reluctance to expand south-bound. Thus in many border
areas Mexican cities have expanded all the way to the politically demarcated international boundaries and in fact they tend to "hug" the border,

Table 7.3 Population of U.S.-Mexico Border Twin Cities, 1930–2020 (projected)

Twin Cities	1930	1950	1970	1990	2020	Annual Growth Rate, 1930–2020 (projected)
Matamoros, Tamaulipas	9,733	45,846	140,660	303,295	736,891	4.8
Cameron-Brownsville, Texas	77,540	125,170	140,368	260,120	554,307	2.2
Reynosa, Tamaulipas	4,840	34,087	140,480	282,666	658,403	5.5
Hidalgo-McAllen, Texas	77,004	106,446	181,535	383,545	1,050,166	2.9
Nuevo Laredo, Tamaulipas	21,636	57,668	152,325	219,465	633,770	3.8
Laredo-Webb, Texas	42,128	56,141	72,859	133,239	407,110	2.5
Piedra Negras, Coahuila	15,878	27,581	40,885	98,184	231,580	3.0
Eagle Pass (Maverick), Texas	6,120	12,292	18,093	36,378	94,495	3.0
Ciudad Juarez, Chihuahua	39,699	122,566	414,908	798,500	2,395,024	4.6
El Paso, Texas	131,597	194,968	359,291	591,610	1,103,065	2.4
Nogales, Sonora	14,061	24,478	53,119	107,937	299,598	3.4
Nogales (Santa Cruz), Arizona		6,153	8,946	29,676	71,796	3.5[*]
Mexicali, Baja California	14,842	65,749	276,167	601,938	1,232,953	4.9
Calexico (imperial Co.) CA	60,903	62,975	74,942	109,303	327,790	1.9
Tijuana, Baja California	8,384	59,952	341,067	747,379	2,676,672	6.4
San Diego, California	209,659	334,387	696,769	2,498,106	3,294,769	3.1

[*]Averaged for the 1950-2020 period.
Source: Table constructed based on information in Pick, Viswanathan and Hettrick (2001: 570, Table 2).

while the American cities have an inclination to keep a distance from border area with either farmlands or uninhabited territories that serve as a natural buffer or security zone (see Photos 7.1–7.3). This spatial northward gravitation of Mexico's urban built environment speaks volumes about the social psychology of a long, unresolved history of Mexican-U.S. relations; the former still considers the territories north of the border part of Mexican territory, while the latter has to guard the annexed colonial territories and keep the "barbarians" at an arm's length.

There is a historical precedent for this uniquely shaped socio-spatial geography. As Nevins (2002: 103) points out, the highly porous nature of the U.S.-Mexico international boundaries up until the late 20th century, as well as the physical and social isolation of border region from centers of population both in the north and the south have contributed to formation of similarly porous racial, ethnic and national boundaries. In addition, the cultural/linguistic, geographic, economic, and architectural characteristics of southwestern United States were not much different from those of the Mexican territories south of the border. Thus as Grebler (1966: 10–11) points out, in their northward movement Mexican immigrants were comforted by the fact that "the distinction between internal and international migration was blurred by climatic and other similarities of the areas on both sides of the border." Gordon (1999: 59) describes the people who resided along the U.S.-Mexico border in the early 1900s as "the Mexican-origin people," a population with a distinct shared identity:

> They lived in a border culture (and many of them in twin towns that straddled the border, like Douglas and Aqua Prieta, Bisbee and Naco, El Paso and Ciudad Juarez); they were not so much bi-national as they were border people, as if border itself were their nationality.

The Border is No Longer: Long Live the Border!

I began this chapter with a brief account of the newly constructed and highly militarized wall/fence along the U.S.-Mexico border, but argued that an appreciation of the rationale for its construction is rooted in the two nations' long and troubled history of political and economic relations mainly in the context of American colonial-imperial interests. I have also tried to demonstrate that by the end of the 20th century the two nations' political economies have become completely interdependent if not fully integrated. I conclude by providing a conceptual framework to make the case that the U.S.-Mexican border line does not demarcate each nation's

Photo 7.1 Border Wall separating Nogales, Arizona on the U.S. side (left) from Nogales, Sonora on the Mexican side (right), 2009 (photo by author).

Photos 7.2 & 7.3 Two sides of the Wall: border Wall and security road in Calexico, California (top photo) and a busy street next to the wall in Mexicali, Baja California on the Mexican side across from Calexico (bottom photo), 2009 (photos by author).

territorial "edge," but rather it now sits right in the midst of two unified political economies and populations.

From a political geography perspective Taylor (1995: 13) envisions trans-state relations as being based on the convergence of two trends: formation of centers of capital control and flow on one hand and creation of a network of global flows of goods and workers on the other—the former transcends state economies while the latter disregards political boundaries. Related to the latter trend the shared histories of el Norte and Mexico south of the border takes Mexican immigrants one step further, and as Rodriguez (1996: 23) argues they enter the United States within a historically constructed "transnational structure" as if "the border did not exist." The numbers are staggering: by 2008 there were 11.8 million Mexican immigrants in the United States, with over half residing without proper documentation.[16] Although southwest border region states are still a magnet for Mexican immigrants, in mapping Mexican immigration patterns since the 1990s Terrazas (2010) observes the emergence of a new pattern:

> Mexican immigrants mainly settle in traditional destination states like California and Texas, which combined are home to well over half of this group. But over the last two decades, the foreign born from Mexico, like other immigrant groups, have begun moving to 'nontraditional' settlement areas. These include states in the South, such as Georgia and North Carolina, as well as Midwestern states such as Nebraska and Ohio.

In addition, each year millions of Mexican citizens enter the United States legally through border crossings in the twin city areas in order to shop, work or visit relatives on the American side of the border region. This is facilitated by the possession of a Border Crossing Card (BCC) that is issued by the U.S. Department of State to Mexican citizens with a valid passport (see Photos 7.4–7.5 and Figure 7.5).[17] Legal Mexican border crossers comprise the majority of those who enter into the American border regions. For instance, in 2006 out of 179 million non-immigrant admissions 148 million were Mexicans (Pew Hispanic Center, 2006). Many "Mexican" residents of the border cities on the Mexican side are also U.S. citizens

---

[16] See Terrazas (2010). The share of foreign born represented by Mexican immigrants almost doubled from 15.6 percent in 1980 to 30.1 percent in 2008 (ibid.).

[17] A Border Crossing Card (BCC) is issued to Mexican citizens holding a valid passport that allows Mexicans to enter the U.S. border region (25 miles deep in California, New Mexico and Texas, and 70 miles deep into Arizona). The BCCs are valid for ten years, allowing the visitors to enter the U.S. border region to conduct business or for pleasure for a stay up to six months. See the U.S. Department of State Foreign Affairs Manual, volume 9-Visas, http://www.state.gov/documents/organization/87208.pdf.

Photo 7.4 Abandoned shopping carts by Mexican day-shoppers who hold Border Crossing Cards (BCCs) in San Luis, Arizona on the U.S. side of the border. Vehicular and pedestrian border entrance to San Luis Rio Colorado, Sonora on the Mexican side is in the background. (photo by author, 2009).

Photo 7.5 Highly fortified entrance to U.S. Border Customs facility on the Mexican side of the border in Mexicali, Baja California. BCC-holding day-shoppers are returning to Mexico from Calexico, California (right), while other Mexican border crossers (on the left) are waiting in line to go through security check before entering the United States (photo by author, 2009).

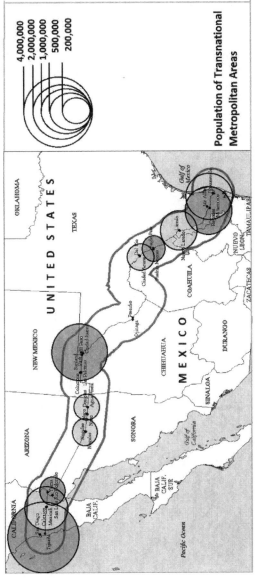

Source for population data: Geo-Mexico (2010), http://geo-mexico.com/?p=4815
Source for original background map: US Government Archives-USA.GOV
http://www.mchb.hrsa.gov/mchirc/dataspeak/events/july_08/materials/notzon_files/ images/image2.png

Figure 7.5 Combined Trans-border Metropolitan Population of Major Twin Cities along the U.S.-Mexican Border Region, 2010. (map by author).

either by birth or through marriage and parental affiliation (Spener and Staudt, 1998: 238). Even if we only focus on the population that resides in the U.S.-Mexican border region, we are dealing with a geographic zone with its own regional political economy that in 2006 had a population of about 12 million, and is projected to double by 2025 (Migration Information Source, 2006) (see Figure 7.5). As neighbors the two nations share almost 2,000 miles of border with each other, but now it begs the question of whether the border is still a valid political boundary separating two independent national entities.

CHAPTER EIGHT

THE GREAT OFFENSIVE WALL OF MEXICO: BORDER BLUES

The U.S.-Mexico border was finalized in 1853 when the United States acquired the southern portion of present-day Arizona and New Mexico for $10 million through the Gadsden Purchase in order to secure a rail route to California (Nevins, 2002: 21; Garcia, 2002: 10). Except for the Rio Grande that provides a natural boundary between the two nations a casual observation of satellite-generated maps of the U.S.-Mexico border reveals the superficial manner in which the remaining political boundaries have been drawn to divide the two territories by a straight line, even on a stretch of rugged mountains along Mexico's border with Arizona. This is typical of all territories that have been subjected to colonial land grabs and expansion without regard to the social, ethnic-cultural and environmental unity and integrity of colonized areas.

There is little documentation on the nature and extent of cross-border population movement during the second half of 19th century. For instance, in the absence of any border control no records were kept from 1886 to 1893 (Grebler, 1990: 19). In fact, as Massey et al. (2002: 25) explain, "One cannot speak of 'international migration' between Mexico and the United States until the twentieth century." During the last century, up until the 1970s the U.S. immigration policy was mostly based on internal cycles of supply and demand for immigrants and migrant workers, particularly the undocumented, and less on controlling the borders to prevent the influx of immigrants. Therefore, the government pursued a rather passive policy of post-migration apprehension of some immigrants who crossed the border without proper documentation.[1]

The idea of stopping northward migration along the U.S.-Mexico border by sealing the border and protecting it through military means gained some currency in the post-WWII years. As early as the 1950s there were ideas floating around to *deter* illegal immigration along the U.S.-Mexican border but they were not materialized. This was a new approach, and a

---

[1] As I mentioned in the previous chapter the apprehended border-crossers were then deported to Mexico with the expectation that most will shortly go through the same cycle again.

radical departure from the hitherto policy of apprehension of border crossers. For instance, in 1953 Lieutenant General Joseph Swing, an INS commissioner, a West Point classmate of president Dwight Eisenhower, and
known as a "professional, long-time Mexican hater" requested $10 million
to erect a "150-mile-long fence to keep Mexicans out" (Acuña, 1981: 156).
But the first serious attempt by the U.S. government to prevent immigration through deterrence along the southern border was made in the
1970s when the border security was strengthened by building fences in
key urban areas. Dubbed as the "Tortilla Curtain," the government constructed flimsy corrugated steel walls to reinforce the existing border barriers along the 13-mile-long stretch in the San Diego sector as well as the
Arizona-Sonora border (Martinez, 2001: 42). But despite this effort, as late
as the early 1990s the U.S.-Mexico border was a porous region with minimal level of control: while Rio Grande defined almost half of the border
on the east, most of the rest was only marked by signs at formal border
crossings. Nevins (2002: 3) provides a vivid observation of the situation in
the San Diego-Tijuana border region:

> What existed in terms of a boundary fence had gaping holes. Large crowds
> of migrants and smugglers gathered each afternoon along the boundary
> waiting to cross at nightfall into the United States extra-legally. "Banzai
> runs"—when groups of unauthorized immigrants would run on the high-
> way through the official ports of entry into the United States—were also
> common (see Photo 8.1).

Later in 1991, the *Office of National Policy* commissioned *Sandia National
Laboratories* (SNL), a subsidiary of Lockheed Martin Corporation and a
governmental laboratory for the *National Nuclear Security Administration*
to study more effective ways to mainly stop the flow of illegal drugs, but
also undocumented migrant workers from Mexico to the United States
(GAO, 1994: 11–12). In fact, as outlined on SNL's web site, the company's
main mission is to "develop technologies to sustain, modernize, and protect our nuclear arsenal, prevent the spread of weapons of mass destruction, defend against terrorism, protect our national infrastructure, ensure
stable energy and water supplies, and provide capabilities to our armed
forces" (Sandia National Laboratories, 2009). Clearly, SNL is part of the
military-industrial complex and its mission statement has no reference to
immigration-related issues to qualify it for a border immigration-control
project. So what was changing in the 1990s that prompted the U.S. government to make a radical policy shift in its management of trans-border
migration mainly along the U.S.-Mexican border?

San Diego, U.S. Tijuana, Mexico

Source: Border Patrol Archives, cf. GAO (1994: 9).

Photo 8.1 Ineffective Fencing in the San Diego-Tijuana Sector in the
Early 1990s.

In the previous chapter I made the case that the maquiladora industries facilitated the incorporation of Mexican and American economies by mainly utilizing Mexican labor south of the U.S.-Mexican border. There is no question that concentration of large number of Mexican maquiladora workers and their families south of the U.S. border has had periodic impact on cross-border migration particularly during recessionary periods. However, as I explain in the following pages it was the trans-border treaty of the North American Free Trade Agreement (NAFTA) that became instrumental in changing the dynamics of migration between Mexico and the United States, unleashing an uncontrollable north-bound flow of migrant workers.

Signed in 1993 by Mexico, the United States, and Canada and implemented in early 1994 NAFTA was intended to open the doors for free trade between the three countries, particularly related to import and export of agricultural products (Zahniser, 2007). The Clinton administration also promoted the idea that NAFTA will be "the ultimate cure for illegal immigration of Mexican citizens to the U.S." (Serrano, 2008: 5). Supporters of NAFTA have argued that its implementation has generated positive growth in Mexico, evidenced for example by an annual average increase of her Gross domestic Product (GDP) during the 1994–2001 period; access to the technology and know-how of her northern neighbors; and an increased demand for both skilled and unskilled Mexican labor in the region. Later, on the 10th anniversary of NAFTA's implementation a sympathetic observer concluded that the agreement has "delivered on its principal promise of creating trade," as between 1994 and 2004 the two-way commerce between the U.S. and Mexico roughly tripled, from $81 billion to $232 billion, respectively (Griswold, 2004). As a neo-liberal, Griswold considered Mexico's break with its past practices of running a centralized, government controlled economy as a positive step. Similar arguments were also made by the U.S. State Department's assistant secretary of state for economic and business affairs, who considered NAFTA as the main conduit for integration of the three North American nations' markets (U.S. Dept. of State, 2004). But analogous to the economic outcomes of the *Maquiladora* Program, market integration was not a two-way street. Rather, it was a program whose policies and regulations forced the Mexican economy to become increasingly integrated with and dependent to that of the United States. A major factor was NAFTA's effects on lowering trade barriers and liberalizing "cross-border movement of goods, capital, raw materials, information, and services" but not movement of labor (Massey, 2005: 5). This was manifested by increasing militarization of the border region and eventual erection and fortification of the fence/ wall along the southern border. Massey (ibid.) points to the fact that by 2002 "the Border Patrol was the largest arms-bearing branch of the U.S. government next to the military itself." Thus the border wall was erected in synch with NAFTA's implementation in order to control, and not stop, the flow of migrant labor.

Contrary to the claims made by neoliberal supporters of NAFTA, its implementation negatively affected the Mexican economy at least in three significant ways. First, despite claims by U.S. officials and heightened expectations that NAFTA policies will curb Mexican immigration to the United States, both legal and illegal, a survey of available data by Passel and Cohn (2009: 12) indicates the opposite. For instance, the number of Mexican-born individuals entering the United States doubled between 2000 and 2009, from 3.7 to 7.4 million, respectively.

Second, in 1993 Mexico's secretary of agriculture predicted that NAFTA's regulations would detach 13 million farmers from their lands. This proved to be prophetic, as NAFTA policies effectively undermined subsistence farming for domestic consumption in Mexico and gradually replaced it with export-oriented commercial and mechanized farming, turning many peasants into day-laborers. This situation was exacerbated by the U.S. government's subsidies particularly to American corn producers who were then able to export their excess produce to Mexico at a much lower price than the corn produced by Mexican farmers (Schepers, 2002). Mexican dairy and meat producers also fell victim to NAFTA's open-door trade policies, and by 2002 Mexico replaced Japan as the main importer of the American beef products and at the same time ranked third among the importers of poultry products from the United States (Ferriss, 2003). Mexican farmers and activists have continued to oppose NAFTA. In early 2008 about 200,000 protesters marched in downtown Mexico City demanding the government to renegotiate this discriminatory aspect of NAFTA with the northern neighbors. The following proclamation, signed by the rally organizers, clearly delineates NAFTA's destructive effects on Mexico's rural and urban economy:

> The ongoing neo-liberal model only increases inequality, poverty, and unemployment for the marginalized sectors of the urban and rural populations, which are the majority in this country. The deterioration of the environment and the handing over of our natural resources to foreign investors only aggravates our social problems, and today it is time for us to stop all that (Rodriguez, 2008).

Third, the pursuit of neo-liberal policies of privatization of Mexican economy and implementation of NAFTA led to the displacement of peasants from rural areas who headed to the cities and northern border maquiladoras and beyond in search of employment; as well as layoffs in the Mexican manufacturing sector that had lost its competitive edge to the maquiladoras in attracting foreign capital and investment. Based on one estimate close to 3 million jobs, mostly in the agricultural sector were lost during the 1990–2000 decade (Ferris, 2003). A former Mexican foreign minister once commented that NAFTA was "an agreement for the rich and powerful in the United States, Mexico, and Canada, an agreement effectively excluding ordinary people in all three societies" (cf. Faux, Salas, and Scott, 2006). For instance, according to the International Monetary Fund (IMF) data the total foreign direct investment in Mexico for the ten-year period prior to implementation of NAFTA (1983–1993) amounted to about $30 billion, while it had a 420% increase for the 1994–2004 period ($156 billion). So it is no surprise that in spite of a considerable increase in foreign investment in post-NAFTA Mexico, the country still faced massive layoffs of its work force.

Faux, Salas and Scott (ibid.) also argue that since NAFTA rules were meant to "protect the interests of large corporate investors" at the expense of "workers' rights, environmental protections, and democratic accountability"; it is no surprise that its impact has been less than positive for American workers. For instance, using the Bureau of Labor statistics and census data they have documented that between 1993 and 2004 U.S. exports accounted for 941,459 jobs while 1,956,750 jobs were "displaced" due to imports (mostly from Mexico); leading to a net job loss of 1,015,290 in the United States. What is more, except for North and South Dakota, Montana, Oregon, Wyoming, Alaska and Hawaii that did not experience high levels of job loss, all other states were hit hard by NAFTA policies. Even the four Southwestern states bordering Mexico that were partners with the maquiladora industries also experienced job losses, with California and Texas particularly being hit the hardest. Bybee and Winter (2006) sum up NAFTA's political and economic objectives, which were definitely not aimed at curbing or completely stopping the flow of illegal immigration between Mexico and the United States:

> NAFTA failed to curb illegal immigration precisely because it was never designed as a genuine development program crafted to promote rising living standards, health care, environmental cleanup, and worker rights in Mexico. The wholesale surge of Mexicans across the border dramatically illustrates that NAFTA was no attempt at a broad uplift of living conditions

and democracy in Mexico, but a formula for government-sanctioned corporate plunder benefiting elites on both sides of the border. *NAFTA essentially
annexed Mexico as a low-wage industrial suburb of the U.S. and opened Mexican markets to heavily-subsidized U.S. agribusiness products, blowing away
local producers* (emphasis mine).

Job losses in the U.S. have been primarily concentrated in the manufacturing sector (Scott, 2003), but as I discussed in preceding sections the agriculture sector has historically been dealing with an acute shortage of farm
laborers particularly at the lower end of skills and pay scale. Related to the
latter sector, Mexican migrant farm workers have effectively filled the vac-
uum, and according to the U.S. Department of Labor statistics (2005: 17)
in the 2000–2001 fiscal year Mexican-born workers comprised 73 percent
of the U.S. agricultural work force. Of those, however, 53 percent were
not authorized to work in the U.S., making the employment of migrant
laborers both profitable and beneficial for both employers and the government for two reasons. First, migrant workers can be paid below the minimum wage if undocumented thus allowing employers to get around labor
laws. Second, undocumented migrant workers pay taxes by consuming
U.S. goods and services yet are denied payment of unemployment insur-
ance and other related benefits, a significant saving for the U.S. treasury
(op. cit.: 54–55). Since the number of immigrants from rural Mexico to
the United States has had a sharp increase from 1994 onward (the year of
NAFTA's implementation), it is hard to assume the link between the two
to be merely a coincident.

Erecting the Offensive Barrier, or 'The Great Wall of Mexico"

In his foreword to Joseph Nevins' book *Operation Gate Keeper: The Rise of
"Illegal Alien" and the Making of the U.S.-Mexico Boundary* Michael Davis
makes an interesting analogy between a border wall and a dam:

> The border is often compared to a dam: defending the fat suburbs of the
> American dream from a deluge of Third World misery. This, of course, mis-
> understands the role of a dam, which is not to prevent the flow of water
> but to control and ration its supply. To the despair of pundits on both sides,
> who would prefer to see a more orderly system of gastarbeiter migration
> strictly controlled by economic demand, the border is a heavy investment
> in the laws of chaos: the Brownian motion of hundreds of thousands of job-
> and-dignity seekers modulated by nocturnal pursuit and detention camps.
> *Realists, of course, understand that a cheap labor flux without the necessary
> quotient of fear and uncertainty imposed by illegality might cease to be cheap
> labor* (2002: x) (emphasis mine).

For the first time in the U.S.-Mexican migration history in the 1990s border crossing became a criminal act to the extent that it was put in the same category of criminality with illegal drugs smuggling and the necessity of coping with it by military means. Not surprisingly this change of strategy coincided with the implementation of NAFTA, and increasing dependence of Mexico's economy and labor market to that of the United States. From this point on there appears to be a major shift in the U.S. government's policy toward immigration from that of "apprehension" to "deterrence," a clear indication of change in strategy from being defensive to waging an offensive against illegal immigration in an almost military fashion (see Table 8.1). The first in a series of such efforts was *Operation Blockade*, initiated and launched by Silvestre Reyes, a Texan Border Patrol Chief who in 1993 doubled the number of border agents along a twenty-mile section of the boundary in an effort to curb the influx of "illegals" in the El Paso-Ciudad Juarez twin city area in Texas.[2] Reportedly, Reyes' strategy proved to be highly effective:

> The strategy represented a radical departure from the prior Border Patrol strategy of pursuing and apprehending unauthorized immigrants after they had crossed the boundary into El Paso area. Almost immediately, Blockade had a significant effect in deterring unauthorized crossings into El Paso; Border Patrol apprehensions fell dramatically. Within one week, in what had been the Border Patrol's second busiest sector (after San Diego), apprehensions fell from a daily average of about 800 per day to about 150 per day (Nevins, 2002: 90).

Operation Blockade was highly effective in reducing the number of unauthorized border crossings into the City of El Paso. But instead of preventing unauthorized entries it forced border crossers to enter the American side from the western end of the blockade area. Furthermore, Spener and Staudt (1998: 235) also find the timing of *Operation Blockade*'s implementation and final negotiation rounds for NAFTA's inauguration more than a coincident:

> That the creation of the free trade area and the blockade took place almost simultaneously constituted an irony that was not missed by human rights activists concerned with the treatment of Mexican migrants: wasn't it a contradiction—and an unjust one at that—to be opening the border to the movement of goods and services but not to people? Didn't economic integration also imply important social integration? Or, as some left activists

---

[2] *Operation Blockade* was later renamed *'Operation Hold-the-Line,'* as "the former proved to be quite offensive to the Mexican government" (Nevins, 2002: 90).

Table 8.1. The Offensive Border Strategy Timeline (*"Prevention Through Deterrence"*), 1993–Present

Operation Name/ Plan	Year	Location	Sponsor	Means
Operation Blockade (later renamed as Operation Hold-the-Line)	1993	El Paso, Texas	Silvestre Reyes, Border Patrol Chief	– Doubled the # of border agents in the El Paso-Ciudad Juarez area
Operation Gate Keeper	1994	San Diego (San Ysidro), CA	Immigration & Naturalization Service (INS) (Clinton admin.)	– More fencing – Increased Border Patrol agents – lighting and surveillance technology
Immigration law enforcement plan	1994	Along the border	Clinton administration	– Increased border security – Deporting criminal aliens – Greater enforcement in the work place
The illegal immigration & immigrant Responsibility Act	1996	Along the border	Congress	– Hiring more patrol agents – Mandating jail time for criminal aliens – Construction of two additional layers of fencing in San Diego – Border states could deputize police forces to uphold immigration laws
House Bill 4437	2003	Along the border	Congress	– called for 700 miles of wall @ an estimated cost of $2.2 billion – made illegal crossing into the U.S. a felony
The Intelligence Reform and Terrorism Prevention Act	2004	Along the border	Bush admin. & Department of Homeland Security (DHS)	– Adding 10,000 new border agents by 2010

Table 8.1 (*cont.*)

Operation Name/ Plan	Year	Location	Sponsor	Means
The Secure Fence Act	2006– present	Along the border	Bush and Obama administrations, the DHS and Justice Department	– building 700 miles of border fencing – Allocating 60+ prosecutors to border districts to prosecute border crimes

Source: Table constructed based on information from Massey et al. (2002: 94–95) and Becker (2008).

> were quick to point out, *wasn't all this open border talk just an ideological veil being lowered over the eyes of the working classes on both sides—a border open to capital but close to workers?* (emphasis mine).

Following a highly favorable publicity of Operation Blockade's success, anti-immigrant politicians in California pushed for implementation of a similar strategy along San Diego-Tijuana boundary. Based on 2008 data the San Ysidro (San Diego)-Tijuana port of entry in California was ranked as the busiest border crossing into the United States with more than 34 million legal annual entries (Bogan, 2009). Consequently, in 1994 the now defunct Immigration and Naturalization Service (INS) during the Clinton administration launched a program called *Operation Gate Keeper* in the San Diego-Tijuana border region. The plan relied on utilization of new equipment such as night vision scopes that helped Border Patrol agents see the border crossers at night, seismic sensors (movement detectors) planted along the trails used by immigrants that alerted agents about suspicious activities, portable radios, and an electronic fingerprinting system nicknamed '*IDENT*.'[3] But in particular, *Operation Gate Keeper* militarized the San Diego-Tijuana border sector by employing a three-tiered deployment of Border Patrol agents in five border stations. A Department of Justice report on Operation Gate Keeper's implementation elaborates on each tier's function:

---

[3] The report admits that seismic sensors were not very effective; however, as they could not "distinguish between human traffic, animals, vehicles, or other ground-shaking disturbances such as earthquakes or thunder" (ibid.).

The first tier was deployed in high visibility, fixed positions along the border and had prevention, apprehension, and observation responsibilities. A second tier of agents located further north in corridors heavily traveled by aliens had more freedom of movement in containing and apprehending illegal aliens who made it past the first tier. The third tier was charged with apprehending any aliens who made it past the Border Patrol's first two lines of defense. Given Gatekeeper's deterrence emphasis, a large number of agents were assigned to fixed positions in the first tier along the border (USDOJ/OIG, 2008).

Both *Operation Gate Keeper* and *Operation Blockade* were pilot projects that were limited to two geographical regions along the U.S.-Mexico border. But as the first and second busiest ports of entry the outcome of these initiatives certainly had an impact on subsequent plans and strategies for immigration control. From then on several immigration bills were passed by the Congress, all emphasizing a sharp increase in the number of Border Patrol agents and reinforcement of border fencing, but this time along the entire border region (see Table 8.1). For instance, while from 1975 to 1995 the number of full-time border agents in the south had a relatively stable growth of about 30 percent every five years; due to a change in strategy from "apprehension" to "deterrence" in 1994 in dealing with illegal border crossings, between 1995 and 2000 the force assigned to the southern border had a 93 percent growth (see Table 8.2).

In his critical examination of the politics of Operation Gate Keeper at national and state levels Nevins (2002: 91–92) argues that the plan was the Clinton Administration's response to a Republican-backed ballot initiative—the infamous *Proposition 187* proposed as a referendum during the 1994 elections in California; an apparent attempt by Democrats

Table 8.2. Number of full-Time Border Agents Deployed along the U.S.-Mexico Border, 1975–2005

Year	Number of Full-Time Border Agents	Five-Year Interval Percentage Change
1975	1,446	
1980	1,975	36.6%
1985	2,624	32.9%
1990	3,226	22.9%
1995	4,410	36.7%
2000	8,525	93.3%
2005	9,857	15.6%

Source: Table constructed based on information in Trac Immigration (2006).

to defeat the proposal. Also known as *Save Our State (SOS)*, and passed by 59 percent of voters, Proposition 187 sought to deny social services, health care and public education to unauthorized, undocumented immigrants. Similar to Spener and Staudt (1998) who find the timing of *Operation Blockade* and implementation of NAFTA as being "ironic," Chomsky (2009) links militarization of the U.S.-Mexico border particularly through *Operation Gate Keeper* as a clear preemptive U.S. policy to tackle the anticipated outcomes of NAFTA's implementation in terms of workers' displacement in Mexico:

> The timing of Operation Gatekeeper was surely not accidental. It was anticipated by rational analysts that opening Mexico to a flood of highly-subsidized US agribusiness exports would sooner or later undermine Mexican farming, and that Mexican businesses would not be able to withstand competition from huge state-supported corporations that must be allowed to operate freely in Mexico under the treaty.

A decade later Representative Duncan Hunter, a California Republican and the Chairman of the Armed Services Committee came up with a more ambitious plan—he advocated erecting a fence along the U.S.-Mexico border stretching nearly 2,000 miles from the Pacific Ocean (San Diego, California) to the mouth of the Rio Grande in Brownsville, Texas. Hunter's proposal for the border fence was part of a larger package to seal the U.S.-Mexico border that included adding thousands of Border Patrol agents and increasing fines of hiring undocumented workers by American employers (Remember The Berlin Wall? 2005). In December 2005 the House passed Congressman Hunter's amendment to the *Border Protection, Anti-terrorism, and Illegal Immigration Control Act of 2005*. But it faced strong opposition in the Senate, leading to another Senate-proposed amendment in early 2006 that only endorsed construction of 370 miles of fence along the U.S.-Mexico border (Dinan, 2006). Supported by the White House, the Senate-passed bill included a comprehensive plan that would have put millions of undocumented immigrants on a path toward permanent legal residency and U.S. citizenship; as well as former President Bush's guest-worker plan which would have allowed Mexican immigrants to legally work in the United States. But in a mid-term crucial election year the House GOP members were not supportive of the Senate bill that contained controversial immigration amnesty clause, and were only willing to support the popular border fence project. Consequently the GOP leaders resurrected their 2005 bill, this time called as *"The Secure Fence Act,"* again pushing for the construction of 700 miles of two-layered fencing along the southwest border with Mexico which was then passed by a 283–138 vote in September 2006 (Montgomery, 2006). The Senate eventually came on board and approved the House plan by an 80–19 vote (SourceMex, 2007).[4] The proposed fence included construction of a 22-mile section near a port of entry in Tecate, California in east San Diego County; 361 miles from Calexico, California to Douglas, Arizona (the longest stretch); 88 miles from Columbus, New Mexico to El Paso, Texas; another 51 mile stretch from Del Rio to Eagle Pass in Texas; and 176 miles from Laredo to Brownsville, Texas (see Figure 8.1). Later, as the border fence construction was near completion in June 2009 the newly elected President Obama met with a bipartisan group of lawmakers and emphasized the need to tighten up borders; crack down on employers who hire undocumented workers; as well as find "an effective way to recognize and legalize the status of undocumented workers" in the United States (Bunis and Terrell, 2009). He also expressed his desire to pass an immigration reform bill by 2010. A year later, in a public speech in El Paso, Texas President Obama reiterated that he has followed the Bush administration's border security policy, and told the audience that "we now have more boots on the ground on

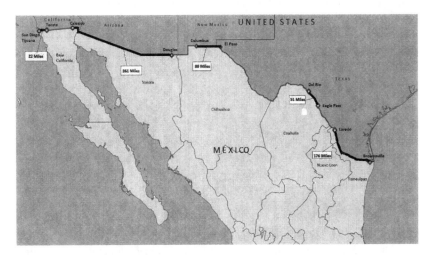

Source: http://news.bbc.co.uk/2/hi/americas/4987784.stm#graphic.

Figure 8.1. Proposed two-layer Fence/Wall along the U.S.-Mexican Border (map by Author).

---

4 See also "U.S. Senate Roll Call Votes 109th Congress—2nd Session," http://www.senate.gov/ legislative/ LIS/roll_call_lists/roll_call_vote_cfm.cfm?congress=109&session=2&vote=00262.

the southwest border than any time in our history"; and that the "fence is now complete" (Fox Nation, 2011).

The Fence/Wall Architecture

As I discussed in the preceding sections the project to study more effective ways of stopping the south-north flow of illegal drugs and undocumented workers along the U.S.-Mexican border was commissioned in the early 1990s to Sandia National Laboratories (SNL) whose expertise is mostly in the area of anti-terrorist military technologies. In its report, the SNL recommended construction of "effective barriers on the flow of traffic" and use of a preventive strategy; instead of the common "apprehension" tactics used by then the INS and Border Patrol agents only after "illegal aliens" had successfully crossed the border. The study also concluded that single barriers "had not proven effective" and recommended instead the construction of "multiple lighted barriers in urban corridor areas" with "patrol roads between the barriers" (ibid.). The proposed fence system included a 10 feet-high opaque preventive wall followed by a 15 feet-high curved fence as a first line of defense. In the cases that the first two preventive/deterrent fences fail and the border crossers are successful to go through these barriers, they would be detected and arrested by Border Patrol before attempting to cross the third 10 feet-high fence (see Figure 8.2).

Eventually, a revised and more refined version of the fence project became part of the Department of Homeland Security's newly announced *Secure Border Initiative (SBI)*, a comprehensive multi-year plan that was launched in November 2005 and aimed at securing U.S borders, particularly with Mexico, in order to stop or at least reduce the undocumented immigration flow. In its advisory report the DHS summed up the SBI plan as an effort to:

> Increase and improve the apprehension, detention, and removal of illegal aliens; a U.S. Citizenship and Immigration Service led plan for expanding the guest worker program and streamlining immigration benefits processes; and a U.S. Customs and Border Protection (CBP) led program to gain control of the nation's land borders. The CBP program, referred to as SBInet, is intended to improve border control operations, deploying more infrastructure and personnel with modernized technology and tactics (Department of Homeland Security, 2006: 2).

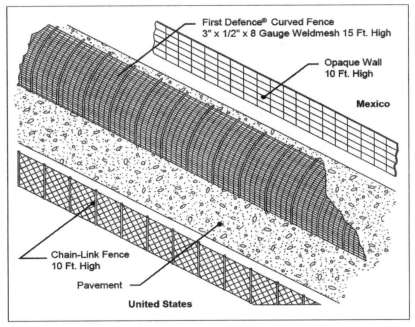

Source: January 1993 Sandia National Laboratories Study (cf. GAO, 1994: 13).
Figure 8.2. Artist's Rendition of the Three-Fence Barrier System.

The SBI had two main components—the *SBInet* which aimed at detecting, identifying, and classifying the threat level associated with attempts for illegal entry to the United States by employing radars, sensors and camera; and the highly militarized *SBI Tactical Infrastructure* (TI) with the objective of enhancing the U.S. Border Patrol agency's ability to deter unauthorized entry attempts by construction of border fences and support structures.

I. *The "Virtual Fence"*

Once completed as planned, the fence/wall will not be a contiguous barrier that effectively seals the border. Rather, it will be comprised of stretches of walls/fences with openings in between particularly in remote rural and mountainous regions. In addition, with only a small portion of it being fenced off, the Rio Grande that runs along 1,255 miles of the border between Mexico and Texas from El Paso to the Gulf of Mexico also needs protection. In those open areas the task of border security was going to be delegated to SBInet's second component, a "virtual fence" system comprised of sensors, cameras, unmanned drones, and integrated surveillance technologies that are monitored by Border Patrol Agents (see Figure 8.3 & Photo 8.2). To gain a complete operational control over the U.S.-Mexican border area the *Secure Fence Act* gave the DHS 18 months to achieve this objective. Five major military contractors, namely, Boeing, Ericson, Lockheed, Northrop Grumman and Raytheon competed to design and deliver the ISBnet's *Virtual Fence* project (Richey, 2006). Similar to other security-related operations such as the prison system and Transportation Security Administration (TSA), the SBI's notable feature is the extent to which the U.S. government has ceded the control of border security matters over to the private sector military contractors. As an example, in a government-sponsored "Industry Day" event in early 2006 DHS's Deputy Director who was a former Lockheed vice-president told a crowd of more than 400 defense contractors that "we are asking you to come back and tell us how to do our business"; further seeking their involvement by adding that *"this is an invitation to be a little bit, a little bit aggressive and thinking as if you owned and you were partners with the CBP"* (Michael Jackson, cf. Richey, 2006; emphasis mine). Eventually, in September 2006 the Boeing Aerospace Company was selected by the U.S. Department of Homeland Security as the main contractor to partner with CBP for a multi-year $2.5 billion virtual fence project (Boeing, 2006). Of note is the credentials of another member of the winning team, the *Elbit Systems of America*—a subsidiary of the Israeli-based company Elbit that has played a significant role in building the separation barrier (the so-called "Apartheid Wall") around the occupied West Bank territories in Palestine (Montgomery, 2006).[5]

The Virtual Fence project has not been very successful, and the only operating project was the prototype "Project 28" near Sasabe, southwest of Tucson, Arizona that back in 2009 was reportedly "plagued with problems" (McCombs, 2009). As early as November 2006, the DHS's Office of Inspector General concluded that:

> The Department does not have the capacity needed to effectively plan, oversee, and execute the SBInet program; administer its contracts; and control costs and schedule. The Department's acquisition management capacity lacks the appropriate work force, business processes, and management con-

---

[5] See chapter 10.

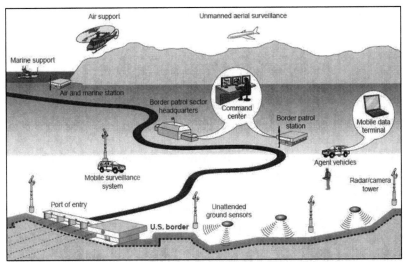

Image source: GAO (2008: 7).

Figure 8.3 Potential Long-Term SBInet Concept of Operations for the "Virtual Fence" project.

Photo: Courtesy of U.S. Customs and Border Protection (CBP).
Image source: http://www.flickr.com/photos/cbpphotos/8492651570/in/set-72157632809681139/

Photo 8.2 A mobile border surveillance tower near the U.S-Mexico border in Nogales, Arizona. The border fence stretches west-east in the lower right-corner.

trols for planning and executing a new-start major acquisition program such as ISBnet (Schulz, 2009).

Yet after two years of experimenting and spending more than $400 million on the 'virtual fence,' in March 2009 the DHS announced that despite failures and disappointments it will actively pursue a new operating system in Sasabe and other parts along the Arizona-Sonora (Mexico) border. For example, a project dubbed as "TUS-1" would install a virtual fence similar to the one depicted in Figure 8.3, comprised of a grid of nine sensors and eight communications towers along with 200 ground sensors in a six-mile stretch, replacing the old and failed Project 28. The towers, "ranging in height from 40 to 120 feet" would have installed cameras and sensors that will utilize microwave technology instead of satellites (McCombs, 2009). In May 2009 the Obama administration also announced its support for the resumption of the virtual fence, thus continuing the policies of previous administration (Hsu, 2009). But in its 2009 annual performance report the DHS declared that it does not plan to extend the border control in 2010 beyond the existing 815 miles in 2009.[6] In addition, citing lack of funding and delays in launching the SBInet's Virtual Fence, the report also indicated that the DHS will move "several hundred Agents from the Southwest Border to the Northern Border to meet the FY 2010 staffing requirements (Department of Homeland Security, 2009: 24). By the end of 2010 Boeing was paid more than $850 million but had only completed 54 miles of the virtual fence (Hing, 2010). The project did not seem to have delivered the expected results:

> The virtual fence was intended to link advanced monitoring technologies to command centers for Border Patrol to identify and thwart human trafficking and drug smuggling. But from the beginning, the program has been plagued by missed deadlines and the limitations of existing electronics in rugged, unpredictable wilderness where high winds and a tumbleweed can be enough to trigger an alarm.... [D]aytime cameras are able to monitor only half of the distance expected. Ground sensors can identify off-road vehicles, but not humans, as initially envisioned by the government (Bennett, 2010).

Subsequently, SBInet's construction was halted by the Obama administration, and in early 2011 the DHS canceled the Virtual Fence altogether by saying that "the effort—on which $1 billion has already been spent—was ineffective and costly" (Preston, 2011). SBInet's cancellation did not end

---

[6] "Border miles under control" implies that the DHS has deployed a combination of personnel, equipment, advanced technology and tactical infrastructure (TI) such as fences and walls along the stated border area.

border militarization efforts. Rather, the DHS Secretary announced that it will be replaced by a new approach "using mobile surveillance system and unmanned drones already in the Border Patrol's arsenal." As an indication of SBInet's egregious expenses, the new alternative plan was estimated to cost "less than $750 million" but cover 323 miles of the Arizona-Mexico border, compared to nearly $1 billion spent on only 54 miles of the Virtual Fence (ibid). However, even the latter plan was a highly expensive undertaking that did not include the cost of building and maintaining the fence/wall along the border.

II. *The Border Fence/Wall*

In its proposed SBInet program the DHS also provided a "fence tool box" comprised of four fencing styles to be erected along the Southwest border—three to stop pedestrian crossing and one to block vehicular border crossing attempts. The 15–18 feet tall pedestrian fence designs include the *picket-style fence* set in a concrete base (Photos 8.3 & 8.4), *bollard fence* (Photos 8.5 & 8.6), and the *post-and-rail with wire mesh* set in concrete foundation (CBP, 2010) (Photo 8.7). In their report to the Congress on border security, Haddad et al. (2009: 21–22) describe picket fencing as being comprised of "metal stakes set sufficiently close together as to be impassable;" and bollard fencing as "vertical installments of solid concrete, metal spheres, or large posts, embedded into the ground at small enough intervals as to be impassable." In some areas *post-and-rail vehicle bollards* similar to those found around federal buildings are installed instead. They consist of steel pipes approximately 6 to 8 inches in diameter placed into the ground and filled with concrete, with horizontal steel rails welded along the tops of the support braces in a horizontal manner (CBP, 2008). The fourth type, the *Normandy-style* vehicle fence stands 4 to 6 feet high and is typically constructed of "welded metal similar to railroad rail" to prevent vehicular border crossings, and are strong enough to resist rolling or being moved manually (Photo 8.8). The U.S. Customs and Borders Protection (CBP) further reiterates that in each border area a specific fence type is selected from the fence tool box in order to "suit the type of environment (urban, rural, or remote) and its geographic and climatic characteristics (hills, rivers, mountains, forests, deserts, etc.) (CBP, 2010).

In addition to the above-mentioned fence types, Haddad et al. (2009: 23) suggest the construction of a "secondary fence" behind the primary fence, similar to the Sandia fence erected in the San Diego border section. The Sandia fence is an angled two-piece fence comprised of a ten feet vertical fence and an extended angle toward the climber to prevent

Photo 8.3 An example of picket-style fence in San Diego-Tijuana border, CA near Freedom Park on the U.S. side, with patrol road and soft pavement to track would-be intruders on the left (photo by author, August 2009).

Photo 8.4 Picket fence, top detail (photo by author).

Photo 8.5 An example of a new bollard fence in Nogales, on the Mexican side. It is built next to the existing older fence constructed with salvaged WWII corrugated metal used for construction of pontoon bridges (foreground, left) (photo by author, August 2009).

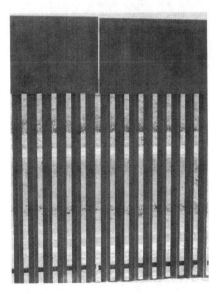

Photo 8.6 Bollard Fence, top detail—on the San Luis/Yuma (AZ)-San Luis Rio, Mexico border (photo by author, August 2009).

Source: CBP, http://www.cbp.gov/xp/cgov/border_security/ti/ti_news/sbi_fence/sbii.xml.

Photo 8.7 A U.S. Border Patrol Agent standing next to an 18-foot tall post-and-rail with wire mesh Pedestrian Fence, Santa Teresa port of entry, New Mexico.

Source: CBP, http://www.cbp.gov/xp/cgov/border_security/ti/ti_news/sbi_fence/sbi6.xml.

Photo 8.8   A Normandy-style vehicle fence near El Paso sector, New Mexico.

climbing "by using gravity and the weight of the climbers against them.[7] However, the authors caution that although most fence types are difficult to compromise, they are expensive to build and maintain, and have to be replaced in about every five years "if the man-made damage to the fence was severe and ongoing."

As construction of the border fence got on its way, so was an increase in the cost of erecting the fence. In its 2007 report to the Congress, the non-partisan *Congressional Research Service* estimated that a 700-mile fence "would cost up to $4.9 billion to build and maintain for 25 years" (Gillman, 2007) (see Table 8.3). But this proved to be a very conservative estimate. By the end of 2008 more than 500 miles of the combined pedestrian and vehicular fences were up along various stretches of the border, with the cost ranging from $2.59 million to $7.425 million per each mile of the pedestrian fence (McCombs, 2009). These estimates however did not include either the costs of purchasing private lands for fence construction, particularly in Texas; or the constant need for fence repair and mainte-nance mainly due to damages caused by border crossers who try to bore through or underneath the barrier. In its March 2011 report the U.S. Customs and Border Protection Agency (CBP) reported that they had to repair 4,037 breaches in 2010 alone, and estimated that "it would cost $6.5 billion 'to deploy, operate and maintain' the existing border fencing over an expected maximum lifetime of 20 years" (Preston, 2011b). During my field visit to bor-der areas in 2009 I observed first-hand this ongoing battle between border crossers and the U.S. Border Patrol agents (see Photos 8.9 & 8.10).

Table 8.3. Completed Border Fence by the end of 2008

State	Total miles Completed	
	Pedestrian	Vehicle
California	91.3	19.8
Arizona	127.8	151.6
New Mexico	14.2	76.2
Texas	44.6	0.04
Total	278	248

Source: Gilbert (2008).

---

[7] The fence is designed by Sandia National Laboratories, a government-owned/con-tractor operated (GOCO) defense facility that works for the U.S. Department of Energy's National Nuclear Security Administration (see http://www.sandia.gov/ERN/global-security/capabilities.html).

Photo 8.9 A rabbit hole underneath the new bollard fence in Nogales-Nogales border on the Mexican side. Note the destroyed concrete base by border crossers (photo by author, 2009).

Photo 8.10 Blow-torched holes on the Mexican side of the old fence in Nogales-Nogales border, with the patched-up areas on the U.S. side. Note the empty water bottles scattered along the Wall (photo by author, 2009).

Although the government has never published the total completed miles of the border fence, most media reports estimate that about 650 miles had been completed by the early 2011.[8] Nor is there any published detailed map of the border fence/wall's exact location. In late 2009 the DHS published a map of completed sections of the border wall on one of its web sites, but it only provided a general sketch without the specifics of the wall/fence locations. As Gilman (2011: 270) points out, "the scale of the map is such that it does not include anchoring landmarks such as towns or state or local parks or reserves" (see Photo 8.11). In particular, in parts of Texas that the wall/fence has been constructed along Rio Grande, it does not show the barrier's distance from the river bank, justifiably a contentious issue of government "land grab" in the eyes of private landowners on the American side of the border. In his investigation of the human rights violations caused by the Texas-Mexico border wall's construction, Gilman (2011: 275–76) points out that the wall's path runs through lands privately owned—a blatant breach of citizens' right to private property guaranteed by the *1948 American Declaration of the Rights and Duties of Man*. But government's land grab for the wall's construction has been discriminatory, as reportedly "the property owners impacted by the wall are poorer, more often Latino and less educated than those not impacted who also live along the border." In a New York Times op-ed, Dear (2013) reiterates that the border barriers in Texas disproportionately run along or through poor communities, "a pattern that is so clear that it sometimes becomes farcical: plans for one fence, for instance, show it ending abruptly at the edge of a billionaire's property." Thus more small landowning individuals and families have lost their properties while "more lucrative developed properties and resorts were not included in the wall's path." Similar to Israel's separation barrier that has annexed Palestinian farmers' land to Israel proper by running the barrier through Palestinian-owned properties, the border wall's path in Texas has often separated landowners from part of their property along Rio Grande that is now cut off by the wall.[9]

The fence portions along the California, Arizona and New Mexico borders were constructed without a hitch. But the fence construction in Southeastern Texas particularly along the Rio Grande Valley proved to be a challenging task both dealing with objections raised by politicians

---

[8] See for instance Carcamo (2011) and Fox Nation (2011).

[9] In his excellent documentary *The Border Wall*, Wayne Ewing (2008) demonstrates the negative effects of the Wall along the U.S.-Mexican border, particularly related to violation of landowners' property rights along the Texas-Mexican border.

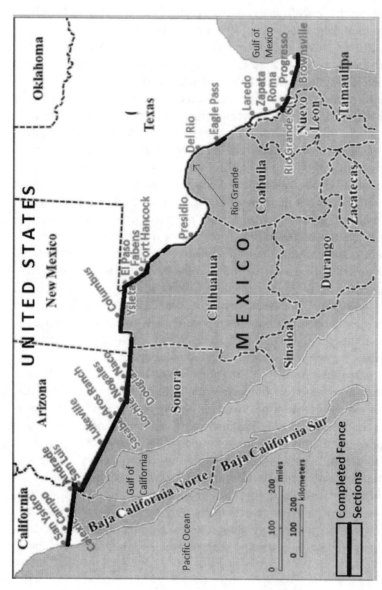

Source: U.S. Customs and Border Protection (CBP), http://www.cbp.gov/linkhandler/cgov/newsroom/highlights/fence_map.ctt/fence_map.pdf.

Photo 8.11 Status of completed Fence/Wall sections along the U.S.-Mexico border as of December 2009 (map by author).

and property owners along the U.S.-Mexico border (Simon, 2009). Using various sources Gilman (2011: 270) reports the average cost of constructing pedestrian fences at about $3.9 million per mile, but adds that 'in the final stages of the project" private contractors hiked the average cost to about $6.5 million per mile. Gilman (ibid.) estimates that the total cost of the wall's construction and maintenance for a twenty-year period amounts to $6.5 billion.

Is the Border Fence/Wall Effective? Notes from the Field

In the summer of 2009, I set out on a two-week field observation to visit the U.S.-Mexican border areas in California and Arizona just as last parts of the Fence/Wall were being completed. I traveled 500 miles and visited four twin-cities along the border, met with many pro-immigrant activists mostly affiliated with religious organizations and churches, as well as governmental and non-governmental immigrant advocate entities and agencies.[10] I started my journey at the border's western-most edge on the Pacific Ocean, a 14-mile-long stretch of newly finished border fence that separates the San Diego and Tijuana metropolitan areas; and then traveled on Interstates 8 and 19 with stops in Calexico-Mexicali (Mexico) in California, and twin cities of Somerton/San Luis-San Luis Rio Colorado (Mexico) and Nogales-Nogales (Mexico) in Arizona. Although before my trip I had done considerable reading and research about the U.S.-Mexican border and immigration issues, the field experience was an

---

[10] Here is the list of organizations and groups:
In San Diego (CA):
  – The Interfaith Shelter
  – American Friends Service Committee
  – Border Angels
In Calexico (CA):
  – Proyecto San Pablo
In Yuma/Somerton/San Luis (AZ):
  – Proyecto San Pablo
  – Chicanos por la Casa
  – Members of the San Luis City Council
In Tucson (AZ):
  – Humane Borders
In Nogales (AZ):
  – Poverty 24/6
  – Catholic Social Mission
  – The Kino Border Initiative

incredible eye-opener and a highly valuable education about 'facts on the ground' related to the border fence.

My first exposure to the U.S.-Mexican border was in San Diego area, when I made a trip in the company of a faith-based organization's director to border area near Friendship Park located on the Pacific Ocean. The park was dedicated by the former First lady Pat Nixon in 1971 as a symbolic gesture of friendship between the two nations. Up until 2009 when the new double fence was constructed, people on both sides that for variety of reasons were unable to cross the border could chat, touch hands and communicate with their loved ones and friends. But now a no-man's land security zone separates the chain-link fence and the historic border marker obelisk on the Mexican side from the newly erected 15-foot tall fence, effectively preventing close communication between people on both sides (see Photo 8.12). A *New York Times* reporter explains how it looked like before 2009:

Photo 8.12 The no-man's land security buffer zone between the new border fence (forefront) and the old chain link fence that used to separate Friendship Park on the U.S. side from Tijuana, Mexico (seen in the background). The old historic border marker obelisk is at the center of the old fence (photo by author, 2009).

Families and friends, some of them unable to cross the border because of legal or immigration trouble, exchange kisses, tamales and news through small gaps in the tattered chain-link fence. Yoga and salsa dancing, communion rites, protest and quiet reflection all transpire in the shadow of a stone obelisk commemorating the area where Mexican and American surveyors began demarcating the border nearly 160 years ago after the war between the countries (Archibold, 2008).

On the way back, as we were driving on a winding road that runs along the border, an unexpected encounter demonstrated the border region's extent of militarization. The area was deceptively calm and peaceful, and there were no indications that our presence was being monitored and watched. I asked my colleague/guide to take me closer to the fence, so she took a dirt road toward the border and stopped right before a "No Trespassing" sign. I got out of the car to have a better view of the border fence complex, but in less than a minute we were surrounded by ICE agents in full military gear riding on two ATV's (all-terrain vehicles) and a border patrol SUV. It was only my guide's familiarity with this kind of situation and her savvy communication skills and experience that got us out of that tense situation without further complications, after she explained to the agents that I was an academic researching the border issues.

The San Diego-Tijuana border area seemed like a formidable high-tech fortress with a newly completed double-fence, motion detector sensors and cameras, stadium lighting, Border Patrol choppers hovering above, and quick-response armed border agents stationed nearby to confront and apprehend the violators (see Photos 8.13 & 8.14). But this seems to be using excessive force to apprehend would-be border crossers. Similarly, driving on I-8 that runs east-west parallel to the border and I-19 later on I had to go through five highly-militarized Border Patrol security checkpoints, where the agents inspect passengers and could search inside the car and the trunk without the occupants' permission and consent.[11]

The fact that the border area on the American side is treated as a war zone and guarded by armed agents is an indication of the constructed barrier's permeability. In the absence of any plans to build a solid border wall and the continued presence of large gaps along the border; and in

---

[11] According to a 1976 Supreme Court ruling, Border Patrol agents have legal authority to stop a vehicle at checkpoints even if there is no reasonable evidence that the vehicle is transporting undocumented immigrants. However, searching a vehicle should be either by the vehicle occupants' consent or based on a probable cause (GAO, 2005–2007). This happened to me at one of the checkpoints, as I later noticed that the Border Patrol agents have opened my luggage in the trunk and checked its contents without my consent.

Photo 8.13 The San Diego-Tijuana border fence on the U.S.-side. Note the combination of virtual fence and the physical barrier, with sensors, cameras and stadium lights (photo by author, 2009).

Photo 8.14 The westernmost section of new picket fence and the patrol road on the Pacific Ocean separating San Diego from Tijuana (the old border barrier can be seen in the background). Photo taken from the Friendship Park on the U.S. side (photo by author, 2009).

light of the documented failure of previous barriers to stem illegal immigration (Nuñez-Neto and Kim, 2008: 2) the newly constructed fence is also a practice in futility. In fact, a recent study by the federal government's General Accounting Office (GAO) indicates that the DHS has failed to access the border fence's effectiveness in order to stop the flow of undocumented immigrants (GAO, 2009: 29). The only outcome of the intensification of border security with the new fence construction has been the diversion of immigration into more remote and dangerous terrain that has led, and continues to lead, to more migrant deaths (Nuñez-Neto and Kim, 2008: 2–3). This is particularly documented by the *Humane Borders*, an immigrant Advocate group headquartered in Tucson, Arizona (see Photo 8.15).[12] As is illustrated in the map, based on official government data in a thirteen-year period from October 1999 to April 2012 there have been 2,269 reported migrant deaths just for those who have attempted to cross the Mexico-Arizona border, with the main causes of deaths being high desert temperatures and dehydration or freezing temperatures during night-time crossings.[13] The total reported migrant deaths in the entire border region vary depending on the reporting agencies and sources. In her report for San Diego's American Civil Liberties Union (ACLU) branch Jimenez (2009: 17) demonstrates the link between the new border fence construction and rise in migrant deaths. For instance, she estimates the death toll for the 1994–2009 period ranging from 3,861–5,607, with a sharp increase from 2005 onward. This grim and fatal reality of border crossing is memorialized in Nogales, Mexico whereby crosses are displaced on the border wall in memory of those who have perished; both known and unknown (see Photos 8.16 & 8.17).

Despite the admirable humanitarian efforts by many immigrant advocacy groups and organizations that try to help immigrants once they cross the border in remote and hard-to-survive border regions, there are many others who not only oppose illegal border crossings but also sadly sabo-

---

[12] In August 2009 I met with the Reverend Robin Hoover who was Humane Border's former Executive Director. This non-profit, church-based volunteer organization has set up more than hundred water stations along various paths used by Mexican immigrants who cross the border into rough and inhospitable Arizona territories. He shared this map with me and explained the difficulties faced by border crossers and the consequences of border fortifications that have redirected immigrants to the more dangerous terrains.

[13] Based on one estimate, of 301 reported migrant deaths with the causes known in FY 2008, 127 migrants died due to the extremes of environmental exposure, 49 of train and motor vehicle accidents, 54 due to drowning, and 71 perished for other reasons such as homicide, suicide, existing diseases and natural disasters (Massey, 2009: 1).

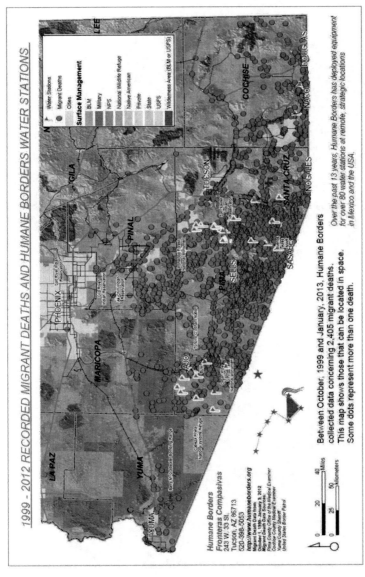

Source: map courtesy of the Humane Borders, Inc.; cartographic design and data development by John F. Chamblee, Michael Malone, and Matthew Reynolds. (permission granted) http://humaneborders.org/news/documents/hb_all_deaths_20120428_letter_download.pdf

Photo 8.15 Recorded migrant deaths along the Arizona-Mexico border, 1999–2012 (each dot represents a recorded migrant death within the American border region).

Photo 8.16 Crosses posted in memory of deceased border crossers on a section of the old border wall on the Mexican side, Nogales, Sonora (photo by author, 2009).

Photo 8.17 A close-up image of crosses with names of the deceased migrants, Border wall on the Mexican side, Nogales, Sonora (photo by author, 2009).

tage the former groups' life-saving humanitarian efforts. I learned of this rather dark side of the border reality first-hand when in 2009 I spent a day with the *Border Angels*, a non-profit immigrant advocate group based in San Diego. Since the newly constructed fence has made it almost impossible to cross the border in the San Diego-Tijuana urban border region, Border Angels' volunteers provide humanitarian aid to immigrants who are forced to move further east and enter the United States in remote rural areas. Our task for that day was to clean up and remove the trash, and place new supplies of fresh water in plastic containers in two migrant camps near the Campo and Jacumba border communities, about 49 and 74 miles east of San Diego, respectively. Upon leaving the Campo migrant camp we were approached by a well-dressed woman in her forties, most likely from the nearby residential community, behind the wheels of a luxury car. In an extremely rude manner she scolded us for aiding and abetting "illegal aliens," and made it clear that she will remove and destroy all of the fresh water supplies that we had just placed at the camp once our entourage leaves the area. She was not bluffing, as the evidence on site indicated that others had slashed plastic water gallons prior to our arrival (see Photo 8.18). This deep resentment about unauthorized border crossers that is often rooted in hatred, prejudice, and above all poverty of sound historical analysis and judgment not only is prevalent among average citizens, but also espoused by the politicians who represent them. For instance, during the Republican presidential campaigns for 2012, Michelle Bachman, an aspirant for presidency declared that she "would build a fence on America's southern border on every mile, on every yard, on every foot, on every inch of the southern border" (Fox News, 2011). Herman Cain, another Republican presidential candidate suggested an even more egregious plan during a campaign stop in Iowa:

> I just got back from China. Ever heard of the Great Wall of China? It looks pretty sturdy. And that sucker is real high. I think we can build one if we want to! We have put a man on the moon, we can build a fence! Now, my fence might be part Great Wall and part electrical technology...It will be a twenty foot wall, barbed wire, electrified on the top, and on this side of the fence, I'll have that moat that President Obama talked about. And I would put those alligators in that moat! (Huffington Post, 2011).

In an Op-Ed published in the *New York Times* Bradatan (2011) makes an interesting point that long after the fall of the Berlin Wall many Germans still refer to it as "Mauer im Kopf" (Wall in the head), a mental inhibitor of unification that still resides in many people's minds mostly out of fear

Photo 8.18 A fresh water plastic container slashed by local residents who oppose humanitarian help provided by volunteer groups, north of the U.S.-Mexican border near rural Campo, about 50 miles east of San Diego, CA (photo by author, 2009).

of an unpredictable outcome. Similarly, related to unauthorized immigration many Americans need the border wall out of fear:

> Walls, then, are built not for security, but for a *sense* of security. The distinction is important, as those who commission them know very well. What a wall satisfies is not so much a material need as a mental one. Walls protect people not from barbarians, but from anxieties and fears, which can often be more terrible than the worst vandals. In this way, they are not built for those who live outside them, threatening as they may be, but for those who dwell within. In a certain sense, then, what is built is not a wall, but a state of mind.

There are indications that a combination of factors including a sluggish American economy that has little to offer to migrant workers, fortification and militarization of the border, and improving economic conditions in Mexico have slowed down the flow of unauthorized migration in the second decade of the New Millennium. Yet many others who have long-established roots and family ties in the United States continue to cross the border. Based on one estimate by the DHS, "56 percent of apprehensions at the Mexican border in 2010 involved people who had been caught previously, up from 44 percent in 2005"; and despite the claims of being an advocate of immigrant groups, by the end of 2011 the Obama administration had deported more than one million immigrants (Cave, 2011). As I have argued in the preceding sections not only the two societies have had a long shared history, but their economies have become so interconnected that the new border fence is now situated right in the midst of an incorporated and almost unified political economy. Border fortification is also keeping millions of unauthorized immigrants who crossed the border before 2005 on the U.S. side and preventing them from returning back to Mexico, a long-established migratory flow that functioned well with the logic of two incorporated political economies. Apparently the border fence has a dual purpose: to keep the criminals and drug smugglers out, and to deter unauthorized immigration. Although a bit condescending, director of the Trans-Border Institute at the University of San Diego has come up with a pragmatic solution: "if you think drug dealers and terrorists are much more dangerous than maids and gardeners, then we should get as many visas as possible to those people, so we can focus on the real threat.... Widening the gates would strengthen the walls" (David Shirk, cf. Cave, 2011).

CHAPTER NINE

ISRAEL AND PALESTINE: A SETTLER COLONY IS BORN

In June 2002, the Israeli Knesset approved the erection of a security barrier or what the government later dubbed as an "anti-terrorist fence," to separate the occupied Palestinian territories of the West Bank from Israel proper. The decision was not made overnight and was a plan in the making since 1992, when the then Prime Minister Yitzhak Rabin brought up the idea of creating a physical barrier in the aftermath of a teenage girl's murder in Jerusalem. But as one advocate notes: "the idea of a fence separating Israelis and Palestinians is, on one level, an admission of failure" (Makovsky, 2004: 50–51). Although in his analysis failure is explained as Israel's inability to prevent infiltration of Palestinian "terrorists" from the occupied territories into Israel, in reality the security fence serves the objective of controlling the flow of Palestinians between the two sides. The fence, similar to what I have discussed in previous chapters related to the U.S.-Mexico border situation, was erected here at the time that the economies of Israel and occupied Palestinian territories were almost fully integrated, so much so that the unhindered movement of Palestinian workers became an unavoidable necessity.

In its report on the separation barrier, *B'Tselem*, the Israeli Information Center for Human Rights in the occupied Palestinian territories provides the following description:

> In most areas, the barrier is comprised of an electronic fence with dirt paths, barbed-wire fences, and trenches on both sides, at an average width of 60 meters. In some areas, the defense establishment decided to build a concrete wall six to eight meters high in place of the barriers. The length of the system—already built, under construction, or in planning—is 709 kilometers, a distance twice as long as the Green Line (B'Tselem, n.d.).[1]

The barrier's architecture and its environs are strikingly similar to those of the demolished Berlin Wall. But while the latter mostly functioned as a defensive barrier, as I will explain later in the following chapter the Israeli

---

[1] "Green Line" here is in reference to the demarcation line that separates Israel proper from the occupied West Bank Palestinian territories captured by Israel in the aftermath of the 1967 Six-Day War.

security fence is an offensive structure by design. This is deeply rooted in the nature of a long-standing and unresolved conflict between Palestinian residents in the region on one hand, and Israeli citizens who have immigrated to Palestine and settled there from mid-19th century onward on the other. Yet understanding Israel's rationale to erect the separation barrier requires a historical appreciation of the way the state of Israel has been established in Palestine. In the following pages I set out to accomplish this objective.

Israel: The Birth of a Nation

I consider the establishment of the state of Israel as a 20th century settler colony project that has evolved and matured not as an independent colonial entity but rather within the context of geopolitical and economic interests of two imperial powers—Britain up until 1948 and the United States ever since. Regardless of initial motivations and pull-push factors for immigration, all settler-based colonies have been historically preoccupied with territorial control, takeover of land in the colonies and further territorial expansion once they pass beyond initial stages of getting settled. In this particular case, scarcity of (suitable) available lands and colonial territories that were set aside in line with British colonial plans created a situation that the land question became main point of contention between Palestinians and Jews.

The genesis of the latter group's obsession with land can be traced back to the Biblical passages used by supporters of the state of Israel that refer to Palestine as *Eretz Yisrael* (Land of Israel), that Palestine was promised by God to Jews who have been displaced and dispersed in the Diaspora.[2] Notwithstanding the lack of validity for any such claim made based on religious texts, one also finds Biblical territorial descriptions of *Erestz Yisrael* quite inadequate, and simply an approximation. For instance, in Genesis 15:18–21 the land promised to Abraham's descendants is described

---

[2] "The term 'Palestine' is applied to Philistia, the land of the philistines. It was only after the Christian era that it seems to have been applied to the whole country. Ptolemy calls it *Palaestina*, later divided as Palaestina Prima, Palaestina Seconda, and Palaestina Tertia. During the middle ages it was known as *Terra Santa*, hence the term Holy Land. But this term, or its equivalent, was ignored by the Arab conquerors who adopted Palaestina Prima as *'fund'* (i.e., military district) *Filastin* and moved the capital from the exposed Caesarea on the coast to the more central inland town of Lydda" (*The Encyclopedia of Islam*, cf. Tibawi, 1961: 1).

as the area running from the Nile River in Egypt to the Euphrates River in Mesopotamia (present time Iraq), while other accounts mention the border of lands to be conquered "for those coming out of Egypt" to be between west of Jordan (the Land of Canaan) and the Mediterranean Sea (see Deuteronomy 1:6–8 and 11:24). As Mahler (2004: 16) points out, "it is not fair to expect that biblical passages should meet standards of detail and exactness required by contemporary historical sources" since "that was not the purpose of their creation" to begin with. In fact, the absurdity of such territorial claims is supported by the nature of land holdings (and not land ownership in a legal sense under capitalism) in pre-capitalist periods and the antiquities that was based on the use-rights and continued presence of individuals, families, and communities on a given piece of land or territory; thus effectively disenfranchising those who had left regardless of their reasons to abandon the said lands and territories (see Figure 9.1).

Palestine has a long history of imperial domination, beginning first by the Persian Achaemenid Dynasty in the 6th century BC, followed by Romans in the 1st century BC, Muslim Arabs in the 7th century AD, the Ottomans from 1517 to 1918, and finally the British from 1918 to 1948. Palestine under the Ottoman rule was divided into five administrative districts known as *Sanjaks*, all of which were incorporated within the Greater Syria Province (Smith, 2010: 19).[3] But our historical journey also begins with the history of British imperial interests in the region, since the state of Israel's establishment took place during the British imperial domination and control over Palestine.

For much of the Ottoman period rule Palestine was off limits to European colonial interests. But during a brief period (1831–1840) it fell into the hands of Mohammad Ali, the Egyptian Mameluk leader who then opened up the "Holy Land" to Europeans—mainly the French, Russians, Prussians and the British. Europeans then sent their colonial 'Trojan horses' in the guise of religious-cultural protection of non-Muslim populations in Palestine who were numerical minorities: The Russians protected the Orthodox Christians while the Catholics were supported by the French. This left the Protestant and Jewish minorities for Prussia and England. The British presence in Palestine was sealed by the opening of British consulate in Jerusalem in 1838. Since having a safe land route from the Mediterranean

---

[3] The five districts were the Sanjaks of Gaza, Jerusalem, Nablus, Lajun and Safad (ibid.).

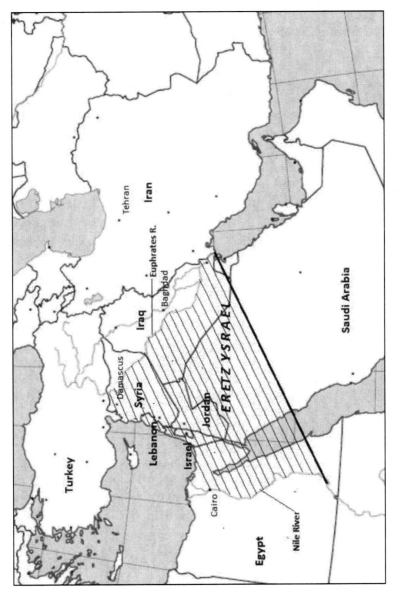

Figure 9.1 Hypothetical Map of Biblical Boundaries of *Eretz Yisreal* (map by author).

Sea to their imperial holdings in India was a crucial matter, the British desired the stability of Ottoman Empire—most importantly the territories that comprise present-time Turkey. But in light of the Russian Empire's ambitions in the region securing a foothold in Palestine became a priority for the British colonial policies:

> Britain's policy was an aspect of what has been called "the Great Game in Asia," a contest in which Russia posed the main threat because its southward expansion threatened the security of India's frontiers. Britain's actions in the Middle East were designed to keep the Russians out of Istanbul in order to forestall the prospects that a Russian fleet stationed there with access to the Mediterranean could cut Britain's imperial lifeline to India (Smith, 2010: 15).

At the time, Jewish presence in Palestine was insignificant. For instance, estimates for 1800 indicate that around five thousand Jews lived in Palestine, or roughly 1.5 percent of the total population that also included about twenty five thousand Christians. By 1880, right before the persecution of Russian Jews during Tsar Alexander III's rule, their numbers had grown to about 25,000—still less than 5 percent of the total population, including 45,000 Christians (Hirschberg, cf. Mahler, 2004: 17, 47 fn.). It is within this context that in the last two decades of the 19th century Zionism evolved as an exogenous movement essentially to find a solution to the long-standing Jewish problem based on two facts: that "Jews were dispersed in various countries around the world, and in each country they constituted a minority." Nathan Birnbaum, the Austrian Jewish writer coined the term "Zionism" in 1885, referring to a return to "Zion" which is one of the Biblical names for Jerusalem (Shlaim, 2000: 1–2). The British interest in protecting Jews was rooted in the Anglican messianic tradition and evangelical doctrine of the early 19th century: "According to this doctrine, the fulfillment of the prophecies about the Last Day was indivisibly linked to the return of the Jews to the land of their fathers, to which they had an inalienable right" (Schölch, 1992: 45). The ultimate objective of course, was "conversion of Jews to Protestant Christianity," which to the British missionaries' surprise was confronted by "insurmountable resistance" and a "minimal" rate of conversion (ibid.: 42).

Although wrapped in religious utopianism, Zionism was a secular nationalist movement fueled by the plight of Jews mostly in Eastern Europe and Russia. In fact, in the aftermath of the 1789 French Revolution and proclamation of the equality of all citizens, French Jews were offered the opportunity to become full citizens by assimilating. As Smith (2004: 27) points out,

Assimilation meant that Jews would presumably give up their commitment to retain their distinctiveness as a separate community adhering to Jewish laws and, with that, their commitment to the idea of a return to Eretz Israel, a hope that had bound them together for centuries.

And so during the 19th century a good majority of Jews in France and many other Western European nations including Austria, England, Germany, Hungary and Italy did choose that route. Meantime, Eastern European Jews particularly in Poland and Russia were facing a growing level of hostility, discrimination and at times persecution that culminated in the 1881–84 Russian *Pogroms*. There were two early Zionist tendencies in the late 19th century before the emergence of Zionism as an organized movement. The first, known as BILU which is an acronym taken from Isaiah 2:5 "envisaged a Jewish state in Palestine founded on the principles of Jewish agriculture and Jewish labor;" while the second, known as *Hibbat Zion* (the Love of Zion) was a cultural movement to safeguard Jewish customs and the Hebrew language by facilitating emigration of Russian Jews and their settlement in Palestine (ibid.: 29).[4] It was the latter group that organized the first wave of Jewish immigration to Palestine, known as *aliya* (meaning 'ascent' or 'going up') that took place between 1882 and 1893. In all, it is estimated that about thirty thousand Jews mostly from Russia landed in Palestine during this period, but their survival largely depended on financial support provided by wealthy Jewish patrons in Western Europe such as Baron Edmund de Rothschild (Fraser, 2008: 6; Mahler, 2004: 21).

There is a consensus to consider Theodor Herzl, a Hungarian-born Jewish journalist as the founder of the Zionist movement that facilitated ensuing waves of Jewish immigration. As an assimilated Jew Herzl did not have any desire to follow the earlier Zionist aspirations. But growing anti-Jewish sentiments in Austria and his exposure to the vicious anti-Semitism of the French society during the infamous Dreyfus Affair in the last decade of 19th century led him to conclude that European Jews had to abandon the Diaspora and find a territory where they can establish a sovereign Jewish state. Herzl articulated his ideas in a little pamphlet *Der Judenstaat* (the Jewish State) published in 1896. For him the Jewish question was neither social nor religious, but rather a national one, yet he initially did not have a preference for Palestine. For instance, in *Der Judenstaat* he asks

---

[4] There is an extensive body of literature on Zionism, but for basic information see Chertoff (1975). Cohen (1950), and Kressel (1973).

"is Palestine or Argentina preferable?" and then immediately comments "the society will take whatever is given and whatever Jewish public opinion favors" (Herzl, cf. Hertzberg, 1960: 215–223). Herzl's vision of a Jewish state established by Jewish immigrants was clearly based on colonization, evident in the following statement when in 1898 he addressed a German-Jewish audience in Berlin:

> Don't you know what a colonial age we are living in? As a consequence of over-population, and of the resultant ever more acute social question, many nations are endeavoring to found overseas colonies in order to channel the flow of emigration there. *This is the policy which England has been pursuing for decades, and which has been regarded as exemplary by many nations* (Herzl, 1973, emphasis mine).

Thus based on above ideas in 1897 Herzl called for a meeting in Basel, Switzerland where participants later formed the World Zionist Organization (WZO). But to his dismay, feared of a backlash in their home countries many assimilated Western European Jews stayed away while delegates from Eastern Europe and Russia dominated the scene. Increasingly the preference was given to Palestine, and during the same period some Zionists began to popularize the fiction that Palestine was an empty land waiting to be colonized. Jewish writers such as Israel Zangwill promoted the slogan of 'a land without a people for a people without a land' (Cook, 2008: 22). The European Jewish communities' reaction to Herzl's *Der Judenstaat* was mixed, leading skeptics to dispatch a fact-finding mission to Palestine to assess the feasibility of Herzl's plan. As Shlaim (2000: 3) notes, the emissaries' findings were not promising:

> After the Basel Congress the rabbis of Vienna decided to explore Herzl's ideas and sent two representatives to Palestine. This fact-finding mission resulted in a cable from Palestine in which the two rabbis wrote, *"the bride is beautiful, but she is married to another man"* (emphasis mine).

The declared goal in WZO's program was "the creation of a home for the Jewish people in Palestine to be secured by public law" (Elon, 1975: 242–243). As Elon indicates, the choice of "public law" and not "international law" was to appease to the Ottoman Court and assure the Sultan that the Zionist movement is not seeking the creation of a self-ruled nation supported by European powers within the Ottoman Empire (ibid.: 242). Earlier, in his *Der Judenstaat,* and in a clearly racist tone Herzl indirectly appealed to the Ottoman Emperor and laid the foundation of WZO's above-stated objective:

Palestine is our unforgettable historic homeland. The very name would be a marvelously effective rallying cry. If his Majesty the Sultan were to give us Palestine, we could in return undertake the complete management of the finance of Turkey. *We should there form a part of a wall of defense for Europe in Asia, an outpost of civilization against barbarism.* We should as a neutral state remain in contact with all Europe, which would have to guarantee our existence (cf. Hertzberg, 1960, emphasis mine).

It is quite fascinating that even before the formation of WZO Herzl envisioned "a wall of defense" that would separate "civilized" Jews from "barbarians," the latter most likely should have been offensive to the Ottomans, as those "barbarians" were the Empire's subjects! Not receiving a positive response from the Ottoman Emperor Sultan Abdul Hamid, in 1902 Herzl courted the British in order to secure the Al-Arish region in the Sinai Peninsula, then part of the Egyptian colony and adjacent to Palestine. But instead, then British Secretary of colonial holdings Joseph Chamberlain offered a territory in British East African colonies located in present-time Kenya. Although as a pragmatist Zionist Herzl found the British offer a plausible one, the Eastern European Jewish adherents of *Hibbat Zion* (the Love of Zion) adamantly opposed the African alternative for the Jewish state and "remained steadfast in their commitment to Palestine" (Smith, 2010: 32).

The Zionist movement became the main impetus for several subsequent Jewish immigration waves ('*aliyot*') to Palestine from the early 20th century to 1948, the year the state of Israel was unilaterally established. Encouraged by WZO's achievements, between 1900 and 1914 the second *aliya* increased the number of Jews in Palestine to about eighty-five thousand (Israel Information Center, 1977: 43). The increase in numbers during the second wave was mostly due to emigration of Russian Jews who left the country in the aftermath of the failed 1905 Russian bourgeois Revolution (Mahler, 2000: 21). Jewish immigrants' creation of Jewish communities did not take place in undeveloped and unsettled lands, but rather right in the midst of Palestinians who have lived there for centuries. At a time when the predominantly Palestinian Arab population was living under the Ottoman rule as imperial subjects and lacking a sense of national identity; Zionism solidified a sense of Jewish nationalism based on a non-existing and yet-to-be created Jewish state. As a consequence, the Palestinian Arabs' response to Zionism was schizophrenic—some were inclined to have dialogue and cooperate with the Zionist settlers, while others remained either indifferent or became increasingly suspicious and hostile to these uninvited guests (see Tessler, 1994: 127–131).

*Advancement of Zionist Settler Colonies in Palestine
under British Occupation*

When in 1914 the Ottomans entered the First World War by joining Austria-Hungary and Germany, they changed the dynamics of British imperialist interests in the Middle East in general and Palestine in particular. Instead of securing a foothold within a stable Ottoman Empire—in this case by protecting the Jewish population in Palestine with the objective of safeguarding their imperial interests in India, now the British had to do all they could to weaken the Ottomans. Thus, negotiating with Emir Abdullah, the Hashemite governor of Mecca in 1915 the British government offered its support for the independence of Arabs in the region if they would join the Allies against the Ottomans (see Friedman, 1970). However, while the Arabs were fighting against the Ottomans, in 1916 the British and French government diplomats met to negotiate their spheres of influence in the Middle East, should the Allies emerge as victors. Kept secret from Arabs in the region, an agreement negotiated between the French diplomat Francois Georges Picot and British Sir Mark Sykes carved out the Arab provinces within the Ottoman Empire north of the Arabian Peninsula into areas of French and British zones of direct control and/or influence. Known as the Sykes-Picot Agreement, the French would control most of present-day Syria and Lebanon, the British would control most of Jordan and Iraq, while what is mostly comprised of current state of Israel to be ruled by a joint Allied condominium (Sachar, 1981: 93). However, with Britain emerging as a stronger Allied power than France toward the War's end, in 1917 the British changed their mind and instead demanded the French to accept a revised plan and recognize a British Protectorate over all of Palestine after the war, since Palestine was a "strategic buffer to Egypt" (Mahler, 2000: 24) (see Figure 9.2).

It was within the above context that the British considered the Zionist movement as a potential alternative ally in the region in order to pursue their imperial objectives. Working closely with then British Foreign Minister Arthur Balfour, Zionist lobbyists in Britain such as Chaim Weizmann and Nahum Sokolow eventually succeeded in getting British approval of the future Jewish state in Palestine. After several revisions by the British authorities and their Zionist counterparts, in November 1917 Balfour sent the following letter to Walter Rothschild, a prominent leader of the British Jewish community:

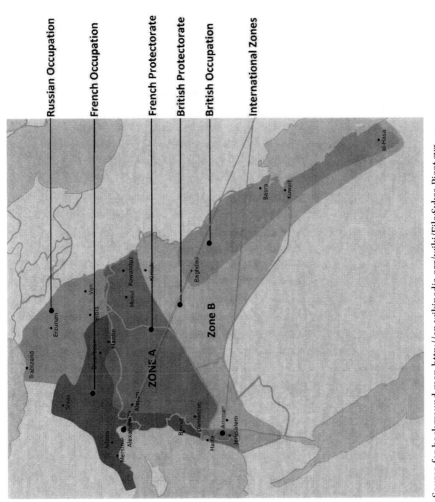

Figure 9.2 Sykes-Picot Agreement of 1916.

Source for background map http://en.wikipedia.org/wiki/File:Sykes-Picot.svg

Dear Lord Rothschild,

I have much pleasure in conveying to you, on behalf of His Majesty's Government, the following declaration of sympathy with Jewish Zionist aspirations which has been submitted to, and approved by, the Cabinet:

"His Majesty's Government view with favour the establishment in Palestine
of a national home for the Jewish people, and will use their best endeav-
ours to facilitate the achievement of this object, *it being clearly understood
that nothing shall be done which may prejudice the civil and religious rights of
existing non-Jewish communities in Palestine*, or the rights and political status
enjoyed by Jews in any other country".

I should be grateful if you would bring this declaration to the knowledge of
the Zionist Federation (cf. Yapp, 1987: 290) (emphasis mine).

The Zionist movement's plan to colonize Palestine was not the only game
in town. As Schölch (1992: 40) points out, "the fact that it [Zionism] did
triumph was not the result of the skill of Zionism's representatives," rather
it was "the consequence of the constellation of World War I powers and
a partial convergence of interests of British imperialism and the Zionist
movement." Shortly after the Balfour Declaration in early 1918 the British
army entered Jerusalem, and with the Ottoman Empire's defeat Britain
occupied Palestine and assumed the territories' *de facto* control. Later in
1922, the newly established League of Nations that two years back was
created by the Supreme Council of the Paris Peace Conference granted
Britain the *de jure* Mandate for Palestine, formally supporting British rule
until 1948.[5] With the League's approval Britain proceeded to subdivide
the region into two colonial administrative areas: the area west of Jordan
River was recognized as Palestine and under direct British colonial rule,
while the territories east of Jordan River became the semi-autonomous
Trans-Jordan region administered by the Hashemite family under British
colonial supervision (see Figure 9.3).

The League of Nations was the first post-WWI international organization that was created with clear objective of protecting European powers'
colonial and imperial interests. For example, article 22 of the League's
covenant states that in the aftermath of the First World War the best
method of governing and administering colonies and territories occupied
and acquired and "*inhabited by peoples not yet able to stand by themselves*

---

[5] A forerunner of the United Nations, the League's principal mission was to maintain
world peace through collective security agreements and disarmament, and settle international disputes through negotiation and arbitration.

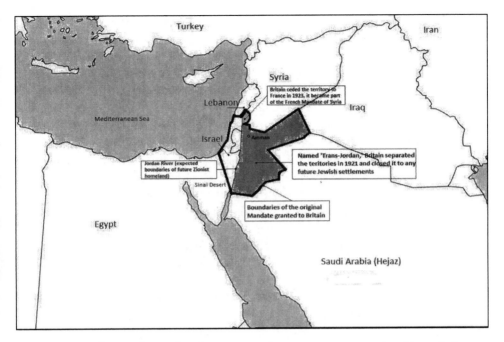

Figure 9.3 The British Mandate (superimposed on contemporary national boundaries, map by author).

under the strenuous conditions of the modern world," is to entrust their tutelage to "*advanced nations who by means of their resources, their experience or their geographical position can best undertake this respon*sibility" (League of Nations, 1920; emphasis mine). Although not considered as an anomaly in Europe at the time, the language of preceding text also denotes the racist tone of colonial policies that were based on prevalent social Darwinist ideas. While the document considered a need for an extended, and almost indefinite, mandate for the populations residing in Central and south-West African Territories as well as the South-Pacific Islands; it held a more favorable position toward territories under former Ottoman Empire's control:

> Certain communities formerly belonging to the Turkish Empire have reached a stage of development where their existence as independent nations can be provisionally recognized subject to the rendering of administrative advice and assistance by a Mandatory *until such a time as they are able to stand alone* (ibid., emphasis mine).

However, the Mandate is also the first international document that utilizes the Balfour Declaration by giving legitimacy to the Zionists and their plans for establishing a Jewish state in Palestine. First, Article 2 of the Mandate declares "the Mandatory shall be responsible for placing the country under such political, administrative and economic conditions as will secure *the establishment of the Jewish national home;*" while at the same time "safeguarding the civil and religious rights of all the inhabitants of Palestine irrespective of race and religion." Second, Article 4 makes a provision for the recognition of "an appropriate Jewish agency" to serve as an advisory body to cooperate with Palestine's British Administration to safeguard "the interests of the Jewish population in Palestine" and "establishment of the Jewish national home," with the Zionist Organization being the legitimate agency recognized by "His Britannic Majesty's government" (ibid, emphasis mine). The Balfour Declaration and Article 6 of the Mandate Charter also cleverly avoided any reference to territorial takeover by immigrant Jews, a necessary prerequisite to establish a Jewish "national home," and put emphasis instead on protection of "civil and religious rights" of indigenous Palestinian populations. If not explicitly, the two documents implicitly indicated the British support of the Zionist movement, while, mindful of expected disappointment by Palestinians and Arabs they skillfully downplayed the prospects of a Zionist settler colony in Palestine. This is what became known as a "dual-obligation" policy by the British, and as Forman and Kedar (2003: 497) have noted,

> Notwithstanding the twists and turns of British policy toward the Zionist project throughout the Mandate, the monumental expansion of Jewish colonization between 1918 and 1948, reflects that *at the end of the day— intentionally or not—government policy was beneficial to Zionist colonization and detrimental to the interests of the country's indigenous non-Jewish population* (emphasis mine).

Zionist Colonization and the Land Question in Palestine

With the blessings of the League of Nations and under British protection the Zionist plan for colonization of Palestine entered a new phase. Emboldened by the Balfour Declaration's implications and British colonial presence, between 1919 and 1923 (the third *aliya*) around thirty-five thousand Jewish immigrants, mostly from Russia arrived in Palestine. The fourth *aliya* (1925–1929) was predominantly from Poland, and by 1929 there were about 160,000 Jews in Palestine. The fifth *aliya* (1933–1936) increased Palestine's Jewish population exponentially, when nearly 160,000 Jews settled in the region. While in 1919 there were only 65,000 Jewish immigrants settled in Palestine, toward the end of the British Mandate in 1948 their numbers was increased by tenfold—with Western European Jews hold-ing the majority status (Mahler, 2004: 21–22). If we only consider legal immigration to Palestine during the Mandate years, more than 92 percent of all registered immigrants were Jewish (Shaw, 1991: 185). Furthermore, between 1922 and end of 1944 the percentage of Palestine's Jewish popula-tion increased from a little more than 10 percent to more than 30 percent (see Table 9.1).

While only a small percentage of indigenous Palestinian Jews were farmers, the future of a Jewish state from the outset depended on the Zionists' success in possession of land in Palestine. As Smith (2010: 124–125) points out, "Zionists were well versed in the intricacies of Arab land ownership even before World War I," and Zionist organizations and agen-cies had "access to external sources of capital" mostly in Europe, a luxury that distinguished them from Palestinian Arab families. In addition, with the establishment of the Jewish National Fund in 1901, Zionist land pur-chases were centralized and coordinated to "ensure that land thus bought would never again be available for sale," and once purchased, "only Jews could work the land" (ibid.: 122, emphasis mine).

Prior to the First World War land laws in Palestine were implemented under the Ottoman Land Code. In general, two distinct land tenure sys-tems were recognized, *mulk* and *miri*. *Mulk* (property) referred to all lands that were considered private property (allodial) with owners having abso-lute ownership rights to its use or disposition. In contrast, *miri* was state or feudal land whereby "the holder or possessor is a usufructuary whose tenure resembles a leasehold, subject to certain limitations on the use and disposition of the land and to the payment of certain fees" to feudal lords or the Ottoman Court (Shaw, 1991: 226). The most common form of *miri* land holding was based on village or clan partnership (*musha'*) whereby

Table 9.1 Jewish Population and Jewish-Owned Land in Palestine, 1922 & 1944

Population	Total	Jews	All Others	% Jewish to Total
1922 census	752,048	88,790	668,528	10.7
Estimated, 1944	1,739,624	528,702	1,210,922	30.3
Total increase	987,526	444,912	542,664	
% Increase by Migration		74	13.3*	

* The rate is actually inflated by migrants of Christian persuasion (29%), while that of Muslim immigrants was only 4 percent.
Source: table constructed based on information in Shaw (1991, Table 3, p. 142; Table 4, p. 376).

each peasant shareholder was allotted a portion of property for cultivation. Smith (2010: 122) reports that by 1923 approximately 75 percent of musha' lands were owned by absentee landlords who lived in towns.[6] As part of reforming the Empire's administration, in 1856 the Ottoman Sultan Abdul Majid issued a proclamation (*Hatti Humayoun*) that granted all citizens equality before the law within the empire. As related to the land question the edict legalized conditional land ownership by foreign subjects contingent on their conforming "to the laws and police regulations, and bearing the same charges as the native inhabitants" (cf. Hurewitz, 1975: 315–318). The reforms were meant to appease the non-Muslim minority populations in order to reduce the separatist tendencies within the Empire. In this context the Ottoman policy toward Zionism was consistent as it allowed Jewish immigrants "to settle as scattered groups throughout the ottoman Empire, *excluding Palestine*" (Mandel, 1976: 2, emphasis mine). However, the official Ottoman policy was rarely implemented in Palestine. For instance, many Jewish immigrants entered Palestine as pilgrims or tourists, and once there they sought the protection of foreign consulates, particularly the British. Related to land acquisition, corruption of local Ottoman authorities and willingness of absentee landowners to sell land to Jewish settlers particularly in northern Palestine helped Zionists to advance their colonization objectives (Smith, 2010: 36–37). Based on one estimate, the proportion of land purchased from large absentee landowners in the 1880–1935 period, both by Zionist agencies and Jewish settlers ranged from about 50 to 90 percent (Aumann, 1976: 121).

There is an ongoing debate among scholars on the extent to which Zionist settler colonies became a component of British colonialism in Palestine. Forman and Kedar (2003: 447–498) identify two camps: those who consider Zionism as a settler movement that served "as a spearhead of Western imperialism" to displace Palestinian residents and take over their lands; and others (mostly Israeli scholars) who see Zionism as a national liberation movement that sought the return of persecuted European Jews to their promised Jewish homeland—the latter group being often at odds with British colonial rule and laws in Palestine. A closer look at the history of British colonial interests and presence in Palestine however will

---

[6] For a more detailed account of Ottoman landholding system and terminologies related to Palestine see Aumann (1976, Appendix 2, pp. 117–27) and Shaw (1991: 225–233).

lend support to the former position, at least up until the outbreak of the Second World War.[7]

As I discussed earlier, in contrast to the Ottoman's opposition to Zionist aspirations, not only did the British government support the establishment of a "national home for the Jewish people" in Palestine (Balfour Declaration); Article 6 of the Mandate Charter also stipulated that the government of Palestine (read 'the British Colonial administration') "shall facilitate Jewish immigration under suitable conditions" and encourage "close settlements by Jews on the land, including state lands and waste lands not required for public purposes" (League of Nations, 1922). As Forman and Kedar (2003: 494) make the case, colonial laws and legal procedures legitimized colonial power relations. For instance, colonial land laws were used as a tool to pacify and govern the colonized which in turn "reduced the need for overt force in maintaining colonial rule." Critical social scientists both inside and outside Israel have emphasized the "intertwining nature of colonial interests and discourses of modernization, which worked to subjugate and marginalize the indigenous population by rendering them primitive, passive, and devoid of development ability or political will" (ibid.: 498).[8]

Related to the land question, the Mandate Legal System in Palestine used Ottoman laws and definitions of land holding and ownership to redefine the land laws under British colonial rule. As Forman and Kedar (2003: 516–517) explain,

> In 1921, Mandate and PJCA[9] officials assumed that all land in question was legally state owned, either *mawat* [dead or undeveloped land] or *mudawwara* (miri) [state or feudal] land that had been transferred to the full ownership of the Ottoman Sultan Abdul Hamid during the last few decades of Ottoman rule and was subsequently appropriated by the Ottoman Treasury) and *that the rights of local residents, if they had any, were strictly "moral"— an imported non-Ottoman term indicating a lack of legal basis* (emphasis mine).

---

[7] For a list of sources on both positions see ibid. (pp. 497–98, footnotes 19–22).

[8] This is not only evident in the language of the 1922 Mandate Charter related to Palestine, but also post-9/11 era, in the way the continuation of American presence in Afghanistan and Iraq in the aftermath of the two nations' occupation and invasion in 2001 and 2003, respectively, has been justified even up to the present time.

[9] In 1891 the Jewish Colonial Association (JCA) was established to help Jews who were emigrating from Eastern Europe to other countries. In 1900, the British Zionist and financier Baron Edmond de Rothschild assigned JCA to administer Jewish colonies in Palestine. JCA was later incorporated into the Palestine Jewish Colonial Association (PJCA) in the mid-1920s (ibid.: 511).

This redefinition of Palestinian legal use-rights to land under Ottoman feudal laws as "moral rights" was a prelude to legal recognition of land ownership in a modern, European capitalist sense. However, in spite of resistance and protests by Palestinian nationalists it also indirectly facilitated Jewish land purchases in Palestine. The majority of Arab Palestinians were small landholding peasants, but Granott (1952: 81–82) contends that a combination of Arabs' willingness to sell and Jewish land purchases in the early 1930s contributed to the emergence of an Arab landless class in Palestine. One factor that galvanized Palestinian peasants was the British government's practice of "dumping," when it opened local markets to European agricultural and consumer goods that were exempt from import tariffs, effectively putting local producers on a disadvantage and pushing many peasants off their lands (Himadeh, 1938: 297).

An unfettered influx of Jewish immigrants, coupled with increasing impoverishment of Palestinians and a general discontent with the British colonial rule in both Palestine and the Arab neighbors sparked Arab revolts and emergence of resistance movements that included pan-Arabists, Palestinian nationalists and militant groups. The main trigger for this unusual hike in Jewish immigration partially lies in an inconvenient historical fact: The *Ha Avarna Agreement* that was concluded between the Nazis and the World Zionist Organization in August 1933 (see Table 9.2). According to the decree's text the agreement was concluded for *"Promoting Jewish immigration to Palestine by releasing the necessary sums* without putting excessive strain upon the foreign currency funds of the Reichsbank, and at the same time for *increasing German exports to Palestine"* (cf. Brenner, 2002: 47, emphasis mine).[10]

With increasing levels of violence and Arab attacks on Jews in 1935 and 1936, and while non-Jewish immigration to Palestine was both negligible and steady, the Zionists demanded an unlimited Jewish immigration and the rights to purchase land, while leaders of Arab resistance movement called for the establishment of an Arab state "where there would be no place for the nearly 400,000 Jews who had immigrated since WWII" (Smith, 2010: 137). This prompted the British government to dispatch a Royal fact-finding commission to Palestine in 1937 known as the Peel Commission, named after its chairman William R.W. Peel. Without any reference to Zionism or British colonial rule, in its report the commission concluded

---

[10] For documentation of the Zionists' collaboration with the Nazis see Brenner (2002). Also see Strauss (1992: 254).

Table 9.2 Jewish and Non-Jewish Immigration to Palestine, 1932–1937

Year	Jews	All others
1932	9,553	1,736
1933	30,329	1,650
1934	42,359	1,784
1935	61,854	2,293
1936	29,727	1,944
1937	10,536	1,939

Source: Table constructed based on information from Aumann (1976: 185, Table 1).

that the Palestine Mandate remains the most viable solution due to the two communities' irreconcilable differences:

> The Arab community is predominantly Asiatic in character, the Jewish community predominantly European. They differ in religion and language. Their cultural and social life, their ways of thought and conduct, are as incompatible as their national aspirations.....[I]n these circumstances to maintain that Palestinian citizenship has any moral meaning is a mischievous pretense. Neither Arab nor Jew has any sense of service to a single state (Palestine Royal Commission report, cf. Fraser, 1980: 22–23).

In the end, the Peel Report concluded that the only alternative solution is to partition Palestine into two separate Jewish and Palestinian independent states with Great Britain remaining as the mandatory power in a zone that included Jerusalem (or the 'holy places') and a narrow corridor that linked the city to the port of Jaffa (see Figure 9.4). As Smith (2010: 138) points out, while some factions within the Zionist movement "cautiously" favored the plan, for very obvious and logical reasons Arabs and Palestinians vehemently opposed it:

> Though the Arab state would comprise about 80 percent of post-1922 Palestine, *the most fertile land had been granted to the Jews*, and 250,000 Arabs living in the Galilee would have to be evacuated. The area awarded to the Jews contained a nearly equal number of Arabs, whereas the Arab area was 90 percent Arab in composition. Palestinian Jews would achieve an independent state but the Arab state might be under Hashemite rule [in Jordan] not Palestinians (ibid, emphasis mine).

With the Peel Partition Plan foiled and the approach of war in 1939 the British needed an Arab support in the region in order to secure oil supplies. This led to publication of the White Paper by the British government with a declaration that "His Majesty's government believes that the framers of the Mandate in which the Balfour Declaration was embodied

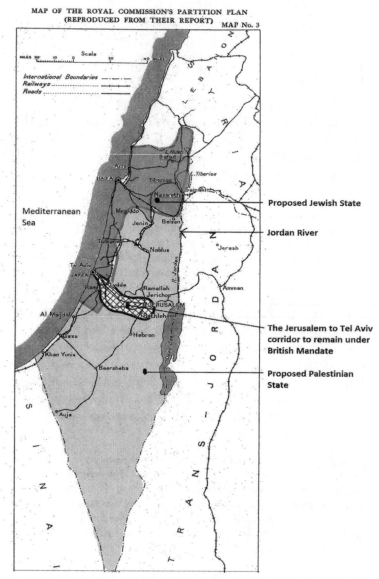

Source: Background map by the Palestine Royal Commission Report, http://en
.wikipedia.org/wiki/File:PeelMap.png.

Figure 9.4 Peel Commission Partition Plan for Palestine, 1937.

would not have intended that Palestine should be converted into a Jewish state against the will of the Arab population" (cf. Hurewitz, 1979: 101). Instead, the new one-state solution in the White Paper envisioned establishment of an "independent Palestine State" within ten years and admission of 75,000 Jewish immigrants and refugees for five years; after which "all further Jewish immigration into Palestine should be stopped forthwith" (the 1939 White Paper on Palestine, cf. Fraser, 1980: 23). Although the White Paper aimed at appeasing the Arab Palestinians, they rejected the plan on the grounds that it did not stop the Jewish immigration, nor did it grant immediate independence to Palestinians. On the other hand, Zionists also opposed the plan considering it in violation of the Balfour Declaration's promises and contrary to international law (Smith, 2010: 146). The White Paper's publication effectively put the British government and the Zionist Agency in Palestine on a collision course.

By the end of World War Two the British Empire's economic and military strengths were on the decline and the Zionists in Palestine were determined to hasten Britain's exit by relinquishing her Mandate even before the 1948 deadline. With increasing level of violence against the British by militant Zionist factions such as Irgun and Haganah, in late 1945 a Joint Anglo-American Committee of Inquiry was appointed by Britain to find a solution for the conflict. In 1946, the Committee's findings were reported back to American diplomats by Dean Acheson, the then U.S. acting Secretary of State. He concluded in a wire communiqué that there is "no hope in countries other than Palestine of substantial assistance in finding homes [for] Jews wishing or forced to leave Europe." Yet similar to the 1939 British White Paper, warning the inappropriateness of narrow nationalist sentiments the Committee also ruled out the two-state solution based on "exclusive claims of Jews and Arabs to Palestine" according to three principles: "Jew shall not dominate Arab in Palestine and vice versa; Palestine shall be neither Jewish nor Arab state; [and] form of government ultimately established shall fully protect interests of Christians, Jews, [and] Muslim faiths under international guarantees" (Dean Acheson, cf. Fraser, 1980: 28–29).

Persisting hostilities and violence between Jews and Palestinians led to Acheson's pessimistic conclusion who did not see the feasibility of establishing a "Palestinian State or states now or some time to come." Hence the Committee's recommendation that "Palestine should continue to be governed under the Mandate, and then the United Nations' trusteeship" as long as the two entities remain hostile" (ibid.: 29). Eventually, since the British could not bring the Zionist agency members and Arab

Table 9.3 Membership Composition of UNSCOP's Two Subcommittees and their Recommendations for Palestine's Future

UNSCOP Sub-Committee	Members	Recommendation for Palestine's Future	UNSCOP Members' Final Vote	
1	U.S., Soviet Union, Canada, Czechoslovakia, Guatemala, Poland, S. Africa, Uruguay, Yemen	Two-state solution and Partition of Palestine with economic unity, with Jerusalem designated as 'special region' to be administered by the UN	For: Against: Abstained:	25 13 17
2	Afghanistan, Columbia, Egypt, Iraq, Pakistan, Saudi Arabia, Syria and Yemen	One single, democratic and independent Palestinian state with provision for minority rights protection	Rejected	

Source: Table constructed based on Fraser (1980: 40–41).

States' representatives to an agreement, they referred the decision on Palestine's future to the newly established United Nations. On May 15, 1947 the UN General Assembly established the Special Committee on Palestine (UNSCOP), charged with the task of finding a solution for the Palestine question.[11] UNSCOP's initial proposed solution was partition of Palestine with the economic union of two states, which Britain promptly rejected. UNSCOP then formed an *ad hoc* Committee comprised of two sub-committees who then reported back with their recommendations. Sub-Committee 1, led by the United States and Soviet Union favored the Partition Plan with economic unity, while Sub-Committee 2 with most of its members still under colonial rule recommended a single democratic and independent state. Eventually the *ad hoc* Committee approved the proposal by Sub-committee 1, which was then adopted and recommended by the UN General Assembly on November 19, 1947 (see Table 9.3).[12]

UNSCOP's adopted plan envisioned the two future states' economic unity. But in reality this unity was not alliance of two political economies of equal strength and status, but that of a much stronger Jewish economy and a less developed and poorer Palestinian economy that according to UNSCOP report at least "during the early days of its existence . . . . . . would

---

[11] UNSCOP membership consisted of Australia, Canada, Czechoslovakia, Guatemala, India, Iran, the Netherlands, Peru, Sweden, Uruguay and Yugoslavia.

[12] This was the adopted UN Resolution 181.

have some difficulty in raising sufficient revenues to keep up its present standard of public services" (UNSCOP's Partition Plan, cf. Fraser, 1980: 46). Thus the UN plan facilitated perpetuation of Palestine's economic dependency on the Jewish state, the former emerging out of a long history of colonization under the Ottomans and the British; and the latter an emerging settler colonial state propped up and aided by colonial and imperial interests. Of note, is the Partition Plan's support by two emerging imperial powers, the Soviet Union and the United States, albeit based on two divergent political economies. Earlier, in September 1947 the U.S. Department of State issued a memorandum pertaining the U.S. policy in the Near East as 'one of higher strategic significance" which necessitated "the maintenance of good will toward the United States on the part of the Moslem world." However, he affirmed his country's "consistent interest in the establishment of a Jewish home" since WWI, reiterating that "the United States has frequently stated its support for large scale Jewish immigration into Palestine and has indicated that it might look with favor upon some arrangement providing for a partition of Palestine (cf. Fraser, 1980: 46). This was a complete reversal of the earlier U.S. position that back in 1945 favored a one-state solution. In his speech to the General Assembly in November 1947, Andrei Gromyko, the then Soviet permanent UN representative also defended his country's support for the partition based on two reasons: "the Jewish people have been closely linked with Palestine for a considerable period in history," apparently rebuking Arab states' opposition to the plan that considered Palestine's partition "an historic injustice;" and the plight of Jews as a consequence of WWII (Gromyko, cf. Fraser, 1980: 60).

Even a perfunctory glance at the partition plan's map will tell the reader that if implemented the conceptualized borders for the two states would have prevented the creation of geographically contiguous territories, resembling M.C. Escher's fantastic illusory drawings that depict impossible spaces (see Figure 9.5).[13] In a closer examination we will notice that the proposed boundaries have created two states that as Shlaim (2000: 25) has observed resembled "two fighting serpents;" and the proposed map's "exceptionally long and winding borders separated the Jewish state from the Arab one, with vulnerable crossing points to link its isolated areas in

---

[13] Maurits Cornelis Escher (1898–1972) is one of the world's most famous graphic artists. He is mostly known for creating impossible structures, transformations and metamorphosis sketches (see Escher's official website, http://www.mcescher.com).

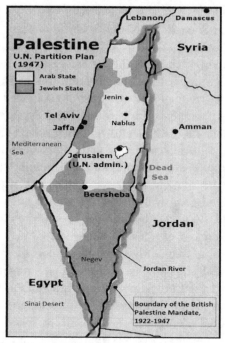

The United Nations' Partition Plan of 1947.

Figure 9.5 Peel Commission Partition Plan for Palestine, 1937.

the eastern Galilee, the coastal plain, and the Negev," that oncce in place would become a "strategic nightmare." Finally, given the Zionists' advantageous econmic position and financial resources vis a vis their Palestinian counterparts and the blessings of the United States and the Soviet Union for a future Jewish state, the more skeptical reader may also conclude that the UN Partition Plan cleverly laid out the grounds for Zionists' future territorial expansion.

Adoption of the UNSCOP Partition Plan, its peculiar spatial arrangement and policy provisions were in fact a prelude to the long-term policy of creating the Greater State of Israel based on Zionist expansionist aspirations. Yet achieving these objectives necessitated either outright land grab by Zionists, or imperial intervention via the Trojan horse of the UN Partition Plan. At the time, Jews owned only 6.67 percent of the land (Tessler, 1994: 174). But considering the magnitude of Jewish immigration to Palestine which by then amounted to almost one-third of total population, the Zionist land purchase policy's success was not impressive—an

indication of Palestinian and Arab nationalists' resistance to Zionist settlers' colonial objectives. By 1947, Palestine's population included 1,293,000
Arabs, Muslims and Christians; as well as 608,000 Jews. Yet the UN plan
proposed allocation of 55 percent of Palestinian territories to the Jewish
state including "the more economically developed part of the country
embracing practically the whole of citrus-producing area." Furthermore,
while there were only 10,000 Jews in the proposed Palestinian State, over
400,000 Palestinians remained within the boundaries of proposed Jewish
State, raising fears among Palestinians that they may be "forcibly removed"
and relocated once the plan was implemented (Abu Nima, 2006: 23–24).

As could be expected, the Partition Plan was embraced by Jews and
Zionists and immediately rejected by Arab states and Palestinians who
considered it as "absurd, impracticable, and unjust" (Shlaim, 2000: 27).
Right after the partition plan's adoption by the UN, a call for general
strike in Palestine by Arab leaders turned violent when angry protesters burned down a Jewish market in Jerusalem (Fraser, 2004: 40); and a
month before the unilateral declaration of the establishment of the state
of Israel a combined force of about one hundred members of Zionist Irgun
and Stern Gang attacked the Palestinian Arab village of Deir Yassin few
miles west of Jerusalem and massacred 250 villagers. Reportedly, half of
villagers killed were women and children "whose mutilated bodies were
stuffed down wells" (Smith, 2010: 199).[14] In retaliation, seventy seven Jewish doctors and nurses in a medical convoy near Jerusalem were killed by
Arabs (Fraser, 1980: 41). Although the British Mandate's official termina-
tion date was May 15, 1948, the Zionist leadership had already proclaimed
the birth of the state of Israel a day before, with the United States being
the first country to immediately announcing its *de facto* recognition at the
United Nations. The Soviets followed suit but this time with *de jure* recognition (Smith, 2010: 200). Although late, Arab states registered their displeasure with Zionists' unilateral declaration, and in a cablegram the Arab
League's Secretary General not only did not acknowledge the proposed
UN Partition Plan, but also recommended "the creation of the United
State of Palestine based upon democratic principles" as the only "fair and
just solution" to the existing conflict (cf. Fraser, 1980: 69). Abandoned
by the British as their colonial protector, a fading imperial power itself;

---

[14] The report was wired by the American Consul at Jerusalem to the U.S. Secretary of
State on April 13, 1948 (cf. Fraser, 1980: 64). But other estimates put the total numbers
killed at 110–115. See for instance, Smith (2010: 199).

and surrounded by weak and disunited Arab states mostly under colonial rule, Arab Palestinians were left on their own to cope with the Zionist aggression. Cognizant of this reality and preparing for a Jewish statehood, from the first phase of the conflict the Zionists were resolved to pursue "a policy of 'aggressive defense' accompanied by economic subversion and psychological warfare." The policy had both "military and territorial objectives"—it aimed at expulsion of Arabs from Palestine and creation of a congruous Jewish-controlled Israeli territory, mainly by systematic capture of land and destruction of Arab villages that dotted the designated Jewish territories under the UN Partition Plan (Shlaim, 2000: 31).

CHAPTER TEN

BANTUSTANS, MAQUILADORAS, AND THE SEPARATION
BARRIER ISRAELI STYLE

A historical understanding of Zionist territorial objectives in Palestine and the State of Israel is an unending map-reading endeavor in futility, based on foregone conclusions of the plight of Palestinians, and probably unrivaled by any other settler colonies of our time. Similar to the previous chapter I do not intend to provide a detailed historical account of the Palestinian-Jewish conflict (or from 1948 onward that between Palestinians and Israelis) and the former's losses and incredible sufferings. This has been done by other scholars and writers more comprehensively and passionately.[1] Rather, my focus here again is on Israel's territorial expansion and the way the two entities' economies have become increasingly entwined to the point of unity—all with the hope in making sense of why Israel erected the Wall around the occupied Palestinian territories.

Israel's First Expansion Phase, 1947–1949

If the Zionists' plan for a "Jewish home in Palestine" was marked by a grand scheme of land grab for a future settler colony, the creation of the state of Israel was predictably a recipe for conflict and bloodshed based on the aggression of Jewish settlers and the Arab Palestinians' resistance. It was in the midst of this undeclared war that the state of Israel was born. This war which Israelis call the War of Independence and Arabs as *al-Nakba* (literally "the disaster") had two phases. The first phase started when the United Nations passed the partition resolution on November 29, 1947 and ended on May 14, 1948, when the State of Israel was unilaterally proclaimed by the Jewish People's Council in Tel Aviv. The UN resolution angered Arab Palestinians who responded with guerilla attacks against Jewish targets. Zionist leaders adopted a hardline "aggressive defense" strategy of capturing as many Palestinian villages and cities as possible

---

[1] See for example, from among many sources, Abunimah (2006), Bennis (2007), Chomsky (1999, 2003 & 2007), Said (1992 & 1995), and Shlaim (2000).

with one clear objective: "to secure all the areas allocated to the Jewish state under the UN partition resolution as well as Jewish settlements outside these areas and corridors leading to them, *so as to provide a solid and continuous basis for Jewish sovereignty*" (Shlaim, 2000: 31, emphasis mine).

The second phase of hostilities began the day after Israel's unilateral declaration of independence, when on May 15, 1948 armies from Egypt, Iraq, Lebanon, Syria, and trans-Jordan attacked Israeli positions from multiple fronts. A truce was reached later in June by Count Folke Bernadotte, the UN-appointed Swedish diplomat, who then traveled to the area to conduct a study of the conflict. He submitted his recommendations to the UN on September 16, 1948 but was assassinated by a member of the militant Zionist Stern Gang the next day.[2] Although the assassin's motives were not investigated, it is not hard to conclude that certain factions within the Zionist movement were displeased with Bernadotte's findings and recommendations. In his telegram to the U.S. Secretary of State, the American Chargé in Egypt referred to Bernadotte's report and his observations of the "appalling" conditions of 300,000–400,000 Arab Palestinian refugees who lived without adequate food, clothing, shelter and basic health care (cf. Fraser, 1980: 72). In Bernadotte's report two recommendations stood out as clearly challenging the future of the Zionist state. First, he emphasized that the UN "should undertake to provide special assurance that the boundaries between the Arab and Jewish territories shall be respected and maintained" based on the partition plan. This clearly would have challenged Israel's excursions beyond demarcated lines and put limits on her future territorial expansions. In fact, it was for this same reason that Israel never adopted a constitution as was called for in the Proclamation of Independence document, as it would have clearly identified state boundaries and in turn delegitimized further future territorial gains beyond prescribed territories.[3] Bernadotte's second recommendation, controversial and unacceptable from the Zionists' perspective, was the full recognition of Arab Palestinian refugees' "right of return" by the UN, including "their repatriation, resettlement and economic and social reha-

---

[2] The Lehi, commonly known as the Stern Gang after its leader was a militant Zionist group that was active during the 1940–1948 period and aimed at forcible eviction of the British from Palestine, securing unrestricted Jewish immigration and creation of 'Eretz-Israel.' One of Lehi's leaders, Yitzhak Shamir eventually became Israel's prime minister in 1983.

[3] According to the Proclamation of Independence document a constituent assembly should have prepared a constitution by October 1, 1948.

bilitation" as well as "payment of adequate compensation for the property of those choosing not to return" (Bernadotte, cf. Fraser, 1980: 74–75). After a short-lived truce an all-out Israeli military offensive swept through Palestine and wiped out the meager resistance pockets by Arab forces; and by the end of 1948 Israel not only reclaimed all territories allocated by the UN plan for the future Jewish State, but also took over additional territories set aside for the Palestinian state (Shlaim, 2000: 28). This effectively placed 78 percent of Palestine under Israeli control and displaced 726,000 Palestinians, who then became refugees on their own lands or in neighboring Arab states (Abunimah, 2007: 25) (see Figure 10.1).

Israeli leaders used the alarming rise of a "menace of Jews" attitude in many European countries and persecution of Jews during the Holocaust as a pretext, while the Proclamation of Independence document declared "Eretz-Israel" a Jewish state "which would open the gates of the homeland wide to every Jew and confer upon the Jewish people the status of a fully privileged member of the community of nations"; thus granting millions of Jews a 'right to return' to a place they have never been to before (cf. Fraser, 1980: 66–67). The document declared assurances that the new state of Israel "will ensure complete equality of social and political rights to all its inhabitants irrespective of religion, race or sex." This led to a massive immigration from both European and non-European nations that doubled Israel's Jewish population between 1949 and 1952 (Smith, 2010: 225). But the 170,000 or so Arab Palestinians who remained and were classified as citizens especially along the militarized armistice lines where frequent incursions by Palestinians was taking place, were still considered as "potential subversives" and subjected to banishment and property confiscation (ibid.). In addition, displaced Palestinians who had lived in Palestine for generations were denied the right to return to their homeland. Israel's urgent need to make room for the influx of Jewish newcomers also made the lands owned by Israeli Arabs an attractive target for confiscation. To give this land grab scheme some legality, in 1950 the Israeli Knesset passed the comprehensive *Absentees' Property Law* based on which most Arab-owned property in Israel was designated as "absentee." The law allowed the state to appoint a Custodian for absentee's property, to whom all property rights were transferred. As Smith (ibid.: 226) explains,

> Any Palestinian Arab could be declared absentee if he had left his usual place of residence on or after November 29, 1947, the date of the United Nations partition resolution. This applied whether the individual had returned to the place of residence on the following day or had fled scenes of combat during the war but had not left what became Israeli territory. *Tens of thousands of*

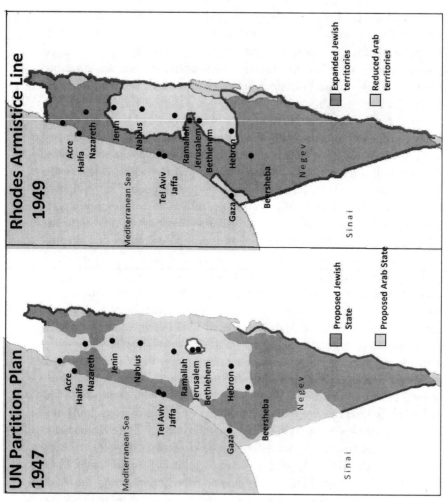

Figure 10.1 The Original 1947 UN Plan (left) and Expanded, Congruous Israeli Territories at the Conclusion of Hostilities in 1949 (right) (map by author).

Israeli Arabs were so classified, only about 1 percent were able to regain some of their property (emphasis mine).

With the conclusion of armistice agreements between Arab states and Israel in 1949 the two entities entered a new phase. Except for 133,000 Palestinians who remained in Israel, more than 700,000 were displaced and forced to leave—of these, 470,000 fled to the Arab Palestine west of Jordan River controlled by Jordanian King and the rest were dispersed into Egypt as refugees (both Gaza Strip and Egypt proper), Jordan, Lebanon and Syria. Yiftachel (2009) calls the 1947–1949 period as the "ethnic cleansing" stage of the Judaization of Palestine project, when Zionists succeeded in uprooting most Arab Palestinians from their land and confiscating the properties they left behind.

Israel's Second Expansion Phase, 1949–1967

Almost a year after Israel's unilateral declaration of independence and despite her flagrant violation of the UN Partition Plan provisions, on May 11, 1949 the UN accepted Israel as a new member. The UN recognition provided Israel with some legitimacy by an institution that back in the 1940s was dominated by a few imperial and colonial powers, with the majority of member states still being under colonial rule. In his little book *Israel a Colonial-Settler State?* Maxime Rodinson (1973: 91–92) remarks that, "colonialists and colonizers are not monsters with human faces whose behavior defies rational explanation, as one might think from reading left-wing intellectuals." As a realist he also concedes that in time colonial projects have become a reality, and that "history is full of *faits accomplis.*" Related to Israel he further writes,

> The Jews of Israel too are people like other people. Some of them have hammered out an illusory ideology to which they have sacrificed themselves as well as a great deal of effort and many human lives. They are not alone. Many are those who have suffered much but have looked with indifference upon the sufferings and rights of others. Many went there because it was the life preserver thrown to them. They most assuredly did not first engage in scholarly research to find out if they had a right to it according to Kantian morality or existentialist ethics.

In spite of all anomalies, irrationalities, and illegalities of a process of nation-building, by all accounts 1949 marks the beginning of a new phase of Israel's growth and development as a settler colony. The settler colony's development from 1949 to the conclusion of the Six-Day War in

1967 drastically increased territories under Israeli control dictated by two parallel political processes. Domestically, the government's "internal colonialist" policies included systematic destruction of Palestinian villages and displacement of their inhabitants in order to build settlements for the new waves of Jewish immigrants. Based on one estimate, out of about 400 Jewish settlements established after 1948 some 350 were built on refugee property. Khalidi (1993) estimates that between 1948 and 1950 about 369 abandoned Palestinian villages were erased in order to build 161 new Jewish settlements. In addition, two-thirds of the cultivated land in Israel was also owned by Palestinians who were forced to flee (Don Peretz, cf. Barakat, 1973: 153). The extreme Zionist expansionist ideas promoted early on by the likes of Jabotinsky were also revived and rehabilitated in the 1960s, with some even pushing for the realization of Greater Eretz-Israel based on Palestine's boundaries during WWI that included Jordanian territories both east and West of Jordan River (Rael, 1980: 139).[4]

Externally, Israel had to deal with imperial rivalries in the region on one hand and emerging pan-Arab nationalist sentiments on the other. In the aftermath of the Suez crisis and with the Soviets' support Egypt and Syria formed a military alliance, albeit fragile, which became a main Cold War era foreign policy concern for the United States and in turn brought the latter and Israel closer together. Militant Palestinian groups such as Fatah and the more mainstream organizations such as the Palestine Liberation Organization (PLO) also added to regional tensions.[5] In particular, Fatah members backed by Syria staged attacks against Israeli installations in the hope of galvanizing Arab states to wage war against Israel. Although based on the U.S. intelligence there were no indications that the neighboring Arab states were preparing for an all-out war against Israel, the latter used this assumption as a pretext to justify her pre-emptive strikes particularly against Egyptian forces. In what is dubbed as the 'Six-Day War,' between June 5 and 10, 1967 Israeli forces swiftly defeated Arab forces and effectively occupied and annexed the remaining 22 percent of historic Palestine—the Gaza Strip from Egypt, East Jerusalem and the West Bank (of Jordan River) territories from Jordan; as well as the entire Sinai Peninsula from Egypt and the strategic Golan Heights

---

[4] Ze'ev Jabotinsky is considered as the founder and ideologue of the Revisionist Zionist movement. I will discuss his ideas at the end of this chapter in more details.

[5] Fatah was formed in 1958 by several young Palestinians who fled Palestine when the state of Israel was created in 1948. Established in 1964 the original PLO was the brain child of the Arab League to represent Palestinian interests (see Sayigh, 1997).

territories from Syria (Matar, 1996). As a consequence, an estimated 300,000 Palestinians fled the West Bank and Gaza, most of whom settled as refugees in Jordan (Sharpe, 2004). Another 80,000–110,000 Syrians were also forced to flee from the Golan Heights to northern Syrian provinces (Morris, 2001: 327) (see Figure 10.2).

The post-1967 period opened up a new chapter in Israel's expansionist history, as in addition to domestic issues of nation-building the successive Israeli governments had to wrestle with colonial administration of the territories occupied during the Six-Day War. Unlike 1947, when the UN Partition Plan set the tone for Israel's unilateral declaration of statehood, this time Israel's military aggression and territorial acquisitions did not sit well within the international community. In November 1967 the UN Security Council unanimously passed the Resolution 242 which explicitly demanded Israel to withdraw its armed forces from the occupied territories and move them behind the armistice (Green) Line; to terminate all territorial claims; and respect the sovereignty and territorial integrity of neighboring Arab states (UN Resolution 244, cf. Fraser, 1980: 117). Yet even if prior to the 1967 offensive the Israelis had assured the United States that they were not after territorial expansion, in a report to the Israeli people right after the Six-Day war's conclusion then Prime Minister Levi Eshkol declared "there should be no illusion that Israel is prepared to return to the conditions that existed a week ago....We have fought alone for our existence and our security, and are therefore justified in deciding for ourselves what the genuine and indispensable interests of our state are and how to guarantee our future" (cf. Neff, 1984: 299).

Israel's Third Expansion Phase, 1967–1991

The two main political entities in Israel, namely, the Likud and the Labor Party may have had different positions in terms of domestic issues. But their policies often colluded when dealing with the occupied territories and the Palestinian question. Between 1967 and 1977 Israel's colonization policy followed the Allon Plan that called for expanding Jewish settlements in East Jerusalem and approximately 40 percent of the occupied West Bank territories, with a clear objective of increasing Jewish settler population in the West Bank without annexation of territories and their Palestinian populations (Matar, 1996: 2–3). While in 1967 there were no Jewish settlements in the West Bank, by 1973 fourteen settlements were established in the occupied territories. During the 1973 election campaign

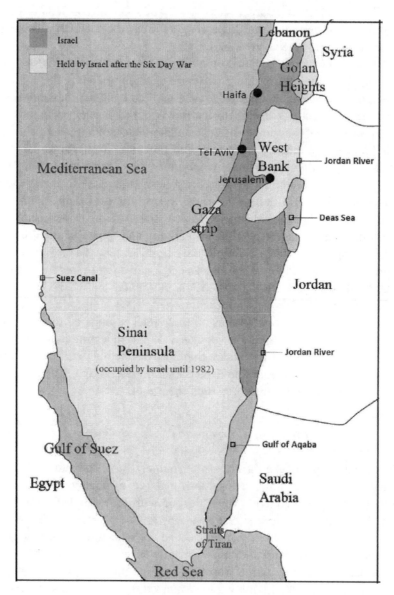

Figure 10.2 Israel and Occupied territories since June 1967 (map by author).

the Labor Party (commonly perceived as Israel's moderate political entity) adopted a controversial platform based on Yisrael Galili's document that supported expansion of Jewish settlements around Jerusalem, the West Bank and Golan Heights; provision of incentives to Israeli industrialists to develop industrial centers near the heavily populated Palestinian areas in the west Bank; permission for land purchases in the Occupied territories; and establishment of a Jewish settlement in the port city of Yamit near Rafah, across from the latter city's southern entrance to the Gaza Strip from Sinai Peninsula (Shlaim, 2000: 317; Smith, 2010: 320). The Galili Document's provisions to expand Jewish settlements in the Sinai Peninsula and Golan Heights alarmed Egypt and Syria, leading to the Yum Kippur War in October 1973. Although Egyptian and Syrian armies made initial advances into their respective territories occupied by Israel, their forces were eventually pushed back with Israel occupying new territories west of the Suez Canal and north of Golan Heights. With American mediation Egypt and Syria signed two "disengagement of forces" agreements with Israel in 1974, but Sinai and Golan Heights continued to be occupied by Israel. Eventually, the Sinai Peninsula was returned to Egypt in 1982 based on the terms of the Camp David Peace Accord between Egypt and Israel that was brokered by the U.S. President Carter in 1978.

The Camp David treaty effectively neutralized Egypt and Jordan and made them partners in guaranteeing Israel's security. It also stipulated a gradual transition from Israeli military rule to a self-governing Palestinian Authority in the West Bank whose local police force were to be supervised by Israeli, Jordanian and Egyptian officers. Ironically, the new Palestinian police were not getting trained to ensure the security of Palestinians in the West Bank, but rather that of Israeli settlers (Camp David agreement of 1978, cf. Fraser, 1980: 171–76). During the 1978–1988 period the die was also cast for creation of Greater Israel as the Israeli regime sped up construction of Jewish settlements in the West Bank which by 1978 totaled 39, housing 7,400 settlers. This was a flagrant violation of several international laws including the 1907 Hague Convention; but particularly the Fourth Geneva Convention of 1949 that was specifically designed to protect the civilian population of occupied areas and prevent the occupiers from permanently changing the status of the territories (Pacheo, 2001: 182). For example, related to demands from Palestinians to participate in political processes or to assume administrative roles under the occupation, article 47 of the Geneva Convention clearly declares "Protected persons who are in occupied territory shall not be deprived, in any case or in any manner whatsoever, of the benefits of the present Convention by ... any agreement concluded between the authorities of the occupied territories and the occupied power" (cf. Pacheo, 2001: 199). This clearly indicates the illegality of Camp David peace Treaty's stated expectations of Palestinians regarding Israel's security. Furthermore, Article 49, paragraph 6 explicitly states "The occupying power shall not deport or transfer parts of its own civilian population into territories it occupies," another explicit indication of the illegal status of Jewish Settlements in all the occupied territories. Thus from 1978 onward all negotiations between Israel and Palestinians are illegal under International laws. However, successive governments in Israel have considered the Jewish settlements as being entirely legal under international laws by invoking the Palestine Mandate adopted by the League of Nations in the 1920s; and rejecting the applicability of Article 49 in the Convention to Palestine by arguing that "no one is being forced to move to the settlements" (Mahler, 2004: 314). But as Margalit (2001: 23) points out, the clear objective of Article 49 is "to prevent permanent colonization of occupied territories, which is undoubtedly the purpose of the [Jewish] settlements ... the rest is sophistry."[6]

By 1987, when the first *Intifada* (literally meaning 'shaking off' or 'uprising' as is translated in English) challenged the legitimacy of the Israeli occupation, 110 settlements were already built in the West Bank housing 57,900 Jewish settlers (Hareuveni, 2010: 9–10, Table 1). The first *intifada* was a militant but unarmed popular uprising that adhered to the principles of nonviolent resistance to the extent it could under the occupation. A traffic accident in which an Israeli truck driver hit and killed four Palestinians in the Gaza Strip is often cited as the 'spark' that ignited the *Intifada*, but Shlaim (2000: 450–451) argues that the seeds of the uprising were sown during two decades of occupation and considers it as "the Palestinian War of Independence":

> In origin the *Intifada* was not a nationalist revolt. It had its roots in poverty, in miserable living conditions of the refugee camps, in hatred of the occupation, and, above all, in the humiliation that the Palestinians had to endure over the preceding twenty years. But it developed into a statement of major political import. The aims of the *Intifada* were not stated on the outset; they emerged in the course of the struggle. The ultimate aim was self-determination and the establishment of an independent Palestinian state,

---

[6] For a detailed account of the fourth Geneva Convention's objectives see Pacheo (2001: 182–188). Although brief, Thomas (2011: 7–8) also provides an interesting overview of Israel's violations of international laws. For Israel's position on the legality of Jewish settlements see Mahler (2004: 310–316).

which had failed to emerge forty years previously despite the UN partition resolution of 29 November 1947.

Although the *Intifada* effectively forced Israeli Jews to reassess their relations with Palestinians and search for a peaceful resolution to the conflict, it was the former group that ultimately dictated the course and terms of negotiations. The process began with the Madrid talks in 1991 which were held under the supervision of the United States and former Soviet Union, along with participation of the European Community representatives. However, the bilateral talks between Palestinians and Israelis quickly deteriorated and failed mainly due to the latter party's refusal to stop the expansion of Jewish settlements in the occupied territories.

Israel's Fourth Expansion Phase, 1993–2000

In 1993 a new round of secret talks between the PLO leaders and Israeli government were held in Oslo, Norway which led to the signing of the Declaration of Principles document (DOP). Article 1 of the DOP document stipulates establishment of "a Palestinian Interim Self-Government Authority" with an elected Council in the occupied territories just for a transitional five-year period, leading to a permanent settlement based on Security Council Resolutions 242 and 338.[7] Without even considering other terms of the Oslo agreement and other treaties that followed, implementation of this article alone was in clear violation of the Fourth Geneva Convention, particularly Article 47, which renders the DOP illegitimate and unenforceable. As one observer points out:

> The harsh experience of the Vichy regime after the Nazi conquest of France provided all-too-familiar reasons for the convention's drafters to prevent the recurrence of such a situation. *The drafters sought clearly and unequivocally to prevent instances whereby the occupying power would prop up a questionable government that would then ostensibly be authorized to make arrangements with the occupying power at the expense of the rights of the occupied civilians* (Pacheo, 2001: 199) (emphasis mine).

Israel's endorsement of the DOP however was contingent on certain preconditions that had to be met by Palestinians. This was accomplished in a letter sent by the PLO Chairman Yasser Arafat to Israeli Prime Minister

---

[7] Text of 1993 Oslo Accords, Declaration of Principles. Retrieved from http://israeli palestinian.procon.org/sourcefiles/1993-Oslo-Accords-DOP.pdf.

Yitzhak Rabin in August 1993. In his letter, Arafat clearly recognized "the right of the state of Israel to exist in peace and security;" accepted UN Resolutions 242 and 388; made unconditional commitment to a peaceful resolution of the conflict; renounced terrorism and violence; and on PLO's behalf made a commitment to terminate the *Intifada* (Rabbani, 2001: 75). Rabin's one-sentence ambiguous, non-committal and arrogant response to Arafat's letter revealed the unequal nature of communication between the colonizer and the colonized: "In response to your letter of September 9, 1993, I wish to confirm to you that, in light of the PLO commitments included in your letter, the Government of Israel has decided to recognize the PLO as the representative of the Palestinian people and commence negotiations with the PLO within the Middle East peace process."[8] Thus in contrast to Arafat's statement, Rabin made no commitment to renounce violence or acknowledge Palestinians' right to exist in peace and security. Later, the 1995 Interim Agreement on the West Bank and the Gaza Strip between the two parties that is commonly referred to as "Oslo II" or the "Taba agreement" moved the negotiations to the implementation phase. Israeli army units were withdrawn from six West Bank Palestinian cities; the occupied territories were partitioned and areas under Israeli or Palestinian control were designated; complex security measures and economic agreements were hammered out; and elections were held for the Palestinian Authority and the Legislative Council seats.

By all accounts, as a clever political scheme the Oslo agreements provided legal justifications for Israel's territorial expansion and increased control over Palestinian economy. In his examination of the Oslo agreement's specific negotiated terms Pacheo (2001: 189–196) identifies several critical legal miscalculations and concessions made by Palestinian negotiators. First, in terms of territorial concessions they allowed Israel's continued control of East Jerusalem that was a prelude to its complete annexation into Israel proper. But more importantly, they made 60 percent of the West Bank territories negotiable. This was based on a map prepared by Israelis that partitioned the West Bank into three separate territorial zones:

> Area A: complete transfer of security and civilian matters to the Palestinian Authority (approximately 17.2 percent by 2001). Area B: Israeli control over security, Palestinian control over civilian matters (approximately

---

[8] Cf. MidEastWeb, retrieved from http://www.mideastweb.org/osloletters.htm.

23.8 percent by 2001). Area C: approximately 59 percent, under Israeli military and civilian control, to be negotiated (p. 190) (see Figure 5).[9]

Although the Israeli military units were to be withdrawn from Area A, this would have changed nothing as they were redeployed outside the city gates. It is like removing the prison guard from an inmate's cell and positioning him/her outside the cell instead! Equally problematic was "the Palestinian concession not to challenge Israel's property rights in Areas A and B," such as lands designated as "Absentee" or areas taken over by Israeli corporations since the 1967 occupation. However, similar legal protections were not granted to Palestinians who owned land in Area C (ibid., pp. 190–191).

The late Edward Said was one of the first observers who detected the Oslo agreements' flaws and deceptive nature. Related to the territorial partition plan he made note of a sad reality that Palestinians all the way through the Oslo negotiation process were "map-less," that is, "they had no detailed maps of their own at Oslo. Nor, unbelievably, were there any individuals on the negotiating team familiar enough with the geography of the occupied territories to contest decisions or to provide alternative plans" (Said, 2001: 33). The partition plan, dubbed by Palestinians as the "Leopard Skin" effectively carved out the West Bank cities, villages and territories into separate entities similar to South African Bantustans under the Apartheid regime. This was a conscious, premeditated effort on the Israeli government's part to create a geography of territorial control by using the old colonial strategy of 'divide and rule':

> A glance at any of the maps reveals not only that the various parts of Area A are separated from each other, but that they are surrounded by Area B, and more important, Area C. In other words, the closures and encirclements that have turned the Palestinian areas into besieged spots on the map have been long in the making and, worse still, the Palestinian Authority has conspired in this: it has approved all the relevant documents since 1994 (ibid.: 38) (see Figure 10.3).

As a by-product of the first legal miscalculation, the second concession by the Palestinian negotiators was to legitimize illegal Jewish settlements particularly in Area C. There are no provisions either in the DOP or the Oslo II documents to stop, restrict or prohibit Jewish settlements in the occupied territories; and the settlements' status remained an open-ended

---

[9] Pacheo (ibid., p. 204 fn. 21) informs the reader that Area C contained "the most important groundwater reserves for the Palestinian population."

Oslo II, 1995

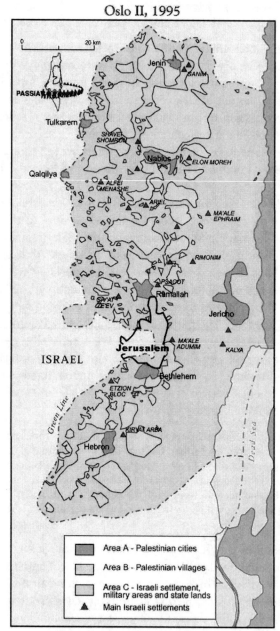

Source: Map courtesy of Palestinian Academic Society for the Study of International Affairs
(PASSIA) http://www.passia.org/palestine_facts/MAPS/Oslo-2.html (permission granted).

Figure 10.3 Cantonization of the West Bank: Palestinian Bantustans under the
Terms of Oslo II Agreements.

issue that was deferred until the final status. Israel's colonial intentions were no secret, and in his report to the Knesset on the Oslo II talks' outcome Israeli Prime Minister Yitzhak Rabin reiterated his commitment to Israel's strategy in the West Bank as to "not to uproot any settlement in the framework of the Interim Agreement, nor to freeze construction and natural growth" (cf. Pacheo, 2001: 192).[10]

The third concession given to Israel was allowing the continued construction of bypass roads in the occupied territories. The origins of bypass roads go back to the 1970s, when Israel began to create a transportation grid mostly in the West Bank with the objective of "bypassing" Palestinian cities and villages, connecting Jewish settlements together as well as to the highway network inside Israel proper (Etkes, 2005). As an example, the stated objectives of constructing bypass roads in the *Settlement Master Plan for 1983–1986* document are revealing. First, the roads are considered as a motivating factor for Jewish settlers to move in and settle in the occupied lands with a sense of security. Second, bypass roads will effectively block Palestinian rural and urban expansion and development by creating impassable physical barriers. The chapter on roads in the *Settlement Master Plan* unabashedly sets the record straight. For instance, in describing the importance of building a bypass road in a mountain ridge area the document states that the road will hold "most of the Arab population in the urban and rural communities;" and "...Jewish settlement along this route (Route 60) will create a psychological wedge regarding the mountain ridge, and also will likely reduce the uncontrolled spread of Arab settlement" (cf. B'Tselem, 2004a: 8). By 2000 the bypass road network was almost complete, dissecting the occupied territories and geographically suffocating many Palestinian population centers.[11] As Pacheo (2001: 193) points out, "this extensive destruction of thousands of acres of Palestinian land for no public or military purpose, but rather to serve the illegal Jewish settler population, was clearly a violation of the [Fourth Geneva] Convention and fell under its war-crime definition in article 147." In an investigative report of the bypass roads B'Tselem (2004b) calls them as "forbidden roads" and puts them in three categories: *completely prohibited roads* built

---

[10] Even up to the present time successive Israeli governments have used the term "natural growth" as an acceptable and legitimate aspect of settlements' expansion, a fictitious term which in fact justifies further illegal expansion of the already existing illegal settlements.

[11] For an excellent compilation of maps related to bypass roads and Jewish settlements in the occupied territories see http://www.btselem.org/maps.

for the exclusive use of Israeli citizens; *partially prohibited roads* on which Palestinians are allowed to travel only with obtaining special permits; and *restricted use roads* that are open to Palestinian vehicles but protected by concrete roadblocks and complete search of vehicles and their passengers (see Figure 10.4). The report also justifiably considers the bypass road network as an instrument of Apartheid based on nationality:

> The roads regime, which is based on separation through discrimination, bears clear similarities to the racist apartheid regime that existed in South Africa until 1994. An individual's national origin determines their right to use various roads. This policy is based on a racist premise: that all Palestinians are security risks, and it is therefore justifiable to restrict their movement. Thus the policy indiscriminately harms the entire Palestinian population, in violation of their human rights and of international law (ibid.).

Palestinian negotiators also made few other concessions during Oslo talks, including legitimization of Jewish settlements in the city of Hebron; permitting the pillage of water resources in the West Bank; and allowing the continued prohibition on population movement by Israel (Pacheo, 2001: 193–197). In summing up the Oslo talks' "fatal flaw" Rabbani (2001: 74) notes that it was ".... neither an instrument of decolonization nor a mechanism to apply international legitimacy to the Israeli-Palestinian conflict, but rather a framework that changes the basis of Israeli control over the occupied territories in order to perpetuate it." In the final analysis I consider Yasser Arafat and Mahmoud Abbas, the main Palestinian negotiators during the Oslo talks to at best being extremely naïve and uninformed in giving up too much and getting too little in return; and at worst collaborators with the occupiers who knowingly betrayed the aspirations of millions of Palestinians who had put their trust in them.

The Second Intifada: *Prelude to the Wall/Fence*

As Israel's Labor Party "peace candidate," in 1999 Ehud Barak was elected Prime Minister who apparently wholeheartedly supported the Oslo Accords (Thomas, 2011: 137). But in reality he was interested in a solution that will not alienate the right-wing Zionists and the settler population. Thus when in 2000 he went to the Camp David summit to offer the Palestinian negotiators Israel's final plan, he was guided by three principles. First, he had no interest in piece-meal steps as was stipulated in the Oslo accords, as in his view Israel was not getting tangible results "without knowing the Palestinians' final demand." Second, he believed Palestinian

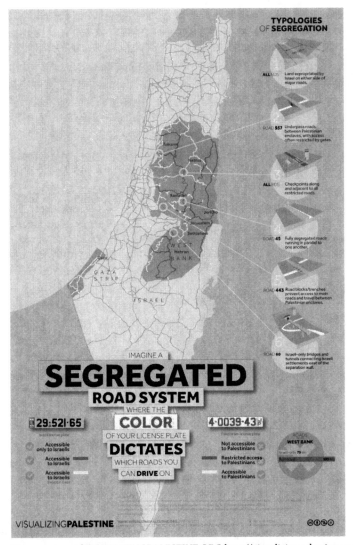

Source: Map courtesy of VISUALIZINGPALESTINE.ORG http://visualizingpalestine.org/info graphic/segregated-roads-west-bank

Figure 10.4. Map of Bypass Roads in the West Bank and Their Connection to Israel's Highway Grid, 2012. Note a network of roads accessible to Israelis only that overpass the 'white' roads designated for Palestinian traffic in the West Bank (the map includes three road categories). The poster's caption "segregated road system where the color of your license plate dictates which roads you can drive on" refers to Israel's dual system of population control that is similar to that of the defunct apartheid regime in South Africa.

negotiators will not accept any proposal which in their view was "unap-pealing." Finally, he wanted to "present all concessions and all rewards in one comprehensive package that the Israeli public would be asked to accept in a national referendum." It was based on this "all-or-nothing" approach that Barak came to the negotiating table with Yasser Arafat and his team (Malley and Agha, 2001). Israelis never presented the details of their proposed package, but based on their past track record it was clear that they would not make any further concessions. Chomsky (2003: 217) sums up the joint U.S.-Israel package that was eventually visualized in the "final status map" in 2001:

> This plan, extending U.S.-Israeli rejectionist proposals of earlier years, *called for cantonization of the territories* that Israel had occupied in 1967, with mechanisms to ensure that usable land and resources (primarily water) remain largely in Israeli hands *while the population is administered by a corrupt and brutal Palestinian Authority (PA), playing the role traditionally assigned to indigenous collaborators* under the several varieties of imperial rule: the black leadership of South Africa's Bantustans, to mention only the most obvious analogue (emphasis mine).

The Camp David proposal suggested a land swap, whereby 9 percent of the West Bank mostly along the Green Line that contained 150,000 Jew-ish settlers and 120,000 Palestinians would have been annexed to Israel in lieu of 1 percent of Israeli territory given to Palestinians. What was not clear, was a plan for relocation of 120,000 Palestinians, and the future of many other Jewish settlements, bypass roads and security zones in the West Bank, as well as the fate of East Jerusalem (Thomas, 2011: 139). By 2001, there were 123 Jewish settlements in the West Bank housing more than 200,000 settlers (Hareuveni, 2010: 9–10).[12] Even a casual observer will realize the strategic location of Jewish settlements that are circling Pales-tinian towns and villages, connected by an extensive network of highways that criss-cross the occupied West Bank territories; which will impede the latter's growth and spatial development and guarantee their geographical isolation. Certainly, this has to be based on careful planning on the Zion-ists' part and not merely a coincidental pattern (see Figure 10.5).

Another problematic feature of the final status map was the fate of a 10-mile wide portion of Area C along the Jordan River known as the *Jor-dan Valley*, roughly covering one third of the West Bank which Israelis

---

[12] This excludes Jewish settlers in East Jerusalem which by 2000 were in excess of 167,000 (ibid.).

Projection of the West Bank Final Status Map presented
by Israel, Camp David, July 2000

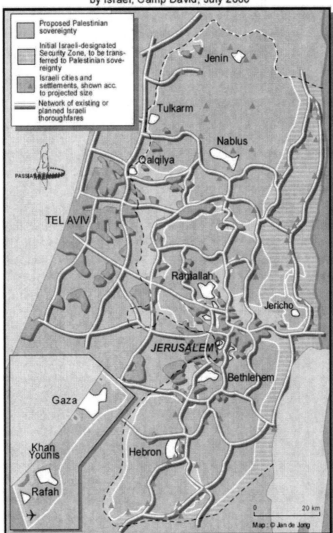

Source: Map courtesy of Palestinian Academic Society for the Study of International
Affairs (PASSIA) http://www.passia.org/palestine_facts/MAPS/images/wbgs_campdavid.pdf
(permission granted).

Figure 10.5 Location of Jewish Settlements in Relation to the Final Status Map of
the West Bank Presented by Israel at Camp David in 2001. Note the network of
Israeli bypass roads and highways in the occupied territories.

earmarked as a security zone remaining under full military control. This almost verbatim followed the plan proposed by Defense Minister Yigal Allon right after the 1967 occupation that designated the Jordan Valley as a military zone to both create a buffer with Jordan and facilitate the West Bank's military control—a clear indication that the final status map was in fact realization of an earlier Zionist plan for 'Eretz Israel.' What was left for the Palestinians was the northern enclaves (or what Chomsky calls "cantons") including cities of Nablus, Jenin, Tulkarm and Ramallah with a narrow corridor that provided a crossing to Jordan via the city of Jericho; and the southern enclave that included Hebron and Bethlehem. The Jericho corridor later became a non-issue when in 1988 Jordan relinquished the West Bank's control to the Palestinians (see figure 10.6).

The proposed package's flagrant design to grant Israel full colonial control over the occupied territories was even beyond Arafat and his negotiating team's tolerance level, which in the course of Oslo negotiations had at times acted as collaborators and made significant concessions. Arafat's "uncompromising no" to Israel's "unprecedented generous offer," as the latter claimed, was then portrayed by Israel and her supporters as a historic missed opportunity to reach a final agreement for peace at Camp David (Malley and Agha, 2001). But even Barak's foreign minister, Shlomo Ben-Ami who participated at Camp David talks later conceded that "if I were a Palestinian I would have rejected Camp David as well" (cf. Mearsheimer and Walt, 2006: 4). The failure of Camp David talks ended Palestinians' hope for a workable solution to the conflict. But it was preceded by almost a decade of broken promises made during the Oslo talks, worsening economic conditions in the occupied territories, and Israel's continued heavy handed administration of the occupied territories using the *closure regime* and *collective punishment*.[13] This pent-up frustration in the occupied territories led to the escalation of violence which is commonly known as the

---

[13] The Internal Displacement Monitoring Centre (IDMC) provides a clear definition of Israel's *closure regime*:

> Closures is a policy of physical barriers in the form of checkpoints, and other road obstacles, and permit requirements.... the closure policy may refer to elaborate system restricting internal movement, as well as external movement between West Bank, Gaza, and Israel (IDMC, 2011).

The Israeli government has used a long-established policy of *collective punishment* whereby a group of Palestinians (such as family members) are collectively punished (such as home demolitions) because of their association with an individual who has in some ways defied the occupation rules.

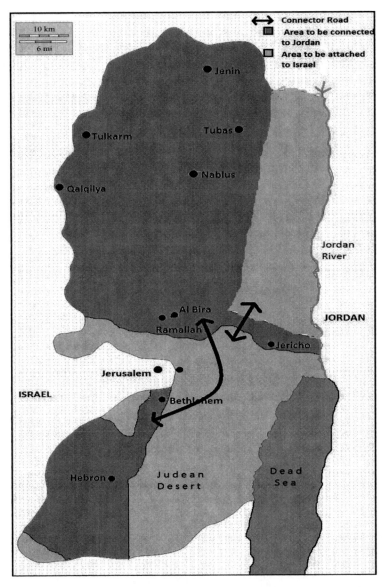

Figure 10.6 The 1967 Allon Plan (map by author). Map constructed based
on information in Tessler (1994: 465–73).

beginning of the second *Intifada*. Thomas (2011: 141) reports, "daily clashes for several months took the lives of 350 Palestinians and 50 Israelis." The disproportionate casualty levels for both sides indicate Israel's superior military might and willingness in using the lethal force. B'Tselem, an Israeli NGO that monitors human rights violations in the occupied territories estimates that 4,789 Palestinians and 1,053 Israelis have been killed during the 2000–2008 period.[14]

The conventional wisdom often blames Ariel Sharon for the escalation of conflict, when on September 29, 2000 he made a provocative visit to the highly contentious Muslim religious site of the Al-Aqsa Mosque and Dome of the Rock on Temple Mount under heavy armed guard of more than one hundred policemen and soldiers.[15] Escalation of violence in the aftermath of Al Aqsa Intifada is also often cited as the reason behind the Israeli government's decision to construct what Israel calls as the "anti-terrorist security fence." In fact, on its web site related to the fence Israel's Ministry of Foreign Affairs (2003) declares that the only purpose to erect the security fence/wall is "to keep the [Palestinian] terrorists out and thereby save the lives of Israel's citizens, Jews and Arabs alike."

Israel's Final Expansionist Offensive: The Separation Barrier[16]

Some observers trace the origins of erecting a physical barrier to separate Palestinians from Israelis to the 1992 stabbing of a teenage Jewish girl in Jerusalem by a Palestinian from Gaza Strip (Makowsky, 2004: 52). At the time, the Labor Party candidate Yitzhak Rabin (known as a Zionist "dove") was running for office; and in a campaign speech he used the incident to declare that in order to avoid further friction between the two entities "Israel must take Gaza out of Tel Aviv" (ibid.). Once elected as Prime minister, Rabin pursued his 'Separation Philosophy' by erecting a security fence around Gaza in 1995, when under the Oslo accords the

---

[14] B'Tselem, *Fatalities*, retrieved from http://old.btselem.org/statistics/english/Casualties.asp).

[15] As a candidate for Prime Minister Post, Sharon's visit to the site was part of his election campaign to attract right-wing voters who at the time were supporting another candidate, Benjamin Netanyahu.

[16] The fence/wall erected by Israel around the West Bank is often referred to by the Israeli government as the "anti-terrorist fence" or "security fence;" while Palestinians call it either the "racial segregation wall" or "the apartheid wall." I will use the more neutral term "separation barrier" in this chapter.

Strip's control was handed over to the Palestinians. In addition, the first section of a separation barrier in the West Bank built of pre-fabricated concrete slabs that formed a mile-long contiguous wall was constructed along the Green Line and parallel to the Trans-Israel Highway #6 between Bat Hefer and Tulkarem in 1994 (ASECOP, 2011). But building a comprehensive separation barrier was not pursued by Shimon Peres and Binyamin Netanyahu, Rabin's two successors who both favored a greater Israel with an integrated economy from the Mediterranean to the Jordan River.[17] Palestinians' increasing frustration with Oslo accords' outcomes and their realization that they have lost more grounds during the negotiations increased the level of mistrust on both sides. Thus the "notion of disengagement" was once again promoted by the newly elected Prime Minister Ehud Barak, who in the aftermath of Camp David's failed talks in 2000 pushed for erecting a "Separation Barrier." Ironically, it was Ariel Sharon, a hard line Zionist "hawk" from Likud Party and a staunch opponent of "Separation Philosophy" and not a Labor Party "dove," who was forced to oversee the construction of the separation barrier. As Makowsky (2004: 54) points out:

> As an architect of the settlement movement, Sharon had long agreed with the settlers that a fence would create a de facto Palestinian state in the West Bank and would mean abandoning those settlements that ended up on the wrong side.

The Security Fence program was approved by Sharon's Defense Cabinet in June 2002, and the adopted plan was "based on the principle of a contiguous obstacle" (Israel's Security Fence, 2007). After several revisions and modifications the barrier's 681 kilometer route was approved in 2005, which according to a UN report 85 percent of the barrier's route was located in the occupied West Bank and only 15 percent followed the pre-1967 Green Line (Lazaroff: 2010). As another of Israel's land grab schemes, this intrusion into the already occupied and carved out West Bank territories has diverged from the Green Line "by anywhere from 200 meters to as much as 20 kilometers," snaking and circling around many Jewish settlements in order to incorporate them into Israel proper while cutting through Palestinian farmlands, towns and villages.[18] When completed, the

---

[17] In line with the Zionists' long-sought ideal of Eretz Israel.

[18] For detailed maps of the separation barrier for various localities in the occupied territories see B'Tselem (2011b), particularly http://www.btselem.org/maps.

barrier will confiscate and physically bring 9.4 percent of the occupied West Bank territories including East Jerusalem to the Israeli side. In a special report prepared for the UN conference on Trade and Development (UNCTAD) Khalidi and Taghdisi-Rad (2009: 21) identify the confiscated land as being "among the richest and most productive agricultural land in the northern West Bank, and as a result of its [the barrier's] construction, access to some of the best water sources in the West Bank have been and continue to be lost" (see Figure 10.7). Sorkin's account of the barrier's route is also revealing:

> The physical wall is marked by its tortured geometry. It follows a remarkably serpentine path, designed not for defense—for which a straight line is more logical—but to reach into the West Bank and capture Israeli settlements for an expanded territory of Israel. Settlements too distant to fall on the "Israel" side of the wall are brought into the system with their own autonomous walls that frame them as floating islands of Israeli territory (2005: x).

In 2003 several Arab nations submitted a proposal to the UN Security Council asking for a vote on barrier's illegality. In a move that has been a signature feature of the American response to UN Security Council's proposals related to Israel since 1949, the U.S. representative vetoed the resolution on the grounds that it failed to condemn Palestinian "terrorist" acts against Israel. Later that year, the UN General Assembly passed a (non-binding, non-enforceable) resolution presented by the European Union that affirmed the barrier's construction was illegal and violating international law.[19] The resolution also encouraged Israel and the PA to respect the terms set forth by the "Road Map for Peace" with the objective of establishing a Palestinian state by 2005.[20] Later in 2004 the Interna-

---

[19] The UN resolution was passed with 144 votes, with 12 abstentions and 4 against (Israel, United States, Marshall Islands, and Micronesia).

[20] In preparation for the invasion of Iraq by the United States in 2002, President Bush needed the support of an Arab coalition. In order to portray the U.S. role and presence more as an arbiter and less as an imperialist power he proposed the "Road Map for Peace" for the establishment of a provisional Palestinian state with the condition of Arafat's removal from PLO leadership with Mahmoud Abbas resuming the leadership role. The Road Map's provision for Palestinians (still under continued occupation) was to denounce all violence against Israel, recognize Israel's right to exist, and maintain law and order in the occupied territories using PA police force. Related to a contiguous Palestinian territory, construction of both Jewish settlements and the separation barrier by Israel made the realization of this provision almost unattainable. Once these conditions were met, Israel was expected to also make a commitment to a two-state solution; freeze the settlement expansion; guarantee territorial contiguity for the Palestinian state; and call to an end to violence against Palestinians. The Road Map's ambiguous language made it unacceptable for Palestinians; and the Israeli Zionists' insistence on a future contiguous Eretz Israel

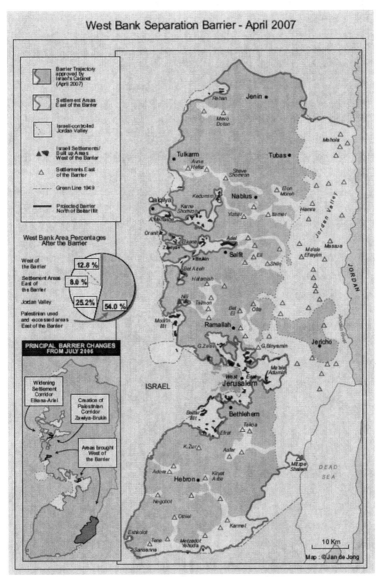

Source: Map design by Jan de Jong, courtesy of Foundation for Middle East Peace (FMEP), http://www.fmep.org/maps/west-bank (permission granted).

Figure 10.7. Map of the West Bank Separation Barrier, 2007.

tional Court of Justice (ICJ) also gave its advisory opinion on the legality of the separation barrier. The court rejected Israel's claim that the barrier was only a temporary security structure and ruled that the barrier's route creates "facts on the ground" that will lead to land confiscation and annexation thus negatively affecting Palestinians' right to self- determination. It also ruled that the barrier's one intent is to assist the illegal settlements, both of which violate Article 49 of the Fourth Geneva Convention. Finally, the ICJ ruled that the barrier limits Palestinians' freedom of movement, invades the privacy of their homes, and usurps their private properties all in clear violation of Article 53 of the Fourth Geneva Convention and Articles 46 and 52 of the Hague Regulations of 1907 (B'Tselem, 2011a). Expectedly, Israel insisted that the international community's choice is the Road Map and that "the International court of Justice in the Hague is not a proper venue to settle the Palestinian-Israeli conflict" (Israel Diplomatic Network, n.d.). The Israeli Supreme Court also put its stamp of approval on the separation barrier by ruling that "the security fence was built for reasons of national security" (Israel's Security Fence, 2007). In his article *"How to Build a Fence"* Makowsky takes a pragmatic approach to the issue and in fact supports the construction of the wall. But he also concedes that "the idea of a fence separating Israelis and Palestinians is, on one level, an admission of failure" (ibid.: 50). Obviously, the failure is that of the Zionist ideal of creating Eretz Israel; but similar to other walls and barriers that have been erected to provide security this one also "marks failed politics and aggressive intransigence" (Sorkin, 2005: vi).

The Separation Barrier's Architecture

Most images of Israel's separation barrier presented by pro-Palestinian activists and media depict long stretches of a high wall built by pre-fabricated concrete slabs that snake around Palestinian towns and villages. But in reality, once completed more than 95 percent of the approximately 680 kilometer-long barrier would consist of a variation of barbed wire and chain-link fence. Israel's Ministry of Foreign Affairs (2004) provides a non-descript account of the barrier, or what is called in Israeli government's lexicon as the "anti-terrorist fence":

---

along with President Bush's lack of resolve to prevent settlement expansion in the occupied territories guaranteed the plan's failure. For a detailed account of the Road Map see for example Fraser (2005: 169–174) and Smith (2010: 500–504).

The anti-terrorist fence forms a strip approximately the width of a four-lane highway. At its center is the chain-link fence that supports an intrusion detection system. This technologically advanced system is designed to warn against infiltrations, as are the dirt "tracking" path and other observation tools. Less than 3% of the fence will be constructed of concrete.

The predominant portion of the separation barrier in the rural areas has a layout similar to the one that separated West Berlin from East Germany, and the U.S.-Mexico border Fence/Wall. It has an average width of 200–300 ft. with a line-up of barbed wire on the occupied territories' side, and a 6–8 foot deep trench followed by a dirt road. The would-be infiltrators are then blocked by a 10-foot electronic chain-fence, fine sand to detect footprints, a paved road for the IDF patrol cars, another fine sand area and finally another line of barbed wire. To top that off, there are sensors and security cameras on regular intervals along the barrier. Cook (2003) provides an actual glimpse of a portion of the fence near the village of Falamiyya in the Qalqiliya Governorate: "The 'fence' begins in the east with a tangle of concertina wire in front of a trench between six and thirteen feet deep. Behind the trench runs an unpaved military road, a chain link fence topped by barbed wire and then a paved military road" (see Figure 10.8 & Photo 10.1). In some areas a pyramid-shaped razor wire barrier is laid out instead of the chain link fence (see Photo 10.2).[21]

In certain areas where Palestinian towns and villages are either too close to Israeli population centers and settlements or have strategic advantage over Israeli areas; tall, pre-fabricated concrete slabs replace the chain link fence. Although much taller, the eight-meter-high (26 ft.) concrete slabs have a clear resemblance to the third- and fourth generation of pre-fabricated concrete slabs used by the former German Democratic Republic in the Berlin Wall's construction.[22] Based on an unclassified 2007 map of the security fence produced by the Israeli Defense Force (IDF), the concrete wall portions of the barrier include a total of roughly ten miles around Jerusalem, separating mostly East Jerusalem from the surrounding West Bank territories; a three-mile stretch on the western edge of Tulkarem along Israel's major north-south highway (Trans-Israel Route #6); a total of three miles separating several sections of Bethlehem from Israel

---

[21] For an interactive descriptive account of the Separation barrier see http://www
.guardian.co.uk/ flash/0,5860,743170,00.html.ß
[22] The average height of concrete slabs used in the Berlin Wall was about 12 feet.

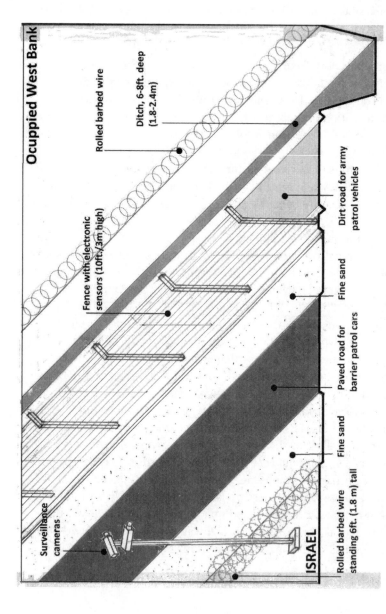

Source used: Israel Ministry of Foreign Affairs (2003). Saving Lives-Israel's Security Fence, http://www.mfa.gov.il/MFA/MFA Archive/2000_2009/2003/11/Saving%20Lives-%20Israel-s%20Security%20Fence Israel-Palestine, http://israelpalestine-speedy .blogspot.com/2010/07/israel-security-fence-wall-of-shame.html.

Figure 10.8. Israel's Separation Barrier-a Typical Chain Link Fence (Sketch by author).

Source: Image courtesy of B'Tselem—The Israeli Information Center for Human Rights in the Occupied Territories, photo by Eyal Raz (permission granted).

Photo 10.1. Israel's Separation Barrier between Rumana, in the West Bank (right) and Umm al-Fahem in Israel. The rolled barbed wire, the ditch and the Israeli patrol road are security obstacles before barrier-crossers reach the chain-link fence.

Source: Image courtesy of B'Tselem—The Israeli Information Center for Human Rights in the Occupied Territories, photo by Yehezkel Lein (permission granted).

Photo 10.2. Pre-fabricated reinforced concrete slabs waiting to be put in place for the Separation Barrier in Jerusalem.

Source: Image courtesy of B'Tselem—The Israeli Information Center for Human Rights in the Occupied Territories, photo by Yehezkel Lein (permission granted).

Photo 10.3. The concrete Separation Wall and an Israeli Defense Force (IDF) watch tower on the Israeli side seen from the town of Qalqilya on the western edge of the West Bank occupied territories.

proper; and a little more than a mile of concrete wall on the western edge of Qalqiliya (see Photos 10.2 and 10.3).[23]

The Defense Ministry's rationale for erecting the concrete wall is two-fold. First, it is argued that "because of the density of housing and other construction in the area, the building of a fence is impossible and, therefore, a concrete barrier becomes necessary." Second, in its many documentations and illustrations the concrete wall is justified as anti-terrorist "life-saver" for Israeli citizens—not only to "stop terrorists from infiltrating," but also to "block them from shooting at Israeli vehicles traveling on main highways alongside the pre-June 1967 line." At regular intervals, the concrete walls are also "crowned" by formidable watch towers equipped

---

[23] For a high resolution declassified map produced by the IDF see http://www.security fence.mod.gov.il/pages/eng/seamzone_map_eng.htm.

with high-tech sensors and cameras that provide the IDF soldiers with high visibility and offensive military capabilities (ibid.).

According to a 2010 UN report there are 57 gates along the barrier that are open on a daily, weekly-seasonal or seasonal basis (Lazaroff, 2010). But the barrier's peculiar path and Israel's repressive means of controlling these crossing points are designed to undermine the Palestinians' freedom of movement and dignity; as well as disrupting the flow of needed services and goods, particularly perishable agricultural produce. In the areas that the barrier cuts through communities it has caused disruptions in Palestinians' daily lives. For instance, in its examination of the barrier's impact in the East Jerusalem area a UN report released in 2011 concludes that Palestinians:

> ....are forced to cross checkpoints to access educational and health services, and even to do their shopping. Their family members from the West Bank cannot visit unless they obtain Jerusalem entry permits (UN News Centre, 2011).

The report also explains the unnecessary hardship imposed on Palestinian farmers who are cut off from their farmlands that is now located in the so-called "Seam Zone"—the West Bank territories that are between the barrier and the Green Line. Since these farmers "depend on Israeli-issued permits to access their land through gates which are only open for limited periods," The barrier has devastated their "agricultural livelihood throughout the West Bank." In highly dense urban centers where the fence is often replaced by concrete walls the barrier not only repressively chokes towns and villages, but also has suffocating psychological effects on the population, a reminder of the Berlin Wall's notorious proximity to neighborhoods and residences. An often-cited example is the Palestinian town of Qalqilya with a population of about 45,000 which is boxed-in by the barrier on all sides (see Figure 10.9):

> One 8 meter-high concrete section of this wall follows the Green line between the city and the nearby Trans-Israel highway. This section, referred to as an "anti-sniper wall," has been claimed to prevent gun attacks against Israeli motorists on the Trans-Israel Highway. The city is accessible through a military checkpoint on the main road from the east, and an underground tunnel built in September 2004 on the south side connects Qalqilya with the adjacent village of Habla (ASECOP, 2011).

The separation barrier is the largest construction project in Israel's history, and a highly costly undertaking. According to one report the project's cost "has ballooned from an expected $1 billion to more than $2.1 billion," with

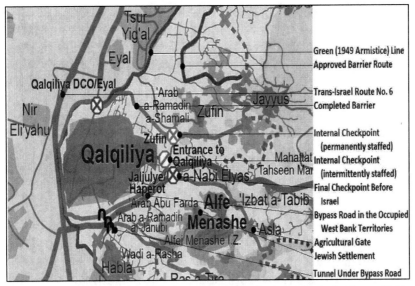

Source: Original map courtesy of B'Tselem—the Israeli Information Center for Human Rights in the Occupied Territories (permission granted). http://www.btselem.org/sites/default/files2/201206_btselem_map_of_wb_eng.pdf.

Figure 10.9. Map of the Separation Barrier surrounding the Town of Qalqiliya in the Occupied West Bank (the Trans-Israel Highway #6 runs parallel to the town's western concrete barrier).

each kilometer of the combined fence and wall construction initially costing approximately $2 million (Bard, 2010). But its construction has not been quick, and by Israel's Defense Ministry's own account by mid-2010 only 64 percent of the barrier had been completed. The year 2010 was the Defense Ministry's previously projected deadline for the barrier's completion, but it no longer provides an end date. Thus even if in the beginning the Israeli government tried hard to justify the urgency of barrier's construction on security grounds, the very slow pace of its completion defies the official Israeli rationale. By all accounts the separation barrier is not a formidable and impermeable line that prevents movement of Palestinians across territories; and like all other walls it is designed to allow for controlled population flow. Thus aside from Israeli government's stated official rationale for erecting the barrier, namely, to avert Palestinian terrorist attacks; we need to look for other possible reasons for its construction. For one thing, since Palestinians have been under Israeli occupation at least since the 1967 six-Day War, why wasn't the barrier needed in the 1970s, 1980s, or 1990s to deter Palestinian "terrorist" attacks? With Israel's control of the eastern stretch of the West Bank along Jordan River and cantonization of occupied territories which are surrounded by Jewish settlements, Palestinians are no longer outside the Jewish state's borders but rather right at the center of Zionists' long-awaited "Eretz Israel." This rather simple but factual observation raises two questions—what makes the turn-of-the current century so special as to require the urgent need to erect the separation barrier; and is the barrier designed to serve a function other than security? In the following section I will attempt to provide an answer for these questions.

The Two Economies Are Now Fully Integrated: Erect the Separation Barrier!

In general, most analyses of Palestinian-Israeli conflict focus on issues of land grab related to deterioration of living conditions in the occupied territories, mistreatment and displacement of Palestinians. But the occupation's economic impact for both Israelis and Palestinians such as the utilization of Palestinian labor for the benefit of Israeli political economy; the settlements' importance as enclaves of production and consumption in their immediate region; and the settlers' means of economic survival are rarely examined in popular discourses. After the Six-Day War a new socio-economic reality was born. A public debate on the future of economic relations between Israel and the newly occupied West Bank and Gaza Strip territories oscillated between supporters of economic separation on one hand and economic integration on the other (Reuveny, 1999: 643). The former advocated preservation of political borders based on the Armistice "Green Line" demarcation and creation of two separate economies; while the latter supported annexation of territories that required removal of the pre-war political borders without granting citizenship to Palestinians. The second position advocated by then Defense Minister Moshe Dayan prevailed and as Arnon (2007: 574) explains,

> [W]ithin a few days after the [Six-Day] war, the borders demarcated by the Green Line, which had been closed to regular economic transactions, were opening while at the same time new economic borders were established. The external borders of the territory now under Israeli control were closed, while within a short time the internal borders practically disappeared as economic transactions crossed the Green Line.

Between 1967 and 1973 the Palestinian labor was infused into Israel's workforce while at the same time the economies of West Bank and Gaza

Strip were subordinated to that of Israel (Smith, 2010: 359–60). Similar to the American trade policies in Mexico, from early on Israel had a clear colonial policy of suppressing economic development in the occupied territories by dumping Israeli agricultural and industrial products into the West Bank at a price that Palestinian farm and cottage industry products could not compete. In addition, the Israeli government "forbade the sale of certain West Bank produce in Israel and placed quotas on others so that they would not compete with Israeli products;" granted extensive subsidies to Israeli citizens; and "reserved the region as a special zone for its industrial goods, to the exclusion of those from other countries" (ibid.). This effectively detached Palestinian farm workers from the land; undermined the political and economic power of Palestinian land-owning class; and as I will discuss in the following pages, gradually integrated the West Bank and Gaza Strip's economies into that of Israel. For instance, between 1968 and 1985 the agricultural labor force in the West Bank and Gaza Strip declined from 46 to 27 percent and 32 to 18 percent, respectively (Bishara, 1989: 226). Finally, even if in the 1970s Palestinian workers in the occupied territories who were mostly employed in low-wage menial jobs sector comprised only 5 percent of Israel's labor force; they were "almost one-third of the labor force in the construction branch, and . . . a majority of unskilled laborers on actual construction sites" (Halabi, cf. Smith, 2010: 360).

The outbreak of the first *Intifada* posed a serious challenge to the occupation's legitimacy. Politically, the *Intifada* forced the Jordanian monarchy to abandon its claim on the West Bank and delegate its administration to Palestinian authorities. With the United States' recognition of the PLO as a legitimate negotiating party on Palestinians' behalf in 1988, as part of the Oslo peace agreements Israel was also forced to follow suit. Yet in spite of a more logical position taken by Israeli politicians on the left that advocated finding a negotiated solution that could lead to an independent Palestinian state; at the end of the day conservative proponents of the 'iron fist' policy within the governing Likud Party prevailed and resorted to violence in order to crush the *Intifada* instead.[24] From the latter group's perspective the uprising posed an existential threat to Israel's ultimate expansionist plans, as the occupied territories were no longer a matter of foreign policy but rather an integral part of Israeli economy. Palestinians were also cognizant of this fact as their means of livelihood increasingly

---

[24] For an extensive chronological analysis of the first Intifada see Lockman and Beinin (1989). Shlaim (2000: 250–260) also provides a critical account.

became dependent on Israel's political economy. For instance, on the eve of the uprising nearly 90 percent of Palestinian trade was with Israel (Reuveny, 1999: 643); and according to one report 45 percent of Palestinian labor force in the Gaza Strip and 32 percent in the West Bank were employed in Israel (Arnon, 2007: 577–78). Although less significant, Israel's economy was also dependent on the Palestinian markets that absorbed about 10 percent of her exports. Thus cognizant of this reality, one of the strategies of Palestinian resistance during the *Intifada* was boycotting Israeli products in the occupied territories. In response, in addition to violent measures taken to confront Palestinian protesters Israelis also imposed punitive economic policies, including closing Israel's labor market to Palestinian workers and replacing them with foreign workers who were hired from South Lebanon and Portugal (Bishara, 1999: 225–227).

In the 1990s the "integration or separation" debate on the future of Israeli-Palestinian economy was once again revived—with the Palestinians mostly favoring economic separation in order to stop further economic dependency on Israel; and the Israel's continuing support of economic integration which was an implicit rejection of the two-state option on their part. As an outcome of the Oslo talks in 1993, in addition to security and administrative issues the DOP also made substantive reference to economic arrangements. For instance, the Palestinian Authority (PA) would be responsible for mostly non-productive sectors such as "education, culture, health, social welfare, direct taxation and tourism"; while Israelis would control the more strategically important economic sectors such as "water, energy, financial development, transport and communications, trade, industry, environment, labor, media and international aid" (Murphy, 1995). The final agreement was signed by the two parties in 1994 which is known as the Paris Protocol. There is a statement in the document's preamble to agreement that at least on paper supports Palestinians' economic development:

> Both parties shall cooperate in this field [a lasting peace] in order to establish a sound economic base for these relations, which will be governed in various economic spheres by the principles of mutual respect.... This protocol lays the groundwork for strengthening the economic base of the Palestinian side and for exercising its right of economic decision making in accordance with its own development plan and priorities (cf. Arnon, 2007; 584).

On this basis, the Palestinian negotiators preferred to establish a Free Trade Area (FTA) similar to the NAFTA agreement between the United States, Mexico and Canada whereby the members "do not share a single exterior border" and each can establish "its own trade regime with the rest of the world".[25] But in reality the Protocol's approach was a continuation of the past Zionist strategy based on a 'no trade border' policy between the two economies, with Israel insisting on imposing a 'customs union' and unilaterally determining the terms of trade and tariffs, workers' mobility (mostly Palestinian workers), and taxation of imported goods (Arnon, 2007: 585). Israeli negotiators also insisted on imposing a monetary union controlled by the Central Bank of Israel not only to have a fiscal monopoly, but to facilitate Palestinian labor mobility between occupied territories and Israel as well (Daud, 2011). In addition, with the pressure from agricultural lobby the Israelis maintained their position that the customs union provide certain protections for Israeli producers of agricultural commodities such as eggs, poultry, and produce against imports to Israel from the occupied territories (Murphy, 1995). Worse yet, Palestinians' trade with other nations also had to be approved by the Israelis.

Overall, despite the provisions made in the Paris Protocol to integrate the two economies, Israel used an increase in the level of violent attacks by Palestinians particularly during the 1994–96 period as an excuse to impose a *de facto* "closure regime," both internal (closure of borders between Israel and the occupied territories) and external (tightening control over Palestinians' ability to trade with other countries). At the same time, with restrictions placed on Palestinian workers to work in Israel, foreign workers were literally flown in from Thailand, Romania and China to replace Palestinians. For instance, the Israeli Labor Ministry's records indicate that in 1993 about 68,000 work permits were issued to Palestinians, with another 40,000 working in Israel without permit (Parks, 1993). This comprised 30 percent of Palestinian labor force in the West Bank and 40 percent in Gaza. In contrast, during the 1994–96 closure regime "the percentage of West Bank workers dropped to 18% and those from Gaza to only 6%," leading to very high levels of unemployment in the occupied territories: 20 percent in the West Bank and more than 30 percent in Gaza (Arnon, 2007: 587). On the other hand, while the share of Palestinians working in Israel as a percentage of her total labor force declined from 8 percent in 1990 to a low 2 percent in 1997; Israel had the ability to replace Palestinian workers with laborers imported from other countries to offset potential economic setbacks (Reuveny, 1999: 647–648). Although not on their own terms, this ironically offered Palestinians an imposed

---

[25] As I have discussed NAFTA's disadvantages for Mexico in previous chapters, Palestinians' preference was not necessarily a dignified one. But I am assuming that in their limited choices between bad and worse they opted for the former.

"economic separation" regime in the occupied territories, further contrib-
uting to their impoverishment.

Availability of cheap foreign labor (virtually slave workers themselves)
also changed the status of Palestinian workers in the occupied territories from the early 1990s onward—from being a highly valuable, available
and abundant cheap, yet hard to replace labor force during the 1967–1987
period; to becoming highly vulnerable and being employed at much lower
wages since they could be easily replaced by foreign workers. This new
phase of globalization of labor thus helped Israel to continue with the
occupation and expansion of Jewish settlements and at the same time
impose the closure regime on Palestinians without impunity; and by the
end of the 1990s the Palestinian economy was completely dependent on
that of Israel. According to a World Bank report, intensification of closures during the 2001–2002 period, coupled by the availability of foreign
workers drastically reduced demand for Palestinian labor in Israel. The
high level of the Palestinian economy's dependence on these employment
opportunities, although mostly low-skill and low-wage jobs, is evidenced
in the high negative correlation between "Palestinian employment in
Israel and domestic Palestinian unemployment" in the occupied territories (The World Bank, 2002: 37).[26] Table 10.1 demonstrates increasing
levels of unemployment and poverty levels for Palestinians in the West
Bank and Gaza Strip in the post-Oslo period. Of note are the very high
levels of unemployment and poverty in the occupied territories in 2002,
the year Israel began constructing the separation barrier.

The separation barrier can therefore be appreciated for the role it plays
in utilizing the impoverished Palestinian workers in a controlled manner, a labor force that is always desperate to find employment in Israel.
Chomsky (2003: 215) contends that long before the Oslo Accords Israeli
industrialists advocated the permanent neo-colonial dependency, in
essence a colonial scheme similar to the former South African apartheid
regime's plan for Bantustans, or "... something like the U.S. relationship
to Mexico or El Salvador, with maquiladoras, assembly plants, along the
border on the Palestinian side of the border." Chomsky's assessment is not
farfetched. For instance, Shlomo Ben-Ami, Israel's foreign minister during
the 2000 Camp David talks quotes Former Prime Minister Ehud Barak
who had stated that the Oslo negotiations served as a stepping stone to

---

[26] According to the World Bank report the correlation coefficient was −0.88 (ibid.).

Table 10.1. Basic Employment Data on the West Bank and Gaza Strip, 1995–2002

Year	West Bank			Gaza Strip		
	Employment in Israel (% of total Employment)	Unemployment	Under the Poverty Line*	Employment in Israel (% of total Employment)	Unemployment	Under the Poverty Line*
1995	20.2	13.9	NA	3.3	29.4	NA
2000	22.4	12.1	18	12.9	18.7	42
2002	13.3	28.2	41	2.5	38.0	68

Source: Table constructed based on information in Arnon (2007: 588, Table 3).
* The World Bank's estimate of the poverty line is $2.10/capita/day.

establish a condition of "permanent neo-colonial dependency" for the occupied territories (cf. Davidi, 2000). In fact, as an outcome of the Oslo Accords in 1998 the Palestinian Authority (PA) enacted a law that established a Palestinian Industrial Estate and Free Zone Authority (PIEFZA) in order to implement policies for developing industrial estates and free economic zones. Initially the law stipulated that both goods supplied to these industries from the occupied territories and products manufactured in the industrial zones should be exempt from import or export taxation. However, the "Final status" Camp David agreement in 2000 effectively shifted the authority from PIEFZA to the Israeli government that by then had assumed control of 60 percent of the West Bank, namely, areas B and C (Bahour, 2010). From then on industrial zones became a part of the occupied territories' economic reality and evolved in three different types: industrial enterprises established near Palestinian cities and towns and scattered throughout the West Bank; Industrial Estates (IEs) with adequate infrastructure and capital housing a variety of industrial enterprises; and Industrial Free Trade Zones (IFTZs) that are established in areas that are both physically and administratively outside Israel's national customs and commercial laws, allowing unrestricted regional and global trade and using cheap labor from the occupied territories (Bahiri and Hazboun, 1995).

Accurate data on the number of illegal factories and industrial zones in the West Bank are scant. One study in 2005 identifies seven major industrial zones in the West Bank (CJPME, 2005), and by 2009 there were at least eighteen illegal Israeli industrial zones (Corporate Watch, 2009b). In addition, with the financial and technological assistance provided by the United states, France, Germany, Turkey and Japan four industrial free trade zones (IFTZs) have been constructed; the al-Jalama near Jenin (Germany and Turkey); the Bethlehem (France); the Jericho Agricultural Park located in the Israeli-controlled Jordan Valley (Japan); and the Tarqomiyya near Hebron (World Bank and Turkey) (Bahour, 2010).[27] In their varied forms most industrial zones are cleverly built in the areas within the occupied territories that under Oslo agreements fall under Israeli administrative and military control (Area C), yet are conveniently located outside the gates of Palestinian urban "Bantustans."[28] The following observation depicts this reality:

> Largely non-residential, Israeli West Bank Industrial Zones are fortress-like hill-top factory complexes connected to nearby hill-top settlements. They are the economic engines of the illegal Israeli settlement blocs.[29] In the best of cases, they provide an industrial base for Israel's illegal colonial development in the territories, exploiting cheap Palestinian labor. In the worst of cases, they offer a particular attraction to industries considered toxic or otherwise undesirable in Israel proper due to the fact that stringent Israeli labor and industrial laws are not applied in the occupied territories (CJPME, 2005).

Israel's unilateral decision to withdraw from the Gaza Strip and evacuate some 8,000 Jewish settlers in 2005, most of whom were then re-settled in the West Bank and given hefty monetary incentives; was part of a long-term plan to create a more secure, contiguous greater Israel by also incorporating main West Bank Jewish settlements into Israel proper. Gaza Strip's explosive high concentration of Palestinian population and limited capacity for the expansion of Jewish settlements made its occupation a volatile and unprofitable undertaking. As early as 2002 the so-called

---

[27] One of the earliest IFTZs was the Erez Industrial Zone established just north of the Gaza Strip-Israel Armistice line/border. At its heyday it employed between 4,000–5,000 Palestinians from Gaza who had to cross the Armistice barrier under tight Israeli security control in order to work. But the complex was abandoned in mid-2004 after it was continuously attacked by Palestinian militants from Gaza strip, and has not been reopened since.

[28] It is not an exaggeration to make an analogy to the location of South African industrial and commercial sites that were also located outside black Homelands (Bantustans) to take advantage of cheap labor under the apartheid regime.

[29] The CJPME factsheet (2005) defines "settlement blocs" as "key instruments of colonization" that are strategically located in order to "1) commandeer natural east-west and north-south transportation routes; 2) seize the hilltops from which to oversee and intimidate the local Palestinian populations; 3) appropriate wells, springs and prime agricultural land; 4) divert aquifer water; and 5) control, disrupt and destroy the flow of Palestinian goods, services and people throughout the territory."

"Gaza Disengagement Plan" proposed by then Prime Minister Ariel Sharon had the blessing of the Bush Administration (Smith, 2010: 506–507). Sharon's plan was based on a foregone conclusion that there was "no Palestinian partner" with whom to sign a bilateral agreement, thus Israel "must initiate a move that will not be contingent on Palestinian cooperation." Sharon also reiterated that "the plan will lead to a better security reality, at least in the long term." He further committed Israel to evacuate Jewish settlers and the military forces from the Gaza Strip, but the latter were then to be redeployed outside the Strip. This according to the plan will leave "no basis for the claim that the Gaza Strip is occupied territory." Finally, while the Gaza Strip was expected to become a demilitarized territory, the plan emphasized that "Israel will supervise and guard the external envelope on land, will maintain exclusive control in the air space of Gaza, and will continue to conduct military activities in the sea space of the Gaza Strip" (Haaretz, 2004). Although the military redeployment was similar to stationing the IDF in Area C that surrounded Areas A and B in the West Bank, by washing her hands of any responsibility for Palestinians' welfare the Strip's social and economic conditions have continued to deteriorate reaching catastrophic proportions. In his critique of Israel's military invasion of the Gaza Strip in early 2009 and foreseeing an impending human disaster Shlaim (2009) provides the following profile:

> Gaza is a classic case of colonial exploitation in the post-colonial era. Jewish settlements in occupied territories are immoral, illegal and an insurmountable obstacle to peace. They are at once the instrument of exploitation and the symbol of the hated occupation. In Gaza, the Jewish settlers numbered only 8,000 in 2005 compared with 1.4 million local residents. Yet the settlers controlled 25% of the territory, 40% of the arable land and the lion's share of the scarce water resources. Cheek by jowl with these foreign intruders, the majority of the local population lived in abject poverty and unimaginable misery. Eighty per cent of them still subsist on less than $2 a day. The living conditions in the strip remain an affront to civilized values, a powerful precipitant to resistance and a fertile breeding ground for political extremism.

With the Gaza Strip being outside Israeli government's responsibility for its residents' welfare, the separation barrier's crucial role in Israel's utilization of Palestinian workers in industrial zones became more clear. First, by boxing in the occupied territories and limiting the entry of Palestinian workers to Israel proper through closures and other security control measures, desperate Palestinian workers in search of jobs have no other choice but to work in "Economic Prison zones"[30] at a rate far below the minimum wage and in an environment similar to the Mexican maqui-ladora factories. This is a bizarre and tragic aspect of the occupation, which the laborers engaged in construction of illegal Jewish settlements and those who work in industrial zones are the Palestinians—thus as the colonized they undermine their own freedom and further diminish the possibility of a future independent Palestinian state.

According to Israel's Civil Administration office in 2009 there were 20,000 Palestinian permit holders working in the settlements, with another 10,000 employed without work permit (Alenat, 2009). By 2012, upwards of 35,000 Palestinian permit-holders were employed in the Jewish settle-ments (Abu-Saadi, 2012). A statement by *Kav LaOved*, an Israeli workers' rights advocacy organization about pay and working conditions in Barkan Industrial Zone near Nablus is revealing:

> According to testimonies from both male and female workers at the fac-tory, their salary ranges from 7–12 shekels an hour (approximately a third of the minimum wage in Israel of 21.70 shekels an hour). The workers do not receive a pay slip as required by Israeli law, nor do they receive other social benefits such as vacation days, sick pay, convalescence pay, overtime, etc. We emphasize that there is no legal dispute concerning the entitlement of Palestinian workers in the settlements to equal rights according to Israeli laws (Corporate watch, 2009a).

The separation barrier's second function is a de facto illegal annexation of an enclosed-zone of the occupied West Bank territories between the barrier and the UN Armistice line (the Green Line), or the so-called "Seam Zone," an area that covers about 143,000 acres or 10 percent of the West Bank and Jerusalem combined.[31] The "Seam Zone" has created several con-tiguous territorial corridors effectively connecting Jewish settlements of Alfei Menashe, Ariel, Beit Arye, Modi'in Illit, Giv'at Ze'ev, Ma'ale Adumim, Beitar Illit and Efrat to Israel proper that house more than 170,000 Jewish settlers (UNCTAD, 2006: 15–16; Human rights Watch, 2005).[32] Currently, at least five industrial zones are located within the Seam Zone providing ideal sites not only for employing cheap labor, both Palestinian and foreign; but also for relocating polluting and environmentally unsafe industries

---

[30] I have borrowed the term from Barhour (2010).

[31] This is in addition to confiscation of 27,000 acres of Palestinian territories that is needed to construct the barrier.

[32] The Seam Zone also includes around 50,000 Palestinians living in 38 villages and towns, who are cut off from the occupied territories (ibid.).

that are not allowed in Israel proper (see Figure 10.10). One example is the Mishor Adumim industrial Zone located east of East Jerusalem that attracts Israeli businesses for two reasons:

> They receive lucrative tax reduction, and both environment and labor regulations are far more lax than inside Israel itself.....for example, Mishor Adumim's main businesses work with plastic, cement,leather tanning, detergents, textile dying, aluminum and electro-plating. Lack of proper checks regarding workers' rights also means companies exploit this loophole to minimize their labor costs (Corporate Watch, 2009b).

Similar to other cases of occupation, the occupiers always find collaborators among the occupied population, mostly for economic incentives. In his book *Globalized Palestine: A National Sell-out of a Homeland*, Khalil Nakhleh (2012) identifies two factions within the Palestinian capitalist class—the "expatriate" and the "indigenous." The former are comprised of those who had earlier left Palestine and made their money mostly in the Gulf States as part of the "Palestinian diaspora" (*Shatat*) but came back after the Oslo talks in the mid-1990s. One glaring example of an "expatriate capitalist" is Abdul-Malek al-Jaber, an educated Palestinian businessman and the head of the Palestine Estate Development Company (Piedco), who has been a key player in the planning and construction of industrial zones inside the occupied territories (in Area C) that employ cheap Palestinian labor and have special "security agreement" with Israel (see Rapoport, 2005). The "indigenous" Palestinian capitalists on the other hand are small family enterprises inside the occupied territories who as colonial collaborators function as local middlemen and contractors by hiring Palestinian workers for Israeli businesses. Alenat (2010) explains the process:

> The workers often do not even know the name of their Israeli employer. The contractor's job is to bring workers to work when needed, to pay them and to make sure they do not demand a raise. In most cases, contractors fire workers, change the workers' workplace and prevent them from demanding their rights. On their part, workers perceive the contractor as a sort of employment agency which can find work for them.

The separation barrier's "brutal irony" is that it is a crucial element in the success of industrial estates based on joint Israeli-Palestinian collaboration: Israel provides security for Israeli businesses in the occupied territories, while Palestinian entrepreneurs pave the way for construction of facilities and facilitate employment of cheap Palestinian labor (Rapoport, 2005). International donor agencies such as the World Bank, USAID, and

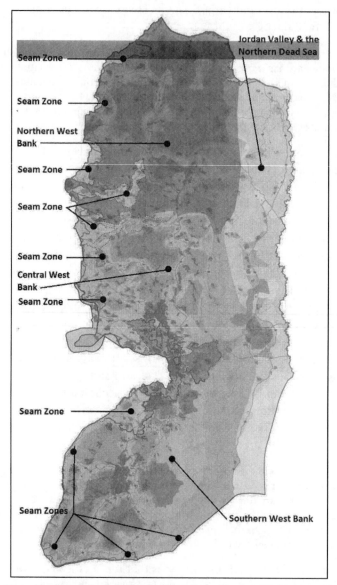

Source: Original background map courtesy of B'Tselem—The Israeli Information Center for Human Rights in the Occupied Territories (permission granted). http://www.btselem.org/sites/default/files2/map/west_bank_fragmentation_map_eng.pdf.

Figure 10.10. Location of Seam Zones.

the British Department for International Development (DFID) have also implicitly accepted the occupation and the separation barrier as part of "facts on the ground," thus accepting and treating Israel as a 'partner' rather than the 'occupier' in supporting industrial zones and other projects in the occupied territories. For these agencies, the PA's role is to ensure security for foreign and Israeli investments and their neo-liberal development projects. It is also tasked "to suppress resistance, under the pretext of enforcing the rule of law thus creating a more suitable environment for development and investment" (The Palestinian Grassroots Anti-Apartheid Wall Campaign, n.d.).

A "Villa in the Jungle"? From Jabotinsky's "Iron Wall" to the Separation Barrier

In a recent article Gabriel Kolko (2012) opened his essay by examining current state of affairs in Israel, that "Zionism was supposed to make Jewish existence 'normal,'....but there is nothing 'normal' in the life and culture of Israel today—which has not lived in peace with its neighbors, much less let the Palestinians have elementary human rights in the lands in which they have lived for thousands of years." He further states that Israel has increasingly become a warrior state that is ironically similar to the United States in seeking peace by pursuing a strategy of perpetual war, which in the former's case is against the Palestinians under occupation and her Arab neighbors. "If war is the criteria of 'normal' existence," he reiterates, "then Zionism has become a failed nightmare" (Kolko, 2012). Israel's current policy toward Palestinians is a far cry from the early Zionist thinking that was based on a realization that establishment of Zionist colonies in Palestine should not violate the basic rights of its Arab population. This in fact was advocated by the Labor Party leaders during the 1950s who were reluctant to consider that the use of military force against Palestinians was a prerequisite to achieve the Zionist movement's objectives. In contrast, Revisionist Zionists whose political lineage goes back to Ze'ev Jabotinsky in the early 20th century adamantly believed that military power was the key factor in establishing the future Zionist state. In his famous essay "*The Iron Wall*" Jabotinsky laid out the ideological foundations of Revisionist Zionism based on two principles:

> The first was the territorial integrity of Ertez Israel, the Land of Israel, over both banks of river Jordan within the original borders of the Palestine mandate. The second was the immediate declaration of the Jewish right to political sovereignty over the whole of the area (Shlaim, 2000: 12).

In addition, Jabotinsky believed that colonization of Palestine was feasible only based on two premises—that "the expulsion of the Arabs from
Palestine is absolutely impossible in any form"; and that Jews and Palestinians have to live together, "provided the Jews become the majority."
But his recognition of Arab Palestinians' rights had an inherent contra-
diction that has brought the Zionist aspirations to a dead end they are in
today. For instance, he asserted that Zionism is based on "the equality of
all nations" and that Zionists "will never attempt to expel or oppress the
Arabs." Yet he was skeptical about achieving Zionist objectives through
peaceful means. For him, peace between Jews and Palestinians did not
depend on the Zionists' relationship with the Arabs, but rather "on the
Arabs' relationship with Zionism" by recognizing and accepting its moral
virtues. Jabotinsky ended his essay by concluding that the only solution
for a peaceful coexistence between the two entities would be the construction of an impermeable "iron wall":

> It is my hope and belief that we will then offer them guarantees that will sat-
> isfy them and that both peoples will live in peace as good neighbors. But the
> sole way through such an agreement is through the iron wall, that is to say,
> the establishment in Palestine of a force that will in no way be influenced
> by Arab pressure. In other words, the only way to achieve a settlement in
> the future is total avoidance of all attempts to arrive at a settlement in the
> present (Jabotinsky, cf. Shlaim, 2000: 14).[33]

Jabotinsky is widely considered as the right wing Likud Party's ideologue.
But since Oslo talks there has been a political collusion between leaders of
Likud and the more liberal Labor Party who have often presented a unified
front in their dealings with the Palestinians. For example, Ehud Barak, the
former Prime Minister and a prominent member of the Labor Party has
often used a similar metaphor in his domestic discussions, that Israel is literally a civilized island surrounded by savages and wild animals, hence his
oft-quoted phrase that "we are a villa in the middle of a jungle" that needs
to be protected (Avnery, 2002). Thus even the Israeli "doves" approve of
Jabotinsky' proposition of creating an "iron wall," which is a variation of
Theodor Herzl's earlier metaphor of "creating a wall against barbarism"
used in his failed attempts back in the late 19th century in order to gain
the Ottoman Court's support for Zionist colonies in Palestine.

In a commentary published in Israel's high-circulation newspaper
Yedioth Ahronoth Alex Fishman, a respected defense analyst provided a

---

[33] Text translated from Jabotinsky (1959: 251–60) (in Hebrew).

chilling account of Israel's "bunker mentality" which he considers as a symptom of a national mental illness:

> We have become a nation that is burying itself behind walls, behind fences. It shows us we are going much more toward isolation; mine is a very patriotic standpoint—and my disappointment comes from this patriotic standpoint. A fence is a kind of weakness. I'm not a psychiatrist but it shows something of the mentality of a nation (cf. Sherwood, 2012).

In fact, except for the southern portion of the eastern border between Israel and Jordan from the Dead Sea to the Gulf of Aqaba, Israel's borders with her neighbors are completely sealed off. The oldest border fence was constructed in the 1960s along the northern Jordanian border which stretches from the Sea of Galilee in the north all the way to the Dead Sea in the south. Israel's northern border is also sealed by two stretches of highly militarized fences; one from the Mediterranean Sea to Syria along the Lebanese southern border, and another that runs along the 1973 cease fire line that separates occupied Golan Heights from Syria. Another highly militarized fence runs for 32 miles and seals Israel's border with Gaza Strip along the 1950 Armistice line; with Israel's latest border fence soon to seal the Egyptian border between the Sinai and Negev deserts at a cost of $400 million (Sherwood, 2012) (see Figure 10.11).[34] The new Israeli-Egyptian border fence design is strikingly similar to that of the separation barrier, and some details make it even more formidable:

> [It] consists of latticed steel, tapped and edged with razor wire, extending at least two meters below ground and in some sections reaching 7 meters above ground. Ditches and observation posts with cameras and antennae will line the route. An electric pulse will run through the fence, setting off an alarm on contact that will allow the Israeli army to locate the exact spot of attempted infiltration. On the Israeli side, a sandy tracking path will show the footprints of interlopers, and an asphalt military patrol road will give unhindered access to army units (ibid.).

Along with border fortifications in January 2012 the Israeli Parliament also updated the Prevention of Infiltration law that was initially enacted in 1954 to prevent Palestinians from entering Israel; but this time to block the influx of several thousand desperate African asylum seekers who if admitted, will threaten Israel's' purity of Jewish identity (Cook, 2012). Today,

---

[34] In February 2012 Benjamin Netanyahu, the Israeli Prime Minister announced that "once construction on the Egyptian border ends, the construction of a Jordanian fence will commence along the Arava" (the Dead Sea-Port of Aqaba stretch) (Israel Defense, 2012).

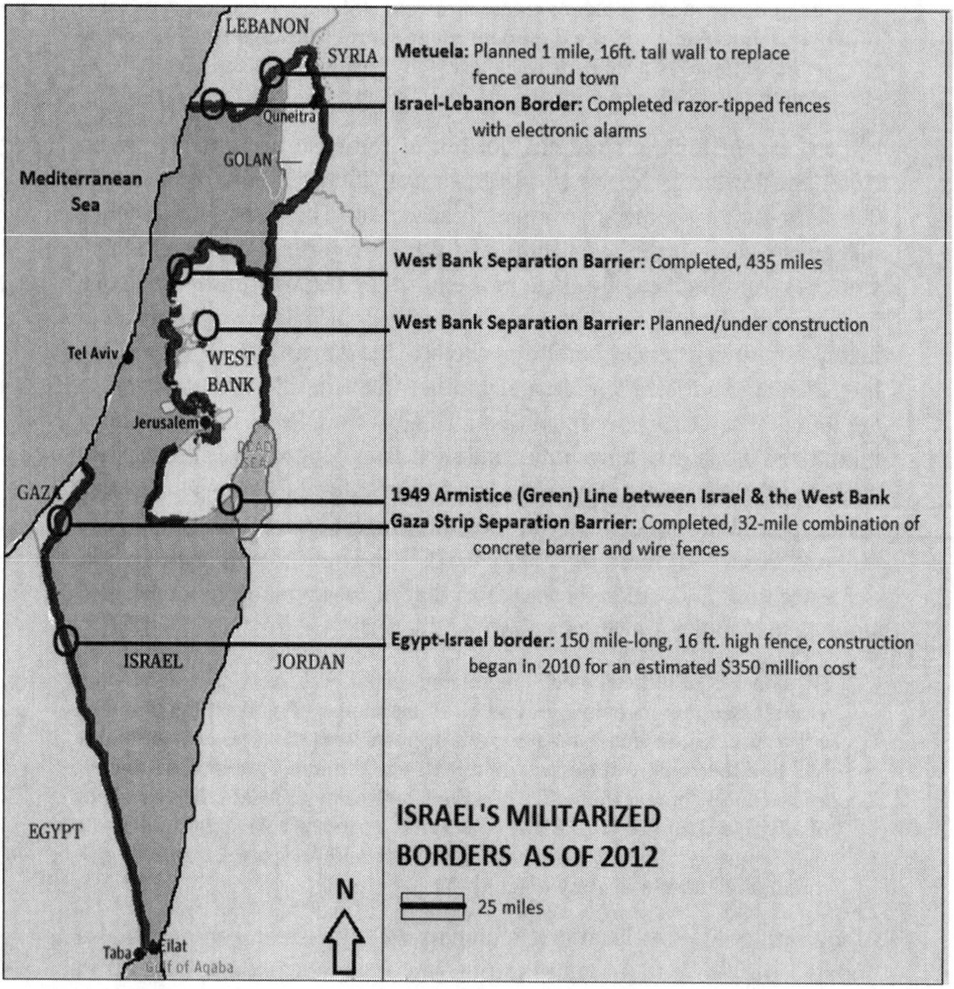
LEBANON
SYRIA
Quneitra
GOLAN
Mediterranean Sea
Tel Aviv
WEST BANK
Jerusalem
DEAD SEA
GAZA
ISRAEL
JORDAN
EGYPT
Taba
Eilat
Gulf of Aqaba
N
Metuela: Planned 1 mile, 16ft. tall wall to replace fence around town
Israel-Lebanon Border: Completed razor-tipped fences with electronic alarms
West Bank Separation Barrier: Completed, 435 miles
West Bank Separation Barrier: Planned/under construction
1949 Armistice (Green) Line between Israel & the West Bank
Gaza Strip Separation Barrier: Completed, 32-mile combination of concrete barrier and wire fences
Egypt-Israel border: 150 mile-long, 16 ft. high fence, construction began in 2010 for an estimated $350 million cost
ISRAEL'S MILITARIZED BORDERS AS OF 2012
25 miles

Source: Guardian (March 27, 2012), retrieved from http://www.guardian.co.uk/world/2012/mar/27/israel-extends-border-fence-critics

Figure 10.11. The Bunker State: Israel's militarized Barriers along Her Borders, 2012 (map by author).

not only has Zionism failed to realize Jabotinsky's dream of establishing Eretz Israel on both sides of Jordan River, but Israel's intransigence in recognizing Palestinians legitimate political rights and demands, despite the two entities' economic integration, is manifested in the erection of the separation barrier. Furthermore, Israel's "perpetual war" policy has also prevented her from achieving peace with Arab neighbors, leading to the creation of what Cook (2012) calls "the world's first bunker state."

CHAPTER ELEVEN

EPILOGUE: CONCEPTUALIZING WALLS AND BORDERS—"GLOBALIZATION FROM WITHIN"

Drawing parallels between a border wall and a dam, Michael Davis makes the following observation in his foreword to Joseph Nevins' book *Operation Gate Keeper: The Rise of "Illegal Alien" and the Making of the U.S.-Mexico Boundary* (2002: x):

> The border is often compared to a dam: defending the fat suburbs of the American dream from a deluge of Third World misery. This, of course, misunderstands the role of a dam, which is not to prevent the flow of water but to control and ration its supply.

Even a cursory historical observation of all the walls, barriers and fortifications built in and around imperial territories will support the above observation made about contemporary barriers, particularly concerning the movements of populations. Within the context of preceding discussions, of the nature of empires and imperial formations and the interdependence of the postmodern *Empire* and the globalization process I will make the following observations that serve as conceptual guidelines for my case studies in this book:

1. Imperial walls and barriers that are constructed and maintained are seldom located on the frontiers. For one thing, frontiers are zones or regions that move and change in space in different time periods (Hall, 2009: 27). The world-systems analysis informs us that all world-systems, and by definition all imperial territories tend to pulsate through periods of expansion and contraction (Chase-Dunn and Hall, 1997). Conceptually, frontiers are also "shaped by processes of interactions among societies," meaning that frontier lines do not move in a unidirectional fashion only (Hall, 2009; 26). Using a biological metaphor Slatta (1997) likens a frontier to a membrane—it has a thickness, is permeable depending on the intensity and direction of population movement, is flexible and most important of all, it moves forward or backward in response to socio-political and economic pressures. Thus for all practical purposes (cost of labor, capital, raw materials, etc.), and regardless

of historical time periods frontiers are not suitable locations to construct and maintain barriers, walls and fortifications.[1]

2. Borders are demarcation lines between two socio-political entities, and up to the point that their economies function independently (in relative terms) there is no need for an intensive border fortification and control. This was the case for the U.S.-Mexico border that up until the mid-1990s was loosely secured whereby unauthorized border crossings prior to the implementation of NAFTA in 1994 were common occurrences even in bright daylight; the Green Line that separated Israel from the occupied territories up until the late 1990s; and the political boundaries between East and West Berlin from 1949–1961. Related to the U.S.-Mexico border, according to Nevins (2002) the Immigration and Naturalization Service (INS) budget for the southwestern portion of the U.S.-Mexico border security enforcement increased from $400 million in 1993 to $800 million in 1997; and Cunningham (2004) reports that the number of border agents more than doubled between 1994 (the year NAFTA was implemented) and 2001 (cf. Wonders, 2006: 79). In this light, border walls and barriers are erected when the two political economic entities have passed beyond a point in their ability to survive independently; and similar to a dam they are always semipermeable allowing a controlled flow and movement of population under the empire's administrative control. This also signals that the two political economies are integrated and the wall/barrier is a tool for imperial intentions.

3. Contrary to the conventional perception the imperial walls and barriers are not erected at the 'edges' of empire, but right in the midst of contested territories (Beck's notion of *globalization from within*). Furthermore, they are not friendly 'fences between neighbors' (see Williams, 2003) since they are never erected and maintained by mutual consent.[2]

Within the above context it is possible to identify at least four types of imperial walls:

Offensive Wall. The imperial-colonial power erects the wall to control the flow of population from subjugated peripheral territories to the mainland

---

[1] My focus here is not on frontier studies. But for a list of literature on comparative frontiers see Hall (2009: 27, f.n. 2).

[2] All the walls examined in this book are pertinent examples.

(center). I consider the wall/fence/barrier along the U.S.-Mexico border and between Israel proper and the occupied Palestinian territories of the West Bank and Gaza Strip as offensive walls.

Empire-Maintenance Defensive Wall. The imperial power builds the barrier to prevent the outflow and exodus of imperial subjects to the outlying yet integrated territories. In this case, the Berlin Wall is the prime example whereby a client state (the German Democratic Republic) serves as proxy for the Soviet Union's imperialist interests by building and maintaining the Wall.

Offensive-Defensive Wall. This type of imperial wall is erected when the imperial integrity is challenged both from within and outside the imperial center. This was certainly the case for the Roman Hadrian's Wall in northern England, and the Gorgan Wall ("*Red Snake*") in northeastern Iran.

Symbolic-Ideological Defensive Wall. At times the imperial subjects and colonized populations also erect walls, always defensive in nature—this time to protect themselves from imperial onslaughts and total subjugation. Since the colonized lack the ability to erect and defend physical barriers that can match the empire's military might, this kind of defensive wall is usually symbolic and cultural that serves as an ideological shield to prevent the colonized to be totally absorbed by the empire. In the post-colonial, globalized period of the Empire the imposition of tribal/Islamic veil (*hijab*) on women and its institutionalization falls under this category, as I have made the case for Muslim immigrants from North Africa in France, or compulsory veiling of women in the Islamic Republic of Iran (see Figure 11.1).

Imperial walls and barriers are therefore ALWAYS violent by nature, with or without the presence of guards, soldiers or border patrol agents; and their mere physical structures invoke a passive-aggressive presence implicitly threatening and challenging the movements of populations or goods. Since imperial formations are always multi-ethnic and multi-national by nature and are maintained by implicit or explicit violence and the use of force, imperial walls and barriers inevitably serve to enforce and maintain ethnic-national inequalities and promote racism and race- and even gender-based discrimination.[3]

Building imperial walls and barriers have to be considered as an effort of last resort, when all else has failed in regulating the population movements within two or more territories of the empire. In this light, erecting walls and barriers should be considered as the first sign of total integration

---

[3] Elsewhere, I discuss and make the case that as a concept 'race' has no social or biological validity (Chaichian, 2006: Introduction), hence I use the term 'ethnic-national' instead of 'racial' or 'racial-ethnic' in my discussion here.

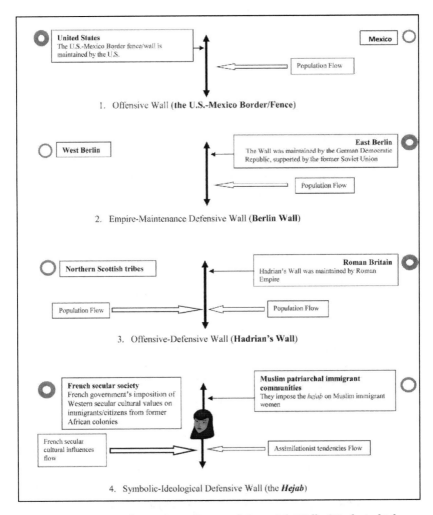

Figure 11.1 Conceptualizing Four Types of Imperial Wall. (Circles' thickness denote relative political/military strength of entities involved in conflict)

of territories and people within which they are situated, meaning that they will eventually become obsolete and doomed to be torn down. There is a lesson to be learned from a recent historical past, and that is to draw parallels between the failed and defunct 'modern' Berlin Wall, and the impending fate of the newly established security walls and fences along the U.S.-Mexico border and Israel-occupied West Bank Palestinian territories.

Post-Wall Berlin

For more than twenty-eight years the Berlin Wall did accomplish its expected task of providing some degree of stability for a system that was increasingly becoming untenable. From that fateful early Sunday morning in August 1961 when the first crude barbed wire fences cut through Berlin, to the night of November 11 in 1989 when West Berliners started to bring down the first piece of the wall at the Brandenburg gate by chiseling away at the concrete slab and taking down the tubing along the top. Yet the formidable structure did not crumble overnight. The following weekend the GDR authorities opened ten border crossings between East and West Berlin. Ironically, the majority of East Germans who immigrated to West Germany either belonged to the post-Wall generation, or were born shortly before the Wall's construction; therefore having no collective memory of the historical context in which the Wall was erected (see Taylor, 2006: 404–406). For example, in their demographic analysis of East Germany Kröhnert and Skipper (2010) report that about 60 percent of "East-West" migrants were 30 years old or younger, a well-educated segment of society who were eager to move to the West in search of jobs and better opportunities.

As border crossings one-by-one became more permeable, so began the Wall's physical dismantling—first by hundreds of "wall peckers" who hurriedly chiseled away at the once notorious concrete barrier and collected their own personal mementoes; and then by bulldozers and heavy machinery that gradually removed the barrier system in Berlin's inner city area by the end of 1990. Yet it took another two years before the demolition of entire outer ring barrier was finished. Now, the path of this portion of the Berlin Wall/fence, often grossly overlooked and not discussed in the Wall narratives and critical discourses demarcates the boundary between the Berlin and Brandenburg provinces within unified Germany (Hertle, 2008: 162).

Many Germans, both in East and West Germany not only found the Wall to be a gold mine that its dismantled portions could be sold off in the market for a hefty profit; but also the vast stretch of land that was used for the Wall's construction as a prime real estate in the heart of unified Berlin. However, except for small number of concrete wall segments that were sold or auctioned off in Germany or abroad, more than 40,000 slabs were crushed and used as gravel in road construction projects. The selected Wall slabs that were slated for sale, all of them the fourth generation design (post-1975), were mostly painted on the side that used to face West Berlin, while their other side (facing East Berlin) were painted white.[4] Of note, is what is dubbed as "the sale of the century" organized by the fading and bankrupt East German government held at the Hotel Park Palace in Monte Carlo, Monaco in June 1990. In one day, eighty-one Wall sections were auctioned off for an average of £6,500 to international clients (Taylor, 2006: 435–36).[5]

From the beginning, the Wall's complete removal became a controversial topic. Some Germans insisted on preserving at least parts of this significant historic artifact of the Cold War era for a more accurate representation of a divided Germany's history. However, others, the majority of them from West Germany, were in favor of complete removal of the Wall and its peripheral infrastructure in order to erase a shameful period of tyranny and repression from German collective memory. The latter group prevailed, and except for few locations the massive Wall structure—the concrete Wall slabs and the fence, the patrol road, the death strip, watch towers and the rest are all gone. Ward (2011: 95) observes that the Wall's total eradication has "willfully dislocated" post-Wall Berlin from its immediate past history. Except for Berliners who are old enough to remember pre-1989 Berlin, the younger generation Germans share the same sentiments that Ward attributes to tourists who come to Berlin to visit the Wall remains:

> Tourists arriving in Berlin, expecting to bring away perhaps their own piece of the Wall that fits in with the popular historical narrative they have received regarding the terror of the Cold War, do not find enough wall remnants to convincingly signal a previous reign of terror (ibid.).

---

[4] White-painted walls made it easier for GDR border patrol guards to detect would-be defectors.

[5] In her coffee table book, *Die Berliner Mauer in der Welt (The Berlin Wall in the World)* Anna Kaminsky (2009) provides a narrative of the contexts in which the Wall slabs are displayed outside Germany.

Although in a different context, my own experience was also close to what Ward describes above. I was not an ordinary tourist when in the spring of 2010 I landed in Berlin. I was there to verify what I knew about the Wall's history, design, and its long path in and around Berlin through a carefully pre-planned field observation. Yet in many occasions I was also at loss to make sense of not only what (little) was left of the Wall; but also of the ways with which it is preserved and displayed. Ward (ibid.: 96) observes that "apart from the four and a half miles of line-markers in the city's center, the path of the Wall is mostly obliterated." The line-marker that she talks about is a double-row of the famous Berlin cobble stone blocks that are in-laid on the paved street surfaces. The line markers do not necessarily run parallel to the curb lines, and except in places that an embedded plaque signifies "Berliner Mauer 1961–1989," the unsuspecting tourist may not even recognize their historical significance (see Photo 11.1).

The few other Wall remnants that have been preserved are also stripped of their inherent authentic historical meanings by the manner they are presented to the public. Ironically, the Wall was erected during the last decade of the modern era; but its dismantling and preservation of few sections took place at the peak of postmodern era of architectural design and urban planning. Citing Alan Colquhoun's interpretation of postmodern urban space (1985), Ward (ibid.: 96) observes that "looking for and valuing Berlin's discordant layers caused by the hot and cold wars of the twentieth century corresponds well with the palimpsest-ideals of postmodern urban planning, which 'looks at the city as the result of temporal accumulation in space, a sequence in which the latest intervention takes its place'." This postmodern interpretation is clearly evident in the '*historicist*' representation of the Wall's remains, as well as the design of new urban spaces and structures on the sites that the Wall structure used to occupy, such as the recently completed project in Potsdamer Platz.[6]

Probably the most significant Wall preservation project is the Berlin Wall Memorial on Bernauer Straße, an elaborate complex that runs an expanse between Oderberger Straße and Garten Straße. This site is one of the most photographed and cited locations when the Wall was being constructed in 1961, as the homes along the east side of Bernauer Straße stood in East Berlin while the pedestrian pavement at their doorsteps remained

---

[6] "historicism" refers to the manner in which postmodern architecture has taken historic motifs from various historical periods and eclectically utilized them in the design of new buildings, disregarding their relevance in the context of a given time period. For a critique of the design and development of Potsdamer Platz see Chaichian (2010).

Photo 11.1   The Berlin Wall's double-row cobble stone line-marker with the embedded signifier plaque near the Brandenburg Gate (photo by author)

in West Berlin side. Designed by Kohlhoff & Kohlhoff, a reconstructed Wall memorial includes a 70-meter (230-foot) preserved section of the Wall that is sandwiched between two steel walls; as well as *representations* of the inner wall, the signal fence, the patrol road, border lights, a watchtower and the Death Strip. But apparently the tourists and visitors were not "getting" this sterile, historicist postmodern "mock-up" memorial at the ground level, which prompted the designers to add an observation platform on the other side of Bernauer Straße so that the visitors could see the "simulated artifact" from above ground level (Ward, 2010: 105–106) (see Photo 11.2). Other notable examples of postmodern representations of the Wall include the East Side Gallery, a 1.3 kilometer-long stretch of the Wall on the east bank of Spree River which in 1990 various German and international artists painted on the wrong side of the Wall slabs facing former East Berlin; painted slabs of the outer Wall similarly painted on the wrong side placed along the Wall's line-marker in Potsdamer Platz; and a replica of the Allied guardhouse installed at the infamous Checkpoint Charlie in 2000 (see Photos 11.3–11.5).[7] These and other "tourist traps" such as photo ops to have your picture taken with fake GDR border guards at Checkpoint Charlie, or having your passport stamped by an East German customs agent replica at Potsdamer Platz were anything but historical sites that could evoke a genuine sense of connectedness to Berlin's not-so-distant past.

What the average tourist or visitor would not see is the long stretch of an equally repressive and deadly border fence installation between former West Berlin and East German territory. But thanks to a German friend who resided in Berlin's northern suburb of Frohnau which used to be part of the French-occupied sector, I had a chance to bike a 40-kilometer (25-mile) stretch of border patrol road that was used by the GDR border guards up until 1989 to secure West Berlin's borders in the suburbs and countryside. Now, paved and used as walking or biking trail by Berliners, the old patrol road snakes through grasslands and wooded areas, with few remnants of the border fence installations—a watch tower here and remains of the inner wall there. Yet looking at a wide strip of overgrown

---

[7] Eberhard Diepgen, former mayor of West Berlin has criticized the East Side Gallery's representation of the Wall by referring to it as a "Disney version of history" (Steininger, 2011). It is important to note that the side of the Wall facing East Berlin was painted white for security reasons in order to make it easier for GDR border guards to spot and arrest would-be defectors, and painting murals on that side of the Wall slabs diminishes the Wall's historical value and authenticity. For a critique of Checkpoint Charlie's postmodern representation see Ward (2010: 98).

Photo 11.2 The Berlin Wall Memorial on Bernauer Straße as seen from the observation platform across the street (the platform is part of the Documentation Center's structure). A segment of the original fourth generation Wall is seen in the foreground between the two steel panels, followed by a reconstructed Death Strip, patrol road, border lights, the watch tower, the signal fence, and the inner wall. The former central (Downtown) East Berlin is visible in the background (photo by author).

Photo 11.3 The East Side Gallery Wall memorial along the Spree River (facing north). Note that the painted side of the wall is facing East Berlin (on the right) which is a historical misrepresentation-this side used to be painted white while the other side facing West Berlin (on the left) was used for murals and graffiti by West Berliners (photo by author).

Photo 11.4 A 'Disneyesque' version of the Wall: Fake East German border agents stamping passports for tourists in front of the painted Berlin Wall slabs at Potsdamer Platz, 2010. Also note that the painted slabs are facing East Berlin, but this side of the Wall was originally painted white for security reasons. Border agents are correctly standing on East Berlin side, but they are issuing East German visas to a traveler who (in reality) is about to enter West Berlin! (photo by author).

Photo 11.5 Another 'Disneyesque' version of the Wall: A replica of the Allied guardhouse at Checkpoint Charlie on Friedrichstraße facing towards East Berlin, installed in 2000. The original guardhouse is on exhibit at the Museum of the Allies in Berlin (photo by author, 2010).

grassland to the east of the trail sent chills down my spine that all other postmodern wall memorial representations in Berlin combined failed to do: this area was in fact the old notorious Death Strip in Frohnau that now runs along residential neighborhoods.

The battle between "modernists" who advocated a more authentic historical presentation of the Wall structure, at least portions of it; and "postmodernist" proponents of a historicist representation of the Wall remains is still alive. On the 50th anniversary of the Wall's construction, West Berlin's former mayor Eberhard Diepgen declared in an op-ed piece that "it was wrong to take all those pieces of Berlin Wall, paint them and send them off into the world as souvenirs of a peaceful revolution"; and proposed instead to rebuild parts of the Wall "as accurately as possible, with barbed wire, watch towers and spring guns, so the brutality of the system is evident." Many readers of his article found his proposal as "bizarre," "ahistorical," and "the wrong signal for the city" (Steininger, 2011); while Klaus Wowereit, Berlin's mayor at the time was quick to denounce Diepgen and what he called as the "newly fashionable leftist view" that tries to promote the notion that building the Wall in 1961 was based on legitimate reasons. He then concluded, "we don't have any tolerance for those who nostalgically distort the history of the Berlin Wall and Germany's division" (Kirschbaum, 2011). Although Diepgen had a valid point in criticizing attempts to eradicate the Wall's history from public memory, realization of his proposal would have created another historicist memorial, a *simulacrum* in its own terms. However, Diepgen's proposal represented a viewpoint that was espoused by a coalition of activists and thinkers when the Wall came down in 1989. As Taylor (2006: 430) points out,

> The idealists who had dared to oppose the [GDR] regime during its last years were not, on the whole, full-blooded capitalists. They were of the Left, and Green, and aimed to build a collaborative rather than a competitive society; to transform the neo-Stalinist experiment that was the GDR into a laboratory for a 'third way' between capitalism and communism.

Similar to other walls in ancient history—the Great Wall of China, the Red Snake in northeastern Iran, or Hadrian's Wall in northern England, the Berlin Wall's demise did not signify one empire or nation's victory and another's defeat; but rather a systemic failure on a much larger scale that victimized the population on both sides of the wall. In his book *The Berlin Wall*, Taylor (2006; 447) ends by telling the sad tale of Conrad Schumann, the young GDR border guard whose iconic photo of leaping over the newly laid barbed wire fence along Bernauer Straße into West Berlin on August 15, 1961 has since become the symbolic image of the ideological and moral triumph of the West (capitalist democracy) over the East (communist dictatorship). His was a success story of a defector who "married a young West German woman," worked "for about twenty years in the Audi car factory," and lived in a "prosperous town" in northern Bavaria in West Germany. With the Wall's demise, he was finally able to visit his family and friends he left behind in what became East Germany, but his visit to his old hometown was anything but a happy ending:

> There, however, he found that he was not entirely welcome. He was the iconic Wall-jumper. Or, as he had been portrayed in the East, iconic traitor and tool of the imperialists. These were the accusations from which the Wall had protected him. Schumann could not reconnect with the friends, and comrades of his youth, the ones he had left behind when he took that impulsive jump to the West all those years ago. With that 'desertion' he had excluded himself from being one of them, and never could be again.
>
> Conrad Schumann hanged himself on 20 June, 1998 in the orchard of his home near Ingolstadt. The family blamed his suicide on personal problems.

I would like to end my book by a quote from Michael Dear, a city and regional planning professor at the University of California, Berkeley. In a recent op-ed in the New York Times titled "Mr. President, Tear Down This Wall" by focusing on the U.S.-Mexico border fortifications Dear (2013) makes a similar argument about the futility and wastefulness of building walls, and urges the President (Obama) to demolish the barrier:

> Of course, whether we act boldly now or not, it will eventually come down, just as other barriers have fallen. The Berlin Wall was demolished virtually overnight, its fragments sold as souvenirs of a bygone Cold War. When it is finally recognized for what it is—a manifestation of a failed immigration policy—our border fence will fall to angry residents, avid recyclers, and souvenir hunters.

REFERENCES

Abdelkrim-Chikh, Rabia. 1990. "Les Femme Exogames: Entre La Loi de Dieu et les Droite de L'Hommes," *L'Islam en France*, Editions Bruno Ettienne, pp. 235–254.

Abu-Saadi, Fadi. 2012. "Palestinian Building of Israeli Settlements: Searching for Alternatives," *Al Akhbar English* (February 16). Retrieved from http://english.al-akhbar.com/print/4272.

Abunimah, Ali. 2007. *One Country: A Bold Proposal to End the Israeli-Palestinian Impasse.* New York; Metropolitan Books.

Acuña, Rodolfo. 1981. *Occupied America: A History of Chicano.* New York: Harper & Row.

Administration of the German Bundestag. 2006. "Elections in the Weimar Republic." http://www.bundestag.de/htdocs_e/artandhistory/history/factsheets/elections_weimar_republic.pdf, accessed 7-21-2010.

Agnew, John. 1994. "The Territorial Trap: The Geographical Assumptions of International Relations Theory," *Review of International Political Economy*, 1: 53–80

Alba, Victor. 1967. *The Mexicans.* New York: Prager.

Alenat, Salwa. 2009. "Palestinian Workers in Israeli West Bank Settlements," *Kav LaOved Workers' Hotline* (March 13). Retrieved from http://kavlaoved.org.il/media-view_eng.asp?id=2764.

Amin Pour. B. 2005. Geometric Survey of the Great Wall of Gorgan and Ancient Jorjan City. Unpublished report, Iranian Center for Archaeological Research, Tehran.

Angulo P.C. 1990. "Foreign Investment and the Maquiladora industry," *Inversión Extranjera.*

Anon. 1985. "Mexico in Historic Move to Join GATT," *the Age*, November 27: 29). *Directa* (direct foreign investment), 139–143. México: Banamex.

Anon. 2004. "The War of the Headscarves," *The Economist* (February 5). http://www.Economist.com/world/Europe/displayStory.cfm?story_id=2404691, accessed 7-4-2008.

Archibolad, Randall. 2008. "U.S.-Mexico Border Fence Will Split Friendship Park," *The New York Times* (October 22), http://www.nytimes.com/2008/10/22/world/americas/22iht-22border.17155357.html?pagewanted=all.

Archick, Kristin; Belkin, Paul; Blanchard, Christopher M.; Ek, Carl; and Mix, Derek E. 2011. *Muslims in Europe: Promoting Integration and Countering Extremism.* Congressional Research Service (September 7), http://www.fas.org/sgp/crs/row/RL33166.pdf.

Arne, T.J. 1945. Excavations at Shah Tepe. Stockholm.

Arnon, Arie. 2007. "Israeli Policy Towards the Occupied Palestinian Territories: The Economic Dimension, 1967–2007," *Middle East Journal*, 61(4): 573–595.

ASECOP. 2011. *Israeli Separation Barrier.* Asociación Europea de Cooperación con Palestina (May 26). Retrieved from http://www.asecop.org/en/articles/93-muro-de-segregacion.

Astier, Henry. 2004. *The Deep Roots of French Secularism.* http://news.bbc.co.uk/i/hi/Europe/3325285.stm, accessed 7-1-2008.

Audley, John J., Papademetriou, Demetrios G., Polaski, Sandra, and Vaughan, Scott. 2004. *NAFTA's Promise and Reality: Lessons from Mexico for the Hemisphere.* Carnegie Endowment for International Peace.

Aumann, Moshe. 1976. *Land Ownership in Palestine 1880–1948.* Jerusalem: Academic Committee on the Middle East.

Babés, L. 1997. *"L'Islam Positif: La Religion des Jeunes Musulmans en France"* (Positive Islam: The Religion of Young Muslims in France). Paris: Édition de L'Aube.

Bahiri, Simcha, and Hazboun, Samir. 1995. "Creating Palestinian Employment in Industrial Zones," *Palestine-Israel Journal*, 2 (3). Retrieved from http://www.pij.org/details.php?id=633.

Bahour, Sam. 2010. 'Economic Prison Zones' Exploit Palestinian Labor, Create Dependency on Isreal," *Middle East Research and Information Center* (November 19). Retrieved from http://www.merip.org/mero/mero111910.

Balakrishnan, Gopal. 2000. "Virgilian Visions," *New Left Review*, 5: 142–148 (September–October).

Balibar, Etienne. 2004. *We the People of Europe: Reflections on Transnational Citizenship.* Princeton, NJ: Princeton University Press.

Barakat, Halim I. 1973. "The Palestinian Refugees: An Uprooted Community Seeking Repatriation," *International Migration Review*," 7(2): 147–161.

Bard, Mitchell. 2010. *Israel's Security Fence.* Jewish Virtual Library. Retrieved from http://www.jewishvirtuallibrary.org/jsource/Peace/fence.html (July 8).

Bayes, Jane H., and Tohidi, Nayereh. 2001. *Globalization, Gender, and Religion: The Politics of Women's Rights in Catholic and Muslim Contents.* New York: Palgrave.

BBC News. 2008. "France Rejects Veiled Muslim's wife" (July 12). http://news.bbc.co.Uk/2/hi/Europe/7503757.stm, accessed 7-13-2008.

Beck, Ulrich. 2000. *What is Globalization?* Cambridge, UK: Polity Press.

———. 2002. "The Cosmopolitan Society and Its Enemies,' *Theory, Culture & Society*, 19 (1–2): 17–44.

———. 2004. "The Cosmopolitan Turn," in Nicholas Gane (Ed.), *The Future of Social Theory*, pp. 143–166. London & New York: Continuum.

Becker, Andrew. 2008. *Immigration Timeline: A look at U.S. Policy toward Immigration and Border Security with Mexico over the Past 60 Years.* PBS Frontline World. http://www.pbs.org/frontlineworld/stories/mexico704/history/timeline.html, accessed 8-6-2009.

Begag, Azuz, and Chaouite, Abdellatif. 1990. *Ecartes d'Identité.* Paris: Seuil.

Bell, Daniel. 1974. *The Coming of Post-Industrial Society.* New York: Basic Books.

Bellah, Robert. 1967. "civil Religion in America," *Daedalus*, 96(1): 1–21 (Winter).

Bennett, Brian. 2010. "Costly Virtual Border Fence in Tatters," *Los Angeles Times* (October 22), http://articles.latimes.com/2010/oct/22/nation/la-na-invisible-fence-20101022.

Bennis, Phyllis. 2007. *Understanding the Palestinian-Israeli Conflict: A Premier.* Northampton, MA: Olive Branch Press.

Berdahl, Daphne. 1999. *Where the World Ended: Re-Unification and Identity in the German Borderland.* Berkeley, CA: University of California Press.

Biddiscombe, Perry. 1998. *Werwolf! The History of the National Socialist Guerilla Movement, 1944–1946.* Toronto.

———. 2001. "Dangerous Liaisons: The Anti-Fraternization Movement in the U.S. Occupation Zones of Germany and Austria, 1945–1948," *Journal of Social History, 611–647 (spring).*

Billington, Ray A. 1956. *The Far Western Frontier, 1830–1860.* New York: Harper and Row.

Birley, Anthony R. 1997. *Hadrian: The Restless Emperor.* London: Routledge.

Bishara, Azmy. 1989. "The Uprising's Impact on Israel," in Lockman, Zachary and Beinin, Joel (Eds.), *Intifada: The Palestinian Uprising against Israeli Occupation.* Boston, MA: South End Press.

Bivar, A.D.H. 2003. "Hephthalites," Encylopedia Iranica, vol. XII, Fasc. 2, pp. 198–201, http://www.iranicaonline.org/articles/hephthalites.

———. 2003b. "Gorgan, Pre-Islamic History," *Encyclopaedia Iranica,* http://www.iranica online.org/articles/gorgan-v.

Bivar, A.D.H., and Fehérvári, G. 1966. "The Walls of Tamisha," *Iran*, 4: 35–50.

Boeing. 2006. "Boeing Team Awarded SBInet Contract by Department of Homeland Security" (September 21). http://www.boeing.com/news/releases/2006/q3/060921a_nr.html.

Bogan, Jesse. 2009. "A Boom at the Border," *Forbes.com* (April 2), http://www.forbes.com/2009/04/01/mexico-texas-economy-business-border.html.

Bouhdiba, Abdelwahab. 1975. *La Sexualité en Islam.* Paris: PUF.

Bourdieu, Pierre. 1979. *Algeria 1960.* New York: Cambridge University Press.

Bradatan, Costica. 2011. "Scaling the 'Wall in the Head'," *The New York Times* (November 27), http://opinionator.blogs.nytimes.com/2011/11/27/scaling-the-wall-in-the-head/.

Brar, Bhupinder. 2005. "A Future Never Fancied: Globalization Theory and the Growth of Majoritarian Nationalism in India," in Käkönen, Jyrki, and Chaturvedi, Sanjay (eds.), *Globalization: Spaces, Identities and (In)Securities*, 145–157. New Delhi, India: South Asian Publishers.

Breeze, David J.; and Dobson, Brian. 1976. *Hadrian's Wall.* London: Allen Lane.

Brenner, Lenni. 1984. *The Iron Wall: Zionist Revisionism from Jabotinsky to Shamir.* London: Zed Books.

———. (Ed.). 2002. *51 Documents: Zionist Collaboration with the Nazis.* Fort Lee, NJ: Barricade Books.

Brett, Michael, and Fentross, Elizabeth. 1997. *The Berbers.* Blackwell publishing.

B'Tselem. 2004a. *Forbidden Roads: The Discriminatory West Bank Road Regime* (complete report). Retrieved from www.btselem.org/download/200408_forbidden_roads_eng.doc.

———. 2004b. *Forbidden Roads: The Discriminatory West Bank Road Regime* (summary report). Retrieved from http://www.btselem.org/publications/summaries/200408_forbid den_roads.

———. 2011a. "Separation Barrier: Opinion of the International court of Justice." Retrieved from http://www.btselem.org/separation_barrier/international_court_decision (January).

———. 2011b. *The Separation Barrier.* Retrieved from http://www.btselem.org/separation_ barrier (January).

Buie, Amanda. 2008. "Mexico's Maquiladoras—Climbing the Ladder of Success," *Prologis Research Bulletin*, 1–12 (spring).

Bullock, Katherine. 2003. *Rethinking Muslim Women and the Veil: Challenging Historical & Modern Stereotypes.* London: The International Institute of Islamic Thought.

Bunis, Dena and Terrell, Jessica. 2009. "Obama Wants Immigration Reform Passed by This Congress," *The Orange County Register*, June 25.

Burns, Thomas S. 2003. *Rome and the Barbarians, 100 BC–AD 400.* Baltimore: Johns Hopkins University Press.

Butler, Ewan. 1955. *City Divided: Berlin 1955.* London; Sedgwick and Jackson Limited.

Bybee, Roger, and Winter, Carolyn. 2006. "Immigration Flood Unleashed by NAFTA's Disastrous Impact on Mexican Economy," *Common Dreams* (April 25). http://www .commondreams.org/views06/0425-30.htm, accessed 8-4-2009.

Calavita, Kitty. 1992. *Inside the State: The Bracero Program, Immigration, and the INS.* New York: Routledge.

Cañas, Jesus, and Coronado, Roberto. 2002. "Maquiladora Industry: Past, Present, and Future," *Business Frontier*, Issue 2. Federal Reserve Bank of Dallas, El Paso Branch, http://www.dallasfed.org/research/busfront/bus0202.pdf, accessed 7-29-2009.

Carcamo, Cindy. 2011. "Arizona Seeks Online Donations to Complete the Fence," *The Orange County Register* (May 9). http://www.ocregister.com/articles/fence-299679-arizona-border.html.

Cardoso, Lawrence A. 1974. *Mexican Emigration to the United States, 1900–1930: An Analysis of Socio-Economic Causes.* Ph.D. dissertation, University of Connecticut.

Castells, Manuel. 1989. *The Informational City: Information Technology, Economic Restructuring, and the Urban-Regional Process.* Oxford: Basil Blackwell.

———. 1990. *The Informational City: A framework for Social Change.* Toronto: University of Toronto Press.

———. 2000. *End of Millennium*, vol. 3 of *the Information Age: Economy, Society and Culture*, 2nd edition. Oxford: Blackwell.

Cave, Damen. 2011. "Crossing Over, and Over," *The New York Times* (October 2), http:// www.nytimes.com/2011/10/03/world/americas/mexican-immigrants-repeatedly-brave-risks-to-resume-lives-in-united-states.html?pagewanted=all.

CBP. 2008. *Section 2.0: General Project Description.* U.S. Customs and Borders Protection (December). http://www.cbp.gov/linkhandler/cgov/border_security/ti/ti_docs/sector/yuma/yuma_300/yuma_cv1a/yuma_cv1a_chpt/cv1a_sec2.ctt/cv1a_sec2.pdf.

——. 2010. *Types of Fence.* U.S. Customs and Borders Protection (January 15). http://www .cbp.gov/xp/cgov/border_security/ti/about_ti/fence.xml.

Cesari, Jocelyne. 2005. "Ethnicity, Islam, and les Banlieues: Confronting the Issues," *Social Science Research Council.* http://riotsfrance.ssrc.org/cesari/printable.html, accessed 7-14-2008.

Chaichian, Mohammad. 1997. "First Generation Iranian Immigrants and the Question of Cultural identity: The Case of Iowa," *International Migration Review,* 31(3): 612–627.

——. 2003. "Structural Impediments of the Civil Society Project in Iran: National and Global Dimensions, *International Journal of Comparative Sociology,* 44(1): 19–50.

——. 2006. *White Racism on the Western Urban Frontier: Dynamics of Race and Class in Dubuque, Iowa 1800–2000.* Lanham, MD: Lexington Books.

——. 2010. *Contested Ideological Urban Landscapes: The Case of Potsdamer Platz in Berlin, Germany.* Paper presented at the International Conference on Spaces and Flows. University of California, Los Angeles, http://f10.cgpublisher.com/proposals/77/index_html.

Chaker, Salem. 2006. *Berber, a 'Long-Forgotten' Language of France* (translated by Laurie and Amar Chaker). http://www.utexas.edu/cola/insts/france-ut/arcives/chaker_english .pdf, accessed 6-30-2008.

Chance, Joseph E., ed. 1991. *The Mexican War Journal of Captain Franklin Smith.* Jackson: University Press of Mississippi.

Charlseworth, Martin. 1987. "Preliminary Report on a Newly-Discovered Extension of 'Alexander's Wall,'" *Iran,* 25: 160–165.

Chase-Dunn, Christopher and Thomas D. Hall. 1997. *Rise and Demise: Comparing World-Systems.* Boulder: Westview Press.

Chertoff, Mordechai. 1975. *Zionism: A Basic Reader.* New York: Herzl Press.

Chomsky, Noam. 1999. *Fateful Triangle: The United States, Israel, and the Palestinians.* Cambridge, MA: South End Press.

——. 2003. *Middle East Illusions.* Lanham, MD: Rowman & Littlefield.

——. 2009. *"The Unipolar Moment and the Obama Era,"* A lecture given at the National Autonomous University of Mexico (UNAM), University City, Federal District, Mexico, September 21. http://www.chomsky.info/talks/20090921%281%29.htm.

Chomsky, Noam, and Achcar, Gilbert. 2007. *Perilous Power: The Middle East & U.S. Foreign Policy.* Boulder, CO: Paradigm Publishers.

CJPME. 2005. 'Factsheet: Industrial Zones and Israel's Colonial Strategy," *Canadians for Justice and Peace in the Middle East,* Factsheet No. 10 (October).

Clark, Victor S. 1908. *Mexican Labor in the United States.* U.S. Department of Commerce Bulletin No. 78. Washington, D.C.: U.S. Government Printing Office.

Clement, Norris, Rey, Sergio J., Fuentes, Noe' Aron, and Brugues, Alejandro. 1999. "The U.S.-Mexican Border Economy in the NAFTA Era: Implications for the Environment," *Network of Border Economics (NOBE)/Red de la Economica Fronteriza (REF)* pp. 55–69, https:// webfiles.uci.edu/chavirar/www/uci/USMexicoBorder/webdocs/WK03MexBorder EconDevelop.pdf.

Cohen, Israel. 1951. *A Short history of Zionism.* London: F. Muller.

Cole, Juan. 2007. *Napoleon's Egypt: Invading the Middle East.* New york: Palgrave-MacMillan.

Collingwood, R.G. 1921. 'The Purpose of the Roman Wall," *The Vasculum,* 8: 4–9.

Colquhoun, Alan. 1985. "On Modern and Postmodern Space," in Joan Oackman, ed., *Architecture Criticism Ideology.* New York: Princeton Architectural Press, pp. 103–117.

Comité Fronterizo de Obreras. 2007. *A Few Facts about the Maquiladora Industry,* http:// www.cfomaquiladoras.org/english%20site/numeralia.en.html, accessed 7-30-2009.

Cook, Catherine. 2003. "Final Status in the Shape of a Wall," *Middle east Research and Information Project* (September 3). Retrieved from http://www.merip.org/mero/mero090303.

Cook, Jonathan. 2008. *Disappearing Palestine: Israel's Experiments in Human Despair.* London: Zed Books.

Corporate Watch. 2009a. "Resisting the Corporations—Exploitation in Israeli Industrial Settlement: a Call for Solidarity with Palestinian Workers (November 18). Retrieved from http://www.corporatewatch.org/?lid=3459.

———. 2009b. "Occupation Industries: The Israeli Industrial Zones (December 2). Retrieved from http://www.corporatewatch.org/?lid=3477.

Cox, Michael, and Kennedy-Pipe, Caroline. 2005. "The Tragedy of American Diplomacy? Rethinking the Marshall Plan," *Journal of Cold War Studies,* 7(1): 97–134 (winter).

Connolly, William. 1995. *The Ethos of Pluralization.* Minneapolis: University of Minnesota Press.

Cramer, Michael. 2008. *German-German Border Trail.* Rodingersdorf: Esterbauer.

Cumberland, Charles C. 1968. *Mexico: The Struggle for Modernity.* New York: Oxford University Press.

Cunningham, H. 2004. "Nations Rebound: Crossing Borders in a Gated Globe," *Identities: Global Studies in Culture and Power,* 11: 329–350.

Daryaee, Touraj. 2008. "The Political History of Ērānšahr (224–651 CE)," *Sasanika,* 2: 1–51. http://www.humanities.uci.edu/sasanika/pdf/Political%20history%20of%20Eranshahr .pdf

Daud, Simone. 2011. "Money for nothing and Occupation for Free: The 1994 Paris Protocols on Economic Relations between Israel and the PLO," *Mondoweiss,* 14 (September 28).

Davidi, Efraim. 2000. "Globalization and Economy in the Middle East—A peace of Markets or a Peace of Flags? *Palestine-Israel Journal, 7 (1–2).*

Davis, Michael. 2005. "The Great Wall of Capital," in Sorokin, Michael (ed.), *Against the Wall: Israel's Barrier to Peace,* 88–99. New York: New Press.

Dear. Michael. 2013. "Mr. President, Tear down This Wall," *The New York Times,* March 10.

De La Cruz, Justino; Koopman, Robert B.; Zhi Wang; and Shang-Jin Wei. 2011. *Estimating Foreign Value-Added in Mexico's Manufacturing Exports.* Washington, D.C.: Office of Economics Working Paper, U.S. International Trade Commission, No. 2011–04A (March), http://www.usitc.gov/publications/332/EC201104A.pdf.

De La Vaissière, Étienne. 2007. "Is there a 'Nationality' of the Hephtalites?" *Bulletin of Asia Institute,* Vol. 17: 119–132.

De Quetteville, Harry. 2008. "Cyrus Cylinder's Ancient Bill of Rights is Just Propaganda," *The Telegraph* (July 16). Retrieved from: http://www.telegraph.co.uk/news/worldnews/europe/germany/2420263/Cyrus-cylinders-ancient-bill-of-rights-is-just-propaganda .html.

Dello Buono, Richard A., and Fassenfest, David (Eds.). 2010. *Social Change, Resistance and Social Practices.* Leiden, the Netherlands: Brill.

Dennis, Michael. 2000. *The Rise and Fall of the German Democratic Republic, 1945–1990.* Harlow.

Denny, Frederick. 1985. *An Introduction to Islam.* New York: MacMillan.

Department of Ancient Near Eastern Art. 2003. "The Sassanian Empire (224–651 A.D.)," in *Heilbrunn Timeline of Art History.* New York: The Metropolitan Museum of Art, 2000–. http://www.metmuseum.org/toah/hd/sass/hd_sass.htm.

Department of Homeland Security. 2006. *Risk Management Advisory for the SBInet Program Initiation.* Washington, D.C.: Office of Inspector General.

Department of Homeland Security. 2009. *Department of Homeland Security Annual Performance Report, 2008–2010.* Washington, D.C.: Department of Homeland Security, Office of the Chief Financial Officer. http://www.dhs.gov/xlibrary/assets/cfo_apr_fy2008.pdf.

Dignas, Beate; and Winter, Engelbert. 2007. Rome and Persia in Late Antiquity: Neighbors and Rivals. Oxford: Oxford University Press.

Dinan, Stephen. 2006. "Bush Backs 370-Mile Fence along Border," *Washington Times,* May 19, p.A1.

Direccion General de Estadistica. 1954. *Compendia Estadistica, 1953.* Mexico: Secretaria de Economica.

Documents on Germany, 1944–1959: Background Documents on Germany, 1944–1959, and a Chronology of Political Developments Affecting Berlin, 1945–1956. 1959. Washington, DC: General Printing Office, http://www.germanhistorydocs.ghi-dc.org/docpage.cfm?docpage_id=2959.

Eduljee, K.E. n.d. "The Wall of Gorgan," Zoroastrian Heritage, http://www.heritageinstitute.com/zoroastrianism/varkana/wall.htm.

——. n.d.b. Merv, Mouru. http://www.heritageinstitute.com/zoroastrianism/merv/merv.htm.

Elden, Stuart. 2006. "Contingent Sovereignty: Territorial Integrity and the Security of Borders," *The SAIS Review of International Affairs*, 26 (1): 11–24.

Elin, Nada. 1997. "In the Making: Beur Fiction and Identity Construction," *World Literature Today*, 71: 47–54 (winter).

Elon, Amos. 1975. *Herzl.* New York.

Engel, Jeffrey A. (Ed.) 2009. *The Fall of the Berlin Wall: The Revolutionary Legacy of 1989.* New York: Oxford University Press.

Etherington, Norman. 1984. *Theories of Imperialism: War, Conquest and Capital.* London & Canberra: Croom Helm.

Etkes, Dror, and Friedman, Laura. 2005. *Bypass Roads in the West Bank.* Retrieved from http://www.peacenow.org.il/eng/content/bypass-roads-west-bank.

Ewing, Wayne. 2008. *The Border Wall* (video recording). Wayne Ewing Films, Inc.

Farrokh, Kaveh. n.d. *Retort to the Daily Telegraph's Article against Cyrus the Great.* Retrieved from: http://azargoshnasp.net/Pasokhbehanirani/kavehcyrusresponse.pdf.

——. 2009. The Great Wall of Gorgan. http://www.kavehfarrokh.com/news/the-great-wall-of-gorgan/.

Fars Foundation. N.d. Golestan Province-Natural Hazards. http://www.iran.farsfoundation.net/en/golestan.html?start=12.

Faux, Jeff; Salas, Carlos; and Scott, Robert E. 2006. *Revisiting NAFTA: Still not Working for North America's Workers.* Economic Policy Institute (September 28). http://www.epi.org/publications/entry/bp173/, accessed 8-5-2009.

Ferris, I.M. 2000. *Enemies of Rome: Barbarians Through Roman Eyes.* Thrupp, England: Sutton Publishing.

Ferriss, Susan. 2003. "Plowing Farmers under Free Trade is Costing Many Mexicans Their Rural Way of Life," *Statesman*, September 7. http://www.statesman.com/specialreports/content/specialreports/mexico_farms/0907mexicofarms.html, accessed 8-5-2009.

Flaig, Dorothee; siddiq, Khalid; Grethe, Harald; Luckmann, Jonas; and McDonald, Scott. 2011. *The Integration of Palestinian-Israeli Labour Markets: A CGE Approach.* Paper presented at the 2011 Agricultural & Applied Economics Association, Pittsburgh, PA.

Flechtheim, Ossip Kurt. 1973. *Die Parteien der Bundesrepublik Deutschland* [*The Parties of the Federal Republic of Germany*]. Hamburg, Translation by Adam Blauhut and Thomas Dunlap, http://www.germanhistorydocs.ghi-dc.org/docpage.cfm?docpage_id=3293, accessed 8-3-2010.

Foley, Neil. 1997. *The White Scourge: Mexicans, Blacks, and Poor Whites in Texas Cotton Culture.* Berkeley: University of California Press.

Forde-Johnston, James. 1978. *Hadrian's Wall.* London: Michael Joseph.

Forman, Geremy, and Kedar, Alexandre. 2003. "Colonialism, Colonization and Land Law in Mandate Palestine: The Zor al-Zarqa and Barrat Qisarya Land Disputes in Historical Perspective," *Theoretical Inquiries in Law*, 4 (2): 490–539.

Fox Nation. 2011. "Obama Claims Border Fence 'Basically Complete' But It's only 5% Finished" (May 10). http://nation.foxnews.com/border-fence/2011/05/10/obama-claims-border-fence-basically-complete-its-only-5-finished.

Fox News. 2011. "On Immigration, Michele Bachmann Says She'll Build a Fence 'On Every Mile' of America's Southern Border" (September 22), http://foxnewsinsider.com/2011/09/22/on-immigration-michele-bachmann-says-shell-build-a-fence-on-every-mile-of-americas-southern-border/.

Fraser, T.G. 1980. *The Middle East, 1914–1979.* New York: St. Martin's Press.

——. 2004. *The Arab-Israeli Conflict.* New York: Palgrave.

Frere, Sheppard. 1987. *Britannia: A History of Roman Britain.* London: Routledge & Kegan Paul.

Friedman, Isaiah. 1970. "The McMahon-Hussein Correspondence and the Question of Palestine." *Journal of Contemporary History,* 5 (2): 83–122.

Friedrich, Otto. 1972. *Before the Deluge: A Portrait of Berlin in the 1920s.* London: Harper & Row.

Frye, R.N. 1977. "The Sassanian System of Walls for Defense, in: Rosen-Ayalon, M. (ed.), Studies in Memory of Gaston Wiet, pp. 7–15. Jerusalem.

Fukuyama, Francis. 1992. *The End of History and the Last Man.* New York: Free Press.

Gane, Nicholas (Ed.o. 2004. *The Future of Social Theory.* London & New York: Continuum.

GAO. 1994. *Border Control: Revised Strategy Is Showing Some Positive Results.* United States Government Accounting Office (December). http://www.gao.gov/archive/1995/gg9530 .pdf, accessed 3-26-2013.

——. 2003. *International Trade: Mexico's Maquiladora Decline Affects U.S.-Mexico Border Communities and Trade; Recovery Depends in Part on Mexico's Actions.* United States General Accounting Office, Report to Congressional Requesters (July).

——. 2007. "Border Patrol: Available Data on Interior Checkpoints Suggest Differences in Sector Performance, 2005–2007. U.S. General Accounting Office.

——. 2008. Secure Border Initiative: DHS Needs to Address Significant Risks in Delivering Key Technology Investment.

Garcia, Alma M. 2002. *The Mexican Americans.* Westport, CT: Greenwood Press.

Garcia, Juan Ramon. 1980. *Operation Wetback: The Mass Deportation of Mexican Undocumented Workers in 1954.* Westport, CT: Greenwood Press.

Geesey, Patricia. 1995. "North African Immigrants in France: Integration and Change," *Substance,* 76/77: 137–153.

Geo-Mexico. 2009. *Secure Border Initiative: Technology Deployment Delays Persist and the Impact of Border Fencing Has Not Been Assessed.* U.S. Government Accounting Office.

——. 2010. The Transnational Metropolitan Areas of Mexico-USA. http://geo-mexico .com/?p=4815.

Ghodrat-Dizaji, Mehrdad. 2011. "Disintegration of Sassanian Hegemony over Northern Iran (AD 623–643), Iranica Antiqua, Vol. XLVI: 315–329.

Gilbert, James. 2008. "500 Miles of Border Fence Completed," *The Sun (Yuma, Arizona),* December 22.

Gilman, Denise. 2011. "Seeking Breaches in the Wall: An International Human Rights Law Challenge to the Texas-Mexico Border Wall," *Texas International Law Journal,* 46: 257–293.

Gillman, Todd J. 2007. "Funding for 700-Mile Border Fence Falls Short," *Dallas Morning News,* February 6.

Gmyrya L. 1995. *Hun Country at the Caspian Gate.* Dagestan: Makhachkala.

Gomez-Quiñones, Juan and Maciel, David R. 1998. "What Goes Around Comes Around: Political Practice and Cultural Response in the Internationalization of Mexican Labor, 1890–1997" in David R. Maciel and Maria Herrera-Sobek (eds.), *Culture across Borders: Mexican Immigration and Popular Culture.* Tucson: the University of Arizona Press, 27–65.

Gonzales, Gilbert G., and Fernandez, Raul A. 2003. *A Century of Chicano History: Empire, Nations, and Migration.* New York: Routledge.

Gordon, Linda. 1999. *The Great Arizona Orphan Abduction.* Cambridge, Mass: Harvard University Press.

Granott, A. 1952. *The Land System in Palestine.* London.

Grebler, Leo. 1966. *Mexican Immigration to the United States: The Record and Its Implications.* Mexican-American Study Project, Advance Report no. 2. Los Angeles: University of California.

Gregory, Derek. 2006. "the Black Flag: Guantanamo Bay and the Space of Exception, *Geografiska Annaler*, 88B (4): 405–427.

Griego, Manuel Garcia. 1996. "The Importation of Mexican Contract Laborers to the United States, 1942–1964," in David G. Gutierez, ed., *Between Two Worlds: Mexican Immigrants in the United States*. Washington, D.C.: Scholarly Resources, 45–85. Griswold, Daniel. 2004. *After 10 Years, NAFTA Continues to Pay Dividends*. Washington, D.C.: Cato Institute (January 8). http://www.cato.org/pub_display.php?pub_id=2489, accessed 8-4-2009.

Haaretz. 2004. The Disengagement Plan of Prime Minister Ariel Sharon (April 16). Retrieved from http://www.haaretz.com/news/the-disengagement-plan-of-prime-minister-arielsharon-1.119737.

Haddad, Chad C.; Kim, Yule; and Garcia, Michael J. 2009. *Border Security: Barriers Along the U.S. International Borders*. Congressional Research Service.

Haddad, Yvonne Y. 1999. "The Globalization of Islam: The Return of Muslims to the West," in John Esposito (ed.), *The Oxford Dictionary of Islam*, pp. 601–641. New York: Oxford University Press.

Hahn, Erich J. 1995. "The Occupying Power and the Constitutional Reconstruction of West Germany, 1944–1989," in *Cornerstone of Democracy: The West German Grundgesetz, 1949–1989, pp. 7–35. Washington, D.C.: German Historical Institute, occasional Paper No. 13.

Hall, Stuart. 1996. "Introduction: Who Needs 'Identity'?" in Hall, Stuart and Paul de Gay (editors), *Questions of Cultural Identity*, pp. 1–17. London: Sage.

Hall, Thomas D. 2009. "Puzzles in the Comparative Study of Frontiers: Problems, Some Solutions, and Methodological Implications," *Journal of World-Systems Research*, 15(1): 25–47.

Hardt, Michael, and Negri, Antonio. 2000. *Empire*. Cambridge, MA: Harvard University Press.

Hareuveni, Eyal. 2010. *By Hook and By Crook; Israeli Settlement Policy in the West Bank*. Tel Aviv: B'Tselem.

Harmatta, J. 1996. "The Wall of Alexander the Great and the Limes Sasanicus," Bulletin of the Asia Institute, N.S., 10: 79–84.

Harrison, Hope M. 2003. *Driving the Soviets up the Wall*. Princeton: Princeton University Press.

——. 2003b. "The Berlin Wall, Ostpolitik, and Détente," *GHI Bulletin supplement*, 1: 5–18.

Hartenian, Larry. 1987. "The Role of Media in Democratizing Germany: United States Occupation Policy 1945–1949," *Central European History*, 20(2): 145–197.

Harvey, David. 1991. *The Condition of Postmodernity*. Cambridge: Blackwell.

——. 2006. *Spaces of Global Capitalism: Towards a Theory of Uneven Geographical Development*. London and New York: Verso.

Hassig, Ross. 1994. *Mexico and the Spanish Conquest*. University of Oklahoma Press.

Haut Conseil à L'Intégration. 2000. *L'Islam dans la République*. Paris: La Documentation Français. http://www.ladocumentationfrancaise.fr/var/storage/rapports-publics/014000017/0000.pdf.

Hemassi, Elbaki. 1987. "French Revolution and the Arab World," *International Social Science Journal*," UNESCO (February).

Hertle, Hans-Hermann. 2008. *The Berlin Wall—Monument of the Cold War*. Berlin: Ch. Links Verlag.

Hertzberg, Arthur (ed.). 1960. *The Zionist Idea: A Historical Analysis and Reader*. New York.

Hervieu-Léger, D. 2000. "Le miroir de L'Islam en France. *Vingtiéme Cièsle*, pp. 79–89 (April–June).

Herzl, Theodor. 1973. *Zionist Writings: Essays and Addresses*, Vol. 1, January 1896–June 1898. Translated by Harry Zohn. New York.

Herzog, Lawrence A. 1990. *Where North Meets South—Cities, Space, and Politics on the U.S.-Mexico Border*. Austin: Center for Mexican American Studies, University of Texas at Austin.

Himadeh, Said B. 1938. "Industry," in Himadeh, Said (ed.), *Economic Organization of Palestine.* Beirut.

Hing, Julianne. 2010. "America's $1.25 Billion Invisible, Unreliable Border Fence is Fallen," *Colorline* (October 22). http://colorlines.com/archives/2010/10/us_debates_1_billion_invisible_unreliable_sbinet_border_fence.html.

Hinojosa, Jose R. 1998. *The Urbanization of the U.S.-Mexico Border Region.* Paper presented at the annual meeting of the Western Social Sciences Association, Denver, Colorado.

Hirschberg, Haim Ze'ev. 1973. "Ottoman Period," in *Israel Pocket Library: History Until 1880,* pp. 212–250. Jerusalem: Keter Publishing.

Hobsbawm, E.J. 1987. *The Age of Empire, 1875–1914.* New York: Pantheon Books.

Hobson, John A. 1902. *Imperialism.* London.

House, James. 2006. "The Colonial and Post-Colonial Dimensions of Algerian Migration to France," *Institute of Historical Research,* University of Leeds. http://www.history.ac.uk/ihr/focus/migration/articles/house.html, accessed 7-14-2008.

Howard-Johnston, J.D. 2006. *East Rome, Sassanian Persia and the End of Antiquity: Historiographical and Historical Studies.* Aldershat, Hampshire: Ashgate.

Hsu, Spencer S. 2009. "In 'Virtual Fence,' Continuity with Border Effort by Bush," *The Washington Post,* May 9.

Huff, Dietrich. 1986. "Sasanian Archaeology: History & Method of Research," The Circle of Ancient Iranian Studies. http://www.cais-soas.com/CAIS/Archaeology/Sasanian/sasanian_archaeology.htm.

Huffington Post. 2011. "Herman Cain Faces Backlash over 'Great Wall,' Alligator-Filled Moat Border Security Solution" (July 11), http://www.huffingtonpost.com/2011/07/11/herman-cain-great-wall-alligator-moat_n_894687.html.

Hultsch, F. 1889. *The Histories of Polybius, Vol. 1,* translated by Evelyn S. Shuckburg. London and New York: Macmillan and Co.

Human Rights Watch. 2005. "Israel/Occupied Territories: Human Rights Concerns for the 61st Session of the UN Commission on Human Rights" (March 10). Retrieved from http://rel;iefweb.int/node/168258.

Hurewitz, J.C. 1975. *The Middle East and North Africa in World Politics.* New Haven, Conn.

Ibn Sa'd. n.d. *Al-Tabaqat al-Kubra.* Beirut: Dar Sadir.

IDMC. 2011. "Closure Regime, Restrictions in Freedom of Movement & Israeli Infrastructure," *Internal Displacement Monitoring Centre* (June 21), http://www.internal-displacement.org/idmc/website/countries.nsf/%28httpEnvelopes%29/901DECF32AFC22E2C125 74B800328550?OpenDocument.

Iran Chamber Society. n.d. Sassanid Empire. http://www.iranchamber.com/history/sassanids/sassanids.php.

Ireland, Douglas. 2005. "Why is France Burning?," *Z Magazine,* http://www.zmag.org/znet/viewarticle/5076, accessed 7-17-2008.

Israel Diplomatic Network. N.d. *The Anti-Terrorist Fence—an Overview.* Retrieved from http://securityfence.mfa.gov.il/mfm/web/main/missionhome.asp?MissionID=45187&.

Israel Information Center. 1977. *Facts about Israel.* Jerusalem: Government of Israel.

Israel Ministry of Foreign Affairs. 2003. *Saving Lives-Israel's Security Fence.* Retrieved from http://www.mfa.gov.il/MFA/MFAArchive/2000_2009/2003/11/Saving%20Lives-%20Israel-s%20Security%20Fence.

———. 2004. *Saving Lives: Israel's Anti-Terrorist Fence—Answers to Questions.* Retrieved From http://www.mfa.gov.il/MFA/Terrorism+Obstacle+to+Peace/Palestinian+terror+since+2000/Saving+Lives-+Israel-s+anti-terrorist+fence+-+Answ.htm#3.

Israel's Security Fence. 2007. *Purpose.* Retrieved from http://securityfence.mod.gov.il/eng/purpose.html.

Jackson, Robert. 2000. *The Global Covenant: Human Conduct in a World of States.* Oxford: Oxford University Press.

Jimenez, Maria. 2009. *Humanitarian Crisis: Migrant Deaths at the U.S.-Mexico Border.* http://www.aclu.org/files/pdfs/immigrants/humanitariancrisisreport.pdf

Johnson, Chalmers. 2006. "Exporting the American Model: Markets and Democracy," *Center for Research on Globalization* (May 5). Retrieved from: http://globalresearch.ca/index.php?context=va&aid=2392.

Johnson, Stephen. 2004. *Hadrian's Wall.* London: B.T. Batsford.

Jonassohn, Kurt. 2000. *On a Neglected Aspect of Western Racism.* Paper presented at the meeting of the Association of Genocide Scholars. Retrieved from http://migs.concordia.ca/occpapers/zoo.htm.

Jones, J. Martin. 1974. "Curbing Communist Expansion: The Truman Doctrine," in Thomas Paterson, ed., *The Origins of the Cold War*, pp. 131–144. London: D.C. Heath and Company.

Kaminsky, Anna (ed.). 2009. *Die Berliner Mauer in der Welt, Bundesstiftung zur Aufarbeitung der SED-Diktatur.* Berlin: Berlin Story Verlag.

Kastenbaum, Michele, and Vermés, Geneviève. 1996. "Children of North African Immigrants in the French School System," *Intercultural Education*, 6(3): 43–48.

Kastoryano, Riva. 2006. Territories of Identities in France," *Social Science Research Council* (June 11). http://riotsfrance.ssrc.org/kastoryano/printable.htm, accessed 7-14-2008.

Kaye, glen. 1994. "The Mexico-USA Border Region: The Filling of an Empty Land," *The George Wright Forum*, 11 (3): 79–88.

Keddie, Nikki R. 2002. *Women in the Middle East: Since the Rise of Islam.* Pamphlet, the American Historical Association. Washington, DC.

Kenyon, Kathleen M. 1970. *Archeology in the Holy Land.* New York: Praeger.

Kerenyi, Carl. 1959. *The Heroes of the Greeks.*

Khaleghi-Motlagh, Djalal. 1996. *Derafš-e Kāvīān.* Cosa Mesa: Mazda.

Khalidi, Raja, and Taghdisi-Rad, Sahar. 2009. *The Economic Dimensions of Prolonged Occupation: Continuity and Change in Israeli Policy Towards the Palestinian Economy.* A special report commemorating twenty-five years of UNCTAD's programme of assistance to the Palestinian people. New York and Geneva: United Nations Conference on Trade and Development.

Khalidi, Valid. 1993. *All the Remains: The Palestinian Villages Occupied and Depopulated by Israel in 1948.* Washington, D.D.: Institute of Palestine Studies.

Khosrokhavar. Farhad. 1997. *L'Islam des Jeunes.* Paris: Flammarion.

Kiani, M.Y. 1982a. "Excavations on the Defensive Wall of the Gurgan Plain," *Iran*, 20: 73–79.

——. 1982b. *Parthian Sites in Hyrcania, the Gorgan Plain.* Archäologische Mitteilungen aus Iran Ergänzungsband 9, Berlin.

Killian, Caitlin. 2007. *Covered Girls and Savage Boys: Representation of Youth of African Origin in France.* Paper presented at the annual meeting of American Sociological Association, New York.

Killian, Caitlin, and Johnson, Cathryn. 2006. " 'I'm not an Immigrant!': Resistance, Redefinition, and the Role of Resources in Identity Work," *Social Psychology Quarterly*, 69(1): 60–80.

Kipling, Rudyard. 1906. Puck of Pook Hill. Kessinger Publishing (2010 facsimile reprint).

Kirschbaum, Erik. 2011. "Berlin Mayor Criticizes Nostalgia for Berlin Wall," *Reuters* (August 13), http://ca.reuters.com/article/topNews/idCATRE77CoT620110813?PageNumber=2&virtualBrandChannel=0&sp=true.

Klausmeier, Axel, and Schmidt, Leo. 2004. *Wall Remnants—Wall Traces.* Berlin: Westkreuz-Verlag.

Klein, Naomi. 2007. *The Shock Doctrine: The Rise of Disaster Capitalism.* New York: Henry Holt.

Knauss, Peter R. 1987. *The Persistence of Patriarchy: Class, Gender, and Ideology in Twentieth Century Algeria.* Praeger.

Kopinak, Kathryn. 1996. *Desert Capitalism: Maquiladoras in North America's Western Industrial Corridor.* Tucson: The University of Arizona Press.

Kressel, Getzel. 1973. *Israel Pocket Library, Zionism.* Jerusalem: Keter Publishing.

Kröhnert, Steffen; and Skipper, Samuel. 2010. "Demographic Development in Eastern Germany," *Online Handbook of Demography*, http://www.berlin-institut.org/online-handbookdemography/east-germany.html.

Kurbanov, Aydogdy. 2010. *The Hephthalites: Archaeological and Historical Analysis*. Doctoral dissertation, Free University, Berlin.

Langerbein, Helmut. 2009. "Great Blunders?: The Great Wall of China, the Berlin Wall, and the Proposed United States/Mexico Border Fence," *The history Teacher*, 43 (1): 9–29.

Lazaroff, Tovah. 2010. "Security Barrier Remains Unfinished," *The Jerusalem Post* (July 8). Retrieved from http://www.jpost.com/Israel/Article.aspx?id=180775.

Le Bars, Stephanie. 2011. "Integration of Islam Perceived as Failure in France and Germany," *Le Monde Fr.* (January 5), Open Source Center EUP20110104029007 ("French Survey Reveals Changing Public Attitudes to Muslim Community").

League of Nations. 1920. *The Covenant of the League of Nations*. Yale Law School: The Avalon Project. Retrieved from: http://avalon.law.yale.edu/20th_century/leagcov.asp#art2

——. 1922. *Mandate for Palestine*. Retrieved from http://unispal.un.org/UNISPAL.NSF/0/2FCA2C68106F11AB05256BCF007BF3CB.

Lenin, Vladimir. 1968. *Notebooks on Imperialism, Volume 39: Collected Works*. Moscow: Progress Publishers.

Lequin, Y. 1992. *Histoire des Étrangérs et de l'Immigration en France*. Paris: Larousse.

Lewis, Bernard (editor). 1980. *The World of Islam*. London: Thames & Hudson.

Lockman, Zachary, and Beinin, Joel. 1989. *Intifada: The Palestinian Uprising against Israeli Occupation*. Boston, MA: South End Press.

Lubin, Alex. 2008. "We are All Israelis," *South Atlantic Quarterly*, 107:4, 671–690 (Fall).

McAdams, A. James. 1985. *East Germany and Détente: Building Authority after the Wall*. New York: Cambridge University Press.

McCain, Johnny M. 1981. "Texas and the Mexican Labor Question, 1942–1947," *Southwestern Historical Quarterly*, 85 (1).

McCombs, Brady. 2009. "Border Fences Grow, As Does Debate that Rages Over Them," *Arizona Daily Star*, March 15.

McGillion, Christopher. 2004. "French Move to Ban Headscarf Veils a Deeper Conflict," *The Sydney Morning Herald* (January 20). http://www/smh.com/cgi-bin/common/popup printarticle.pl?path=/articles/2004/01/19/1079360695620.html, accessed 1-12-2008.

MacMaster, Neil. 1997. *Colonial Migrants and Racism: Algerians in France, 1900–62*. Basingstoke.

Maddrell, Paul. 2009. *Exploiting and Securing the Open Border in Berlin: The Western Secret Services, the Stasi, and the Second Berlin Crisis, 1958–1961*. Woodrow Wilson International Center for Scholars: Cold War International History Project, working paper #58. http://www.wilsoncenter.org/topics/pubs/CWIHPWP58_maddrell.pdf, accessed 8-6-2010.

Madison, G.B. 1998. *The Political Economy of Civil Society and Human Rights*. London: Routledge.

Mahamedi, H. 2004. "Walls as a System of Frontier Defense during the Sassanid Period," in Daryaee, T. and Omidsalar, M. (eds.), *The Spirit of Wisdom[Mēnōg ī Xrad], Essays in Memory of Ahmad Tafazzoli, pp. 145–159. Costa Mesa, California*.

Mahler, Gregory s. 2004. *Politics and Government in Israel: The Maturation of a Modern State*. Lanham, MD: Rowman & Littlefield.

Maillard, Dominique. 2005. "The Muslims in France and the French Model of Integration," *Mediterranean Quarterly*, 16 (1): 62–78.

Makovsky, David. 2004. "How to Build a Fence," *Foreign Affairs*, 83 (2): 50–64 (March).

Maksimychev, Igor. 2008. 'How the Berlin Wall Fell," *International Affairs*, 54 (3): 164–181.

Malley, Robert, and Agha, Hussein. 2001. "Camp David; the Tragedy of Errors," *the New York Review of Books* (August 9).

Manchaca, Martha. 2001. *Recovering History, Constructing Race: The Indian, Black, and White Roots of Mexican Americans*, The Joe R. and Teresa Lozano Long Series in Latin American and Latino Art and Culture. Austin, TX: University of Texas Pres.

Mandel, Neville J. 1976. *The Arabs and Zionism before World War I.* Berkeley and Los Angeles.

Mann, John C., and Breeze, David J. 1987. "Ptolemy, Tacitus and the Tribes of North Britain," *Society of Antiquaries of Scotland*, 117: 87–91.

Martin, Colin. 2003. "Hadrian's Wall," *British Heritage*, 26–35 (September).

Martin, James J. 1981. *Charles A. Beard: A Tribute.* Institute for Historical Review. Retrieved from: http://www.ihr.org/jhr/v03/v03p239_Martin.html.

Martinez, Oscar J. 2001. *Mexican-Origin People in the United States: A Topical History.* Tucson, AZ: University of Arizona Press.

Masoudian, Mohsen; Gholami, Mohammad Ali; Meshkavati-Toroujen, S. Javad; and Fendereski, Niayesh. 2011. "Functioning of Garkaz Earth Dam, Gorgan Wall and its Channel as an Ancient Flood Diversion Project," *International Commission on Irrigation and Drainage*, R.57.2.04.

Massey, Douglas S. 2005. *Backfire at the Border: Why Enforcement Without Legalization Cannot Stop Illegal Immigration.* Washington, D.C.: Cato Institute, Center for Trade Policy Studies (June 13). http://www.freetrade.org/pubs/pas/tpa-029.pdf, *accessed 6-4-2009.*

———. 2009. *Testimony before the US Senate Committee on the Judiciary* (Washington, DC: May 20, 2009), http://judiciary.senate.gov/hearings/testimony.cfm?id=3859&wit_id=7939.

Massey, Douglas S., and Felipe Garcia España. 1987. "The Social Process of International Migration," *Science*, 237: 733–38.

Massey, Douglas S.; Durand, Jorge; and Malone, Nolan J. 2002. *Beyond Smoke and Mirrors: Mexican Immigration in an Era of Economic Integration.* New York, NY: Russell Sage Foundation.

Matin, Philip. 2003. *Promise Unfulfilled: Union, Immigration, and Farm Workers.* Itacha: Cornell University Press. Excerpt from http://hnn.us/articles/27336.html, accessed 7-17-2009.

Matlack, Carol. 2005. "Crisis in France: How Welfare State Economies Failed a Generation," *Business Week* (November 21). http://www.businessweek.com/print/magazine/content/05_47/b3960013htm?chan==gc, accessed 6-5-2008.

Mattar, Ibrahim. 1996. *Jewish Settlements, Palestinian Rights, and Peace.* Washington, D.C.: The Center for Policy Analysis on Palestine, Information Paper Number 4.

Mattingly, David. 2006. *An Imperial Possession: Britain in the Roman Empire, 54 BC–AD 409.* London: Penguin Books.

Mearsheimer, John, and Walt, Stephen. 2006. "Letters," *London Review of Books*, May 11.

Menander. 1987. *The History of Menander the Guardsman*, ed. and transl. by R.C. Blockley. Liverpool: ARCA.

Mernissi, Fatima. 1991. *The Veil and the Male Elite: A Feminist Interpretation of Women's Rights in Islam.* New York: Addison Wesley.

Merseburger, Peter. 2004. *Willy Brandt, 1913–1992.* Munich.

Migration Information Source. 2006. "The U.S.-Mexico Border" (June). http://www.migration information.org/feature/display.cfm?ID=407.

Miles, David. 2005. *The Tribes of Britain.* London: Weidenfeld & Nicolson.

Millett, Martin. 1990. *The Romanization of Britain: An Essay in Archaeological Interpretation.* Cambridge: Cambridge University Press.

Mitchell, Maria. 1995. "Materialism and Secularism: CDU Politicians and National Socialism, 1945–1949," *The Journal of Modern History*, 67: 278–308 (June).

Moffat, Alistair. 2005. *Before Scotland: The Story of Scotland Before History.* London: Thames and Hudson.

Moghissi, Haideh. 1994. *Populism and Feminism in Iran: Women's Struggle in a Male-Defined Revolutionary Movement.* New York: St. Martin's Press.

Montgomery, David. 2006. "House Votes to Build 700 Miles of Fence along the U.S.-Mexico Border," *Knight Ridder* Washington Bureau (September 14). http://www.accessmylibrary.com/coms2/summary_0286-17637951_ITM, accessed 7-14-2009.

Morawska, Eva. 1990. "The Sociology and Historiography of Immigration," in *Immigration Reconsidered: History, Sociology and Politics*, edited by Virginia Yans-McLaughlin. New York; Oxford University Press.

Morris, Benny. 2001. *Righteous Victims*. New York: Vintage Books.

Mothersole, Jessie. 1922. *Hadrian's Wall*. London: John Lane.

Mueller, Carol. 1999. "Escape from the GDR, 1961–1989: Hybrid Exit Repertoires in a Disintegrating Leninist Regime," *American Journal of Sociology*, 105 (3): 697–735.

Müler, Christian. 2005. "France and the Challenge Posed by Islam," *Qantara*, http://qantara .de/webcom/show_article.php?wc_e=476&wc_id=298, accessed 7-14-2008.

Murphy, Emma. 1995. "Stacking the Deck: The Economics of the Israeli-PLO Accords," *Middle East Research and Information Project*, Vol. 25 (July–August).

Nakhleh, Khalil. 2012. *Globalized Palestine: the National Sell-Out of a Homeland*. New Jersey: Red Sea Press.

Naravane, Vaiju. 2005. "Flashpoint in France," *Frontline*, 22(24), November 19–December 02. http://www.flomnet.com/fl2224/stories/20051202000905300.htm, accessed 6-5-2008.

Nasr, S.V.R. 1999. "European Colonialism and the Emergence of Modern Muslim Societies," in John Esposito (ed.), *The Oxford History of Islam*, pp. 549–599. New York: Oxford University Press.

Nevins, Joseph. 2002. *Operation Gatekeeper: The Rise of the "Illegal Alien" and the Making of the U.S.-Mexico Boundary*. New York, NY: Routledge. New York Times. 1889.

NISES. 2004. *Total Population*. National Institute for Statistics and Economic Studies. http://news.bbs.uk/2/hi/Europe/4385768.stm#france, accessed 7-11-2008.

Nokandeh, Jebrael. 1999. *Preliminary Report: Archaeological Survey at the Golestan Dam, Gonbad-e Kavus* (in Farsi: *Gozaresh Moghadamati va Tousifi Barresi Bastanshenasi Sadd-e Golestan, Gonbad-e Kavus*). Unpublished report, Iranian Center for Archaeological Research, Tehran.

Nokandeh, Jebrael; Sauer, Eberhard; Omrani Rekavandi, Hamid; Wilkinson, Tony; Abbasi, Ghorban Ali; Schwenninger, Jean-Luc; Mahmoudi, Majid; Parker, David; Fattahi, Morteza; Usher-Wilson, Lucian Stephen; Ershadi, Mohammad; Ratcliffe, James; and Gale, Rowena. 2006. "Linear Barriers of Northern Iran: The Great Wall of Gorgan and the Wall of Tamishe," *Iran, Journal of Persian Studies*, Vol. 44: 121–173.

Norman, Albert. 1946. *Our German Policy; Propaganda and Culture*. New York.

Nuñes-Neto, Blas, and Kim, Yule. 2008. *Border Security: Barriers along the U.S.-International border 1–2*. Congressional Research Service, RL33659.

Ohmae, Konichi. 1995. *The End of Nation State: The Rise of Regional Economies*. New York: The Free Press.

Omrani Rekavandi, Hamid; Sauer, Eberhard; Wilkinson, Tony; and Nokandeh, Jebrael. 2008. "Secrets of the Red Snake: The Great Wall of Iran Revealed," *Current World Archaeology*, No. 27: 11–22.

Open Society Institute. 2002. *The Situations of Muslims in France*. http://www.eumap.org/ reports/2002/eu/international/sections/France/2002_m_france.pdf, accessed 7-17-2008.

Opper, Thorsten. 2008. *Hadrian: Empire and Conflict*. Cambridge, MA: Harvard University Press.

Pacheo, Alegra. 2001. "Flouting Convention: The Oslo Agreements," in Carey, Ron (Ed.), *The New Intifada: Resisting Israel's Apartheid*. London: Verso.

Palestinian Grassroots Anti-Apartheid Wall Campaign. n.d. *Occupation, De-development and Normalization*. Retrieved from http://www.stopthewall.org/downloads/pdf/Pales tinian%20Economy%20FS.pdf.

Parks, Michael. 1993. 'Israel Discovers its Dependence on Palestinians: with Occupied Territories Closed, Industry is Suffering Without Cheap Labor," *Los Angeles Times* (April 10).

Passel, Jeffrey and Cohn, D'Vera. 2009. *Mexican Immigration: How Many Come? How Many Leave?* Pew Hispanic Center Report (July 22). http://pewhispanic.org/files/reports/112 .pdf, Accessed 8-5-2009.

Paterson, Thomas. 1974. "The Marshall Plan Revisited," in *the Origins of the Cold War*, pp. 167–74. London: D.C. Heath and Company.

Petras, Elizabeth M. 1981. "The Global Labor Market in the Modern World," in *Global Trends in Migration; Theory and Research on International Population Movements*, edited by Mary M. Kritz, Charles B. Keely, and Silvano M. Tomasi. New York: Center for Migration Studies.

Pew Forum on Religion and Public Life. 2011. "The Future of the Global Muslim Population" (January 27). http://www.pewforum.org/future-of-the-global-muslim-population-regional-europe.aspx

Pew Hispanic Center. 2006. *Fact Sheet: Modes of Entry for the Unauthorized Migrant Population* (May 22). http://pewhispanic.org/files/factsheets/19.pdf.

Pfeiffer, Gerd, and Strickert, Hans-Georg (eds.). 1957. *Outlawing the Communist Party*, translated by Wolfgang P. von Schmertzing. Cambridge, MA. http://www.germanhistory docs.ghi-dc.org/ docpage.cfm?docpage_id=3422, accessed 8-3-2010.

Pick, James B., Viswanathan, Nanda, & Hettrick, James. 2001. 'The U.S.-Mexican Borderlands Region: A Binational Spatial Analysis," *The Social Science Journal*, 38: 567–595.

Piore, Michael. J. 1979. *Birds of Passage: Migrant Labor in Industrial Societies.* New York, NY: Cambridge University Press.

Pirnya, Hassan. 1934. *Iran-e Ghadim, ya Tarikh-e Mokhtasar-e Iran ta Engheraz-e Sassanian (Ancient Iran, or Iran's Concise History to the Downfall of the Sassanids).* Tehran: Roshanaee Publishing (in Farsi).

Portes, Alesandro, and Borocz, Josef. 1989. "Contemporary Immigration: Theoretical Perspectives on Its Determinants and Modes of Incorporation," *International Migration Review, 23(3): 606–630.*

Portez, Alejandro, and Walton, John. 1981. *Labor, Class, and the International System.* New York: Academic Press.

Preston, Julia. 2011. "Homeland Security Cancels 'Virtual Fence' after $1 Billion is Spent," *The New York Times* (January 14), http://www.nytimes.com/2011/01/15/us/politics/15fence.html.

——. 2011b. "Some Cheer the border Fence as Others Ponder the Cost," *The New York Times* (October 19), http://www.nytimes.com/2011/10/20/us/politics/border-fence-raises-cost-questions.html.

Procopius. 1914. *History of the Wars, Vol. 1, Books 1–2: The Persian War.* Translated by H.B. Dewing. Loeb Classical Library.

Rabbani, Mouin. 2001. "A Smorgasbord of Failure: Oslo and the Al-Aqsa Intifada," in Carey, Ron (Ed.), *The New Intifada: Resisting Israel's Apartheid.* London: Verso.

Rael, Jean Isaac. 1980. *Party and Politics in Israel: Three Visions of a Jewish State.* United Kingdom: Longman.

Rapoport, Meron. 2005. "Israel: Industrial Estates along the Wall," *Le Monde Diplomatique* (June 5). Retrieved from http://mondediplo.com/2004/06/05thewall.

Razi, Abdullah. 1968. *Tarikh-e Kamel-e Iran: az Ta'sis-e Selseley-e Mad ta Asr-e Hazer (Iran's Comprehensive History: From Mad Dynasty to the Present).* Tehran: Eqbal publishing (in Farsi).

Reisler, Mark. 1976. *By the Sweat of their Brow: Mexican Immigrant labor in the United States, 1900–1940.* Westport, Conn.: Greenwood Press.

Remember Berlin Wall? Now, Think Mexico (2005). Editorial, *the Miami Herald*, November 17.

Reuveny, Rafael. 1999. "The Political Economy of Israeli-Palestinian Interdependence," *Policy Studies Journal*, 27(4): 643–664.

Richey, Joseph. 2006. "Privatizing Immigration Control," *CorpWatch* (July 5), http://www.corpwatch.org/article.php?id=13845.

Roberts, Charles M. 1959. "Accord on Talks May Ease Tensions," *Washington Post* (September 27). http://www.washingtonpost.com/wp-srv/inatl/longterm/summit/archive/sept59.htm, accessed 8-6-2010.

Robertson. Roland. 1992. *Globalization; Social Theory and Global Culture.* London: Sage.

Rodinson, Maxime. 1973. *Israel A Colonial-Settler State?* New York: Monad Press.

Rodriguez, Angie. 2008. "Thousands of People Protest NAFTA and Defend Food Sovereignty in Mexico," *Food First*, Institute for Food & Development policy (February 18). http://www.foodfirst.org/en/node/2050, accessed 8-5-2009.

Rodriguez, Gregory. 2007. *Mongrels, Bastards, Orphans, and Vagabonds.* New York: Pantheon Books.

Rodriguez, Néstor. 1995. 'The Battle for the Border: Notes on the Autonomous Migration, Transnational Communities, and the State," *Social Justice*, 23 (3): 21–37.

Rottman, Gordon L. 2008. *The Berlin Wall and the Intra-German Border 1961–89.* Oxford: Osprey.

Rühle, J., and Holzweißig, G. 1988. *13 August. Die Mauer von Berlin.* Köln: Verlag Wissenschaft and Politik.

Rumford, Chris. 2006. "Introduction; Theorizing Borders," *European Journal of Social Theory*, 9(2): 155–169.

Sachar, Howard. 1981. *A History of Israel: From the Rise of Zionism to Our Time.* New York: Alfred A. Knopf.

Said, Edward. W. 2001. "Palestinians under Siege," in Carey, Ron (Ed.), *The New Intifada: Resisting Israel's Apartheid.* London: Verso.

———. 1999. *The Question of Palestine.* New York: Vintage Books.

———. 1995. *Peace and Its Discontent; Essays on Palestine in the Middle East Peace Process.* New York: Vintage Books.

Salway, Peter. 1981. *Roman Britain.* Oxford: Clarendon Press.

Salway, Peter. 1993. *The Oxford Illustrated History of Roman Britain.* Oxford: Oxford University Press.

Salway, Peter. 2002. *The Roman Era: The British Isles 55 BC–AD 410.* Oxford: Oxford University Press.

Sandia National Laboratories. 2009. *Mission Areas.* http://www.sandia.gov/mission/index.html, accessed 8-6-2009.

Sandoval, Daniel. 2003. *Maquiladora along the U.S.-Mexico Border: Pat, Present, and Future.* EDGE: Poverty and Global Development.

Sassen, Saskia. 1988. *The Mobility of Labor and Capital: A Study in International Investment and Labor Flow.* Cambridge: Cambridge University Press.

———. 2000. "New Frontiers Facing Urban Sociology at the Millennium," *British Journal of Sociology*, 51(1): 143–60.

———. 2004. "Space and Power," in Nicholas Gane (ed.), *the Future of Social Theory*, pp. 125–142. London & New York: Continuum.

Sauer, E.W., Omrani Rekavandi, H., Wilkinson, T.J., Nokandeh, J. et al., 2013. *Persia's Imperial Power in Late Antiquity: the Great Wall of Gorgān and Frontier Landscapes of Sasanian Iran.* Oxford, Oxbow: British Institute of Persian Studies Archaeological Monographs Series II.

Sayigh, Yezid. 1997. *Armed Struggle and the Search for State: The Palestinian National Movement, 1949–1993.* Washington, D.C.

Schepers, Emile. 2002. "NAFTA Devastates Mexican Farmers," *People's Weekly World Newspaper*, December 14. http://pww.org/article/view/2518/1/125 Accessed 8-5-2009.

Schick, Jack M. 1971. *The Berlin Crisis 1958–1962.* Philadelphia: University of Pennsylvania Press.

Schmidt, Erich F. 1940. *Flights Over Ancient Cities of Iran.* Chicago.

Schnapper, Dominique. 1991. "La Frace de L'Intégration: Sociologie de le Nation en 1990," *Coll. Bibliotèque des Sciences Humaines.* Paris: Gallimard.

Schölch, Alexander. 1992. "Britain in Palestine, 1838–1882: The Roots of the Balfour Policy," *Journal of Palestine Studies*, 22 (1): 39–56 (Autumn).

Schulz, G.W. 2009. "Homeland Security USA: Building a Border Fence Costs a Fortune," *Center for Investigating Reporting* (February 18). http://www.centerfor-investigativereporting.org/blogpost/20090218homelandsecurityusathe-outtakespartv, accessed 7-1-2009.

Scott, Robert E. 2003. *The High Price of 'Free Trade.'* Economic Policy Institute (November 17). http://www.epi.org/publications/entry/briefingpapers_bp147/, accessed 8-6-2009.

Scullard, H.H. 1979. *Roman Britain: Outpost of Empire.* London: Thames and Hudson.

Seljuq, Affan. 1997. "Cultural Conflicts: North African Immigrants in France," *International Journal of Peace Studies*, 2(2). http://www.gmu.edu/academic/ijps/vol2_2/seljuq.htm, accessed 6-5-2008.

Sereny, Gitta. 1996. *Albert Speer: His Battle With Truth.* Vintage.

Serrano, Simon. 2008. *The Great Wall of Mexico: NAFTA and Illegal Immigration.* Florida Coastal School of Law, http://works.bpress.com/simon_serrena/1, accessed 5-25-2009.

Shahidian, Hammed. 2002. *Women in Iran: Emerging Voices in the Women's Movement (Volume 1).* Westport, CT: Greenwood Press.

Sharp, Heather. 2004. "Right of Return: Palestinian Dream," *BBC News*, retrieved from http://news.bbc.co.uk/2/hi/middle_east/3629923.stm

Shaw, J.V.W. (ed.). 1991. *A Survey of Palestine: Prepared in December, 1945 and January, 1946 for the Information of the Anglo-American Committee of Inquiry* (volume 1). Institute for Palestine Studies.

Sherwood, Harriet. 2012. "Israel Extends New Border Fence but Critics Say It is A Sign of Weakness," *The Guardian* (March 27), retrieved from http://www.guardian.co.uk/world/2012/mar/27/israel-extends-border-fence-critics.

Shlaim, Avi. 2000. *The Iron Wall; Israel and the Arab World.* New York: W.W. Norton.

———. 2009. "How Israel Brought Gaza to the Brink of Humanitarian Catastrophe, The *Gguardian* (January 6). Retrieved from http://www.guardian.co.uk/world/2009/jan/07/gaza-israel-palestine.

Silverstein, Paul. 2004. "Headscarves and the French Tricolor," *Middle East Report.* http://www.merip.org/mero/mero013004.html, accessed 4-2-2008.

Simon, Stephanie. 2009. "Border-Fence Project Hits a Snag," *The Wall Street Journal*, February 4, p. A4.

Simons, Hans. 1951. "The Bonn Constitution and its Government," in Hans J. Motgenthau, ed., *Germany and the future of Europe*, 114–130. Chicago.

Sklair, L. 1989. *Assembling for Development.* Boston; Unwin Hyman. SourceMex. 2007. "U.S. Senate Approves 700-Mile Wall along U.S.-Mexico Border," *SourceMex Economic News & Analysis on Mexico* (March 12). http://www. allbusiness.com/north-america/mexico/3897266-1.html, accessed 7-14-2009.

Slatta, Richard W. 1997. *Comparing Cowboys and Frontiers.* Norman: University of Oklahoma Press.

Slavesky, Filip. 2008. "Violence and Xenophobia as Means of Social Control in Times of Collapse: The Soviet Occupation of Post-War Germany, 1945–1947," *Australian Journal of Politics and History*, 54(3): 389–402.

Slusser, Robert M. 1973. *The Berlin Crisis of 1961: Soviet-American Relations and the Struggle for Power in the Kremlin, June–November 1961.* Baltimore: The John Hopkins University Press.

Smith, Charles D. 2010. *Palestine and the Arab-Israeli Conflict: A History with Documents.* Boston: Bedford/St. Martin.

Snyder, Louis L. (ed.). 1958. *Documents in German History.* New Brunswick: Rutgers University Press.

Sondage Ifop. 2001. "L'Islam en France et les Réactions aux Attentats du 11 Septembre 2001," *Le Monde/Le point* (October). http://www.ifop.com/Europe/sondage/OPINIONF/islam.asp, accessed 7-4-2008.

Sorkin, Michael. 2005. "Introduction: Up Against the Wall," in Sorkin, Michael (ed.), Against the Wall: Israel's Barrier to Peace, vi–xxi. New York: The New Press.

Spener, David, and Staudrt, Kathleen. 1998. "Conclusion: Rebordering," in Spener, David, and Staudt, Kathleen (eds.), *The U.S.-Mexico Border: Transcending Divisions, Contesting Identities*, pp. 233–257. London: Lynn Rienner.

Spiegel Online. 2007. "Herero Massacre: General's Descendants Apologize for 'Germany's First Genocide'." October 8. http://www.spiegel.de/international/world/0,1518,druck-510163,00.html.

State of the Border Region 2010. 2011. "Indicator Metadata and Data Tables (May). http://www.semarnat.gob.mx/informacionambiental/documents/sniarn/pdf/frontera_meta dato_2010_ingles.pdf.

Steininger, Michael. 2011. "Berlin Wall Turns 50—and Some Want to Rebuild It, Barbed Wire and All," *The Christian Science Monitor* (August 13). http://www.csmonitor.com/World/Europe/2011/0813/Berlin-Wall-turns-50-and-some-want-to-rebuild-it-barbed-wire-and-all.

Stiglitz, Joseph E. 2002. *Globalization and Its Discontents.* New York: W.W. Norton & Co.

Strauss, Herbert A. 1992. "Jewish Immigrants of the Nazi Period in the USA," in Strauss, Herbert A. (Ed.), *Jewish Emigration from Germany, 1933–1942: A Documentary History.* New York: K.G. Saur.

Taboada-Leonette, Isabel, and Lévy, Florence. 1978. "Femmes et Immigrées: L'Insertion des Femmes Immigrées en France," *Migrants et Société*, No. 4. Paris: La Documentation Français.

Tannenbaum, Frank. 1950. *The Struggle for Peace and Bread.* New York: Alfred Knopf.

Taubman, William. 2004. *Khrushchev: The Man and His Era.* W.W. Norton & Co.

Taylor, Frederick. 2006. *The Berlin Wall: A World Divided, 1961–1989.* New York: Harper-Perennial.

Taylor, Peter J. 1995. "Beyond Containers: Internationality, Inter-Stateness, Inter-territoriality," *Progress in Human Geography*, 9 (1): 1–15.

Terrazas, Aaron. 2010. "Mexican Immigrants in the United States," *Migration Information Source* (February). http://www.migrationinformation.org/usfocus/display.cfm?ID=767.

Tessler, Mark. 1994. A History of the Israeli-Palestinian Conflict. Bloomington, IN: Indiana University Press.

Thomaneck, J.K.A., and James Mellis (eds.). 1989. *Politics, Society and Government in the German Democratic Republic: Basic Documents.* Oxford: Berg, http://www.Germanhistory docs.ghi-dc.org/docpage.cfm?docpage_id=3249, accessed 8-3-2010.

Thomas, Baylis. 2011. The Dark Side of Zionism: Israel's Quest for Security Through Dominance. New York: Lexington Books.

Thompson, Lester. 1938. "Geological Evidence for Ancient civilization on the Gurgan Plain," *Bulletin of the American Institute for Iranian Art and Archaeology*, Volume 3.

Tibawi, A.L. 1961. British Interests in Palestine, 1800–1901. New York: Oxford University Press.

Time-Life Books. 1994. *Rome: Echoes of Imperial Glory.* Alexandria, VA: Time-Life Books.

Todaro, Michael P., and Lydia Maruszko. 1987. "Illegal Migration and U.S. Immigration Reform: A Conceptual Framework," *Population and Development Review*, 13: 101–104.

Todd, Malcolm. 1999. *Roman Britain.* Malden, MA: Blackwell.

Tomasek, Robert D. 1957. *The Political and Economic Implications of Mexican Labor in the United States under the Non-Quota System, Contract Labor Program, and Wetback Movement.* Ph.D. dissertation, University of Michigan.

Tote des 17. Juni 1953, http://www.17juni53.de/tote/recherche.html; and *17. Juni 1953 Der Volksaufstand in Ostberlin*, http://www.17juni1953.com/pdf/17juni1953.pdf, accessed 8-5-2010 (both documents in German).

Trac Immigration. 2006. *Border Patrol Expands but Growth Rate after 9/11 Much less Than Before: Division Between North/South Border Little Changed.* http://trac.syr.edu/immi gration/reports/143, accessed 8-6-2009.

Tribalat, Michéle. 1995. Faire France: Un *Enquête sur les Immigrés et leur Enfants.* Paris: La Déconverte/Essais.

———. 1996. *De l'Immigration á l'Assimilation; Enquête sur les Population d'Origine Etrangér en France.* Paris: La Déconverte/INED.

UN News Centre. 2011. "Israeli Barrier Isolates Palestinian Communities in East Jerusalem, Says UN Report" (July 11). Retrieved from http://www.un.org/apps/news/story .asp?NewsID= 39006& Cr=palestin&Cr1.

UNCTAD. 2006. "The Palestinian War-Torn Economy: Aid, Development and State Formation. New York: the United Nations Conference on Trade and Development.

Urry, J. 2000. *Sociology Beyond Societies: Mobilities for the Twenty-first Century*. London & New York: Routledge.

U.S. Department of Labor. 1916. "Report of the Commissioner General of Immigration," *Report of the Department of Labor*. Washington, D.C.: U.S. Government Printing Office.

——. 2005. *Findings from the National Agricultural Workers Survey (NAWS) 2001–2*. Research Report No. 9 (March). http://www.doleta.gov/agworker/report9/naws_rpt9.pdf, accessed 8-5-2009.

U.S. Department of State. 2004. *State Dept. Official Hails Benefits from NAFTA*. April 20, http://www.america.gov/st/washfile-english/2004/April/20040420162429AEneerGo . 7202722.html, accessed 8-4-2009.

U.S. Department of State, Division of European Affairs. 1943. *National Socialism. Basic Principles, their Application by the Nazi Party's Foreign Organizations, and the Use of Germans Abroad for Nazi Aims*. Washington, DC: United States Government Printing Office.

USDOJ/OIG. 1998. *Operation Gatekeeper: An Investigation into Allegations of Fraud and Misconduct*. Department of Justice, Office of the Inspector General Executive Summary (July). http://www.justice.gov/oig/special/9807/exec.htm.

Väisse, Justin. 2004. "Veiled Meaning: The French Law Banning Religious Symbols in Public Schools," pp. 1–6, in *The Brookings Institution: US-France Analysis series*. http://www .brookings.edu/fp/cusf/analysis/vaisse20040229.pdf, accessed 7-2-2008.

Van Alstyne, Richard W. 1974. *The Rising American Empire*. New York, NY: Norton.

Vargas, Lucinda. 1998. "The Maquiladora Industry in Historical Perspective (Part 2)," *Business Frontier*, Issue 4, http://www.dallasfed.org/research/busfront/bus9804.pdf accessed 7-29-2009.

Vaughn-Williams, Nick. 2008. "Borders, Territory, Law," *International Political Sociology*, 2: 322–338.

Veh, O. (ed.). 1970. *Prokop, Perserkriege, Greichisch-Deutsch*. Munich.

Vidal, Gore. 2002. *Perpetual War for Perpetual Peace*. New York: Nation Books.

Vogt, Timothy. 2000. *Denazification in Soviet-Occupied Germany: Brandenburg, 1945–1948*. Cambridge, MA.

Von Oppen, Ruhm (ed.). 1955. *Documents on Germany under Occupation, 1945–1954*. London and New York: Oxford University Press.

Walker, R.B.J. 1993. *Inside/Outside: International Relations as Political Theory*. Cambridge: Cambridge University Press.

Ward, Janet. 2011. *Post-Wall Berlin: Borders, Space and Identity*. New York: Palgrave-McMillan.

Watt, W. Montgomery. 1961. *Muhammad: Prophet and Statesman*. New York: Oxford University Press.

Wells, Peter S. 2005. "The Limes and Hadrian's Wall," *Expedition*, 47(1), 18–24.

Wilkes, John J. 2005. "Hadrian's Wall," in Ganster, Paul and Lorey, David E. (Eds.), *Borders and Border Politics in a Globalizing World*, 1–10. New York: SR Books.

Williams, John. 2003. "Territorial Borders, International Ethics, and Geography: Do Good Fences Still Make Good Neighbours?," *Geopolitics*, 8 (2): 25–46.

Winter, F.E. 1971. *Greek Fortifications*. Toronto: University of Toronto.

Wonders, Nancy A. 2006. "Global Flows, Semi-Permeable Borders and New Channels of Inequality," in S. Pickering and L. Weber (eds.), *Borders, Mobility and Technologies of Control*, pp. 63–86. Springer.

World Bank. 2002. *Long-Term Policy Options for the Palestinian Economy*. Jerusalem: West Bank and Gaza Office. Retrieved from http://unispal.un.org/pdfs/WB_policy_200207.pdf.

Yahhaoui, Abdessalem. 1989. "Crise d'Identité, Crise Idéologique et Pratique Religieuse; L'Islam en milieu Maghrébin," *Identité*, 7–15.

Yapp, M.E. 1987. The Making of the Modern Near East 1792–1923. Harlow, England: Longman.

Yiftachel, Oren. 2009. "Creeping Apartheid in Israel-Palestine," Middle East Research and Information Project, volume 39 (winter).

Yousef, Ahmed. 1998. *The Fascination of Egypt: From the Dream to the Project.* Paris: Harmattan.

Zahniser, Steven. 2007. *NAFTA at 13: Implementation Nears Completion.* http://www.ers .usda.gov/publications/wrso701/wrso701.pdf, accessed 7-30-2009.

INDEX

Abbas, Mahmoud   294n20
Achaemenid Dynasty   248
Acheson, Dean   265
Adenauer, Chancellor   128
Afghanistan   15, 59, 65, 145, 261n8, 286
Aghabad Canal   78
Al-Aghsa Mosque   292
Alborz Mountains   86–87
Alexander of the Macedon   55
Alexander's Barrier   55
Algeria   18, 154–156, 158–89, 161–165, 171
Allied forces   96–99, 107, 110, 138
Allon Plan   277, 291
Allon, Yigal   290
Al-Nakba   271
American Civil Liberties Union (ACLU)
   240
American Friends Service Committee
   xxvi, 235
American Military Government in
   Germany, the   99
   See also AMG
AMG   99–101, 103, 107
   *See also the American Military
      Government*
Amnesty International   8
Amu Darya   56, 59, 62, 66,
   *See also Ochus River, Oxus River, and
      Jeyhoun*
Ancient Greeks   1, 10, 28, 165n
anti-immigration sentiments   182, 183n,
   185
Antonine Wall   39, 53
Antoninus Pius   39
Arab conquests   56
Arab League, the   269, 276
Arafat, Yasser   281–282, 286, 288, 290, 294
Atrak River   67
Austria   92, 146, 250-251

Bachman, Michelle   243
Bactria   65
   See also Balkh
Bahram V   62
Balfour, Arthur   254
Balfour Declaration   256, 257–258, 261, 265
Balkh   65
   See also Bactria

Bantustans (Israel)   xxi, 271, 283–284, 288,
   308, 310
Barak, Ehud   286, 288, 290, 293, 308, 316
Barbarians   xx, xxiv, 5, 14, 24, 26, 28, 30,
   40, 42–43, 49–50, 60n, 178, 199, 245, 253
Barrier of Peroz   55
Beard, Charles   14
Belfast   1
BCC   202–204
   See also Border Crossing Card
Bell, Daniel   12
Ben Bella, Ahmed   155
Benwell   38–39
Berlin Ultimatum, the   115–116
Berlin   xxiv, xxvi, 1, 90–92, 96n4, 97–98,
   101, 106, 110, 111n24, 112–113, 115–132,
   135–139, 142–144, 146, 252, 297, 321,
   323–326, 328–332
Berlin Wall
   architecture   129
   as a defensive wall   128, 143, 147,
      322–323
   as a sign of East Germany's weakness
      139
   Berlin Wall Memorial   326, 329,
   dog runs   136–137
   downfall of   146
   First generation   129, 138, 141
   Fourth generation   131, 133, 135–137,
      297, 325, 329
   inner border security barrier   138
   "Operation Rose"   117–119, 126
   postmodern representation of remains
      325–326, 328, 331
   Sale of the Century   325
   Second generation   129–131, 141
   Third generation   131–132, 137-140
Bernauer Straße   326, 328–329, 332
Beur, the   161–162, 168
BIP   188-189
   *See also National Border
      Industrialization Program*
Bismarck, Otto von   92
Bojnourd   86
Bonaparte, Napoleon   154
Border Angels   xxvi, 235, 243
Border Crossing Card   202–203
   See also BCC

Borders
  Between East and West Germany 143
  external 304
  imperial 17
  internal 18
  mobile 18
  open 139
  political 15, 304
  territorial 15–16
Boumedienne, Houari 155
Bourdieu, Pierre 165–166, 168
Bowness-on-Solway 32
Bracero era 181, 184
Bracero program 181, 184–188
  See also Mexican Farm Labor Supply
  Program
Brandenburg Gate 119, 121–125, 138, 324, 327
Brezhnev Doctrine 146
Britain xx, 23–24, 26, 28n6, 29–32, 36, 40, 42, 49, 51–52, 90, 94, 97, 247, 250, 254, 256, 263, 265–266, 323
British Department of International Development (DFID) 315
British Empire 4, 265
British frontiers 39, 48
British Mandate 257–58, 269
British Museum 23n, 50
Brittunculi 31
B'Tselem 292–293, 296, 299–301, 303, 314
Budapest 146
Bukhara 66
Bundestag 95
Burqa 153
Bush, G.W. 10n10, 215–216, 218–219, 294, 296, 311
bypass roads (in the Palestinian occupied territories) 285, 287–289

Caesar, Julius 23, 25
Cain, Herman 243
Caledonia 28
Caledonian(s) 40, 43, 58
Calexico xxvi, 195, 198, 201, 204, 219, 235
Camp David Peace Accord 279
Cárdenas, Lázaro 183
Carlisle 32, 36, 40, 50
Casablanca Conference, the 96–97
Caspian Sea 53–54, 56, 59n10, 60, 65, 67, 78, 86–87
Cassivellaunus 23
Catholic Social Mission 235
Catuvellauni 23

Cawfields 34–35, 45–46
CBP 220, 222–223, 225, 228–230, 234
  See also Customs and Border Protection
Celtic tribal societies
  Brigantes 26–28, 36, 49
  Caledones (Caledonii) 28
  Damonii 26
  Novante 26, 49
  Selgovae 26, 49
  Votadini 26
Chai Ghushan Kuchek Canal 79–83
Chamberlain, Joseph 253
Charlottenburger Chaussee 121
Chavéz, Cézar 187
Checkpoint Charlie 328, 330
Chesters 39
Chicanos por la Casa 235
Chionites 59
Chirac, Jaques 152
Chomsky, Noam 218, 271, 288, 290, 308
Christian Democratic Union (CDU) 108–109
civil society 9, 12
Claudius 23
Clinton administration 20, 215–217
Coalition of the willing 10
Cold War xxvi, 13, 105–106, 110, 115–117, 131, 145, 147, 276, 325–326, 333
"Collective Guilt" Policy, the 99–100
Communist Party of Germany, the 94, 100, 108, 146
  See also KPD
Control Council, the 97–98, 104
Corbridge 32, 34, 39
cross-border migration 195, 210
Cuba 145, 147
Customs and Border Protection 220, 223, 230, 234
  See also CBP
Cumbrian Coast 38–39
Cyrus Cylinder 3
Czechoslovakia 146, 266

Dacians 24
Dahae Confederacy 56
Daniel 12, 55
Danube 24, 49
Darband (Derbent) 55
Davis, Michael 18, 213, 320
Dayan, Moshe 304
Dear, Michael 333
Declaration of Principles (DOP) 281
Deir Yassin 269

Department of Homeland Security   175,
  215, 220, 222, 224
  See also DHS
Denazification   99
Der Judenstaat   251–252
DHS   175n1, 215–216, 220, 222, 224–225,
  233, 240, 245
  *See also Department of Homeland
  Security*
Diaz, Porfirio   179–180
Diepgen, Eberhard   328n, 331–332
Dio Cassius   28
Dome of the Rock   292
Domitian   24
Dreyfus Affair, the   251

East Berlin   xxvi, 106, 112, 121–122, 124–128,
  136, 143, 323, 325–326, 328–330
Eastern Europe   90, 104–105, 145, 148,
  250–253, 261
East German Politburo   145
Economic Cooperation Administration
  (ECA)   104
Economic Recovery Program (ERP)   104
EDC   110–111
  *See also the European Defense
  Community*
Eisenhower, Dwight   116, 208
el Norte   195, 202
el Paso   179–180, 195, 198–199, 214–215,
  219, 221, 229
Empire   1–14
  and hybrid identities   9
  as a decentered and deteritorializing
    apparatus   9
  as a metaphor   2
  hybrid identities as multitudes   9
  hybrid identities as people   9
  neo-liberal   2
  rule of   xx
  the age of empire   3, 6
Enabling Act, the   95–96
Ephthalites   59–60
  See also Hephthalites and White Huns
Era of Enganche   180–181
Eretz Yisrael   247
Escher, M.C.   267
Eshkol, Levi   277
Euphrates River   248
European Charter of Regional Minority
  Languages (ECRML)   157
European Defense Community   111n34,
  110
Exposition Universelle   5

Fanon, Franz   xx
Fatah   276
Fertile Crescent (northern Iran)   86, 88
Firdawsi   55
First World War   4, 94, 254, 256, 259
Fishman, Alex   316
Forth-Clyde isthmus   24, 26, 28, 32, 39
Fourth Geneva Convention   279–281, 285,
  296
Français de Souche   157, 169
France   xx, xxv, 10n8, 18, 90, 92, 94,
  97, 151–165, 168–170, 172, 251, 254, 281,
  309–310, 322
Framework Convention for the Protection
  of National Minorities (FCNM)   157
Free Germany   100
French Muslims   151–153, 157, 158n6, 164,
  168–169
French Republicanism   156, 161
Friedman, Milton   12
Fukuyama, Francis   12

Gadsden Purchase   180, 207
Galili, Yisrael   279
GATT   190–192
  *See also General Agreement on Tariffs
  and Trade*
Gaul   23, 50
Gaza Strip   19, 275–276, 279–280, 282,
  292, 304–306, 308–311, 317, 322
GDR   92, 94–95, 107–109, 112–113, 115–117,
  119–120, 126–129, 131, 136–140, 142–148,
  324–325, 328, 332
General Accounting Office (GAO)   240
General Agreement on Tariffs and Trade
  191
  See also GATT
German Democratic Republic, the   xxiv,
  92, 94–95, 107–108, 110, 113, 118n, 127, 297,
  322–323
  See also GDR
German Empire, rise and fall   92–93
Germany   90–92, 94–103, 110–113, 115, 119,
  127, 143, 147–148, 251, 254, 309, 325, 332
  divided   90–91, 107, 118, 325
  East   92, 97, 112, 115–116, 127, 136, 138–140,
    142–143, 145–146, 297, 324, 332
  Federal Republic of   106, 107n21, 108, 138
    See also FGR   106, 138
  neutral   111
  occupied   101–106
  West   92, 97, 109–113, 115, 118, 138, 143,
    146n28, 324–325
  unified   106, 110–111, 324

Glasnost   146
global capitalism   6, 11–13
globalization   xix, 14–19, 153, 164, 172
    of labor   308
    from within   3r 20–321
Great Wall of China   xxvii, 2, 53, 243, 332
Great Wall of Gorgan   xxv, 2, 53
    architecture   58, 66
    as a defensive wall of barrier   55,
        58–60, 65, 78
    as a physical barrier   86
    associated hydraulic structures   78–85
    brick kilns   58, 68, 76
    brick wall   67, 69–70
    ditch   78–87
    forts   67–68, 71, 75–76, 83, 85–87
    gates   77
    standardized bricks   56, 68
Golan Heights   276–77, 279, 317
Golestan Province (Iran)   xxvi, 53, 56, 65,
    73, 82, 84, 86
Gonbad-e Kavus   58, 80
Gorbachev, Mikhail   138, 145–148
Gorgan   xxvi, 65n16, 76, 86, 88
    See also Hyrcania
Gorgan Plain   67, 76, 78, 86–87
Gorgan River   54, 67, 78–79, 81–83
Gorgo (Jorjan)   65
Great Britain   xx, 97, 263
Great Depression   95
Greater Berlin   97–98
Green (Armistice) Line   xx, 246, 277, 288,
    293, 302, 304, 312, 321
Gromyko, Andrei   267
Guadalupe Hidalgo Treaty   176
Gumishan   53, 67

Ha Avarna Agreement   262
Habitation á Loyer Modéré   159
    See also HLN
Hadrian   24, 26, 30–32, 34, 38–40, 42, 49–51
Hadrian's Wall
    architecture   32
    as a means to control population
        movement and flow   48
    as a military defensive structure   42
    as a symbol of imperial might   48
    forts   26, 28, 32, 34, 36, 38–40, 45, 49
    gates   26, 34, 38, 45, 48
    geopolitics of   31
    milecastles   34, 38–39, 42–43, 48
    parapet, the   32, 34, 43–44
    turrets   34, 38–39, 42–43, 48
    valuum   36, 38, 43, 45–46, 48–49

Haganah   265
Han Dynasty   xxiii
Harkis   156, 161
Harvest of Shame   187
headscarf controversy   151, 168
Hebron   286, 290, 310
Hephthalites   55, 59–60, 62, 65–66, 89
    See also 'white Huns' and 'Ephthalites'
Herzl, Theodor   251–253, 316
hijab
    as a defensive wall,   151–172
    as a curtain   166–167, 172
    as a liberating tool   167
    as a protective tool   166
    controversy   156, 169–170
    in urban settings   163
    its three interwoven dimensions   167
    resurgence of   169
Hitler, Adolf   90, 95
HLM   159–160
    See also Habitation á Loyer Modéré
Hobsbawm, E.J.   3–5
Hobson, John   4
Holocaust   273
Housesteads   43–44, 47
Humane Borders   xxvi, 235, 240–241
Hungary   146, 251, 254
Huns   59
Hunter, Duncan   218
Hyrcania   67, 86, 88
    See also Gorgan

Ibn Sa'ad   163, 170
ICD   98–99, 105
    See also the Information Control Division
ICE   237
ICHTO   xxvi, 56, 58, 67–68, 82
    See also Iranian Cultural Heritage and
        Tourism Organization
Ideological wall   xxv, 170, 172
IDF   297, 301–302, 311
    See also Israeli Defense Forces
IMF   xix, 17, 190, 192, 212
    See also International Monetary Fund
Immigration and Naturalization Service
    216, 321
    See also INS
imperial formations   2–3, 6, 13, 17, 320, 322
imperialism   4–5, 256, 260
Information Control Division   98
    See also ICD
INS   185–186, 215–216, 220
    See also Immigration and Naturalization
        Service

integration or separation debate (Israel) 306
Interfaith Shelter, the xxvi, 235
Internal Displacement Monitoring Center (IDMC) 290n13
International Court of Justice 296
international migration 199, 207
International Monetary Fund 17, 190, 192, 212
See also IMF
Intifada 280–282
First 280, 305
Second 286, 292
Iranian Cultural Heritage and Tourism Organization xxvi, 56
See also ICHTO
Iranian revolution 156
Irgun 265, 269
Islam
and orthopraxy 168
its alleged violent nature
its compatibility with Western values 153
its theological doctrine 154
Islamic
cultural values 164, 168–169
dress 164
Empire 59
ethos 163
fundamentalism 162
headscarf 153
hijab (veil) xxv, 18, 152
militancy 151
movement 164, 167
Republic of Iran 169–170
[Shiite] morality 170
teachings 164
theology 168
version of civil religion 153
Islamic-Arab conquest of Iran 59
Israel
Absentees' Property Law 273
as an apartheid regime 283, 286–287, 308, 310
as a settler colony 275
as the world's first bunker state 318–319
closure regime 290, 307–308
final expansionist offensive 292
first expansion phase 271
fourth expansion phase 281
its colonization policy 277
second expansion phase 281
third expansion phase 277

unilateral declaration of independence 272, 275
Israeli Defense Forces 297, 301
See also IDF

Jabotinsky, Ze'ev 276, 315–316, 319
Jericho 1, 290, 310
Jerusalem 1, 246, 250, 256, 263, 266, 269, 276–277, 279, 282, 288, 292, 294, 297, 300, 302, 312–313
Jewish Colonial Association (JCA) 261n9
Jewish immigration to Palestine 262–263
aliya 251
fifth aliya 258
fourth aliya 258
magnitude 268
promoting 262
second aliya 253
third aliya 258
Jewish National Fund 259
Jewish People's Council 271
[Jewish] Settlement Master Plan 286
Jewish settlements 272, 276–277, 279–281, 283, 285–286, 288–289, 293–294, 304, 308, 310–312
Jordan River 256, 275–276, 288, 304, 319
Jordan Valley 288, 290, 310
Judaism 168
Just-in-time production 12
Jeyhoun 59, 62
See also Amu Darya, Ochus River and Oxus River

Kabyle, the 7, 163–166, 168
Kennedy administration 117, 128, 187
Kennedy, John F. 117, 125, 127–128, 130, 187
Khrushchev, Nikita 115
Kidarites 59
Kipling, Rudyard 42–43, 45
Kopeh Dagh Mountain 62
KPD 94–95, 99–100, 108–109
See also the Communist Party of Germany
Kurfürstendamm 126

Labor Party (Israel) 277, 279, 286, 292–293, 315–316
Laïcité 157
See also secularism
Laredo 195, 198, 219
League of Nations 256-258, 261, 280
Lehi, the 272
See also Stern Gang
Lenin, Vladimir Ilyich 4, 6, 94
Lernaean Hydra 10–11

les banlieues 159
Les Trentes Glorieuses 159
Liberal Party [Germany] (LDPP) 108
Likud Party 277, 293, 305, 316
Limes, the 49–50
Lille 18, 159

Macedonia 2, 56
Maghreb 154, 156n, 158
Maghrebi 153, 159–160, 162, 165, 168–169
Maghrebin 156n, 159–160, 164, 172
Manifest Destiny 178
maquiladoras 189–192, 195, 197, 212, 271, 308
maquiladora industries 11, 188–190, 192, 195, 197, 210, 212
maquiladora program 188–189, 210
Maksimychev, igor 146n29, 147
Mandate Legal System 261
Marshall, George 104–105
Marshall Plan 104–105
McClure, Robert 99
McCloy, John J. 117
Mecca 167, 254
Medina 167
Menander 60
mercantile capitalism 3
Mernissi, Fatima 163, 166–167, 170
Merv 62–63, 86
Mesopotamia 3, 24, 58–59, 248
Mexicali 195, 198, 201, 204, 235
Mexico 176, 178–199, 202, 204, 207–215, 218, 220, 222, 224, 227, 235–236, 240, 245, 305–306, 307n, 308
Mexican American War of 1846–1848 176
Mexican Farm Labor Supply Program 184
See also Bracero Program
Mexican independence 176
Ming Dynasty xxiii
Mitte district 112n26, 126
Morocco 7, 18, 154, 158, 163n, 171
multiculturalism 18, 30, 154, 156
Murghab River 62

NAFTA xix, 10, 16, 191-192, 195, 197, 210–214, 218, 307, 321
See also North American Free Trade Agreement
National Border Industrialization Program 188
See also BIP
National Liberation Front of Algeria (FLN) 155
National Socialist Party 94n, 95
See also NSDAP and the Nazi Party

Nativist sentiments 183
NATO xix, 49, 115, 127, 146n29
NATO Pact 115
New Deal 184
Nazi party 95–96
See also the National Socialist party and the NSDAP
Nazism 96, 98–100
Neo-liberal 210
development projects 315
economic policies 12, 17, 191, 212
Empire 2
global capitalism 11
interpretations 17
lexicon 13
model 211
states 12
Neo-liberalism xix
Netanyahu, Binyamin 292n15, 293, 317
Network Society 15–16, 18
NGO 8
Nile River 248
Niqab 153
Nixon, Pat 236
Nogales (Arizona) xxvi, 195, 198, 200, 223, 231–232, 235
Nogales (Mexico) xxiv, 195, 198, 227, 231–232, 240, 242
North Africa 151, 153, 155, 160, 162, 164–165, 322
North American Free Trade Agreement 16, 192, 197, 210
See also NAFTA
NSDAP 95–96
See also the National Socialist Party and the Nazi Party
Nuevo Laredo 195, 198

Obama, Barak 216, 219, 224, 243, 245, 333
Obama administration 216, 224, 245
Occupied territories (Palestine)
Area A 282–283
Area B 282–283
Area C 283, 288, 310–311, 313
Ochus River 56
See also Amu Darya, Jeyhoun and Oxus
Operation Blockade 214–218
Operation Gate Keeper 213, 215–218, 320
Operation Wetback 186
Ottoman Empire 252, 254, 256–257, 260
Ottoman Land Code 259
mawat 261
miri 259, 261
mulk 259
musha' 259–260

Oslo Accords   286, 292–293, 305, 308–310
Oslo talks   286, 290, 306, 308, 313, 316
Oslo II   282–285
    See also Taba Agreement
OXFAM   8
Oxus River   62, 66

Palestinian Authority   279, 282–283, 288, 306, 309
Palestinian economy
    closure regime   290, 307–308
    dependence on Israel   306
    free economic zones   309
    Free Trade Area (FTA)   306
    foreign workers replacing Palestinian workers   306–308
    Gaza Strip   304–306, 308–311
    illegal factories in the West Bank   309
    Industrial Estates (IE)   313
    Industrial Free Trade Zones (IFTZ)   309–310
    Jewish settlements in the occupied territories   311
    Palestinian capitalist class   313
    Palestinian entrepreneurs   313
    Palestinian Industrial Estate and Free Zone Authority (PIEFZA)   309
    Palestinian labor mobility   307
    Palestinian workers   246, 305–308, 311–313
    Palestinians working in Jewish settlements   309–310, 312
    permanent neo-colonial dependency   308–309
    perpetuation of economic dependency   267
    poverty   308–309, 311
    Seam Zones   302, 312, 314
    Separation Barrier and its role/function   308–311
    unemployment   307–309
Palestine   xxv, 1, 19, 222, 246–248, 250–254, 256, 258–273, 275–276, 280, 284, 287, 289, 298, 313, 315–316
Palestine Liberation Organization (PLO)   276
Palestine Jewish Colonial Association (PJCA)   261n9
Palestinian refugees   272
Palestinian workers   305–308, 311–313
Paris   5–7, 18, 151, 156n, 159, 162
Paris Protocol   306–307
Parnesius   42, 45
Parni tribe   56

Parthian period   56
Parthians   56, 58, 59
Peel, William R.W.   262
Peel Commission   267
Peel Partition Plan   263–264, 268
Peel Report   263
People's Republic of China   xxiii
Peres, Shimon   293
Perestroika   146–148
Peroz   55–56, 62, 65–66
perpetual war for perpetual peace   14
Persia   2, 56, 60, 87
Persian Empire   3, 53, 57–59, 61, 65n15, 89
Picot, George   254
Picts Nation, the   40
Pishkamar Mountain   53–54, 67, 75–76
Potsdam Agreement   106, 110–111, 115
Potsdamer Platz   121, 326, 328, 330
Poverty 24/6   xxvi, 235
Prague   146
Prophet Mohammad   166
Proposition 187 (California)   217–218
Proyecto San Pablo   xxvi, 235
Prussian Kingdom   92
Psychological Warfare Division   98
    See also PWD
Ptolemy   28n5, 247n
PWD   98
    See also the Psychological Warfare Division

Qaleh Qarniareq   76, 78
    See also Qizlar Qaleh
Qalqiliya   297, 301, 303
Qizil Allan   53
    See also the Red Snake and Great Wall of Gorgan
Qizlar Qaleh   76
    See also Qaleh Qarniareq

Rabin, Yitzhak   246, 282, 285, 292–293
Reagan Ronald   138
Red Snake   xxv, 53, 55n2, 59, 66, 71, 78, 85
Reichsbank   262
Reichsrat   96
Reichstag   95–96
Reyes, Silvestre   214–215
right of return   272
Rio Grande   186, 195, 207–208, 218, 221, 233
Road Map for Peace   294
Roman Britain   23–24, 26, 30n, 323
Roman Empire   5, 14, 23, 25, 40, 48, 50–51, 59, 61, 323
Romanization   30–31, 52

Roosevelt, Franklin Delano   96, 184
Rushdi, Salman   151
Russian Pogroms   251

Sbzavar   86n33
Sadd-I Garkaz Dam   79, 81–83
Said, Edward   283
Sandia National Laboratories   208,
    220–221, 230
    See also SNI
San Diego   xxiv, xxvi, 179, 195, 198,
    208–209, 214–216, 218–219, 225–226,
    235–240, 243–245
Sanjaks   248
San Luis Rio Colorado   xxvi, 203, 227, 235
Sarkozy, Nicholas   153
Sarl-I Maktoom Canal   78–79
Sassanian Empire   62, 85, 89
    See also Sassanid Empire
Sassanid (s)   53, 55–56, 58–59, 62, 66, 76,
    83, 85–87
Sassanid Empire   55, 59–60, 66, 86, 89
    See also Sassanian Empire
Sassanid era   56, 83
Satanic Verses   151
SBI   175, 220–222
    See also Secure Border Initiative and
        SBInet
SBInet   220–225
    See also SBI and the Secure Border
        Initiative
Schumann, Conrad   332–333
Scotland   24, 27–28, 38–40, 50
Scythians   56
Second Reich   92, 94, 103
Second World War   96, 261
    See also WWII
Secularism   157, 170
Secure Border Initiative, the   175, 220
    See also SBI and SBInet
Secure Fence Act   180, 216, 218, 222
Security Fence (Israel)   246–247, 292–293,
    296–298, 301
    See also Separation Barrier (Israel)
Seleucids   56
Separation Barrier (Israel)
    architecture   296
        barbed wire   246, 296–297, 299
        chain-link fence   296–297, 299
        concrete slabs   293, 296–297, 300
        military road, paved   297
        military road, unpaved   297
        trench   246, 297

    as an anti-terrorist fence   246, 292,
        296–297
    as an offensive structure   247
    Israeli-Egyptian border fence   317
    Prevention of Infiltration Law   317
    Seam Zones   302, 312, 314
Seyhoun River   59
    See also Syr Darya
Shadravan Dam   85n30
Shahpour   85n30
Sharon, Ariel   292–293
Silk Road   62, 64
Sinai Peninsula   253, 276, 277
Six Day War, the   246n, 275–277, 303–304
SNL   208, 220
    See also Sandia National Laboratories
Social Democratic Party (of Germany)
    92, 94, 96n4
Socialist Unity Party of Germany (SED)
    109
Somerton/San Luis   235
Spartakist League   94
SPD   92, 94–95, 108–109
Soviet Military Administration in
    Germany, the   100, 109, 112
    See also SVAG
Soviet Union   12, 90, 92, 94, 97, 100–101,
    104–105, 107–112, 115–117, 119, 127, 138, 143,
    145–148, 266–268, 281, 322–323
Staci, Bernard   152
Staci Commission   152
Stalin, Joseph   110–113, 137
Stalin-Alee   112
Stanegate   31–34, 36, 45, 49
Stanwix   39–40
Stern Gang   269, 272
    See also the Lehi
Suez crisis   276
SVAG   100–101
    See also the soviet Military
        Administration in Germany
Swing, Joseph   208
Sykes, Mark   254
Sykes-Picot Agreement   254–255
Syr Darya   59
    See also Seyhoun River
Sisyphus   xxiv

Taba Agreement   282
    See also Oslo II
Tabaristan   86
Tacitus   28n5
Tel Aviv   271, 292

Texas 176, 178-180, 185-186, 195, 198, 202, 212, 214-215, 218-219, 221, 230, 233
   See also Coahuila y Tejas
Third Reich 95-96, 99, 110
Third World 18, 188, 213, 320
Three Powers West German Zone, the 103
Tijuana xxiv, 195, 197-198, 208-209, 216, 226, 235-239, 243
Toulie House Museum 50
Trajan 24
Trans-Israel Highway 293, 302-303
transnational corporation 8, 17
Transportation Security Administration 222
   See also TSA
Trapos 118
Treaty of Versailles 94-95
Treaty of Westphalia 15
Truman Doctrine 104-105
TSA 222
   See also Transportation Security Administration
Tsar Alexander III 250
Tulkarem 293, 297
Tunisia 154, 158, 171
turf walls 32, 38-39, 49
Turkmenistan 53, 59-60, 62, 65
twin cities (along the U.S.-Mexico border) xxiv, 195, 197-198, 205, 235
Tyne-Solway isthmus 27, 28n5, 31

Ulbricht, Walter 94-95, 108, 112-113, 116-117
United Nations 3n1, 10n10, 14n16, 256n5, 265-266, 269, 271, 273
United Nations Special Committee on Palestine 266
   See also UNSCOP
United States xx, xxv, 10, 14, 16, 30, 90, 92, 97-98, 104, 109-111, 116-117, 127-128, 145, 147, 175n2, 176, 178-190, 194, 199, 202, 204, 207-208, 210-214, 216-219, 221, 243, 245, 247, 266-269, 276-277, 281, 294, 305-306, 309, 315, 323
University of Edinburg 56, 58, 67-68, 82
UN Conference on Trade and Development (UNCTAD) 294
UN Partition Plan 268-270
   See also UNSCOP Partition Plan
UN Resolution 242 277, 281-82
UN Resolution 338 281
UNSCOP 266-268
   See also United Nations Special Committee on Palestine

UN Security Council 277, 294
Unter den Linden 121, 123-126
USAID 313
U.S. Department of Labor 182, 185, 187, 213
U.S. Department of State 96, 119, 202, 267
U.S.-Mexico border xxiv, xxvi, 11, 19, 48, 175, 178, 180, 186, 192n15, 195-199, 207-208, 217-218, 234-235, 246, 297, 321-324, 333
U.S.-Mexico border fence 178, 297, 323
   Architecture
      Bollard fence 225, 227, 231
      Normandy-style Vehicle barrier 225, 229
      Picket style 225-226
      Post-and-Rail 225, 228
      primary fence 225
      Sandia fence 225
      secondary fence 225
      virtual fence 221-225, 238
   as an offensive wall 207, 321-323
   as a war zone 237
   "Tortilla Curtain" 208
   total cost 235
   See also the U.S.-Mexico border Wall
U.S.-Mexico border Wall 11
   See also the U.S.-Mexico border fence
Uzbekistan 59, 62

Veil xxv, 18, 151-153, 163, 166-167, 170
   See also hijab
Vidal, Gore 14
Vietnam 15n, 147
Vindolanda 31

Wall of Tamishe 87-88
Wallsend 38
Warsaw Pact 115-117, 127, 146
Weimar Republic 94
West Bank (occupied Palestinian territories) xxv, 1, 19, 222, 246, 276-277, 279-280, 282-290, 292-295, 297, 299, 301-307, 309-312, 314, 322, 324
West Berlin xxiv, xxvi, 90, 96n4, 106, 113, 115-119, 121, 124-129, 131, 135-139, 142-143, 297, 321, 323-325, 328-332
Whin Sill (Crags) 32, 35
white man's burden 154
White Huns 59
   See also Hephthalites and ephthalites
White Paper (British) 263, 265
World Bank, the xix, 193, 308-310, 313
World Trade Organization 17, 191-192
   See also WTO

World Zionist Organization   252, 262
  See also WZO
Wowereit, Klaus   331
WTO   xix, 17, 191–192
  See also World Trade Organization
WWII   15n, 94–97, 103, 159, 207, 227, 262,
  267
WZO   252–253
  See also World Zionist Organization

Xusro   55

Yum Kippur War   279

Zionism   250, 256, 262, 315–316
  as a bunker mentality   317
  as a failed nightmare   315

as a national liberation movement   260
as a secular nationalist movement   250
as a settler movement   260
as an exogenous movement   250
as an organized movement   251
and Jewish nationalism   253
Ottoman policy toward   260
Revisionist   315
the Iron Wall of   315–316
Zionist colonization   258
Zionist movement   251–254, 256, 258, 263,
  272, 276n4, 315
Zionist settler colonies   254, 260
Zionist tendencies
  Bilu   251
  Hibbat Zion   251